NEW READINGS OF THE AMERICAN NOVEL

Narrative Theory and its Application

NEW READINGS
OF THE
AMERICAN NOVEL

Narrative Theory and its Application

Peter Messent

St. Martin's Press   New York

© Peter Messent 1990

All rights reserved. For information, write:
Scholarly and Reference Division
St. Martin's Press, Inc., 175 Fifth Avenue,
New York, N.Y. 10010

First published in the United States of America in 1990

Printed in Singapore

ISBN 0–312–04653–7

Library of Congress Cataloging-in-Publication Data
Messent, Peter B.
New readings of the American novel : narrative theory and its
application / Peter Messent.
   p. cm.
ISBN 0–312–04653–7
1. American fiction—History and criticism.   2. Narration
(Rhetoric)   I. Title.
PS371.M47   1990
813.009—dc20   90–8042
                                                   CIP

Contents

Acknowledgements

My interest in some of the materials developed here was first raised within the University of Nottingham Critical Theory Group. I would like to thank friends and colleagues within that group who offered helpful comments on individual sections of my manuscript: most especially – Elizabeth Boa, Diane Knight, Elaine Millard, and Douglas Tallack. I tested out some of the critical approaches represented here with my students. My thanks for their patience, cooperation, and ideas. Gavin Cologne-Brookes, working under my supervision toward his Ph.D. on William Styron's novels, discussed Bakhtin with me at length. I hope our conversations were as useful to him as they were to me.

My special thanks to two colleagues from my department whose help has been even more substantial. Richard King was ever-willing to read chapters and part-chapters for me in draft form. His good advice and warm encouragement were invaluable. So, too, were David Murray's. He read both separate sections of the book as I was proceeding, then the complete text at manuscript stage, and his comments were always incisive, always constructive. I consider myself privileged to have such colleagues and friends. With the help of all those named above, this book is much better than it would otherwise have been.

I also wish to thank Caroline Egar and Moira Eminton for the concern and care which she brought to this project; and Freda Duckitt, our departmental secretary, whose speed and accuracy in typing the book, despite other tasks at hand, was greatly appreciated. John Clements, the best of friends, provided the basketball, bourbon and good talk which gave much needed temporary relief in the throes of writing. William and Alice, my children, always special, showed real interest in what I was doing; both encouraged me and put up without complaint as I retreated yet again to work on this manuscript. My love to them. And also, of course, to Penny Craig to whom I owe a thousand thanks.

April, 1989

The author and publishers wish to thank the following who have kindly given permission for the use of copyright material: Basil Blackwell Ltd. for extracts from *Narrative Discourse* by Gerard Genette, 1986; The Bodley Head and Charles Scribner's Sons, an imprint of Macmillan Publishing Company for extracts from *The Great Gatsby* by F. Scott Fitzgerald. Copyright © 1925 by Charles Scribner's Sons; copyright renewed 1953 by Frances Scott Fitzgerald Lanahan; Georges Borchardt, Inc. and Hill and Wang, a division of Farrar, Straus & Giroux, Inc. for extracts from *S/Z: An Essay* by Roland Barthes. Translation copyright © 1974 by Farrar Straus & Giroux, Inc; Curtis Brown Ltd. and Random House, Inc. for extracts from *The Sound and the Fury* by William Faulkner. Copyright © 1929 and renewed 1957 by William Faulkner; Harper & Row, Publishers, Inc. for extracts from *Mules and Men* by Zora Neale Hurston. Copyright © 1935 by Zora Neale Hurston; renewed 1963 by John C. Hurston; W. W. Norton & Company, Inc. for extracts from *The Portrait of a Lady* by Henry James, A Norton Critical Edition, ed. Robert D. Bamberg. Copyright © 1975 by W. W. Norton & Company, Inc; Charles Scribner's Sons, an imprint of Macmillan Publishing Company, for extracts from *The Sun Also Rises* By Ernest Hemingway. Copyright © 1926 by Charles Scribner's Sons; copyright © renewed 1953 by Ernest Hemingway; University of Texas Press for extracts from *The Dialogic Imagination: Four Essays* by M. M. Bakhtin, edited by Michael Holquist, translated by Caryl Emerson and Michael Holquist © 1981; Virago Press Ltd. and Harper & Row, Publishers, Inc. for extracts from *Their Eyes Were Watching God* by Zora Neale Hurston. Copyright © 1935 by Zora Neale Hurston; renewed 1965 by John C. and Joel Hurston; and with Alfred A. Knopf, Inc. for extracts from *A Lost Lady* by Willa Cather. Copyright © 1923 by Willa S. Cather; renewed 1951

*To My Parents
John and Rosa Messent
with all my love*

Introduction

The book that follows will provide an introduction to a variety of theoretical models for the reading of narrative. I will apply these models to seven American novels to show how they work in practice. My intention in so doing is to present those who compose my audience with a series of textually informed readings which will then be available for them to negotiate to suit their own critical needs.

These are the bare bones of my project and, set out like this, my plans may sound both mechanical and over-ambitious. In fact, I cannot hope, given the nature of my survey, to explain all aspects of the critical approaches on which I base my study. Neither can my treatment of my chosen texts be comprehensive. By design it will be partial. For while I will attempt to give a clear and accessible explanation of my theoretical sources, I will focus on those aspects which I find most immediately useful in approaching the literary text and most helpful in informing my own critical practice. I intend, therefore, in my chapter on Bakhtin, to explain some of the critical terms he uses, and to attempt to show their implications when applied to Mark Twain's *Huckleberry Finn*. I shall not try, however, to provide a systematized version of a writer whose wide ranging critical activity, marked by a type of 'internal incompletion'[1] reflected in his own spiralling style, is built to resist such a project. In my chapter on reader response, likewise, I will not attempt to 'cover' what is a large and complex field. I will rather concentrate on the two critics, Wolfgang Iser and Stephen Mailloux, who allow me good critical access to the novel I wish to discuss, Willa Cather's *A Lost Lady*. Such tactics are highly selective.

My study of the literary texts to which these theories are applied will also be partial. I do not order these texts chronologically but rather, to a certain extent, choose my text to suit my theory. Faulkner's *The Sound and the Fury* has time as its central concern. It thus suggests itself as a suitable field for the examination of chronological representation in narrative. *Huckleberry Finn*, with its relation between black slave, ill-educated white boy, and dominant social structure, is particularly amenable to Bakhtinian analysis. This is not, though, to suggest that such methods can be applied only to the works of the cited authors. Far from it. These analyses are to be seen as models which can be applied elsewhere. My final chapter, in which I will apply a range of the critical approaches previously used to the one novel, *Their Eyes Were Watching God* by Zora Neale Hurston, will serve as practical example of this. My intention too will be to demonstrate in each chapter how a particular critical tack throws light on various aspects of a narrative, rather than to offer a comprehensive analysis of the text in question. In the majority of cases, however, such a selective approach will have wider implications.

My own critical approach in this book is pluralistic in so far as there will be no attempt to reduce the theories I use to one common denominator, or to insist on the supremacy of any single one. No text, though, literary or critical, is value-free, and mine will be no exception. In explaining how I choose to use and organize my material, my own critical biases will, I think, become clear.

My first three chapters will follow a structuralist model, in so far as the novel examined in each will be analyzed against the background of the literary system of which it is a part; its effects and meanings seen as a product of a certain 'underlying set of laws' to which all narratives, however complex, adhere. My initial emphasis, then, will be on the text itself, to show how 'the literary work . . . is a *construct*, whose mechanisms [can] be classified and analyzed'[2] by any committed and comparatively skilful reader. One of the strengths of such a model lies in its demystification of the business of literary criticism. For in insisting that complicated narrative strategies are subject to critical explanation it encourages a shift away from 'interpretation'. I will pursue this point further in my first chapter.

I do not, however, wish to lose hold of interpretation entirely. I see is as an essential part of my project to modify what I see as the more sterile aspects of structuralism. For in its most rigid manifestation its tendency is to treat literature as a *self-sufficient* system. Some structuralist critics, in their rigorous analysis of the laws and conventions which compose the literary system, divorce literary texts from their cultural siting, from the social and historical conditions which finally give them their fullest meaning. Terry Eagleton argues for a broader approach when he writes that 'the meaning of the text is not just an internal matter: it also inheres in the text's relation to wider systems of meaning, to other texts, codes and norms in literature and society as a whole. Its meaning is also relative to the reader's "horizon of expectations"'.[3]

My opening chapters, then, will constitute an attempt not only to show how the meanings of a text are created internally, produced within a textual system, but also to show how those meanings relate to, and overlap with, a set of wider meanings which exist outside that text. So when, for example, I come to use Rimmon-Kenan's discussion of character construction as my model in Chapter Three, I will attempt, at key points, to show how the insights which emerge from the use of her mode of analysis take on larger resonance when brought into relationship with wider systems of cultural meaning.[4]

Chapter Four is, in several ways, a pivotal chapter in this book. For here, as I discuss reader response theory, I shift ground considerably from critical methods which place their primary stress on the text itself and on how its effects are created, to one which focuses on our readerly activity as we encounter the text, and on the social and historical frames which condition both our understanding and reception of it. Different aspects of these concerns will be pursued, though in different form, in the next two chapters. This section will thus serve as a bridge from a mode of criticism which emphasizes narrative autonomy to one with a more developed cultural and political thrust. It is also pivotal in its focus on a text, *A Lost Lady*, which foregrounds issues of gender and sexuality. Such concerns will surface earlier, in the chapter on Hemingway. From this point, however, they will be subject to more sustained critical examination.

I will, accordingly, use my chapter on Barthes – whose

radical version of reader response theory in *S/Z* [5] gives up
any notion of critical 'objectivity' in its call for readerly
'collusion/collision' [6] with the text – as a point of entry
for discussion of those issues of sexuality, power, economics,
and gender role which circulate both in Henry James' *The
Portrait of A Lady* and in Edith Wharton's *The House of Mirth*. I
will then move away from a stress on the reader in my sixth
chapter, on Bakhtin, but will retain – and indeed intensify
– my developing concentration on the social and historical
contexts which frame the literary text.

For Bakhtin's dialogic theory places central attention on
the importance of 'the actual historical situation of each individual utterance'[7] in our constructions of textual and social
meaning. It sees language as a site of conflict where different
social groupings struggle for power. His theory provides, then,
a fitting final voice in the series of overlapping and often
conflicting voices which I use to compose my own critical
meanings. For it is here that the relation of the literary text
to issues of social power and historical meaning is developed
most explicitly. In applying Bakhtin to *Huckleberry Finn* the
issue of race will be introduced as significant to my study.
And in my final chapter, I will use Hurston's *Their Eyes Were
Watching God* both as a type of testing ground for the critical
approaches thus far introduced, and as a point of further
discussion of both race and gender. This will be put into
the context of that suppression and marginalization of black
voices and women's voices which has marked, until recently,
both the construction of the American literary canon and that
social reality it reflects. For there is no denying a large measure
of truth to Paul Lauter's statement that the 'literary canon' is
'in short, a means by which culture validates social power'.[8]
What starts out as a pedagogic exercise will, therefore, end
as a political one. I in no way see the two as incompatible.
In line with Myra Jehlen, my study points towards the recognition 'that the political categories of race, gender, and class
enter into the formal making of American literature such that
they underlie not only its themes, not only its characters and
events, but its very language',[9] and towards the re-definition
of the American tradition which accompanies such a recognition.

My study, therefore, will move in several directions. It will use structuralist theory to show how the effects created in a narrative might be accurately described. It will show how all the theories used can be related, to greater or lesser extent, to an understanding of the studied texts in the context of their broader cultural framework. It will suggest the need to widen our literary horizons; to revise the canon to include types of writing until now marginalized or excluded. These aims are complementary to a degree. There is, however, a critical gap in what I will be trying to do which needs acknowledging, though I will not try to fill it.

For the majority of texts I will study are part of the established American literary canon. I limit myself to the period 1881 (*The Portrait of a Lady*) to 1937 (*Their Eyes Were Watching God*). This reflects my particular field of interest. It also results from my sense that, despite some notable exceptions, texts which belong in the American realist tradition and the modernist one which developed from it, have tended to resist new readings. The canonic writers – Twain, Hemingway, Fitzgerald, in particular – seem to lie there solidly, subject to challenge by some feminist critics, but with their importance for the most part taken for granted. Unable to be muscled aside, part of every survey course on American literature, texts by these writers have come to seem unnegotiable, subject to a set of more or less fixed interpretations, having the status of monuments rather than inspiring fresh challenge in the light of present critical concern.[10] Part of my intention here is to examine such texts in the light of recent theoretical developments to attempt to produce some small example of that type of critical practice suggested by Russell Reising when he quotes Bakhtin as follows:

> Every age re-accentuates in its own way the works of its most immediate past. The historical life of classic works is in fact the uninterrupted process of their social and ideological re-accentuation. Thanks to the . . . potential embedded in them, such works have proved capable of uncovering in each era and against ever new dialogizing backgrounds ever new aspects of meaning.[11]

I cannot agree with all of what Bakhtin appears to propose here, for no work, classic or otherwise, can of itself 'uncover' meaning from one historical period for another. I do however think that there are certain 'classics' which speak significantly across time, which reveal meanings 'hidden' in them for each new generation of readers to discover, depending on the critical tactics and ways of reading brought to bear on the texts at issue.[12] This is not to deny the fact that political and cultural determinants, as Paul Lauter and Nina Baym, for example, suggest, help to form this canon. Nor is it to deny that literary 'values' can change.[13] It is, though, to suggest that novels like *Huckleberry Finn* and *The Sound and the Fury* will be around and judged 'classic' for some time yet. What I will try to do here is to use recent theory to renegotiate such works, to 're-accentuate' them: to illustrate their continued importance by showing how 'new aspects of meaning' still remain readily discoverable in them.

My other intention in examining the literature of this period, is to begin to point the way towards that expansion and re-accentuation of the American literary tradition as a whole of which Russell Reising speaks in *The Unusable Past: Theory and the Study of American Literature* (1986). Though these two projects can and will be put together, this is, I think, where my critical inconsistency comes in. For one activity, renegotiating the multiple meanings which a classic text spills out, is here replaced by another, in which the critic becomes the giver of value – seeing a text's importance in terms of its regional, ethnic, gender or class difference.[14] The thrust of such criticism is political, seeing literature as a general field of cultural production in which all voices should be equally recognised.[15] In terms of our need for a democratic re-evaluation of the literary community this means extending (or even abolishing) the canon to bring in previously suppressed voices: black, women's, native American, working class, etc. It means evaluating these voices primarily in socio-historical, rather than aesthetic terms. I am drawing fine distinctions here. Texts like *Their Eyes Were Watching God* and *Narrative of the Life of Frederick Douglass* which are now, as it were, 'recuperated' have perhaps been chosen for such treatment partly because of their obvious 'literary' merit; while my reading of *Huckleberry Finn*, for example, is one which stresses a way of reading it in a socio-political manner. There is, however, a theoretical hole here which is perhaps unfillable between the notion of the classic text and the notion of the text as expression of American heterogeneity.

This is the stressed word in much modern American criticism. Such a re-accentuation of the American literary frame leads towards the fulfilment of that vision Sacvan Bercovitch has of a 'capturing' of 'the heterogeneity of America'.[16] Reising, too, argues for 'a new appreciation of the heterogeneity of American literature, a heterogeneity often blurred or denied by the polarization of canonical/noncanonical, major /minor, aesthetic/social'. While I see the blurring of which Reising speaks as for me, at least, at present unavoidable, the arguments which I wish to make in my book, the way I structure it, will constitute a small, but I hope significant move in the direction of that 'democratization of American literary studies' for which he calls.[17]

1
Speech Representation, Focalization and Narration in *The Great Gatsby*

I

In *The Great Gatsby* [Fitzgerald] found truth in the beauty
of art, and beauty in its truths
(Robert Sklar)[1]

The knowable is at the heart of the mysterious
(Gérard Genette)[2]

Most students are stopped dead in their critical tracks when
they meet words like 'truth' and 'beauty'. When it comes to
writing about a literary text such terms, which suggest a
semi-mystical conception of the work of art, are off-putting
rather than helpful. They are evaluative not analytical, and
as such can be described as 'merely subjective noises'.[3] Such
subjective noises, however, have one noticeable effect: in their
clear assumption of privileged knowledge both about a text
and a philosophical and aesthetic field (truth, beauty, art)
they close down possible responses to that text on the part of
others. How can I approach a novel which has already been
so grandiloquently and conclusively assessed by Sklar?

Gérard Genette in *Narrative Discourse* (1972) takes a very
different critical tack, and one which I think enormously
liberating. His intentions are in tune with what Gerald

Prince describes as the general 'goals of narratology': 'to discover, describe, and explain the *mechanics* of narrative' (my emphasis).[4] The stress is not on the *meaning* of an individual text (its contents), but on its mechanics; the way 'meaning is produced'.[5] Boris Uspensky, the Soviet formalist, is centrally concerned in *A Poetics of Composition* (1970) with 'the laws which govern the structural organization of the artistic text'.[6] All narrative fiction, according to such an approach, is part of a general *system*, and as such, is subject to a set of basic rules or laws. If we can isolate and define these laws, we can start seeing how any one text gains its artistic effects. Genette takes Marcel Proust's *A la recherche du temps perdu (Remembrance of Things Past, 1913–27)* as his case study. He refuses, however, to do so in a reductive manner:

> It seems to me impossible to treat the *Recherche du temps perdu* as a mere example of what is supposedly narrative in general . . . The specificity of Proustian narrative taken as a whole is *irreducible* . . . the *Recherche* illustrates only itself. But, on the other hand, that specificity is not *undecomposable*, and each of its analyzable features lends itself to some connection, comparison, or putting into perspective (pp. 22-3).

Mystery and knowledge are not incompatible for Genette: by de-composing Proust's text, by showing how artistic effects are established by the complex use of the mechanics of narrative which are in themselves both accessible and readily explained, he illustrates how the construction of the 'text's polished surface' is 'at least partly the result of sophisticated handling of the most basic tools of narrative'.[7]

The appeal of such a method is precisely in its demystifying qualities. Most students when faced, for example, with the mass of critical interpretations of *The Great Gatsby* (1926) throw up their hands at the idea of presenting a reading of the novel which is in any way 'original': what tends to emerge in their essays is a patchwork of received critical ideas stitched together with greater or less skill and ability to give a coherent, if profoundly unoriginal, reading of the text. An alternative type of analysis which focuses on the 'way in which individual narratives can be studied as unique realizations of the general system'[8]; which examines how, for example, character is constructed or chronological effects are created both generally and in one specific textual case – allows any committed reader to:

> carry out structuralist analyses with enthusiasm and skill and . . . arrive at independent observations surprising in their scope . . . The 'magically' acquired (class restricted?) 'feel' for literature [is replaced by] a sophisticated handling of texts . . . The supposedly scientific grid can be applied without complexes, yet inevitably leads to the heart of the complicated narrative strategies that may well be the secret of the text's 'mystique' in the first place.[9]

I wish to attempt to illustrate such a practice in this chapter, by discussing how Genette and other critics who are working in the area of narratology – most especially Boris Uspensky in *A Poetics of Composition* and Shlomith Rimmon-Kenan in *Narrative Fiction* (1983) – approach the areas of focalization, speech representation, and narration. I wish to show in attempting to apply parts of their work to *The Great Gatsby* how such a 'scientific' approach helps to reveal the operating principles behind a dense and complex text:

> Loosely subjective talk [is] chastized by a criticism which recognize[s] that the literary work, like any other product of language, is a *construct* whose mechanisms [can] be classified and analyzed like the objects of any other science.[10]

My analysis particularly directs itself towards Nick Carraway's position in the novel. His perspective on events, the way the words of others are filtered through his own, the tactics he uses as narrator of the story: all these suggest his control, indeed domination, of the materials at his disposal. That his is both an unreliable and politically suspect stance will become evident in the course of my chapter. As a means of suggesting the way in which a study of the mechanics of narrative relates to larger frames of reference, I retain until the end of my chapter a section which should more properly go earlier. For in the examination of the ideological facet of Nick Carraway's focalization which I place there, I make the transition to that different level of contextual and interpretive analysis which narratology can prompt. In the chapter on Faulkner which follows this, I will again suggest how such a move can be realized.

Before I start my study of *The Great Gatsby*, however, I should point out the unusual technical vocabulary Genette uses in his work. This will be introduced as and when relevant in this chapter. His use of such terms (the substitution of analepsis for flashback, for instance) is part of his attempt to construct a comprehensive 'technical vocabulary' [11] for narrative. It serves both 'to highlight distinctions which looser, more commonsensical terms might obscure', and to help sharpen the boundary lines between the 'internal laws and logic'[12] of the fictional system itself and that external reality which frames it. Genette is, however, refreshingly playful when he writes of his use of scientific terms, speaking of his project in metaphoric terms taken straight from his subject matter (Proust) as 'a sort of periodic diversion, like the insomniac turning over and over in search of a better position' (p. 23). He accepts his 'technology' as 'surely barbaric to the lovers of belles lettres' (p. 263), but there is no apology in such a state- ment – a democratization and demystification of literature is, as I have suggested, implicit in his project. He is also happy to see such terms consigned to oblivion, going 'to join other packaging, the detritus of Poetics', once they have outlived their usefulness: his is a very pragmatic poetics.

II

Genette uses the categories of tense, mood, and voice to approach the field of narrative. He uses these terms, which belong to the grammar of verbs, since he sees narrative in its basic form as 'the expansion of a verb' (p. 30). *Huckleberry Finn* can thus be reduced in its barest bones to *Huck takes a journey down the Mississippi*; *The Great Gatsby* to *Nick charts his record of Gatsby*. *Tense*, then, concerns itself with the relationship between past, present and future time in narrative fiction; the 'order, pace and frequency of events and their telling'.[13] This will be the subject of my second chapter. *Voice* is the category which contains the narrating activity itself. In grammatical terms, voice has to do with 'the subject of the statement'.[14] In terms of his narrative grammar, Genette identifies this with the position and identity of the narrator, the circumstances of the narrating, and the way in which any narrative can be composed of various levels of narrating activity. *Mood*, with which I commence, concerns the way in which narrative information is regulated, and the varying degrees of its provision: 'the narrative can furnish the reader with more or fewer details, and in a more or less direct way'.[15] Genette divides mood into two main aspects, distance and perspective (or focalization). Speech representation, the main subject of the following subsection, comes within the former category.

Modal distance: showing/telling and speech representation

The view I have of a picture depends for precision on the distance separating me from it (Genette, p. 162).

In his section on distance, Genette discusses how the narrator's mediations relate to the presentation of the story; the degree to which it is presented in indirect or condensed form, or as 'detailed, precise, "alive"' (p. 164). Fitzgerald, like Proust, achieves the difficult and 'paradoxical'[16] task of combining both positions. He uses a retrospective narrator whose selective role in the presentation of events is most evident. *Telling* is the conventional name for such a technique:

a presentation mediated by [a] narrator who, instead of directly and dramatically exhibiting events and conversations, talks about them, sums them up, etc.[17]

Yet he still maintains the mimetic illusion (*showing*) in the novel – 'the illusion that events "literally unfold before the reader's eyes"'.[18] Literature apparently here *imitates* reality, 'the narrator seeming to disappear . . . the reader being left to draw his own conclusions from what he "sees" and "hears"'.[19]

The apparent disappearance of the narrator in *The Great Gatsby* results from the way in which so many of the story's events are filtered (focalized) directly through the perceptions, cognitions, and emotions of that Nick who participates in them. The novel shares with the *Recherche du temps perdu* – certainly for its most part – the 'marvel' that Genette describes; that despite the distance resulting from retrospective narration (which, in turn, frames other retrospective narrations):

> this *temporal distance* between the story and the narrating instance involves no *modal distance* between the story and the narrative: no loss, no weakening of the mimetic illusion. Extreme mediation, and at the same time utmost immediacy. That too is perhaps symbolized by the rapture of reminiscence (pp. 168–9).

Fitzgerald, while insisting on the story's status as *memory* (with the 'explicit mediation' of the narration thus introduced), achieves a sense of absolute immediacy in the party scenes, re-introduction of Daisy and Gatsby, hotel scene, etc. Like Proust, he produces a text 'simultaneously at the extreme of *showing* and at the extreme of *telling*',[20] collapsing the traditional difference between the two forms.

This effect is created in part by the way in which temporal distance between story and narrating activity is eclipsed by the slidings which take place between Nick as 'source, guarantor, and organizer' of the narrative, and the scenes he then presents to us in which his younger self participates. Nick Carraway, as narrator, takes the floor at the start of the novel: 'In my younger and more vulnerable years . . . '. His voice as retrospective narrator – 'when I came back from the East last Autumn' – shifts almost imperceptibly into his voice as narrative participant, with the chronological transition marked more obviously by the textual lay-out (the gap that occurs after the introductory statement) than by any immediate change in verbal form. For verbs remain in the past tense, leaving an adverbial marker to first directly signal the stylistic change: 'the Middle West *now* seemed . . . '[21] (my stress). Nick's position as earlier participant in the story cannot be clearly distinguished from, merges with, that as narrator. Such a technique will recur as I shall later show: it is, however, one very obvious but highly effective way in which the narration/story gap – the distance between telling and showing – is smoothly bridged in the text.

Where modal distance does vitally appear in *The Great Gatsby* is in the area of speech representation. For the rendering of speech in a literary text is directly related to the way in which the narrator mediates the words of others in presenting the story. As narrator, Nick represents the speech, emotions, and thoughts of others in two ways:

(a)   by allowing the characters in his narrative (including his earlier self) to speak without any mediation. Direct access is given to the uttered speech (*direct discourse*) of the protagonists: ' "You make me feel uncivilized, Daisy", I confessed', ' "Civilization's going to pieces", broke out Tom violently' (pp. 17–8). This is the 'most "mimetic" form [of speech] where the narrator pretends literally to give the floor to his character'.

(b)   by using indirect forms of speech and thought which give the reader no 'guarantee . . . of literal fidelity to the words "really" uttered'.[22] Whenever Carraway reports on the words or thoughts of another, we are faced with a real question as to how far he is expressing their thoughts in their own style, or *in his own style*; how much distance mediating narrator is interposing between us and them? Whether, more radically, he is actually imposing his own words, and thoughts, on them? Let me give a fairly long example which will help illustrate my meaning. The night of Myrtle's death, Gatsby tells Nick 'the strange story of his youth . . . he wanted to talk about Daisy':

> She was the first 'nice' girl he had ever known. In various unrevealed capacities he had come in contact with such people, but always with indiscernible barbed wire between. He found her excitingly desirable . . . what gave [her house] an air of breathless intensity, was that Daisy lived there – it was as casual a thing to her as his tent out at camp was to him. There was a ripe mystery about it, a hint of bedrooms upstairs more beautiful and cool than other bedrooms, of gay and radiant activities taking place through its corridors, and of romances that were not musty and laid away already in lavender but fresh and breathing and redolent of this year's shining motor-cars and of dances whose flowers were scarcely withered. It excited him, too,

that many men had already loved Daisy – it increased her value in his eyes. He felt their presence all about the house, pervading the air with the shades and echoes of still vibrant emotions.

But he knew that he was in Daisy's house by a colossal accident. However glorious might be his future as Jay Gatsby, he was at present a penniless young man without a past, and at any moment the invisible cloak of his uniform might slip from his shoulders. So he made the most of his time. He took what he could get, ravenously and unscrupulously – eventually took Daisy one still October night, took her because he had no real right to touch her hand . . .

But he didn't despise himself and it didn't turn out as he had imagined. He had intended, probably, to take what he could and go – but now he found that he had committed himself to the following of a grail . . . He felt married to her, that was all . . .

When they met again, two days later . . . Gatsby was overwhelmingly aware of the youth and mystery that wealth imprisons and preserves, of the freshness of many clothes, and of Daisy, gleaming like silver, safe and proud above the hot struggles of the poor.

'I can't describe to you how surprised I was to find out I loved her, old sport. I even hoped for a while that she'd throw me over, but she didn't, because she was in love with me too. She thought I knew a lot because I knew different things from her . . . Well, there I was, 'way off my ambitions, getting deeper in love every minute, and all of a sudden I didn't care. What was the use of doing great things if I could have a better time telling her what I was going to do?' (pp. 141–3).

There is a huge difference here – in both conception and mode of speech – between committing oneself 'to the following of a grail' and being ''way off [one's] ambitions'. Gatsby's own language is repetitious, lacks specificity and rhetorical eloquence. He speaks vaguely of 'doing great things', and knowing 'different things from her'. The language preceding this direct discourse is noticeably more specific and more eloquent. In what is a highly distinctive mixture of direct speech, 'tagged indirect thought'[23] ('it excited him that', 'he knew that') and free indirect speech ('There was . . . a hint of bedrooms upstairs . . . '), the 'documentary autonomy of . . . quotation'[24] clashes noticeably with the narrator's imposed verbal and conceptual presence. The metaphoric play concerning snagging and restrictive social barriers and the donned evasive mantles of invisibility just do not fit with the simpler vernacular discourse attributed directly to Gatsby: 'as if I was some kind of cheap sharper', 'getting deeper in love every minute'. Gatsby's 'threadbare . . . phrases', which move in the text at large between repetitious clichés ('trying to forget something sad that had happened to me', 'the sad thing that happened to me'), crass tactlessness ('look here, old sport, you don't make much money, do you?'), and downright lies ('I thought you inherited your money?' 'I did, old sport', he said automatically, 'but I lost most of it in the big panic – the panic of the war'), reveal little evidence of the heightened rhetoric to be found in Nick's supposed reports of his words and thoughts. When Gatsby wants to describe his 'rich cream' coloured car 'bright with nickel, swollen . . . with triumphant hat-boxes . . . ', he calls it 'pretty' (just as he calls Daisy 'nice' here): it is Nick who gets descriptively carried away. In the quoted passage, phrases like 'ripe mystery', 'breathless intensity', 'vibrant emotions', 'flowers . . . scarcely withered', 'romances . . . redolent of this year's shining motor-cars', suggest a romantic sensibility and an extravagant turn of phrase more in line with that Nick who talks of Gatsby's 'glowing garden', the 'romantic possibilities of his parties', his 'romantic readiness', his 'dispens[ing] of starlight to casual moths', than anyone else.

As Nick himself implicitly suggests, Gatsby may speak at two levels of discourse: his 'elaborate formality of speech' (seemingly implied by the marker 'old sport') and 'elegant sentences' not absolutely incompatible with the 'threadbare' content of an 'appalling sentimentality'. However, when Nick apparently reports Gatsby's speech, the words used bear no relation to any example of direct discourse given:

His heart beat faster as Daisy's white face came up to his own. He knew that when he kissed this girl, and

forever wed his unutterable vision to her perishable breath,
his mind would never romp again like the mind of God. So
he waited, listening for a moment longer to the tuning-fork
that had been struck upon a star. Then he kissed her. At
his lips' touch she blossomed for him like a flower and the
incarnation was complete (p. 107).

We do not know whose voice speaks here. There is, moreover, a clear note of ambiguity about the status of the words
themselves. While at the passage's conclusion, Nick speaks
of 'all [Gatsby] said', at its start we are told, 'He talked a
lot about the past, and I *gathered* that he wanted . . . ' The
stressed word suggests rather that Nick is sifting and sorting
materials that are not fully coherent. Where too, we ask, is
Gatsby's 'appalling sentimentality'? Tuning-forks struck on
stars, Daisy's (redundant) flower-like blossoming, perhaps,
but apart from this, the tone and linguistic control of the
passage are remarkable. In both my quoted examples we
can easily transpose certain words to Gatsby's mouth ('I
just felt married to her, old sport'), but the idiolect as a
whole is suspiciously close to that Nick uses throughout the
novel. Gatsby's own speaking voice, his own actual language,
may in fact be thoroughly marginalized. The quasi-religious
discourse of both passages – 'incarnation', 'following of a
grail' – is nowhere directly attributed to Gatsby. It is Nick
alone who talks of 'the sacredness of [Gatsby's] vigil', Nick's
words which constantly filter Gatsby's story.

When Gatsby does speak in direct discourse – 'Can't repeat
the past? . . . Why of course you can! . . . I'm going to fix
everything just the way it was before' (p. 106) – his words
appear to trigger Nick's rhetorical imagination. Nick feeds
off Gatsby; his Yale education with its 'literary' bent allows
him to rhetorically extend Gatsby's one-liners. They form a
double act, with Gatsby as formally ill-educated (two weeks
in St Olaf's; five months at Oxford) straight-man who supplies
the initial few words on which Nick's more abstract and
rhetorical flights depend. They form complementary parts of
one voice:

'[Daisy's] got an indiscreet voice', I remarked. 'It's full
of – ' I hesitated.

'Her voice is full of money,' he said suddenly.
That was it. I'd never understood before. It was full
of money – that was the inexhaustible charm that rose
and fell in it, the jingle of it, the cymbals' song of it . . .
High in a white palace, the king's daughter, the golden
girl . . . (p. 115).

Because of Fitzgerald's use of indirect speech within the
novel, it is finally impossible to say to what extent the
narrating instance (Carraway's voice) obliterates character
(Gatsby); exactly how far Nick integrates the latter's words
'into his own speech, and thus *expresses* them in his own style'.
I would argue strongly, though, on the basis of the examples
given, that Carraway's voice 'blend[s] with, to the point of
amounting to, [Gatsby's] language'.[25] This is no criticism –
rather part of the novel's powerful effect whereby Carraway,
narrator-protagonist, takes charge of, univocalizes, all the
materials at his command. Modal distance is very considerable here. Nick, in gathering up 'the whole kitty' of memories
available to him – his own and those of others – takes over
Gatsby's story, transmits it, and gives it its meaning, putting
his stylistic and interpretive signature (verbal and ideological
focalization: see next section) firmly on it; the novel becomes,
like Proust's, 'a fine example of narrative egocentrism'.[26]

III

Focalization

Genette describes perspective as, after distance, 'the second mode of regulating information' (p. 185) in narrative
fiction. It is an aspect of mood in so far as it concerns
the way in which such narrative information is screened
through a number of different channels, told '*according to
one point of view or another*' (pp. 161–2) which can be more
or less restricted. Focalization, then, is a matter of whose
'point-of-view' controls or orients the narrative at any particular textual point. Genette's replacement of the latter term
constitutes an attempt – if not a completely successful one
– to escape the stress on the visual connoted by 'point of

view'. In discussing this area, Genette makes an important and fundamental initial distinction between *focalization* and *narration* in any text: between 'who sees?' and 'who speaks?' A straightforward example of this difference can be seen at the beginning of William Faulkner's 'Barn Burning':

> The store in which the Justice of the Peace's court was sitting smelled of cheese. The boy, crouched on his nail keg at the back of the crowded room, knew he smelled cheese, and more: from where he sat he could see the ranked shelves close packed with the solid, squat, dynamic shapes of tin cans . . . [27]

Here, the narrator who tells the story refers to the boy, through whose eyes (and nose!) we perceive the room, in the third person. This clearly signals the gap between voice and mood, narration and perspective. It is the boy who sees: he therefore is the focalizer.

Rather than constructing a typology of all the different possible forms of narration and focalization,[28] I will focus only on my core text. Immediate problems in separating off the two areas become apparent in the fact of Fitzgerald's use of a retrospective 'first person' narrator, Nick Carraway. For Nick speaks *and* sees in *The Great Gatsby*, is both narrator and focalizer. This is, of course, not uncommon in narrative fiction, and does not prevent us from looking at Nick in terms of each category in turn. As focalizer in the narrative Nick does, however, hold a dual position, for his 'point of view' is represented from two temporal perspectives. This causes a 'double focalization'[29] effect to be produced. As narrator-focalizer, Nick, the retrospective narrator, knows the full story; knows Gatsby more intimately than anyone else. His perspective is that of a narrating agent separated off in terms of both time and knowledge from the younger Nick who appears within his narrative. The introduction to the story, and later statements such as 'I see now that this has been a story of the West, after all', 'West Egg . . . still figures in my more fantastic dreams. I see it as a night scene by El Greco' (p. 167), and 'After two years I remember the rest of that day . . . as an endless drill of police' (p. 155), show both in their use of the present tense and in their other temporal markers ('still', 'now') that we are being presented with Nick's focalization from the narrating present, what Nick feels when writing. Nick, however, also has the status of internal focalizer within the narrative told by his older self: as that Nick who participates as a character in the narrated story, who has not the knowledge of that narrating self; who initially – for example – does not even recognise Gatsby when he is speaking to him ('This is an unusual party for me. I haven't even seen the host', p. 49). His focalization is represented from two positions: that of the narrating present, what Nick feels and knows when writing; that of a narrated past, what Nick felt and saw at the time of the events described. Such focalizing tactics produce a narrative situation which can be described by applying to Fitzgerald, in modified form, Genette's comments on Proust:

> Between the information [of the internal focalizer, the actor-observer Nick Carraway who comes East 'in the spring of twenty-two'] and the omniscience of the novelist is the information of the narrator [Nick who tells the story after Gatsby's death, after his own return from the East], who disposes of it according to his own lights and holds it back only when he sees a precise reason for doing so (p. 206).

The movement between – and overlap within – these two focalizing positions accounts for some of the text's most interesting effects.

Types of focalization

Internal focalization (who sees?) in any narrative text implies restriction:[30] seeing narrative events through a single frame. Focalization is not necessarily restricted to one person. Particularly in modernist novels, changes in focalization are common: in Genette's words, 'any single formula of focalization does not . . . always bear on an entire work, but rather on a definite narrative section, which can be very short' (p. 191).[31] When, for example, Nick speaks of the 'number of young Englishmen dotted about' at Gatsby's party who were 'agonizingly aware of the easy money in the vicinity and convinced that it was theirs for a few words in the right key' (p. 43), the focalization is theirs: their knowledge or 'point of view' is the one briefly presented.

The example, however, raises the issue of the different types of focalization to be found in a text; why 'point of view' with its stress on vision alone is too narrow a term to be wholly satisfactory. Here, for instance, we are not concerned with those young Englishmen's perceptions, what they hear, see, or touch, but rather with their cognitions, what they know and believe. Such a distinction is drawn by Shlomith Rimmon-Kenan, who is, in turn, modifying Uspensky's schema in *A Poetics of Composition*. Drawing on both these sources, I want to briefly suggest some of the different facets of focalization[32] directly relevant to Fitzgerald's novel.

(a) Focalization: the spatial, temporal and perceptual facet

'The spatial [and] temporal coordinates from which the narration is conducted' (Uspensky p. 57); the point – in time and space – at which the focalizer is situated. An external narrator-focalizer, one located outside the represented events, is often associated with the type of panoramic 'birds-eye view' with which Forster's *A Passage to India* (1924) opens; the kind of 'simultaneous focalization' which occurs when the reader is offered views of what is happening in a number of different places at one particular time (Rimmon-Kenan gives Patrick White's *Voss* (1957) as her example). As external narrator-focalizer in *The Great Gatsby*, Nick is located in the mid-West. From this spatial position he 'panoramically' describes the location of his earlier self prior to the commencement of the main story – in this same city, in his father's office, in Europe. Though the narrative returns to this spatial focalization at certain points, for the most part its locating importance recedes into the background as Fitzgerald makes use of what Uspensky calls a 'concurrence of the spatial position': Nick the narrator metaphorically holding a camera behind the head of that earlier version of himself who is a protagonist in the described story. The narrator, in Uspensky's terms, seems to be 'attached' to the character 'and thus holds the same spatial position as [him]. For example, if the character enters a room, the narrator describes [it]' (p. 58).

Nick's spatial position as internal focalizer, as character and participant in the story, is a limited one. This is what is, therefore, presented to the reader for the majority of the novel. It is limited to his actual ability to see, hear, etc. – where he is placed in relation to the depicted event. The restrictive nature of Nick's spatial perspective as narrative participant is clear when he watches Tom and Daisy after Myrtle's death through 'a rift at the sill' beneath the drawn blind of their kitchen window. He sees 'Daisy and Tom . . . sitting opposite each other . . . ' (p. 138), but his angle of vision is narrow because of his location. The notion of such restriction is reinforced by the fact that he watches them through glass. He suggests that they are conspiring together, but that reading is a pantomimic one, based on gesture and appearance, not words.[33]

Nick reports elsewhere on Daisy and Gatsby's appearance together in Louisville in 1917. As Nick was not himself present there, any knowledge of events then occurring must be focalized by one whose spatial position allowed access to them, one who *saw or heard* what happened (Jordan, positioned 'five feet away' from the roadster in which they both sit). The emphasized words point up the connection between the spatial facet of focalization and what Rimmon-Kenan calls *the perceptual facet*: what is heard, seen, smelt, etc. This latter is the most obvious sign of focalization: as Jordan says regarding the Louisville years, 'I didn't *lay eyes on* him again for over four years' (my stress). This sentence also makes clear the very close relationship between the spatial and temporal facets of focalization: where one sees from and when one sees go hand-in-hand together.

As external narrator-focalizer, Nick's position in terms of chronological location is retrospective: he knows in advance, as evidenced at the novel's start, all the events which are to occur in the text. As internal focalizer, his position is 'synchronically related to the past events',[34] limited to what he sees and knows at the time the events occur. The description is carried out from a position contemporaneous to the action occurring. So, when Nick sees Gatsby reaching towards what 'might have been the end of a dock' the restrictions which accompany chronological contemporaneity are obvious: as retrospective narrator-focalizer (rather than as internal focalizer), Nick knows exactly what Gatsby is reaching for, what the green light signifies. This situation, where Nick, relating the story from a chronological position of full knowledge, presents us with his earlier (ignorant) self is a tactic which Genette would see as a type of transgression.

Transgression is a central notion in his study of narrative. For the term effectively points to the way in which a novelist breaks 'the limits of his own narrative "system"'' (p. 208). Transgressions constitute shock-effects, ruptures of limits, a shaking of 'the traditional equilibrium of novelistic form' (p. 259). Such violations of literary norms are key areas of interest for Genette, suggesting as they do stress points where – consciously or unconsciously – novelistic needs are so deep as to push against and disrupt the very boundaries of the generic tradition. Here Fitzgerald's transgressive tactic is one which Genette would call paraliptic – the 'lateral ellipsis' (p. 52) or narrative sidestepping of a given element. In this case such 'sidestepping' consists of the autobiographical narrator silencing himself concerning information available to him at the time of writing. *The Great Gatsby* is a novel which makes consistent use of such paralipsis, since Nick's whole position as narrator depends on such (vital) suppressions.

As a footnote to my comments on the limitations of Nick's position regarding the spatial and temporal facets of focalization, the widening of angle at the novel's end is significant. Nick, in summing up his experiences, though still chronologically and spatially restricted (his last night in the East; on the shore), moves beyond these narrow boundaries, in speculative flight towards an all-embracing spatial and temporal ('panchronic') view – one more normally associated with narrative omniscience. He takes the reader with him through history, from the Dutch sailors to Gatsby and beyond, and geographically reaches from Long Island to the whole American continent. This shift suggests something of the way in which Nick escapes those restrictions with which the focalizing activity is associated; how his perspective stretches beyond its (reasonable) limits. If, on this occasion, the range of his 'vision' is partly validated by the speculative quality of some of his remarks, nevertheless the movement from tiptoeing in the dark, peeping through a crack in a frame, to this panoramic and panchronic position suggests an abrupt and highly revealing shift in focalizing level, suggests a totalizing tendency which stamps full and final meaning on what has previously been fragmentary and restrictive. Such a tendency, as we have seen in the section on speech representation, consistently marks Nick's activity in this text.

(b) Focalization: the psychological facet

Uspensky distinguishes between 'objective' description and subjective, 'some psychological point of view' (p. 82). This subjective psychological focalization is to be distinguished from the perceptual facet. The latter concerns the focalizer's sensory range. The former can be divided into two spheres: mental and emotional.[35] The mental field is that of cognition, what a character believes, knows, conjectures, remembers, conceptualizes: Myrtle's 'I knew right away I made a mistake . . . when I married [George]'. On a much wider scale, Nick's remembrances, which form the bulk of the text, constitute another such example. The story is formed by Nick, the narrator-focalizer's 'remembrance of things past' with all the subjectivity such filtering activity reveals.

Rimmon-Kenan describes the emotional component of focalization in terms which echo Uspensky's description of this general field as '"subjective" (coloured, involved)'[36] rather than an uninvolved neutrality. Nick's language – as I will later show – reveals his emotional empathy with Gatsby. Nick is also the channel through which the emotions of others are funnelled. 'Tom', he tells us, 'was feeling the hot whips of panic' (Tom's focalization); Myrtle's eyes were 'wide with jealous terror' (Myrtle's focalization). The double process of focalization occurring here is one which operates through the whole text and again suggests just how dominant Nick's position is:

   (i) cognitive focalization: what Nick knows concerning the focalized (object of focalization), Tom and Myrtle.

   (ii) emotional focalization: what Tom and Myrtle feel.

Problems arise here as to Nick's trustworthiness: how can we know he, as internal focalizer, interprets the feelings of others correctly? Uspensky suggests that in the case of a 'first person' narrator, both author and reader often seem to 'consolidate with him, and to identify with his image'.[37] This is true enough here. We trust our narrator unless there are clear signals not to: nothing in the above instances is subjectively at stake for Nick. He describes the feelings of others 'objectively' – bases his knowledge on the behaviour of those he describes. Such a situation is not always the case.[38]

It is important to note that these categories of focalization are not necessarily discrete. A glance at the 'eyes of Dr. T. J. Eckleberg' explains my meaning. Michaelis describes the eyes, objectively, as an advertisement (Michaelis' focalization-perceptual facet). Wilson responds to them with the words 'God sees everything' (p. 152), while Nick describes them as 'brood[ing] on over the solemn dumping ground' (p. 26). Wilson and Nick's responses belong to both the perceptual and psychological facet of focalization. What they objectively see (perceptual) is swiftly informed by a subjective response to that object. Wilson transposes his personal and marital failures to the realm of divine arbitration. Nick reads the landscape symbolically: ashes versus riotous nature, dumping ground versus carnival, entropy versus devotion and fervour of a quasi-religious kind. These descriptions belong to the mental facet of focalization, for Nick's use of connotative words (brood, solemn dumping ground) suggests a symbolic reading, or conceptualization, of reality.

The descriptions, however, equally belong to the emotional facet of focalization. Wilson's belief that the eyes represented in the advertisement are the eyes of God, suggests his unbalanced mental and emotional state following his wife's death. Nick's conceptualization of the eyes and the scene they survey in terms of binary oppositions (dumping ground versus grail quest, etc.) suggests a polarizing tendency which operates at an emotional as well as a mental level. The description of 'ash-gray men', of brooding eyes – not objective language, this – indicates the kind of sinking of the heart which is recurrently contrasted in the text to Nick's delight in romantic fulsomeness. His emotive celebration of Gatsby is matched by a similarly emotive dismissal of the rottenness of those who surround him, the 'foul dust' which 'floated in the wake of his dreams' (p. 8). The associative link between 'foul dust' and valley of ashes endorses the emotional connotations of his earlier description.

(c) Focalization: the verbal facet

Shifts in language often reveal shifts in focalizing position. Even the way names are used reveal source of focalization.[39] Gatsby is called – at various textual points – Jimmy, Jay, Mr Nobody from Nowhere. Even without the framing contexts, we would know whose words are being used, whose focalization is involved (Gatsby's father's, Daisy's, Tom's). Specific phraseological characteristics attach themselves to individual characters, thus Gatsby's affectation of upper-class Englishness: 'old sport'. In this novel there, at first glance, appears to be a very obvious correlation between specific verbal traits and the character to whom they belong, because of the use of direct quotations; and consequently this verbal facet would seem redundant in terms of the pinpointing of the focalizing position. My examination of speech representation has, however, already shown how the language of the text raises real questions concerning the nature of such a position.

In my section on speech representation I was concerned with how Nick mediated the words of others. Here my stress is on his words (both written and spoken): how his language signals an emotional and ideological involvement with Gatsby. For Nick's whole life as represented in the text comes to focus on his relationship with, and his curiosity about, Gatsby. His whole project as external narrator-focalizer is to explain what he has come to see of value in him. What Genette calls a 'hidden strain' is inflicted here on the principle of point of view in terms of 'the difficulty [Nick] experiences in satisfying his curiosity [about Gatsby] and in penetrating into the existence of another' (p. 205). For Nick has only partial access to Gatsby's motivations. His assessment of him is highly subjective, biased. It is Nick's focalization which is crucial to this text, and his attitude to Gatsby becomes a consistent one, shared by Nick both as the story is progressing and after it is over.

Nick's subjective attitude (psychological facet of focalization) to Gatsby is revealed in his language (verbal facet) as internal focalizer. This can be seen first in the way Nick's words clearly signal his personal involvement with him. When Nick, for example, tells Gatsby 'you're worth the whole damn bunch put together' (p. 146), the expression – containing the only profanity, however mild, Nick uses in the text – reveals his strength of feeling. Gatsby smiles in response to his remark, and the wonderful phrase follows, 'as if we'd been in ecstatic cahoots on that fact all the time'. 'Cahoot' is a word 'used in the [American] South and West to denote a . . . *partnership*'[40] (my stress). Nick's personal involvement with Gatsby is clear, from his acting as 'go-between' who makes possible the resumption of Gatsby and Daisy's presumably adulterous relationship to his gesture, later to be copied by Holden Caulfield, of erasing the obscene word from Gatsby's step (the silencing of 'an alternative form of writing'?).[41] Nick's 'romance' with Jordan is a pale imitation of that he sees Gatsby pursue; he calls the whole thing off with Gatsby's death. His Prufrockian realization of the encroaching years ('a thinning list of single men to know . . . thinning hair' p. 129) directly relates to that 'youth and mystery' Nick claims Gatsby recognizes and tries to recapture in Daisy. Nick's personal involvement with Gatsby is indisputable, resonates everywhere, too, in his language.

Such involvement can be particularly noted, also, in Nick as narrator-focalizer, and his use of what Genette calls *modal locutions*: the way in which words such as 'perhaps, undoubtedly, as if, seem, appear' are used. Such modalizing locutions 'allow the narrator to say hypothetically what he could not assert without stepping outside internal focalization' (p. 203). They function as 'unavowed paralepsis'. Paralepsis is a transgressive giving out of more information than is immediately accessible to the focalizing centre at the time of the action – 'giving information that should be left aside' (Genette, p. 195). Here it is 'unavowed' in that this giving of information consists of guesswork or speculation, which constitutes a move beyond a position of ignorance or limitation to that of interpretation. Such locutions allow Carraway to hypothesize about Gatsby's secret centre, tell what he cannot – as internal focalizer – actually know.

Such modal locutions swamp *The Great Gatsby*. Two key examples are on the occasion of Gatsby and Daisy's re-meeting when Nick says:

There *must have been* moments even that afternoon when Daisy tumbled short of his dreams – not through her own fault, but because of the colossal vitality of his illusion. It had gone beyond her, beyond everything . . . (p. 92)

and after Myrtle's death, where he comments:

I have an idea that Gatsby himself didn't believe it [Daisy's telephone call] would come, and *perhaps* he no longer cared. *If that was true he must have felt* that he had lost the old warm world . . . *He must have looked* up at an unfamiliar sky through frightening leaves and shivered as he found what a grotesque thing a rose is . . . (p. 153)

In the examples of indirect speech previously mentioned, Nick's words seem to eat up Gatsby's; so here, too, Nick's conception of Gatsby's romantic quest endows very heavy significance to what, on Gatsby's part – in both instances – is only silence. Gatsby says nothing: Nick is on both occasions heavily interpreting. Nick's use of modals swamps the literal facts and direct observations he has available to him. In the second passage, for example, we have only interpretation, no objective description. Nick's own value scheme (ideological facet of focalization) is at issue as well as Gatsby's, here. Though Gatsby believes you can 'repeat the past', it is Nick who imposes a thoroughgoing romantic credo on Gatsby. His allusion here is to the perfect romantic moment. Time is halted, and the rose is held in perfect condition with delicate bud just opened. The clock starts and the rose blows, withers, and fades. Gatsby is left metaphorically holding a withered and 'grotesque' remnant of what he once had. Such readings suggest an evaluative stance which may bear more relation to Nick's own value scheme and sensibility than to Gatsby's.

Linguistic and ideological aspects of Nick's focalization coalesce as he converts Gatsby's experience finally to a level of metaphoric significance which (paraleptically) shatters all the previously formulated conceptual frames of the narrative. I will only highlight the most significant parts of the ending, but a clear use of modal locutions ('man *must have held* his breath', Gatsby's 'dream *must have seemed* so close') launches a set of metaphorical parallels between the green light on

Daisy's dock, the green breast of the new world which flowered
for the Dutch sailors, and the green light which represents
'the orgastic future'; between Gatsby's 'wonder' and that of
those same sailors; between Gatsby's story and America's.
Such modal locutions finally seem to completely vanish as
what begins as speculation ends as (paraleptic) firm conviction,
fact/information Nick cannot know: 'Gatsby believed', 'we will
run faster' (pp. 171–2). Nick's interpretation of Gatsby has
swallowed up any literal knowledge of him in an act of metaphoric transcendence.

All this shows how, as the text proceeds, Nick's exploitation
of the possibilities of indirect discourse, his pressing against
the limits of what he can actually know and see, leads to a
powerful processing of the narrative through the controlling
medium of his language (verbal facet of focalization), his
reading of reality (ideological facet), and his attitude towards
it (psychological facet). Gatsby – who is framed by Nick in a
series of fixed images (arms stretched towards Daisy's dock;
on his porch, 'hand up in a formal gesture of farewell' after
his party p. 56) – is finally incorporated into a mythic reading
of his story that feeds off, and leaves far behind, the literal
and objective presentation of the figure within that frame.
Such focalizing tactics should lead us to take some kind of
a rain-check on just how far we, as readers, can go along
with Nick's point of view. After all, this is the period when
great use is being made of the ironic monologue, and John F.
Callahan argues strongly for a reading of the text in accord
with 'the same principles of distance and detachment between
Carraway and Fitzgerald that critics generally are willing to
respect with Prufrock and T. S. Eliot'.[42]

(d) Focalization: the ideological aspect

As has emerged in the foregoing discussion, the verbal and
ideological aspects of focalization are intimately connected.
Ideological, in Uspensky's terms, is equivalent to 'a general
system of viewing the world conceptually' (p. 8): thus a system of values or world view.[43] Ideological evaluation can be
carried out from one dominant viewpoint. In *The Great Gatsby*,
Carraway's is obviously such a perspective: his evaluations
are presented overtly at commencement and closure of the

text, covertly throughout it. Different ideological focalizations (which may be revealed through a character's words and actions) may be subordinated to this dominant perspective. Thus Tom's racism, male chauvinism, and self-centredness are clearly textually apparent, clearly evaluated from Nick's hierarchically superior position: 'They were careless people, Tom and Daisy . . .' (p. 170). A fuller discussion of Nick's ideological focalization will take place in the final section of my chapter.

What became clear in my description of the verbal facet of focalization was, however, the overlap between these two areas. For just as the language used in a text can often indicate a character's emotional position, so can it indicate his or her value system: 'the world view of a character . . . may be defined through stylistic analysis of his speech'.[44] Tom's first words, 'I've got a nice place here . . . it belonged to Demaine, the oil man . . . We'll go inside' (p. 13), reveal his self-satisfaction with the material comforts his wealth has bought. His mode of speech, though, also reveals a solipsistic base to personality and world view. He speaks these words as a final statement: no opinion is solicited, no approval is sought. An inherent sense of authoritativeness and superiority (based solely on material and social status) is established here, to be repetitively signalled throughout the text. This connection between language and ideology again suggests the overlapping nature of the categories Uspensky uses (without devaluing their usefulness).

IV

Narration

Although Genette's distinction between narration and focalization is a useful one, it is not absolutely watertight, as my discussion of Nick as narrator-focalizer in the last sections – one who both speaks and sees – suggests. For the way in which Nick sees inevitably affects, informs, the way he speaks. I now wish to focus more fully on the telling of the narrative in this section of the chapter, and will conclude it by giving final illustration of this narration/focalization overlap.

In briefly focusing on aspects of the narrating activity in *The Great Gatsby*, I will again suggest the ways in which this text creates its totalizing effects. I will then return in my final section to focus again on Nick's ideological focalization (one which affects everything connected with the telling of his story) but in more detail.

Time of the narrating

Tristam Shandy spends a year writing to describe one day of his life:

> he observes that he has gotten 364 days behind, that he has therefore moved backward rather than forward, and that, living 364 times faster than he writes, it follows that the more he writes the more there remains for him to write; that, in short, his undertaking is hopeless.

Sterne comically highlights the fact that writing takes time. In most narratives, however:

> the fictive narrating . . . is considered to have no duration; or, more exactly, everything takes place as if the question of its duration had no relevance. One of the fictions of literary narrating . . . is that the narrating involves an instantaneous action, without a temporal dimension.[45]

Carraway's narrating act is unusual in that it is not freed from the order of time. Marcel's, on the other hand, in Proust's *Recherche* is, as Genette points out, 'instantaneous', 'rapture', ' "a minute freed from the order of [T]ime" ' (p. 223). The time scheme of this story's occurrences is clear enough. Nick comes East in the spring of 1922. The main events happen that summer, with Myrtle's death day/Nick's thirtieth birthday occurring right at that summer's end: 'almost the last, certainly the warmest, of the summer' (p. 109). Gatsby's death occurs between half-past two and four o'clock the next afternoon, a day when 'an autumn flavor [was] in the air' (p. 146). Late in October, Nick meets Tom again in New York, and leaves for the West soon after. Narrating time is also clear, though the time scheme is less explicit. Nick starts writing within a year of returning home. He is finishing the narrative some two years after Gatsby's death.[46] Though Fitzgerald's use of narrating time here is highly unusual, it does not seriously disrupt the normal effect of 'final convergence' found in retrospective first person narrations. I will shortly show how such an effect, where story 'overtake[s] the narrating',[47] is produced in the text's final passages to give an impression of absolute final coherence and conclusion.

Narrative levels

A brief run through the terms Genette uses to describe the different levels of narrative, and the position of the narrator with respect to these narrative levels, is necessary at this point. In accord with my previous policy, I will define these terms only to the extent that they apply to, and clarify, the text at hand. A comprehensive typology of Genette's terms can be found in his *Narrative Discourse*, and also in Rimmon-Kenan's *Narrative Fiction*.

In *The Great Gatsby* there are various narrative levels apparent. Genette used the term diegetic, which he takes from Plato, as the base from which he constructs his typology of such levels. The term essentially means *the telling of a narrative*, the spatial-temporal boundaries of that narrative, the events and participants contained within it. Diegesis designates, in terms of narrative levels, 'the universe of the first narrative',[48] that story commencing in this case 'In my younger and more vulnerable years'.

Narrative levels operate in hierarchic relation to one another: one frames another. So when any fictional character within the diegetic frame tells a story, we move onto another level which Genette calls the metadiegetic. So, for example, 'One October day in nineteen-seventeen – (said Jordan Baker that afternoon . . . ' (p. 72) constitutes 'a second degree narrative', or metadiegesis (meta here meaning 'proceeding from'). If a further level of narration were to be found within the frame of Jordan (or anyone else's) second degree narrative, it would be called a meta-metadiegesis, etc.

The above metadiegesis (Jordan's story) functions in explanatory and thematic relationship to the diegesis.[49] Thus, her narrative explains Daisy and Gatsby's past relationship, and thematically establishes a contrast between Gatsby's 'romantic' behaviour and Tom's philandering which parallels that on the diegetic level. Such relationships also exist where, rather than directly quoting the stories of others, Nick 'absorb[s] them into his own': 'She was the first "nice" girl he had ever known . . . '. This kind of absorption, where a narrator on the diegetic level takes charge of a second level narrative, produces an ambiguous level of narrative which Genette terms the *pseudo-diegetic*.[50] The majority of both metadiegetic and pseudo-diegetic narratives in this novel function to explain Gatsby's past (are thus metadiegetic or pseudo-diegetic analepses – analepsis equalling 'flashback' in Genette).

Narrators are described by Genette in terms of the level on which they operate. Narrators can be either heterodiegetic or homodiegetic; extradiegetic or intradiegetic. Nick Carraway is an *extradiegetic homodiegetic narrator*. He narrates from a position of retrospective knowledge 'superior to the story he narrates', a narrator 'in the first degree'[51] (and thus extradiegetic or standing outside the diegesis); but he is also present as a participant in the story he tells (thus homodiegetic). Furthermore, as he plays a central, rather than a marginal role in this story, we can narrow our definition one stage further to call him an *extradiegetic autodiegetic narrator*. A useful rule in terms of the relation between narration and narrative levels, is Rimmon-Kenan's 'narration is always at a higher narrative level than the story it narrates. Thus the diegetic level is narrated by an extradiegetic narrator, the metadiegetic level by a diegetic (or intradiegetic) one.'[52] Thus, Jordan in the previous example is an *intradiegetic homodiegetic* narrator (she plays a minor part in the story she tells); pseudo-diegetic narratives of the 'One autumn night, five years before . . . ' type ('when he kissed this girl and forever wed his unutterable visions . . . ') waver between the categories of extradiegetic heterodiegetic narration (Nick, first level narrator, absent from the story he tells), and intradiegetic homodiegetic narration (Gatsby, second level narrator, present in the reported story).

The way in which Fitzgerald exploits the possibilities open to him in terms of both the relationship between narrative levels, and the handling of time in the text, can be seen in the final paragraphs of the novel where he creates that effect of final convergence to which reference has been made. For here extradiegetic narrator (that Nick who stands outside the frame of the main narrative, retrospectively telling his and Gatsby's story) and internal focalizer (that intradiegetic Nick who is experiencing the story's events as they occur) are suddenly and effectively fused.

Such a fusion is transgression in the form of what Genette calls *metalepsis* – an 'effect of strangeness' marked by an unexpected transition between one narrative level and another.[53] For here the narrating voice finally overlaps/blurs with that of the internal focalizer, Nick, through whose experiencing eyes we metaphorically look; narrating instance and narrated event are welded almost imperceptibly together. At the novel's conclusion, Nick as internal focalizer sits on the sand near Gatsby's house before leaving the East:

> . . . as I sat there brooding on the old, unknown world, I thought of Gatsby's wonder when he first picked out the green light at the end of Daisy's dock. He had come a long way to this blue lawn, and his dream must have seemed so close that he could hardly fail to grasp it. He did not know that it was already behind him, somewhere back in that vast obscurity beyond the city, where the dark fields of the republic rolled on under the night.
>
> Gatsby believed in the green light, the orgastic future that year by year recedes before us. It eluded us then, but that's no matter – tomorrow we will run faster, stretch out our arms further . . . And one fine morning –
>
> So we beat on, boats against the current, borne back ceaselessly into the past (pp. 171–2).

Diegetic boundaries are crossed here as one voice flows into another. We lose our sense of where one narrative frame ends and the other begins as – concurrent with this crossing of narrative levels – internal focalizer merges with narrator-focalizer. For this is Nick speculating on Gatsby's story, but it is also Nick two years later, ending his book where he started it, celebrating Gatsby's romantic readiness.

If we look closely we can see where the two voices cross over. A switch in tense and a move from first person to third occurs in the 'Gatsby believed . . . ' paragraph. The shift in person is not, however, by itself a clear marker of a change in voice: it could be explained in terms of a rhetorical change in speculative gear on the part of the internal focalizer. The tense change is also masked by the fact that the paragraph in which it occurs begins in that past tense which has been the norm until then. I do not want to labour the point too much, merely to indicate that there is no textual break here; that one voice becomes another almost imperceptibly. The words which come to us from the internal focalizer and the voice of the extradiegetic narrator blur at the text's end. Appropriately enough, given the content of the story, time disappears. The temporal gap in the two positions is elided as the narrator, rhetorically finishing his text with a final flourish, merges almost indistinguishably with that earlier version of himself whose values he completely shares. To point out a transgression such as this is not to criticize. The challenge to novelistic form contained in it suggests a textual need to allow one voice and one voice only to be finally authoritative (and authoritarian?), one single voice which subtly but undeniably drowns out all others, in which all self divisions are (apparently) obliterated. Carraway's narrating voice carries all before it.

The power of this narrating presence is also illustrated in the way in which Nick transgresses the limitations of his position as narrator and tells that which cannot theoretically be available to him. This is a form of paralepsis (giving more information than is available in principle).[54] Nick shows evidence of narrative omniscience in this text – he knows too much about the story, passes beyond the frame of that narrating position available to him. We can see how such transgression operates by looking briefly at the narrative sequence beginning 'Now I want to go back a little' (p. 148) in Chapter Eight.

This sequence traces events which occur when Nick is absent from the scene. We are not directly told who gives Nick this information, who tells him the story of what happened the night before Gatsby's death. Nick recreates the story from a variety of sources, tells it in his voice. An aura of immediacy, though, is given to the scene by the use of direct discourse (the dialogue between Michaelis and

Wilson) which distracts the reader from the narrator's absence. Speculating on Nick's information source is quite possible though. Michaelis is present throughout the sequence, and after an initial refusal to pin down the source of narrative informattion and of focalization ('*They* had difficulty in locating the sister . . . ', '*Someone* . . . took her in his car', '*everyone* who came into the garage glanced irresistibly through [the door]. Finally, *someone* said it was a shame'), the passage settles into perceptual/spatial focalization through Michaelis ('Michaelis heard a car . . . ', 'Michaelis saw with a shock'). If Nick has, as seems likely, gained his information from him, there still seems something transgressive concerning the detailed quality of this information. He may have received from Michaelis reports of his and Wilson's conversation, but to be able to quote exactly? This objection is, however, provisionally answered by Nick's later references to 'newspaper reports' and 'Michaelis's testimony at the inquest'. These sources could account for this kind of detail, as well as the tracings of Wilson's movements which follow. However, hints remain that Nick is going beyond the limits of his position as narrator-focalizer. The description of Wilson's 'glazed eyes' turning:

> out to the ashheaps, where small gray clouds took on fantastic shapes and scurried here and there in the faint dawn wind (pp. 151–2).

is Nick's, not Michaelis'. It is of a piece with his prior description of the valley of ashes as 'fantastic farm' with its 'spasms of bleak dust'; its descriptive richness and irrelevance to the matter at hand – Wilson's behaviour – suggests, like the earlier description of 'the hard brown beetles . . . thudding against the dull light' (p. 149), the transgressive presence of an omniscient narrator.

Similar transgressions occur in two other passages. In Chapter Seven, Nick reports on Myrtle's death:

> The mouth was wide open and ripped a little at the corners, as though she had choked a little in giving up the tremendous vitality she had stored so long (p. 131).

Nick sees the corpse but we are given no sharp detail concerning it – it is wrapped in blankets on a table, masked by Tom's figure. Some first-hand witness (Michaelis) could later have described the physical appearance of the corpse, but the modal locution ('as though') is Nick's alone. Such paralepsis occurs, too, in Chapter Eight, when Nick repeats Gatsby's story of his earlier relationship with Daisy. While Gatsby is sent to Oxford instead of returning home as he so 'frantically' wished to do, Daisy:

> began to move again with the season; suddenly she was again keeping half a dozen dates a day with half a dozen men, and drowsing asleep at dawn with the beads and chiffon of an evening dress tangled among dying orchids on the floor beside her bed (p. 144).

The final touch of the 'dying' orchids, with its implication of perceptual presence, again suggests the way Nick tells us more than he can possibly know, gives us more information than was available to him at the time of the events; than has become available since. Nick's story may be based on facts (what he or others see, hear, know) but it goes beyond them.

I have here been speaking of Nick's narration, the way in which 'the sovereign *authority*'[55] of Nick's authorial presence stamps itself on this text; the narrating performance itself. But in describing the transgressive effect of such a narrator having too much knowledge at his disposal (noting the 'dying orchids' by the bed of a Daisy who neither he, nor the person supposedly giving him his information, is anywhere near!) I have used a term, paralepsis, which Genette restricts to the area of mood, not narration. This is significant. For narration cannot here be separated off from focalization. What Nick, as narrator, sees, knows, feels, etc. is crucial to the novel. Narration and focalization inextricably overlap. This overlap goes unrecognized by Genette, since it blurs the lines between his categories of mood and tense. He rather invents a new category, testimonial/ideological function of the narrating voice,[56] to contain the narrator's feelings and knowledge. To do this, however, is to deny the connection between Nick as internal focalizer (participating as character in the narrated story) and

Nick as narrator-focalizer (narrating the story but still having a *perspective* on the events he describes; a perspective he *shares* – see my comments on the novel's ending – with that earlier version of himself). Focalization and narration cannot finally be divorced in the way Genette suggests. This narrator both tells *and* sees ('I see now that this has been a story of the West, after all –' p. 167). Thus, my use in this chapter of the term narrator-focalizer which Rimmon-Kenan introduces.

It is, however, in transgressing his limits as narrator-focalizer (giving us scenes at which neither he himself was present, nor anyone else behind whose head he can metaphorically hold his camera [*focalize*]) that Nick alters the status of his *narrative*, shatters the boundaries which separate supposed historical accuracy from fictional artifice. Nick converts history into fiction: not what he sees but what he imagines becomes important. His totalizing vision is an artistic one (as well as an ideological and emotional one): it gives shape to the narrative he writes. Nick becomes a kind of non-fiction novelist, who in telling us what he factually sees and knows of Jay Gatsby (history), is always ready to pass the baton, to use Mailer's phrase,[57] to Nick the fiction writer. In this latter guise, Nick creates an imaginative world which fits his artistic needs (to produce a satisfactory narrative) rather than fitting the requirements of known truth. Nick's focalizing presence shapes the materials at his command to the fulfilling of his own requirements – emotional, ideological, and artistic. His narrative voice gives practical shape to such a project. So is the reader entirely sucked both into Nick's vision of the world and the narrative web he spins.

V

Nick's focalization: ideological facet

Vision and voice, therefore, coalesce in *The Great Gatsby*. In this last section of my chapter I wish to examine Nick's ideological facet of focalization to see what may be suggested as to the larger nature of his informing vision. I leave this section until now due to its comparative length, but also because this is the one point in the chapter where my concern with the mechanics of narrative leads to further contextual and interpretive levels of analysis.

Uspensky's main stress in treating the ideological facet of focalization is on how 'different evaluative systems [world views] assume definite relationships to each other, forming a complex design of oppositions and identifications' (p. 9) within a narrative. To follow this through in *The Great Gatsby* we might see Tom's arrogant eccentricity and physical power in terms of his status as a member of the dominant social and economic group. Gatsby's attractiveness appears in contrast a result of his romantic and 'spiritual' potential, here functioning in the only realm available, the materialistic and socially divided America of the 1920s, and unfortunately focused on an unworthy object of desire, Daisy. Nick in such a scheme operates as one who is a divided figure, a curious blend of the romantic and moralist; one who can celebrate and appreciate Gatsby's potential, but whose traditionalist values are appalled by the Eastern world in which that potential is betrayed.

This is reasonable, as far as it goes, though already I am interpreting: much of the above is never stated in the text. My interpretation is however heavily dependent on Nick's 'single, dominating point of view',[58] its distortions subject to no kind of corrective balance. Such distortion, signalled particularly in the emotive sweep of the final section where Nick removes Gatsby from his historical frame by the use of 'seductive, romantic . . . paralytic discourse',[59] suggests Nick's focalization needs very careful handling instead.

And it is this use of language (verbal aspect of focalization) which might allow us a way of approaching an evaluative position (Nick's) which is not subject to any kind of challenge within the text. This self-enclosed narrative world can only be framed by reference to the type of larger contextual frame I will suggest as I proceed. Nick's use of heightened rhetoric and romantic discourse is, as I have shown earlier, a feature of the text as a whole, but it is stepped up a notch at the novel's end ('last and greatest of all human dreams', 'transitory enchanted moment', 'capacity for wonder', etc.). Nick has made Gatsby a hero on a romantic quest throughout his narrative. This results in a tendency, confirmed in this ending, to remove his story to the level of the abstract, the emotional, and the personal:

to create a Keatsian world which lacks historical referent. In doing this, he removes Gatsby out of history.

Gatsby's story can, however, be read in terms of what it does reveal about the conditions of American life in the 1920s. There are other ways of approaching it than Nick's. Stuart Ewen, writing about this period, draws links between the notion of the socially constructed self (the self not as solid, coherent, genuine, but as an 'empty vessel to be filled and refilled according to the expectations of others and the needs of the moment')[60] and the world of advertising expanding so fast at the time. These are connections open to the reader to pursue: connections Gatsby himself would appear to have made. For, in order to cross class lines, he has constructed a self to fit the needs of others. This is nothing unusual; it is a classic American paradigm from Ben Franklin onwards. What is new is the way that self, the Jay Gatsby he has invented, is bolstered through the techniques and props borrowed from the world of advertising and commodification. The notion of 'personal magnetism',[61] a prime value in an other-directed 1920s incorporated America, fitted neatly with that of 'commodity self'; the self perfected through the use of commodities, to attain success. A toothpaste advertisement of the period ran, for example, 'A flashing smile is worth more than a good sized bank account. It wins friends'.[62] Commodity self easily becomes the self as commodity. Daisy shows a touch of real intuition when she recognizes the packaged product Gatsby has made of himself: 'You resemble the advertisement of the man . . . You know the advertisement of the man . . . ' (p. 114).

Gatsby's 'self', I would suggest, can be seen in such terms: as commodity self, constructed to meet the circumstances he is to encounter. As such, his appeal to 1920s consumption-oriented America is readily understandable. The white flannels, marble steps, champagne glasses bigger than finger bowls, sunken baths, etc., all add to the impression of desirability he conveys. Daisy sobs over his 'beautiful shirts' (p. 89), part of the array of props which support/compose his persona. But Gatsby also creates the self as commodity to sell to Cody, Wolfsheim, Daisy, and to Nick (who has become in turn, by the time of writing, his PR man). Gatsby sells this commodity both socially and in the business realm, succeeding through his made image. Perhaps that is what he had learnt best from Franklin. Gatsby's 'flashing smile' – one of those 'rare smiles with a quality of eternal reassurance in it' (p. 49) – wins both good sized bank account and friendship. If Gatsby's autobiography gives Nick the impression of 'skimming hastily through a dozen magazines' (p. 65), so does his persona: he is the man in all the adverts, the 'man with the kindly face',[63] whose smile makes him into 'an ecstatic patron of recurrent light' (p. 86).

This constructed image, despite certain flaws, is by and large convincing. Why does he fail? Gatsby evades the pro-letarian world to which he was born, slips between social and economic barriers, because of his implicit understanding of the power of the image and of advertising in American culture in the 1920s. It is in directly challenging Tom, the only member of the dominant class so confronted, that Gatsby's made image is deconstructed. Nick puts 'Jay Gatsby' in quotation marks after the hotel scene in which Tom, placed under threat, cuts through Gatsby's 'front'. And Richard Godden sketches, in deliberately exaggerated form, the set of socio-economic reasons which can be called on to explain Gatsby's final defeat:

> Tom Buchanan, having disembodied his own wife for purposes of display, needs to approach denied satisfactions through the body of the working-class female; an upwardly mobile Gatsby seeks status via the release and theft of the feminine leisure class body. In response, Tom extends the hegemony of his class to the abused industrial male . . . The double death secures Buchanan's grip on the leisure class 'token' and releases him from the growing threat of his own uneasy liaison with the industrial class. Along the way vengeance is enacted by the leisure class female on the offending body of her working-class counterpart – one of Myrtle's breasts is left flapping, the blood drains away and her vitality is conspicuously evacuated.[64]

Nick does not explain Gatsby in such terms. Indeed, there is no reason why he should. He is not a Marxist, rather a middle-class conservative from the Mid-West. In making such distinctions, however, we do get a line on

Nick's ideological focalization. He does not come up with such a decidedly 'unromantic' explanation; does not analyze the conditions of contemporary American history to explain Gatsby's goals (why Daisy is the one 'object' on the 'market place' he desires) and defeat. Rather he retreats, 'cuts and runs' to adapt Callahan's words,[65] to the realm of myth.

Myths are, in Richard Slotkin's words, 'stories, drawn from history, that have acquired through usage over many generations a symbolizing function central to the culture of the society that produces them'.[66] Nick converts Gatsby's story into an old American narrative: the failure of the dream of perfection.[67] In this scenario, Gatsby replays the Dutch sailors' story, focusing eyes of innocent wonder on the green light of unrealizable desire. Nick 'freezes experience'[68] here into unchanging repetition (that which has happened before, is going to happen again). Historical process, the world of social praxis represented in the text, is replaced by stasis. This myth-making falsifies experience; is, in Slotkin's words, 'partial representation masquerading as the whole truth'. Consigning Gatsby's story to the realm of the eternal and timeless ('so we beat on . . . ceaselessly into the past'), Nick appeals to 'ritualized emotions, habitual associations, memory, nostalgia', rather than questioning the real historical meaning of the events which have occurred. In doing so, he denies the possibility of 'interpreting and controlling the changing world'.[69]

This denial may be related to Nick's final step back to his mid-Western world, essentially that of the past (of 'my father['s] . . . advice', the 'fundamental decencies', etc.). Nick's shaping of the text to fit his own emotional and ideological needs may tie in with this (implicit) conservatism, the nature of his own social and economic position. For though Gatsby swiftly by-passes the proletarian world by his creation of a deeply attractive version of the modern American self, the general lack of such movement is implicit in every detail of the narrative. Brief references to a 'cobbled slum' near Port Roosevelt (p. 66), 'the hot whistles of the National Biscuit Company' (p. 109), never allow us to completely forget that a world of production lies beneath that of leisured consumption highlighted in the novel. Nick's allusion to 'my Finn' (note the possessive) who lives among 'soggy whitewashed alleys' (p. 81) is part of a series of sporadic references to those who form the working base – chauffeurs, caterers, gardeners, grocers – on which rest all the social relations so casually depicted in the text. Nick, middle class and traditional, whose final retreat is to the old values, the world of his father, has no stake in explicitly revealing the injustices and power relations on which American life is based.[70] He, after all, is reasonably well off, and content with his socio-economic lot. To tell Gatsby's story as 'class-battle', one whose attempt to climb the class divide ('I'll be damned if I see how you got within a mile of her [Daisy] unless you brought the groceries to the back door', Tom says, p. 125) is wrecked by a reassertion of power on the part of those at the apex of the socio-economic system, is just not in his conservative nature. Tom and Daisy become 'careless people', nothing else.

Nick's consignment of Gatsby's story to the realm of the eternal and timeless may be a way of avoiding such historical realities. It may be more personal, a laying on of 'meaning', a hyperidealization of Gatsby, in response to his own (failed) life. The emotional freight which accompanies his removal of Gatsby to the level of romance and of myth may reflect his own emotional need to step out of history (which, in a sense, he finally does);[71] to impose personal patterns of meaning which exist independently of it. Readings of Nick's ideological perspective remain tentative. They do suggest, however, that any study of 'ideology' in a text cannot be separated out from a larger frame of historical reference. To examine the mechanics of narrative (here the ideological facet of focalization) is not necessarily to preclude the possibility of interpretation and historical contextualization. It can indeed, inspire them. Both Genette and Uspensky, in their concentration on the closed world of the text, resist – to varying degree – such a move. This subject is one to which I will return in my next two chapters.

2

Time and Narrative: Faulkner's *The Sound and the Fury*

I

On the wall above the cupboard, invisible save at night, by lamplight and even then evincing an enigmatic profundity because it had but one hand, a cabinet clock ticked, then with a preliminary sound as if it had cleared its throat, struck five times.

'Eight o'clock,' Dilsey said.[1]

Clock time may be artificial, 'the position of mechanical hands on an arbitrary dial' (p. 74), but it is inescapable. Based as it is on the natural measure of the passing of the day, it cannot be stopped: twisting off the hands of your watch is a gesture of futility. Time is shared; is public. In a narrative it is that which the protagonists have in common, and by which their interactions are measured. Time, according to Paul Ricoeur, is also 'a mystery'. It is enigmatic in that it is both repetition and change, 'the observations that are to be made regarding it cannot be unified'.[2] Day repeats day, season repeats season, in circular and eternal pattern, yet time is the agent of all change. 'Time "is"', paradoxically, repetition within irreversible change'.[3]

Both repetition and change figure strongly in *The Sound and the Fury*. The Compson family disintegrates yet repetitions

44

and duplications abound. When Quentin, Caddy's daughter, runs away from home, Mrs Compson immediately equates her behaviour with that of Quentin, her son: 'Find the note . . . Quentin left a note when he did it' (p. 251). Doublings of actions come on top of doublings of name.[4] The end of the novel takes us back to its beginnings. A cyclical view of history is implicit in Benjy's final drive past the Confederate monument to the graveyard. Monuments of the past, both public and private, orient this journey, a journey which is itself a weekly ritual. The reader is led back into the past, 'from effect to cause',[5] at the same time as the end result of the Compson family history, the idiot Benjy, is displayed to her or his eyes.

Time is central to narrative fiction in a number of ways. 'To tell a story' is, as Jean Verrier says, 'to represent a series of events, to represent time'.[6] *The Sound and the Fury* not only represents time: it is also a novel which has time as a major theme. In this respect, it falls into that category of modernist novels like Virginia Woolf's *Mrs Dalloway* (1925), Thomas Mann's *The Magic Mountain* (1924) and Marcel Proust's *Remembrance of Things Past* (1913–27) of which Ricoeur says:

> All fictional narratives are 'tales of time' inasmuch as the structural transformations that affect the situations and characters take time. However only few are 'tales about time' inasmuch as in them it is the very experience of time that is at stake in these structural transformations (p. 101).

Clock and calendar time are juxtaposed in such texts with internal time, personal experiences of time 'pulled back by memory and thrust ahead by expectation' (Ricoeur, p. 105). Internal time is the 'time of consciousness' (p. 107), the way our thoughts and feelings succeed one another as we negotiate the world of clock and calendar time. It is the way we capture time's flow in our minds; how our thoughts range freely between past and future. Public time then, represented in *The Sound and the Fury* by the striking of clocks, the naming of dates, is set against the various internal experiences of time (Benjy's, Quentin's, Jason's) juxtaposed in the text. The similarities and discordances which result can be explored, according to Paul Ricoeur, *only* in the medium of fiction:

Shall we say once again that the hour is the same for all? Yes, from outside; no, from inside. Only fiction, precisely, can explore and bring to language this divorce between worldviews and their irreconcilable perspectives on time, a divorce that undermines public time (p. 107).

The Sound and the Fury foregrounds the divorce of which he speaks. A full and difficult text, my analysis of it is bound, therefore, to be partial. I will give attention to all four sections of the narrative, but most especially to Benjy's and Quentin's. These are, of course, those in which the disruptions of convention and chronology are most noticeable. Benjy's section will be of particular importance when I come to the subject of voice, and the way a character's experience of time relates to a work's meaning, in the final section of my chapter.

In her discussion of the study of time in narrative in French secondary schools, Jean Verrier points out the advantages of systematically describing and rigorously analyzing exactly how temporal structuring works in a narrative. Such a process starts with the 'matter of picking out all the temporal references in a given novel' (p. 32) – or, I would add, part of a novel. She works on the principle I introduced in my first chapter, that 'it is know-how rather than knowledge that we propose the students should acquire', and that the application of an analytic model both 'sharpens the reading process' and whets the reading appetite (p. 43). She goes on to state, in a passage which confirms my own textual approach in the first chapters of this book:

> the analysis of temporal structures is only one part of a more complex system which includes the analysis of point of view, voice . . . representation of the spoken word, etc. On another level, structural analysis can be put back into a historical perspective (the same stories are not always told in the same way, people do not always conceive of time in the same way), an ideological perspective (every society tells itself the stories which it needs to solve its contradictions at a given moment of its history), a psychoanalytical perspective (the most universal stories, that of Oedipus, for example, are perhaps also the most personal) (p. 44).

I wish to suggest something of the same movement in my chapter. First, I will examine Genette's model of how to approach the structuring of time in the novel. This, I hope, will provide the kind of analytic tool which will prove useful to any student of literature and will take up the main part of my chapter. I will, secondly, move my attention to Paul Ricoeur's claim that Genette downplays the issue of voice and focalization in his treatment of time in narrative; to the way in which a character's handling of time, sorting it into 'meaningful and unmeaningful' segments, relates to 'the meaning of the work as a whole' (p. 83). Such a focus on what Auerbach calls the 'remembering consciousness'[7] takes me beyond temporal structuring as literary technique alone to touch, in my final section, on those areas of psychoanalysis and history of which Verrier speaks.

II

Genette crucially distinguishes in his *Narrative Discourse* between two types of time in narrative which, following Rimmon-Kenan, I call text time and story time. Text time is, in theory, the time it takes us to read a given text. This is, however, dependent on the reader. The spatial equivalent of this chronological time becomes our measure, the way we linearly count off the text, page by page, sentence by sentence, chapter by chapter. This is how text time is defined – the 'one-directional and irreversible . . . linear presentation of information'[8] of the written narrative. This sequence of events is usually discordant with story time, 'the time of the thing told'.[9] Story time focuses on how long events last within the narrative, how the reader reconstructs those events in their chronological order. So, a page in a novel (text time) can tell of five years in a protagonist's life (story time). Genette describes the relations between text time and story time under three headings: order, duration, and frequency. It is in the discordances between the sequence of events as they are presented in the text and the amount of textual space given to their description (text time), and the reconstitution of these events in their original chronological sequence and the temporal extent of their various occurrences (story time) that Genette's (and my) interest lies.

Order

The reader uses the temporal markers contained in a narrative to reconstitute the textual events in their original chronological order, as far as that may be possible. Textual time can be arranged in the same order as story time, as at the start of Section Four of *The Sound and the Fury* where day dawns, Dilsey opens the door of her cabin, goes to the kitchen, then to the woodpile, etc. Of more interest are those relationships 'of contrast or of dissonance' (p. 35) which Genette sees as absolutely crucial to narrative fiction, where these two types of time are not synchronized. Such disjunctions he entitles narrative *anachronies*. Anachronies are of two main kinds – analepsis and prolepsis.

(a) Analepsis and prolepsis

Rimmon-Kenan justifies the use of these terms in their avoidance of the psychological and the 'cinematic-visual' connotations of the 'flashback' and 'anticipation' of more conventional usage. She defines them as follows:

> An *analepsis* is a narration of a story-event at a point in the text after later events have been told. The narration returns, as it were, to a past point in the story. Conversely a *prolepsis* is a narration of a story-event at a point before earlier events have been mentioned. The narration, as it were, takes an excursion into the future of the story (p. 46).

These anachronies are always defined in relation to the narrative starting point. In Benjy's section, then, this point would be that moment on April 7, 1928, when Benjy is watching the golfers through the fence; in Quentin's, between seven and eight o'clock on the morning of June 2, 1910, when he first sees the shadow of the sash on the curtains of his Harvard bedroom. Already a problem arises as to the size of the narrative sequences with which we decide to deal. If we wish to represent the relations between story time and text time by alphabetical means, with a and b (Quentin and Jason's sections) as analeptic, then the four separate sections of the novel form a sequence c, a, b, d. I find it most useful to treat each section of the text separately, while fully recognizing both the alternative strategies available, and the need not to lose sight of the full narrative pattern.

Benjy and Quentin's sections provide, as most readers soon discover, real difficulties in our attempts to reconstitute story time in relation to text time. Temporal indicators are apparent as we make our linear way through these two sections, but they are hard to follow and to coordinate, are disguised and often deferred. Benjy's section 'mosaically projects (in memory) the "action"' of the whole novel: we are subject, as readers of a novel which 'begins in the mind of an idiot',[10] to kaleidoscopic switchings of voice, scene, and chronology which can only be retrospectively subject to any kind of ordering. Quentin's section presents different problems, but is similarly confusing. The reader finds her or himself immersed within the workings of a tortured consciousness where distinctions between present moment and the various remembrances of past events, between internal dialogue and conversation with others, blur and shift disturbingly. My tactic at this point is, rather crudely, to examine a part of Benjy's section to show just how its temporal structurings operate, to illustrate the anachronic relationships between text time and story time to be there discovered.

Benjy's section is of course particularly confusing. The notion of anachrony takes as its grounding point a clear notion of the difference between past, present and future. In both Benjy and Quentin's sections such a temporal consciousness fails to exist. We consequently get embroiled in a web of different time sequences, presented (as Genette says of Proust) 'in such a way as to leave the "simple" reader, and even the most determined analyst, sometimes with no way out' (p. 79). The kind of effects which result from Faulkner's adoption of the convention that allows the interior discourse of an 'idiot child'[11] control of the narrative are seen on the first page of the novel. Benjy moans on hearing the word 'caddie' though the cause and effect relation between the two events is not signalled. This relation, explained by the fact that for 'caddie'

Benjy hears 'Caddy', cannot be possibly understood by the reader until Caddy herself is textually introduced (in the following scene). A type of textual advance notice is being given (someone called Caddy will soon appear), an advance notice though of a narrative participant whose part in the story now being related is already over (whose status is analeptic). Thus the very stress on her absence. The effect here is contorted, but can finally be described quite simply in a statement of the following type: 'Caddy had already been lost to Benjy, as will be explained later'.[12]

Benjy's section, taken by itself, is constantly interrupted by jumps and analepses. Readerly difficulty is compounded by the narrative contortions which result from the siting of the narrative in the mind of one to whom 'past and present are scarcely distinguishable'.[13] The reader has to wait for the following sections to make chronological sense of Benjy's. The carpet is whipped from under our readerly feet: we have to temporarily abandon our position as stable reader, recuperating meaning from fictional disorder. Such a position can only be fully recovered when all four sections of the novel have been read.

When this has occurred, we can build up some picture of the order of Benjy's section. Marking the points of chronological change, I will proceed through the first twenty-five pages of the text, detailing the anachronies which are to be found. Following Genette, I will first name alphabetically (A, B, C, etc.) the sequence of events as they are arranged linearly on the printed page (text time). I will then number the chronological position of each textual segment according to its temporal order in the reconstructed story (story time). Anachrony, to recap, is charted in relation to the point at which the 'first narrative'[14] starts, here with Benjy watching the golfers. I base my reconstitution of story time largely on the detective work of George R. Stewart and Joseph M. Backus, using a simplified version of the dates they give for the events described.[15] Though the specificity of some of the dates given below may be challenged, the general chronological order is retrospectively unproblematic (now see chart, p. 51).

We can condense this patterning by grouping together alphabetically (thus shifting the previous alphabetical base) those events which occur in the same, or roughly the same,

start of textual sequence	*page number*	*events as occur in textual sequence*	*events as occur in chronological order of the story*	*approximate date*
Through the fence. . . .	11	A	18	April 7, 1928
Caddy uncaught me	12	B	8	December 23 (about 1904)
'It's too cold out there'	12	C	5	as above
What are you moaning about	14	D	19	April 7, 1928
'What is it.' Caddy said	14	E	6	December 23 (about 1904)
Can't you shut up	16	F	20	April 7, 1928
Git in, now, and set	16	G	17	December 23 (about 1904)
Cry baby, Luster said	19	H	21	April 7, 1928
'Keep your hands'	19	I	7	After Mr C's death, before Roskus'
Mr Patterson was chopping	20	J	9	Spring or summer, 1908
'They ain't nothing'	20	K	22	April 7, 1928
and Roskus came	23	L	2	December 23 (about 1904)
She was wet	23	M	1	Damuddy's death, Fall, 1898
What is the matter	25	N	23	As above
Roskus came	25	O	2	April 7, 1928
See you all at the show	25	P	24	Damuddy's death, Fall, 1898
'If we go slow'	25	Q	3	April 7, 1928
The cows came jumping	26	R	10	Damuddy's death, Fall, 1898
At the top of the hill	27	S	4	April 7, 1928
There was a fire in it	32	T	12	Damuddy's death, Fall, 1898
Taint no luck on	33	U	11	After Quentin's death, June, 1910
Take him and Quentin	34	V	13	Mr C's death, 1912
Disley was singing	34	W	15	as above
'That's three, thank the Lawd'	35	X	14	as above
You can't go yet	36	Y	16	as above
Come on, Luster said	36	Z	25	April 7, 1928

seven temporal periods; A being Damuddy's death day or thereabouts, B being December 23, about 1904, etc. (I have elided together sequences set around the time of Mr Compson's death and the one scene occurring sometime after his death but before Roskus' as time period F). So we end with the following formula:

$$G18 - B8 - B5 - G19 - B6 - G20 - F17 - G21 - B7 -$$
$$C9 - G22 - A2 - A1 - G23 - A2 - G24 - A3 - D10 -$$
$$A4 - E12 - E11 - F13 - F15 - F14 - F16 - G25.$$

In this formula G is the period of present action (April 7, 1928) thus events proceed in numerical sequence, G18, G19, etc. The numbers here still relate to the events as they occur in reconstituted story time. Such a sequentiality does not necessarily occur within other temporal groupings; so B8 precedes B5 since the latter in text time, Benjy's going out of doors with Versh, precedes the former in story time, Caddy being out there with him on that December 23 date. Certain hierarchal interlockings between these textual segments result from their various positionings. It is the return to the time of the 'first narrative' (G) which both contains and gives continuity to the sequence, but other forms of connection become apparent on further condensing the formula above. In this condensation, I show how one temporal sequence contains another in the following way. Square brackets [ ], signal a move from the time of the first narrative. The use of round brackets ( ), mark further temporal subordination. The symbol < > indicates the move to yet another level of such subordination. So:

$$G18 \; [B8, 5] \; G19 \; [B6] \; G20 \; [F17] \; G21 \; [B7(C9)] \; G22 \; [A2,1] \; G23$$
$$[A2] \; G24 \; [A3 \; (D10) \; A4 \; (E12, 11 \; <F13, 15, 14, 16>)] \; G25$$

The comings and goings of the text are now available in formulaic terms. The conclusions may seem self-evident to one who is *au fait* with Faulkner criticism. I suggest, though, that for one trying to get to critical grips with Faulkner for the first time, a simple version of this exercise – ordering, for instance, any ten pages of text in such a way – can provide both a means of understanding what is occurring at the textual surface (literally, what is happening), a way to start discussing the differences between one narrator's attitude to time and another's, and a means of seeing exactly how Faulkner constructs his narrative and the implications of such a practice.

Here, what is first evident is the complete absence of prolepsis. As in Quentin's section, all movement is between present and past. The future is closed. The structural complexity of this section is clear from the formula, as is the fact that the swing from one time sequence to another follows no set pattern. A fairly regular movement between present and past is broken at the end of this textual segment when analeptic shifts to four different temporal periods are contained within the time of the first narrative. This bracketed sequence (between G24 and G25) is interesting in that it pulls together what might be termed the four central 'monuments' of the Compson family history, the three deaths and one marriage which in many ways provide the centre to the entire narrative. The absence of a fifth such monument, the birth of Quentin, is significant in terms of the stress on loss in the text as a whole. A sequence describing the time of Caddy's marriage (D10: *The cows came jumping*) is the only one to be wholly enclosed by two other past sequences from the same chronological period – significantly again that of Damuddy's death. The relation between the two, the 'overwhelming' of the one by the other, suggests not only a cause and effect relationship between them, but also a stress on death at the expense of future prospects.

It is noticeable that Damuddy's death is, and will be, the first event – in terms of story time – described in the narrative. Everything springs from that temporal point. Caddy's taking on of her conflicting roles of mother–sister–lover trace back to this event. The image presented here of 'the little girl's muddy drawers',[16] which Faulkner saw as the genesis of the whole book, is also at the genesis of its story time scheme. The whole process of chronological to-ing and fro-ing also speeds up at the textual points centering around crises in family history: five time shifts in two pages around Damuddy's death and Caddy's wedding (pp. 25–6); seven time shifts in four pages around Quentin's and his father's deaths (pp. 32–6). This perhaps suggests the disturbance still

associated by Benjy with their memory. Death days liberally
sprinkle this narrative. Benjy's repetitive trips to the cemetery
(F17) mark the family graves out as 'the "con-text" or "what
is written" ';[17] that which already determines present action
and history, what is being written 'now'.

Such exercises as the above can be carried out with either
large or small scale textual sequences. Edmond Volpe, for
example, charts twenty chronological shifts on just one page of
Quentin's narrative.[18] It is noticeable, though, that while the
first two sections of the novel are entirely past oriented, Jason,
in the third, constantly looks to the future. His anticipations
are, however, often either unrealized, speculative, fantastic,
or a mixture of the last two. Parodic speculation on his own
death concludes with his telling his mother, 'and then you
can send Ben to the Navy I says or to the cavalry anyway,
they use geldings in the cavalry' (p. 176). Such unrealized –
and often unrealizable – anticipations might, perhaps, be
termed pseudo proleptic, evoking in advance an event that
might, or possibly could, take place later, rather than one that
definitely will. Genuine prolepsis occurs in the final section of
the novel, where the third person narrator speaks of the three
mulberry trees beside the Compson house with 'fledged leaves
that would later be broad and placid as the palms of hands
streaming flatly undulant upon the driving air' (p. 237).

(b) Reach and extent. Returns and recalls

In his treatment of anachrony, Genette discusses both
reach and extent. Reach marks the temporal distance of the
anachrony from the 'present' moment.[19] Quentin's section is
difficult to pin down in terms of exact time of an event's occurrence, though an approximate chronological sequence (story
time) can be reconstituted.[20] However, Quentin's evocation
of his fight with Dalton Ames can be given an approximate
reach. The fight, the summer before Caddy's wedding, is recounted on the day of Quentin's suicide – a reach of ten to
twelve months. Its extent, the duration of the anachrony (if we
mark it from 'finally I saw him' to 'for a long time', pp. 143–9),
is one part of a day; from Quentin seeing Ames in the barber-
shop, to meeting him at the bridge over the creek at one o'clock,

to recovering from his fainting against a tree afterwards, Caddy joining him.

The status of *The Sound and the Fury* as a text which in its first three sections makes use of interior discourse as a narrative technique, means that Genette's other comments on narrative order are not always easy to apply. I adopt his categories as best I can to meet the case at hand. He, for example, separates analepsis into two types – completing analepses (or 'returns') and repeating analepses (or 'recalls'). Returns are 'retrospective sections that fill in, after the event, an earlier gap in the narrative' (p. 51). Recalls are when the narrative retraces its own steps, alludes back to its own past.[21] Returns and recalls are crucial to *The Sound and the Fury* but cannot be divided off in the above manner. Without them we would be left with a narrative of present action alone. The whole point of Faulkner's art is to trace the effect of past on present. His 'haunted chambers of consciousness' recapitulate, refer back to 'actions that are past, that are lost, that are dead, and have become the materials of prolonged elegy'.[22] Unsurprisingly, therefore, such returns and recalls are a central part of his formal armoury. Right from the second page of Benjy's section ('*Caddy uncaught me*') lacunae in story time are being filled in. The reader starts on her or his repair work, taking all the bits and pieces offered to fill in narrative gaps. This is the very way Faulkner works.

In theory, the difference between completing and repeating analepses is that between first (or only) time filling in of past details and recurring tracings of them. This distinction breaks down in Faulkner's text. Indeed, the very blurring of the relationship between the two is central to the structuring of the novel. Benjy's opening section establishes the conditions for such overlappings. Totally destroying conventional notions of narrative coherence, Faulkner plunges his reader into a 'remote and strange world ... where sensations and basic responses are all we have',[23] and where (in terms of story time) chronological sequence is all awry. Almost all the events which have occurred prior to the time of the first narrative are first narrated in this section, but in fragmentary form, with a lack of chronological signposting.

These are the factors which lead to the breaking of the boundary lines between completing and repeating analepsis.

No such convenient categorizations apply here. Each analeptic reference to one particular past scene adds something further to our knowledge of it, thus all 'complete' to some extent. At the same time, even the first reference to such a scene cannot be defined solely as 'completing'. Far from it. The free floating nature of such narrative fragments means that narrative gaps remain incomplete, chronological location uncertain. Only once further analeptic sequences have occurred can such locating work, such gap-filling, be done. In other words, even the first completion (filling in of past detail) is also what Genette calls an 'anticipatory recall' (p.83) – 'it had already happened, as we will see later' – needing a later narrative tracing of the same event to give it proper sense. Likewise that later tracing is a recall, in that it refers back to that already narrated, but also a return, in that it fills a narrative gap which has not yet been closed.

Returns and recalls thus merge in Faulkner's text, and it is by way of such a disruption of narrative conventions that some of his most powerful and radical effects are realized. The conveyance of such effects can be noted in relation to one particular sequence. T.P.'s statement 'Me and Benjy going back to the wedding' (part of the scene beginning '*the cows came jumping out of the barn*', p. 26) exists in a narrative vacuum until it can be positioned in the context of later analepses, both within and without the frame of this particular section. Its status as a return (referring to a wedding which has happened at some point prior to the first narrative) cannot even be confirmed until later information allows us such contextualizing power. Its status as anticipatory recall is thus evident. The scene takes more shape with Benjy's return/recall '*Then I saw Caddy, with flowers in her hair, and a long veil like shining wind. Caddy, Caddy*' (p. 42). This textual filling in/retracing is then continued in T.P.'s reference to '*Miss Caddy done gone long way away. Done get married and left you*' (p. 52).

The narrative complexity becomes further evident at this point in that this latter return/recall (the first fully explicit reference to Caddy's wedding which nonetheless retraces the earlier analepses) is, in fact, a minor part of another analeptic sequence treating Benjy's desire to go down to the gate. And moving into Quentin's section, we find similar crossovers and blurrings occurring as Faulkner continues to stretch the temporal conventions of the novel form. His memory of the receipt of Caddy's wedding invitation and his response – letting the announcement sit on his table, envisioning it as a bier, for three days – looks textually in two directions, backwards to her wedding, and forwards to his suicide which it prompts. At the same time it fills in gaps in two separate narrative sequences: that relating to Caddy's wedding in Mississippi (eventually filling in both date and marital partner) and that relating to Quentin's behaviour in Harvard at a previous point.

The circular and overlapping quality of these analeptic returns/recalls is entirely appropriate to a narrative in which obsessive recollections and repetitious retracings can never quite fill in its absent centre (Caddy); where all that finally marks such desperate narrative efforts is the constant recovery of signs of coming loss:

> Mr and Mrs Jason Richmond Compson announce the marriage of their daughter Candace to Mr Sydney Herbert Head on the twenty-fifth of April one thousand nine hundred and ten at Jefferson Mississippi . . . Aren't you even going to open it? . . . *It lay on the table a candle burning at each corner upon the envelope tied in a soiled pink garter two artificial flowers* . . . (pp. 87–8).

The type of completing/repeating analepsis here illustrated is one of Faulkner's prime means of textual construction in *The Sound and the Fury*. Genette points out that when analepses are repeated, much of the effect conveyed is a product of the comparison to be made 'between two situations that are similar and also different' (p. 55). Such comparative effects are especially pronounced in the kind of analeptic circlings which compose so much of Faulkner's text. The analepsis which refers in Benjy's section to Caddy's kissing of Charlie gains dramatic resonance when set beside the later one in Jason's narrative dealing with the same or similar incident. The focus in Benjy's initial presentation of this past episode is on his reactions – his cries, his pulling at her dress, and his response to Caddy's restoration of the bond between them: ' "I won't any more, ever. Benjy. Benjy." Then she was crying, and I cried, and we held each other . . . Caddy took the kitchen soap and washed her mouth at the sink, hard. Caddy smelled like trees' (p. 49). When Jason recalls and completes the scene, or one very similar occurring at the same temporal period, he speaks rather of his mother's response:

> like that time when she happened to see one of them kissing Caddy and all next day she went around the house in a black dress and a veil and even Father couldn't get her to say a word except crying and saying her little daughter was dead and Caddy about fifteen then only in three years she'd been wearing haircloth or probably sandpaper at that rate (p. 205).

Benjy and his mother both cry in response to Caddy's action. This pattern of Caddy as prime mover with family as reactors runs throughout the text. Both family members here are repressive in their refusal to allow Caddy to grow up, to grow away from the family centre, to develop in response to natural sexual needs. Their position mirrors Quentin's in this respect. Mrs Compson's extreme attitude is more open to ethical critique than Benjy's – her status as rational adult makes her response to Caddy's emergent sexuality difficult to justify in its self-centred and guilt-inducing quality. Benjy's response, though, is perhaps more difficult for Caddy to cope with. There is an internal division implicit in the irresolvable conflict between her own sexual desire and related need to move beyond kinship relationships and her status as neglected child playing both a sisterly and maternal role to another neglected (and helpless) child. Jason's cynical reaction to the whole incident is entirely in line with that misogyny and emotional coldness evident throughout a section beginning 'Once a bitch always a bitch, what I say', grotesquely comic in contrast to Quentin's prior tortured speculation on virginity, purity, honour, and the like 'fine dead sound[s]' (p. 158). Contrast and analogy operate strongly in any consideration of the type of analepsis which operates in this text. Meaning circulates in the novel as a result of such shifts of retrospective focus.

The analeptic modes which operate in the novel function in a way which Genette confines to recall alone. Recall can, for him, 'modify the meaning of past occurrences after the event . . . by making significant what was not so originally'. The whole principle of 'deferred . . . significance [or] inter- pretation' (pp. 56–7) suggested here is the mechanism by which Benjy's section operates both in its individual segments and in its entirety. Benjy's description of Luster putting him to bed on April 7, 1928, concludes when the latter goes:

> to the window and looked out. It came out of Quentin's window and climbed across into the tree. We watched the tree shaking. The shaking went down the tree, then it came out and we watched it go away across the grass. Then we couldn't see it (p. 71).

The reader has to wait for the recall/return in the fourth section to realize that what is described here is Quentin's flight from the house with the money taken from Jason's room to meet the circus man in the red tie.[24] It is on the basis of such analeptic tactics that the reader engages in constant redeciphering of the Compson family and its history.

(c) Achrony

Genette describes in his exploration of Proust one last type of anachrony, where events are 'not provided with any temporal reference whatsoever, events that we cannot place at all in relation to the events surrounding them' (p. 83). He gives the term achrony to these. In Benjy's section some clue is usually given by the context of an anachrony as to its temporal placing. Such clues come in a variety of forms: references to Benjy's change of name (from Maury) by the age of five, to the selling of the pasture, to Caddy's wedding and various deaths, etc. This is equally the case in Quentin's section. Indeed, a major part of readerly activity consists in working out the jigsaw puzzle of information given in scattered form to reconstitute the original story time, picking up the contextual clues offered which enable one to do so.

The one event in Quentin's section which cannot be chrono- logically located is his conversation with his father concerning the supposed 'incest' with Caddy. No details at all are given to fix this occasion in chronological context, no reference is made to the location or to any contemporaneous occurrences which would enable us to place this dialogue in relation to the time scheme of the section as a whole. Achrony is 'dateless and ageless' (p. 84) for Genette: our readerly mystification about when this conversation occurs suggests that the spatial and temporal kinships which are marked out in other elements of the narrative are not a governing priority in the case of this event. This, in turn, leads us to look for some other principle of organization appropriate to this particular episode. Given the intensity of Quentin's mental activity in his section, it would seem appropriate to place this episode in relation to the logic of Quentin's internal world, a desperate spinning of the mind as he plays out scenarios which might enable him to stop that 'clock-time' which he sees as so destructive. The complete lack of contextual detail would endorse such a reading. Spatial or chronological proximity is not the organizing principle here: the location of this episode is in Quentin's mind only – this is the 'logic' appropriate to this whole achronic sequence. This interpretation might be supported by Faulkner's answer to a question asked him at the University of Virginia some years later:

> *Q.* Did Quentin . . . actually have that conversation with his father about sleeping with his sister, or was that part of his — ?
> *A.* He never did. He said, if I were brave, I would – I might say this to my father, whether it was a lie or not, or if I were – if I would say this to my father, maybe he would answer me back the magic word which would relieve me of this anguish and agony which I live with. No, they were imaginary. He just said, Suppose I say this to my father, would it help me, would it clarify, would I see clearer what it is that I anguish over? [25]

III

Duration

Genette's second category in his discussion of narrative temporality is that of duration. To compare a text's 'duration' to that of the story it tells is, as Genette says, a very tricky operation, since it is, in fact, impossible to measure the former in chronological terms.[26] We are rather dealing with two different types of duration – textual space, the linearity of a text as measured in pages and lines, and story time, the chronological duration of the story, 'the time of the thing told'.

The relationship between these two types of duration (that of text and that of story) can be measured, according to the conventions Genette describes, exactly by setting story time against textual linearity. The length of time an incident, or sequence of incidents, takes to occur is placed against the textual length devoted to it or them. This relation defines the pace or *speed* of a narrative, thus: 'the speed of a narrative will be defined by the relationship between a duration (that of the story, measured in seconds, minutes, hours, days, months, and years) and a length (that of the text, measured in lines and in pages)' (pp. 87–8). Comparing a text's spatial duration with story duration as measured in clock or calendar time, we can then measure both the tempo and the rhythm of a narrative – its drastic slowings down, its rapid accelerations, its recurring stresses – against a hypothetical norm. This norm consists of a narrative whose pace is constant, where the relation between 'duration-of-story/length-of-narrative would remain always steady' (p. 88). An illustration of this would be when each day in a character's life (story time) was described in one page of text (text time) throughout a narrative.

Such a norm is hypothetical because of the difficulty of imagining a narrative with no change of pace. Once it is established, however, we can discern a novel's major rhythms by examining the accelerations and decelerations which occur therein. In Rimmon-Kenan's words:

> the effect of acceleration is produced by devoting a short segment of the text to a long period of the story, relative to the 'norm' established for this text. The effect of deceleration is produced by the opposite procedure, namely devoting a long segment of the text to a short period of the story (pp. 52–3).

Acceleration and deceleration effects in a narrative are graduated by Genette as running from ellipsis at the one pole to descriptive pause at the other, with summary and scene positioned accordingly on the continuum between.

(a) Ellipsis

Ellipsis, where story time has no equivalent in text time, is the maximum speed of any narrative. It occurs where the linear continuity of the narrative is temporarily broken; where a 'chronological lacuna' (p. 108) occurs.[27] Ellipsis seems an unhelpful term to apply to Faulkner's novel. The linear continuity of this narrative – especially in its first two sections – is subject to multiple disruptions. In fact, the broken rhythms of the novel's first half are created precisely by these fractures. However, no chronological lacunae occur as a result. The narrative jumps in temporal sequence are cuts from the time of the first narrative back to the past. To call them ellipses would be to mislead. These cuts do not mark a gap in 'present' story time: rather another time or series of times come flooding into that of the first narrative. This is what disrupts it: too much information rather than too little.

In Quentin's section a gap in story time does seem to be evident when he joins Gerald and Mrs Bland on their picnic expedition. At one moment in the first narrative Mrs Bland is speaking of wine as 'a necessary part of any gentleman's picnic basket' (p. 135). The next textual reference to the same scene ('It kept on running for a long time', p. 149) is to the point in story time when Quentin's eye is smarting after the (unmentioned) fight with Bland.[28] This is not ellipsis, though. No chronological lacuna occurs in terms of story time. Rather, Quentin's overfull and overflowing consciousness spills its contents on top of ongoing first narrative, effaces that narrative as a solid object stands directly before, and hides, its shadow. Story time has its equivalent in text time. The ticking of the clock in 'present' story time continues. The text time which contains the discovery of Caddy's loss of virginity and the fight with Dalton Ames that follows, matches the story time which stretches from the moment Quentin withdraws into what Ricoeur calls 'internal time',[29] the time of consciousness, to the moment when he emerges from it.

If ellipsis does occur in the first two sections, it is in rather different ways. In Benjy's section the ellipsis is not one which relates to chronological duration. Rather it is the ellipsis of logic and understanding. When we read '*Benjy, Caddy said, Benjy. She put her arms around me again, but I went away*' (p. 43), we process a verbal sequence which omits one stage in the logical description of what has happened. To fill in this type of ellipsis would be to normalize the abnormal and thus to destroy exactly what creates the remarkable effects of Benjy's section. Full meaning is recuperable, though, by completing the chain of understanding which Benjy can only elide: 'She put her arms around me again, but I closed my eyes so as not to have to look at her, so it seemed as though I went away'. This is clumsy in the extreme: it suggests something, though, of what the reader must accomplish throughout the section.

Similarly in Quentin's section, the kind of ellipsis which does occur does not represent a gap in story time. It is rather a type of syntactical ellipsis which represents the swift and elliptic slides of consciousness itself. The fusing and confusing of voices which occurs with the removal of punctuation markers, for example, when Quentin rehearses the conversations about incest and suicide with his father, is a way of syntactically representing the uninterrupted flux of Quentin's mental process. The short circuitings of grammatical forms, which occur in Quentin's replaying of the conversation he had with Herbert Head prior to his sister's wedding, illustrates the jumps of his consciousness in action while simultaneously containing a satirical thrust at Head's clichéd and desperately false discourse:

> let's you and I get together on this thing sons of old Harvard and all I guess I wouldn't know the place now best place for a young fellow in the world I'm going to send my sons there give them a better chance than I had wait don't go yet let's discuss this thing (p. 101).

No time is unaccounted for here. The acceleration effect is a result rather of pushing too much mental accounting into the story time (that in which the thought can take place) available. Interior monologue creates its own acceleration and deceleration effects, according to the intensity (or lack of it) of the mental activity which occurs.

Ellipsis does occur in the final section of the narrative,

but the containing of its action to the course of one day, its
focus on the sequence of events in that one day, means that
such ellipsis ('He . . . got in the car again and sat there. After
a while two negro lads passed', p. 277) is neither pronounced
nor significant.

(b) Descriptive pause

At the other extreme from ellipsis, which represents the
maximum acceleration of narrative speed, comes 'the absolute
slowness of descriptive pause'[30] where a segment of text corresponds to a suspension of story time. Story time, according to
Wallace Martin, 'stops, in a sense, in passages of commentary
and description'.[31] The description of Osmond's villa in *The
Portrait of a Lady* illustrates such a pause.[32] Such totally static
descriptions are usually avoided in modern narratives. When
Faulkner finally makes use of description in the last section
of *The Sound and the Fury* it is noticeable that though story time
decelerates (a very brief period in terms of story duration is
treated at some length) it never quite stops. Dilsey is described
as wearing:

> a stiff black straw hat perched upon her turban, and a
> maroon velvet cape with a border of mangy and anonymous
> fur above a dress of purple silk, and she stood in the door
> for a while with her myriad and sunken face lifted to the
> weather, and one gaunt hand flac-soled as the belly of a
> fish (p. 236).

Story time still flows here: she stands 'for a while' and lifts
her face to the weather prior to its (soon to follow) reversion
to normal position. The clock ticks on in what Genette would
call a 'detailed scene'[33] not a descriptive pause.

Faulkner's narrative, even when it describes purely mental activity (as it does to varying extent in the first three
sections), never comes to a standstill. The narrative then
becomes one of the activity of consciousness. The unfolding
of textual movement – even at seemingly 'static' moments as
when Quentin narrates the (imaginary) conversation with his
father – corresponds to the length of time it takes to process
thoughts through a consciousness. The tracing of mental

process matches the ticking off of story time on a second by second, minute by minute, basis.[34] At the same time – and this is the peculiar double movement to Faulkner's narrative to which I will return – these tracings offer exactly that information which allows for the reconstitution of story time in its larger context, outside the frame of the 'first narrative' in which those moments of mental activity occur. Descriptive pauses are, however, absent from this text.

(c) Summary and scene

Between the extremes of ellipsis and descriptive pause there are, in theory, any number of possible narrative speeds. In practice, narrative convention has reduced such possibilities to two: summary and scene. Summary, according to Genette, is 'the narration in a few paragraphs or a few pages of several days, months, or years of existence, without details of action or speech' (pp. 95–6). Sited near the end of the scale of narrative speed marked by ellipsis, acceleration is produced by condensing any story period into very limited textual space by giving a relatively brief account of its main details. Nick's family history in *The Great Gatsby* is introduced through summary: 'My family have been prominent, well-to-do people in this Middle Western city for three generations . . . '(p. 8). Like Proust, and unlike more traditional novelists, Faulkner rejects summary as the 'connective tissue'[35] of his novel. Instead, he presents in the first two sections a series of scenes and fragments of scenes separated by temporal shifts into other scenes and fragments of scenes. The connective tissue of these sections is, as I will argue later, metaphor. The accelerations and decelerations in them result not so much from moves between the four conventional narrative speeds, but more from the relative rapidity of the scene shifts, the relative length of the scenic fragments presented, the particular narrative style in which a given scene is written.

It is scene, then, that defines the whole of Faulkner's novel. Usually, scene is associated with the use of dialogue with a minimum of framing commentary, where 'story-duration and text-duration are conventionally considered identical' (Rimmon-Kenan, p. 54). Genette broadens this definition by contrasting scene with summary: scene here becomes associated with the dramatic, 'the strong periods of the action coinciding with the most intense moments of the narrative' (p. 109) as opposed to summary, linked to the non-dramatic and those weak narrative moves captured accordingly by means of 'large strokes'. Non-dramatic, weak narrative moments tend to disappear in the compressed intensity of the modernist text. Such texts depend exactly on the juxtaposition of one dramatic moment against the other. Even where the narrative moves of *The Sound and the Fury* are not 'intense' (Benjy's 'first narrative' describing mundane details of Luster's teasing; Dilsey's emergence from her cabin, making breakfast, in the final part), scene still seems a more appropriate term than summary to describe them. Rimmon-Kenan's offered definition 'a detailed narration of an event' (p. 54) gives, despite its looseness, the most practical definition of the term.

Thus Faulkner abandons what Genette calls 'the traditional . . . rhythmic system of novelistic narrative' (p. 112) in *The Sound and the Fury*. The novel's rhythms are dictated largely by other means. Summary is redundant where the movement between past and present is a matter of mental process sited within the frame of interior monologue. This helps explain the novel's difficulty: not just that the abrupt movement between scenes makes it hard to follow, but that we get none of the readerly 'breathing space' that a summary offers. We cannot 'idle' at all. The siting of each narrative section around the events of one day means that, even when the interior monologue is not used in the final section, the need for summary recedes.

(d) Narrative speed and internal time

The relationship between internal time (the activity of consciousness: 'internally experienced time measured not by clocks . . . but according to one's internal consciousness')[36] and clock time, public time, provides, as I have said, the source of the peculiar double movement of Faulkner's narrative in terms of duration effects. Two different 'time schemes' play off against one another within the novel, with different acceleration/deceleration effects. Clock time (time measured by an external standard) provides the frame for the 'first narrative' of each section of the novel: one day is the equivalent textually of between forty-eight and eighty-nine pages. In terms of internal time, by which the first three sections also operate, Benjy's sixty-one page section covers thirty years of such time; Quentin's eighty-nine pages, twelve years; Jason's seventy-two pages, some twenty-two years.

The balance between internal time and clock time (the passing present) is variable in these three sections. A rough count, difficult to make because of the acute fragmentation of the opening sections, puts the ratio of 'time of the first narrative' to 'time prior to the first narrative' at just over one to four, almost one to one, and approximately five to one, respectively. Clock time becomes progressively more insistent as the novel continues and becomes dominant in the final section. The undermining of public time, particularly evident in the opening sections, runs counter to the 'reality' principle. This latter principle is only fully asserted with the use of the third person narrator of the fourth section. Here, the fixing of the narrative back in clock time runs concurrent with a first detailing of the external appearance (what the public world sees) of both the Compson family members and that symbolically crumbling house, 'square, paintless . . . with its rotting portico' (p. 264), which they inhabit.

The relationship between internal time and clock time in the novel complicates any measurement of the narrative's speed. The longest uninterrupted scene in Quentin's section, for example, is that charting his reaction to Caddy's loss of virginity and his consequent first meeting with Ames.[37] Its importance is to be measured both in its textual length and its dramatic intensity. The scene can be measured in terms of its chronological duration (clock time).[38] How long it takes to pass through Quentin's mind is, however, indefinite. The difficulty of measuring internal time (and thus assessing narrative pace by conventional methods) is highlighted when we examine the imagined conversation concerning Caddy's virginity which occurs between Quentin and his father where external temporal markers drop away entirely. If this is an act of consciousness alone, how can its time scale or 'speed' be measured? If, though, we attempt to reconstitute the conversation according to 'realist' criteria, remembering fragments of it are scattered throughout Quentin's section, we might allow it to have taken five minutes; on the other hand, it may have been drawn out over several days or weeks. Standard ways of measuring a narrative's speed and rhythm cannot work where internal time is concerned.

Even when we recover the story time (the entire sequence of narrative events in their original chronological order) according to 'realist' criteria (the history of the Compson family), the measurement of narrative speed according to Genette's criteria is difficult, at least in the first two sections. For though it is often possible to roughly trace the chronological duration of scenes (though not always – twenty sections of Benjy's narrative relate to his change of name but the period of story time covered is unspecified), the determination of text time devoted to those scenes is made extremely difficult by their fragmented nature. Volpe traces some 195 scene shifts in Quentin's section alone.[39] Any attempt, then, to measure text time against story time becomes not just an uneconomical exercise (counting the lines of all the various segments which relate to one narrative 'scene') but also a pointless one. The use of the fragmentation principle also disrupts traditional notions of narrative speed.

Acceleration and deceleration effects in *The Sound and the Fury* cannot be measured by conventional means. The pace of Jason's section, for instance, is a product of his narrative style. This relates to Faulkner's use of interior monologue, where it is the character's voice (and the frame of mind it represents, the interior landscape it depicts) which controls narrative pace, rather than the sequence of events described (chronological time in relation to text time). Jason's mode of self-presentation, syntactical habits, create the furious speed of his section. As Sundquist comments, what marks his narration is his 'compulsive "I says", simmering with rage and maintaining the drive of his narration at a pace and a pitch furiously, mercenarily intent on making up for the lost time of childhood'.[40] The juxtaposition of fragments that constitute the rhythms of the novel in the first two sections likewise reflect the interior landscape of their narrators. Narrative rhythms are controlled, too, by scene length. Textual time devoted to a particular incident (however long its chronological duration) marks its centrality in the narrator's mind. This principle, which again arises from the use of interior monologue, explains the rhythmic patterns of the analeptic sequences.

Thus, in Jason's section, the only long analeptic sequence centres on one incident, in turn marked out by the textual space devoted to it. In this sequence, which contains the bringing of Quentin back to Jefferson, the father's funeral, and Caddy's returns, at least eleven chronological shifts occur. The central sequence is however clear – four pages of text devoted to his meeting with Caddy at the cemetery and what directly follows: his agreeing to let her see Quentin 'a minute' for $100, his holding Quentin up in the back of the carriage as he is swiftly driven past Caddy, their meeting the next morning.[41] The textual weight given the sequence validates its narrative centrality. While signalling the start of that triangular relationship between Jason, Caddy, and Quentin (Quentin held as hostage by Jason to Caddy's money) which motivates so much of his present action, it also alludes to themes of crucial import to the entire novel: Jason's cruelty, greed, and resentment; the shifting family balance signalled by the father's death.

The text's pace and rhythms undoubtedly relate, then, in the first three sections to the speed of the cross-cutting from one chronological sequence to another and the relative textual length of those sequences rather than to the duration/length ratio of any particular sequence. They also relate, though, to the relative types of intensity (Jason's furious, Quentin's poetic) of narrative voice. The number of episodes devoted to any scene also, in the first two sections, help to establish the scene's importance. The rhythms of the narrative flow around various fixed and central points: thus the centrality of Damuddy's death in narrative terms is suggested by the number of times it is 'recalled' (eighteen) in the opening section. I will return to this rhythmic effect, so vitally important to this narrative, in my next section.

Traditional ways of measuring narrative pace are then inappropriate to Faulkner's novel. The rhythms of his narrative are created by other means. Even in the final, more conventional section of the novel this remains true. The deceleration with which it commences can be explained by traditional means – story time passing slowly in relation to text time. This, however, does not remain true as we move from the slow pace of the Easter service to the rapid pace of Jason's chase after Quentin. The pace of the narrative is not controlled by the

text time/story time ratio. Indeed, story time remains vague
as far as the service goes. It is spatial cross-cutting plus the
amount of movement taking place in the separate locations
which control narrative pace here. The church scene focuses
around a point of almost absolute stillness, Dilsey sitting:

> bolt upright, her hand on Ben's knee. Two tears slid down
> her fallen cheeks, in and out of the myriad coruscations of
> immolation and abnegation and time . . . In the midst of the
> voices and the hands Ben sat, rapt in his sweet blue gaze.
> Dilsey sat bolt upright beside, crying rigidly and quietly in
> the annealment and the blood of the remembered Lamb
> (pp. 262–4).

This scene is placed in obvious and effective juxtaposition
with the speed of that detailing Jason's chase, the 'rush' of
violent action that marks this section – 'he raced the engine,
jamming the throttle down and snapping the choker in and out
savagely' (p. 271) – and the rapid movement within the scene
which accompanies it. Pace is also varied by the transitions
between conceptual activity (focusing on sheer mental process,
the tickings of consciousness, what is being thought), and perceptual activity (what is seen and heard), dialogue, and action.
It is Benjy's inability to function in the initial area which gives
his section its relatively constant speed. This is all to suggest
that the speed of Faulkner's narrative is controlled not by
traditional novel movements between descriptive pause, scene,
summary and ellipsis; rather that he finds new and radical
methods to give his narrative a cadence which, like Proust's,
is 'unprecedented' (Genette, p. 112). Like Proust, too, though
in a distinctly different way, it is in the narrative's 'frequency'
effects that such rhythms are realized.

IV

Frequency

The final category Genette discusses in his treatment of
time in narrative fiction is that of frequency: 'the relation
between the number of times an event appears in the story

and the number of times it is narrated (or mentioned) in the text' (Rimmon-Kenan's *Narrative Fiction*, p. 56). This aspect of temporality is obviously crucial to *The Sound and the Fury* whose textual circlings and re-circlings around the figure of Caddy, entirely absent from the 'first narrative', are what gives the novel much of its charge.

In her article on 'The Paradoxical Status of Repetition', Shlomith Rimmon-Kenan points out that it is *difference* which lies 'at the heart of repetition . . . we can say nothing about it except through a discussion of differences'. What she is pointing to here is the fact that the re-telling of an event or incident gets its meaning from the variations it introduces on the original telling: the kind of variations dependent on narrator, focus, extent of amplification, place in the narrative continuum, etc. Even when an event is re-told by exactly the same narrator using the same words and the same focalization, 'difference is introduced through the very fact of repetition, the accumulation of significance it entails, and the change effected by the different context in which it is placed. We never go into the same river twice, and no pure repetition exists'.[42] These remarks must be held firmly in mind when considering repetition in Faulkner's novel: at its most simple level, the repetition of the name Caddy becomes the point of departure for revealing the differences in the attitude of the first three narrators towards her. This is the very principle on which the narrative works. The repetition of incident and event becomes a point of departure for a readerly examination of the notion of difference. The rhythms of the narrative movement are most centrally those of repetition.

Genette discusses the various types of frequency effects which can occur in a narrative, paying his main attention to repetitions both of story event and of textual statement (the same pattern of words used). He defines four kinds of frequency.

(a) Narrating once what happens once

This is the most common narrative form to which he gives the name 'singulative narrative' (p. 114). Examples are scarcely needed: the Easter service in Section Four, though, will serve.

(b) Narrating n times what happened n times

Chatman names this form of repetition 'multiple-singulary':[43] several tellings, each telling that of a story event which is repeated several times. Genette's example is the statement: 'Monday, I went to bed early, Tuesday I went to bed early, Wednesday I went to bed early, etc.' (p. 115). Interestingly, all three of the Compson brothers' narratives follow this unusual pattern to some extent.

Thus Benjy particularly is associated with repeated tellings of what happened on repeated occasions. The opening reported words in his section are 'Here, caddie' which spur Benjy's 'moaning'. Later the same day, Luster, teasing Benjy as he repeatedly does, says ' "You want something to beller about. All right, then. Caddy." he whispered. "Caddy. Beller now. Caddy" ' (p. 55). The multiple-singulary, the call (Caddy) and response (moaning/bellowing) effectively marks out Benjy's entrapment within patterns of repetition and loss.

And such patternings are one of the distinctive features of his section in which the same event or response occurs on repeated occasions.[44] Indeed, such multiple-singularies become a major organizing principle of his narrative. Thus, in five consecutive episodes which alternate between the name changing scene and the time of the first narrative, Benjy's 'looking at the fire' is described or implied five times on five separate occasions (pp. 56–7). The telling of a story incident thus both spurs the association with other such story incidents – so motivating a jump in story time – and confirms the previous analysis of Benjy's entrapment. The closing of the fire door by Luster on two occasions in this same sequence signifies the withdrawal of comfort and of pleasure; and confirms the relationship between repetition and loss which drives his narrative. Other examples of the same frequency effect can be found within Benjy's section. The smell of trees and leaves; Benjy's crying in its absence; his reaction to the smell of death; the narrative returns to those other comforters, slipper and mirror; all these operate in a similar way here.

Quentin and Jason's sections also operate, though to lesser extent, through multiple-singularies. Significantly in both cases such repetitions relate to their separate neuroses.

Quentin's repeated references to walking 'upon my shadow, tramping it' (p. 111), 'tramping my shadow into the dust' (p. 104), relates to what John Irwin calls 'the substitutive punishment, upon his own person, of the brother seducer . . . by the brother avenger';[45] of that part of him which harbours incest desires by that which wishes to punish that desire. His re-tellings of the hearing of, and avoidance of, clocks speak of his related desire to step outside time's limits, to suspend that process which leads inevitably towards spoilage and loss. In Jason's case the returns, at different intervals, to 'country suckers', New York Jews, Eastern sharks and the cotton market, suggest both his paranoid tendencies and his material acquisitiveness (endorsed by constant returns to money matters throughout the section). The fact that the concluding section of his narrative contains the words with which it started – 'Like I say once a bitch always a bitch' (p. 234) – suggests both the misogyny and brutality within which he too is trapped. Multiple-singularies become one of Faulkner's major methods for both organizing the cyclic rhythms of the novel itself, and at the same time, suggesting that compulsion to repeat within which all three brothers are trapped. I will return to this subject later, with particular reference to Benjy.

(c) Narrating n times what happened once

The third type of frequency defined by Genette is also central to the circular and spiralling rhythms of Faulkner's narrative. This type he calls 'repeating narrative' (p. 116). In her article on the status of narration in *Absalom, Absalom!*, Rimmon-Kenan speaks of that narrative as 'trying to capture through the act of repetition that which escapes and eludes'.[46] This seems exactly to describe, too, the narrative technique of Faulkner's earlier novel. Both within sections and between sections we spiral back to certain key events in the family history, the different ways of then circling around those events providing modes of interpreting, even recovering what is now missing. In *Absalom, Absalom!*, Henry's murder of Charles Bon is narrated thirty nine times in all, sometimes without changes in focalization or style.[47] Though such acute over-determination is absent from *The Sound and the Fury*, a similar technique is at work. We are led as readers to circle back over key moments; the weddings, deaths, name-change, and so on. In Benjy and Quentin's sections particularly, 'first narrative' is constantly interrupted by such recalls.[48] They – together with multiple singularies – are primarily responsible for the narrative's rhythms. To illustrate, we might look at narrative repeats which focus on Caddy's wedding. Jason only recalls it briefly, and then in relation to the memory of that lost job in the bank which compulsively informs his present actions. Benjy and Quentin's narratives, however, recall the event frequently. This, after all, represents the moment of loss for both of them. Their similarity of response is suggested by two complementary passages describing Caddy on that day:

> *Then I saw Caddy, with flowers in her hair, and a long veil like shining wind. Caddy. Caddy* (p. 42).

> *Only she was running . . . running out of the mirror the smells roses roses the voice that breathed o'er Eden. Then she was across the porch I couldn't hear her heels then in the moonlight like a cloud, the floating shadow of the veil running across the grass, into the bellowing* (pp. 77–8).

The triple repetition of 'running' in the passage from Quentin's section marks the narrative moment at which Caddy disappears from the family centre. We are left with 'the floating shadow of the veil' – a trace of a trace of her presence. Sundquist, who calls this 'lyrical' passage 'the wondrous center of the book', sees Caddy 'vanishing from the mirror of Quentin's narcissism into the wrenching mindless vacuum of Benjy's bellowing'.[49] I would rather stress the similarities of their response to her. The language of both is lyrical. Full presence is defined in Benjy's passage by the repetition of the name: what the reader sees are the flowers in the hair, the veil, both of which are repeated, at least by association ('roses, roses') in Quentin's description. Quentin's reference to Edenic myth is at least potentially reinforced by the metaphysical quality of the simile Benjy uses to describe the veil, 'like shining wind'. The strength of their mutual feelings towards Caddy, the magical quality of her presence for them, their move from plenitude to loss (Benjy's reaction to this vision is to bellow), is revealed by such a narrative tactic. Quentin's 'elopement' scenario (*'we can go away you and Benjy and me where nobody knows us'*, p. 114) significantly includes Benjy whose interest – Caddy's remaining in 'the timeless realm of family relationships'[50] – he shares. Caddy's loss, according to Sundquist:

> represents the crucial generative event in the book – in fact, the event that forecloses generation. It is the moment of discovered grief that brings death, actual and metaphorical, into the psychological worlds of Benjy and Quentin; it is the moment of potential but elusive tragedy, envisioned deep within the novel's mind, from which the increasingly furious and distorted saga of the Compsons follows.[51]

(d) Narrating once what happened n times

The final frequency effect Genette describes is that which he calls iterative narrative, where 'a single narrative utterance takes upon itself several occurrences together of the same event' (p. 116). As Genette explains, he is not referring here to the recounting of just one occurrence which then serves to represent a number of others, rather to a synthetic process where a number of incidents are conjoined in one. Rimmon-Kenan offers the opening of Lawrence's *The Rainbow* (1915) as an example, the annual cycle of activity of the Brangwen men narrated just one time. Huck Finn's description of his sufferings at the Widow Douglas' hands provides another.[52] The mode is not applicable to this Faulkner text, though it is to *Light in August*. The 'sharp sense of habit and repetition' (p. 123) Genette connects with this mode is captured here, instead, by the use of multiple-singularies and repeating narratives.

V

Faulkner's use of these particular repetition effects – multiple-singularies and repeating narratives – provides my point of departure for the final section of this chapter. Genette is concerned throughout his discussion of narrative time with the twofold relationship between text time and story time. When

Paul Ricoeur assesses Genette's system in *Time and Narrative* he suggests the need to examine narrative temporality not as a two-tiered, but rather as a three-tiered scheme. To story time (a narrative's events reconstituted in their original chronological order) and text time (the time represented spatially by the linear sequentiality of the written text), Ricoeur adds a third category entitled 'the fictive experience of time', which he ties to the twin areas of narrative voice and focalization.[53] The thrust of his argument is that an examination of anachronic variation which results from disparities between text time and story time leads to a further area of examination: why these anachronic variations are introduced into the narrative in the first place? What is their ultimate end? How, in other words, does the use of analepsis in Faulkner, for example, relate to *'the meaning of the work as a whole'*? (p. 83, my emphasis).

He thus moves a step away from Genette's very rigid form of structuralism. Genette attempts to draw his working categories from the closed narrative, from temporal features discovered within the examined text (or series of texts). Ricoeur argues that to do this is tacitly to reject the way in which a narrator, or a character whose focalization that narrator adopts, fictively experiences time.[54] This fictive experience – the temporal distortions attributable directly to a narrator or focalizing centre – can only be explained by setting it in the context of what Ricoeur calls 'the time of life' (p. 81), the temporal experience of the reader. The types of temporal experience explored in fiction (through the adoption of a particular voice and/or perspective) constitute what Ricoeur calls a 'refigur[ing]' (p. 158) of time that can only have *meaning* when set against the way we, as readers, situate ourselves in time. It is in the meaning which results from this 'intersection of the world projected by the text and the life-world of the reader' (p. 160) that Ricoeur sees the full significance of the literary work as lying. And this is where narrative voice is so important. For it presents us, as readers, with the fictive experience of time. Such an experience does not exist in a textual vacuum: it is addressed, via narrative voice, to us as readers. 'Reading', as Ricoeur says, 'marks the point of intersection between the world of the text and the world of the reader . . . Every point of view [focalization] is the invitation addressed to readers to direct their gaze in the same direction as the author or the characters' (p. 99). We refer to our own temporal norms as a way of assessing the meaning of the text, the meaning of a character's fictive experience of time.

I have, in fact, already travelled some way in this direction in my interpretation of character in my discussion of frequency effects in *The Sound and the Fury*. I now wish to develop this approach more fully by referring to various parts of the novel, most especially its first and last sections, to illustrate the point Ricoeur makes: that the fictive experience of time – which comes to us through a number of voices and focalizations – relates uncompromisingly to the work's overall meaning.[55]

To do this, I wish to return to the question of repetition effects in the novel. Rimmon-Kenan's discussion of the paradoxes of repetition offers a codification of currently accepted conventions regarding the subject. As such, her discussion fits into the frame of a cultural code, to use Barthes' term, that the Western reader shares. In Ricoeur's words, the time Rimmon-Kenan is speaking of is 'the time of life', part of our common frame of reference, of 'the life-world of the reader'. One of the paradoxes of repetition she lists is that 'constructive repetition emphasizes difference, destructive repetition emphasizes sameness (i.e. to repeat successfully is not to repeat)'. This paradox provides an important starting point from which to consider Benjy's voice and focalization – his fictive experiences of time as represented in Faulkner's novel. As an example of constructive repetition, Rimmon-Kenan relates Freud's speculations concerning the child's game of 'throwing the reel away and then pulling it back as an enactment of his mother's departure and return'. This Freud saw as:

a successful, constructive, ultimately pleasurable repetition, because by passing from a passive situation of being overpowered by his mother's absence to an active situation where he inflicts the same fate on the various objects within his reach, the child gains mastery over the disagreeable experience.[56]

Such a successful repetition (due to the measure of difference described above) might be placed in the context of Benjy's fictive experience of time in *The Sound and the Fury*. When Benjy takes the 'baby's play pretty' (p. 34), the spools the infant Quentin is playing with, it is not, we can assume, to play any such game. Benjy never learns to cope with absence. Benjy's keeping 'of that old dirty slipper' (p. 68), even bringing it to the table with him, is – in Freudian terms – his form of compensation for the nurturing Caddy's absence. No mastery though is gained over the disagreeable experience of her going: we never see him playing such games with objects within his reach as described above. Rather, these objects always, repetitiously, retain their status as comforters. Any removal of them brings, repetitiously, cries of pain. Benjy never learns to transform loss into pleasure. He remains caught in patterns of repetition which can only be read in negative terms: repetition without difference.

So, too, with his inability to communicate through language. We, as readers, accept Faulkner's use of the novelistic convention by which one who cannot express himself socially is allowed 'speech' via the literary device of interior monologue. In Benjy's section 'the anarchic arena of remembered voices'[57] which composes his consciousness contrasts strongly with his own linguistic inadequacy. Communication for him is restricted to moans, cries, and howls. Freud's analysis of the game with the reel described above notes the child's verbal responses: an 'expressive o-o-o-o [interpreted as "fort" by Freud and the child's mother]' as the reel was thrown over the side of the cot to disappear from view, and a 'joyful "da" [there]' as it was pulled back into view.[58]

This 'fort/da game' is central to the psychoanalytic theory of Jacques Lacan who sees the child's birth into language as coincident with 'the utilization of the symbol' (the game as symbolic representation of the mother's absence and reappearance). A twofold displacement thus occurs – the mother's absence and presence symbolized by the game; linguistic differentiation in turn symbolizing the disappearance then reappearance of the reel. 'Such an experience' as Anika Lemaire comments 'may be considered the inaugural moment of all future displacement, all metaphors and all language'. The child's action, and the language which in turn symbolically represents that action, re-produce reality. They replace 'lived experience . . . substituting a sign for reality'.

This substitution marks the entry of the child into what Lacan calls 'the Symbolic order', the order of the 'social given, a culture, prohibitions and laws'. Benjy never makes the full transition from what Lacan calls the Imaginary – 'the dual relationship, the merging of self and other . . . the absence of mediation between the self . . . and the object of desire [the mother/Caddy]' – to the Symbolic order.[59] He does symbolically recognize Caddy's absence. His desire for her is marked both by the noises he makes when he hears her name, when he instinctively recognizes signs of her disappearing presence from his life, and by his clinging to the slipper which becomes his token of substitution for her loss. But he never accepts that loss; never 'master[s] his privation', 'negatives the field of forces of desire',[60] through such symbolic acts as the child in the case study does. He remains trapped, making the same scarcely differentiated sounds, the same compulsive actions; never passes fully into the Symbolic order to become a social being, an individual, a member of society; is never fully born into language.[61]

Benjy's failure to translate from the realm of the Imaginary to that of the Symbolic is marked by those repetitions of his which lack any sense of difference. He repeats the same acts, same noises, over and over again; barred access to language and to the 'I', Benjy lives in a world of ever-sameness. This in terms of Rimmon-Kenan's argument is destructive repetition, that associated with what Freud saw as the death instinct rather than the life instinct. Benjy's failure to fully come to consciousness is marked by the repetitive patternings associated with him. Complete repetition (with no difference) is, however, the equivalent of death – no change, no process, no development.[62]

Benjy's whole narrative, then, must be contextualized according to our own temporal norms as readers – this is what gives it its meaning. His entrapment in a world of repetition without difference must be measured against our understanding of the life instinct as composed exactly of change and difference. Formally, Faulkner makes use of the frequency effect of the multiple-singular both to give the novel one of its basic rhythms and also to suggest exactly the entrapment of his characters within the realm of sterile repetition. This, too, is the function of his use of metaphor as organizing principle in terms of the temporal shifts of the first two sections.

For it is metaphor which is the principle of composition that lies at the heart of these sections. Genette discusses the junctions between anachronies and 'first narrative' in his section on temporal order. In Faulkner's novel, these junctions are often both abrupt and verbally unacknowledged as a result of his use of interior monologue. Shift of time sequence is often difficult to locate and pin down. And though such ruptures are textually marked by use of italics in the first two sections, this is not always so. In Benjy's section, furthermore, italics sometimes mark the beginning of a temporal shift, sometimes its entirety (with further shift signalled by a return to normal type). The threads of the narrative are connected up not by metonymic progression (the linearity of time's chain) but by metaphor. Both Ricoeur and Docherty pick up on this figure of speech as the vital one in examining temporal dislocation and disjunction in modernist narratives;[63] the root explanation for (and signal of) the disruptions of story order which occur in such texts. Genette discusses the way in which narrative junctures take place in Proust and the various tactics employed.[64] Ricoeur and Docherty considerably develop his stress on the importance of metaphor as connective device, and in doing so offer a way of penetrating more swiftly to the core of Faulkner's narrative.

Metaphor has as 'one of its secret sources of power' its ability to 'equate almost anything with anything else'. Linear logic is disrupted, temporal distance is 'annulled' by the 'erosion of . . . boundar[ies]' which metaphor allows, 'the superimposition of one element upon another in a magical, wishful, or powerful way, with no regard for Realistic logic or coherence'.[65] In metaphor consists what Genette calls the 'quasi-miraculous fusion' (p. 70) between the time of narration and the time of the recounted event, the two merging as one. 'Archipelagos of unrelated memories' – the phrase is Ricoeur's (p. 135) – are coordinated through a series of relay stations (a name, a word or phrase, a sight or smell, an action, a thought) which join those fragments the one to the other.

Once metaphor is recognized as the basis for chronological disjunction in *The Sound and the Fury*, then narrative junction can be reduced to a word, a thought, an event. At its most

obvious, Gerald's 'blowing off . . . about his women' (p. 151)
connects with Quentin's memory of Ames, his attempt to
protect his sister's honour; the blow he strikes analogous
to that made earlier. Benjy's memory of his interruption of
Caddy and Charlie on the swing similarly connects with his
present action of interrupting Quentin and the man with the
red tie in the same place. Temporal boundaries break down.
The chronological jumps and cuts, then, take secondary status
to a situation in which 'two passages . . . are linked by repetition, thematic similarity, or memorial association on the part
of a character, and the two passages share in the one moment
of present apprehension or creation of a fictional character by
the reader'.[66]

The vital thing about metaphor, though, as a connective principle, is that it hinges on an awareness both of
similarity and difference. Two points in time may be linked
by their mutual associations, but they are at the same time
distinct and dissimilar in other respects. Faulkner's narrative
technique, certainly in the first two sections of *The Sound and
the Fury*, brilliantly plays with this device. For the reader
sees the metaphoric connection between events, while the
focalizer-narrator fails to do so. What is different for us is
identity or sameness for Benjy and Quentin, both caught in a
fixed and unchanging world which centres on Caddy. What are
chronological shifts for us – able to see the difference between
one time and another, between one incident and another, as
well as their similarities – fuse as one sequence, one moment,
in their abnormal minds. When the reader comes across the
name 'Caddy', he or she recognizes the metaphoric connection
(the point of similarity) between that name and the 'caddie'
which Benjy has heard shouted on the golf course. But the
reader also recognizes the difference between them. Benjy fails
to recognize this difference and that is why he moans: for him
'caddie' *is* 'Caddy'. Caught in a world of sameness, he is unable
to differentiate between different moments in time, unable to
make the distinction between similarity and sameness in each
group of scenes or incidents. The breakdown of his sense of
time relates to this. He lives in a kind of continual and kaleidoscopic present precisely because he identifies the stimuli
he encounters with the exact same rendition of those stimuli in
the past. His inability to distinguish present from past lies in

his failure to recognize that difference round which metaphor operates. So, too, for Quentin, though for other reasons. His sense of time is also disrupted. At points of stress all is in flux in his mind – the fight with Ames in the past co-present with that with Bland in the present. The notion of difference temporarily disappears. He, too, has lost the ability to make true metaphoric connections. Both men are caught in worlds in which time has stopped – worlds not of metaphor, but of undifferentiated repetitions.

We start to recover the novel's meaning, then, by laying the characters' fictive experience of time, as represented both in the narrative and in its very organizing principles, against our own understanding of time. Repetition without difference becomes to us a clear mark of inertia, of 'oversameness', life-denying abnormality. Both Quentin and Benjy are caught within such repetition compulsions which both mark them as aberrant and cut them off from the world of public chronology in which we, as readers, live. This 'public time' is counted off by calendars and clocks throughout the novel. Quentin's 'supremely private' act of suicide[67] cannot counter its passing. The dates which frame each narrative, the 'clock in the Unitarian steeple' (p. 110), the courthouse clock in Jefferson, mark off what Ricoeur calls 'monumental time' (p. 106), the official time of history itself of which the reality principle consists.

It is in terms of this principle which recognizes both repetition and change that both Quentin and Benjy's abnormality is evident. Dilsey's characterization also – in a very different way – is associated with that repetition without development which marks inertia. For Rimmon-Kenan defines 'complete repetition' not just in terms of death, but also 'if one prefers', in terms of 'eternity'. Both death and eternity she defines as 'being . . . beyond life and beyond narrative'.[68] This comparison between a death instinct, marked by stultifying and life denying repetition, and eternity, casts an interesting light on the final section of the novel which focuses so strongly on Dilsey. Dilsey is associated with repetition. Her 'I seed de beginnin, en now I sees de endin' (p. 264) stresses her status as still centre of a changing world. Repetition here, however, goes hand in hand with difference. She cares for Quentin just as she had previously cared for her mother, Caddy. She operates to a Sunday routine the description of which opens the section. But strong attention is also drawn to the effects of time's passing. Her former physique, 'a big woman once', has been eroded by time ('only the indomitable skeleton was left rising like a ruin or a landmark above the somnolent and impervious guts', p. 236). She herself recognizes the process of dissolution which has accompanied temporal process: from first to last, 'beginnin' to 'endin'. The last male descendant of the family, is, in Myra Jehlen's words 'a mental incompetent castrated for the sake of public security',[69] the 'big man' described in the last section 'who appeared to have been shaped of some substance whose particles would not or did not cohere to one another or to the frame which supported it' (p. 244).

Change (difference) in this novel is for the worse. Successful psychoanalysis, as Richard King points out in *A Southern Renaissance*, leads away from repetition towards transcendence.[70] The note of transcendence introduced into the final section of the book is not, however, similar to Ike McCaslin's act of '*historical* consciousness' (my stress) in *Go Down, Moses*, but operates only in a religious frame. The black preacher sees 'de resurrection en de light; sees de meek Jesus sayin Dey kilt Me dat ye shall live again . . . sees de doom crack en hears de golden horns shoutin down de glory, en de arisen dead whut got de blood en de ricklickshun fo de Lamb!'. Dilsey cries 'rigidly and quietly in the annealment and the blood of the remembered Lamb' (pp. 263–4). This is a move outside of history. Dilsey, too, looks beyond life and beyond narrative to that lack of differentiation ('the sempiternal repetition of the Same' [Ricoeur, p. 130]) which is eternity. Her 'solution' is no more satisfying to the secular reader than Quentin's whose other-worldly corollary it is. Both find 'salvific meaning'[71] only in forms of death. As Jehlen comments:

The famous Dilsey episode, something of a Hallelujah chorus, is really no more redemptive than any other section. Perhaps Faulkner realized that no degree of endurance by a nigger mammy could reverse the disintegration of the aristocratic South.[72]

It is not endurance, but rather anxiety – anxiety about narration and anxiety about time – which prevails in *The Sound and the Fury*. Faulkner's repetitious re-tellings of the same story ('I finished it the first time, and it wasn't right, so I wrote it again . . . that wasn't right. I wrote it again . . . ')[73] suggest – despite the difference between narrators, between points of view – a kind of paralysis which results from an inability to position the Compson family psychodrama (which centres around the figure of Caddy) in the context of what Myra Jehlen calls 'social relationships [and] historical situations',[74] the ongoing process of Southern history which encircles it. Anxieties about both time and its meaning emerge in the later Appendix Faulkner wrote to the novel. This commences with Faulkner's reference to Ikkemotubbe, the Indian chief who originally owned the Compson land. Ikkemotubbe's title meant 'The Man' in English. This is translated to 'L'Homme' by his (unlikely) foster brother, 'a Chevalier of France'. 'L'Homme' was, in turn, anglicized by Ikkemotubbe to 'Doom'.[75] This later (metaphoric) equation of man and doom fits a novel about the doom of a family. It fits, too, a novel which can be retrospectively (analeptically) read – but only when put in 'the explosive historical setting' of *Absalom, Absalom!* – as also about 'the doom of the South'.[76] Faulkner's own repetitions of the word 'doom' entirely suit a narrative where time's passing coincides with 'the defection that ravages love',[77] where the repetitions that mark a family history (and will be later shown to mark that of the 'social–cultural order' it represents),[78] are compulsive, marked not by difference but by a life-denying over-sameness.

Such an entrapment, in the shape of a 'blind insistence'[79] on a futile re-enactment, is what concludes the novel. Here Benjy, on his way to the graveyard (site of the triumph of the death instinct, place of final inanimation and inertia), repeats a pattern that is both regular ('ev'y Sunday') and absolutely sterile in its lack of variation. When Luster does vary the routine, by swinging the carriage to the left of the monument of the Confederate soldier in the town square (rather than to the right as normal), Benjy's bellows register his outrage at the disturbance of the proprieties: 'Bellow on bellow, his voice mounted, with scarce interval for breath. There was more than astonishment in it, it was horror; shock; agony eyeless, tongueless; just sound' (p. 283). This 'sound and fury' signifies nothing bar the disruption of a completely meaningless routine. Jason re-establishes the order of an idiot, the carriage turns, peace is restored as 'cornice and facade flowed smoothly once more from left to right; post and tree, window and doorway, and signboard, each in its ordered place' (p. 284). The fictive experience of time with which the novel ends is of a repetition of the same which occurs on the way to that 'boneyard y'all headed fer' (p. 283). The concluding moment is that of duplication. Time and history are contained by 'a kind of circular plot'[80] which negates the prospect of change, difference and development. Narration itself becomes repetition as textual present merges with the earlier trip to the graveyard described in Benjy's section, that past which can only now recur in repeated and relentless form. The meaning of the novel only becomes fully evident when the fictive experiences of time it contains are revealed.

3

Slippery Stuff: The Construction of Character in *The Sun Also Rises*

I

There was a story around that I had gone to switserland
[sic] to avoid being shot by demented characters out
of my books.
(Hemingway to Fitzgerald, March 31, 1927)[1]

'I'm going back to Mike.' I could feel her crying as I held
her close. 'He's so damned nice and he's so awful. He's
my sort of thing.'[2]

'Character', Joel Weinsheimer writes, is an 'extraordinarily slippery term'.[3] Definitions of character in a literary text can be equally slippery. How, for example, can we 'label' Mike in *The Sun Also Rises* given the paradoxical nature of Brett's description? Such a description, moreover, is one he shares with Robert Cohn of whom Bill says: 'The funny thing is he's nice, too. I like him. But he's just so awful' (p. 101). Not only then are we faced with the problem of paradox, but also that of similarity: if two characters are described in like manner the lines between them start blurring. Can either be described in terms of that coherent and unique individuality which has been the basis for traditional notions of what character in the novel means?

86

Such traditional notions which insist on character in terms
of unique identity, of unchanging and essential qualities, have
been rigorously challenged. The very idea of 'continuous
character', of character as stable and unchanging, has been
discredited by critics. Weinsheimer refers to such a concept
as 'lyrical and atemporal – almost divine, almost ridiculous'.[4]
Recent experimental fiction goes so far as to deconstruct the
notion of character entirely, replacing it with:

> fragmentary 'instants of subjectivity' none of which seems
> to be related to each other, and none of which seem ever
> to develop into a more stable self.[5]

The idea of even treating character in fiction according
to mimetic criteria, has been challenged by semiotic theory.[6]
It takes issue with any theory of characterization which gains
its validation from extra-textual sources; rejects any identification with character as a kind of 'ghostly person, having all
the attributes of people except bodily existence[7] – one who
transcends all fictional boundaries (Hemingway running to
Switzerland to evade his characters' wrath!).[8] Such theory
approaches the literary text as a closed and self-sufficient
system. To treat characters as if living human beings is
seen as 'a sentimental misunderstanding of the nature of
literature'. Marvin Mudrick describes such theory, rather, in
terms of its treatment of fictional characters as 'only more or
less efficient patterns of words subordinate to larger patterns'.[9]
Weinsheimer speaks of characters as 'marks in a book . . . segments of a closed text . . . patterns of recurrence'.[10] Barthes in
his seminal 'Introduction to the Structural Analysis of Narratives' argues that they are 'essentially "paper beings"'.[11]

To see literary character as merely a pattern of words
is, however, inadequately to account for the reading experience. Bernard McGuirk stresses 'the *inevitability* [my stress]
of a reader's propensity to "naturalize" linguistic structures
into associations with "lived" experience, with recognizable
psychologies'.[12] Shlomith Rimmon-Kenan, whose model I will
use extensively in this chapter, accepts the critical usefulness
of the semiotic approach to character; as a highly artificial
construct composed from those 'verbal scraps (physical

appearance, thoughts, statements, feelings)'[13] encountered as the textual surface of the narrative is scanned. She never loses sight, however, of character as an end product. If textual details provide indications of character, such details are assimilated and composed by the reader to produce an overview which allows characters to be seen 'at once as persons' as well as, in the former sense, as 'parts of a design'.[14] Barthes, writing in 1970, altered his previous stance in acknowledging such activity: 'to read is to struggle to name';[15] textual scraps are always subject to readerly attempts at cohesion. To admit that a complex character is not 'realistic' and rather a composed fictive construct is not to deny that we 'naturalize' the text according to what Garvey calls 'life information',[16] conceptions of 'personality . . . familiar to us in life and art'. These provide the models for our drive towards synthesis.[17] Recent critical attention to the decentering or fragmentation of the subject may disturb such a drive. It does not, however, disrupt such a 'naturalizing' process. Rather it suggests a new conception of character is called for which recognizes 'identity' as something both provisional and multi-faceted, recognizes the individual as subjected to a constitutive social order.

I will commence my study of *The Sun Also Rises* by first examining the way in which character can be approached as subordinate to action, and the usefulness and shortcomings of such a critical tactic. I will then take up Rimmon-Kenan's two way approach and apply it selectively to the novel. She maintains methodological rigour by processing the information available at the surface level of the text in terms of indicated character traits. Such traits are implied, she suggests, in a number of different ways; are then reinforced by means of analogy. She uses this base to lay out a type of categorizing model which can usefully be applied to any representational text. She retains, though, the stress on the importance of character as a projection of a whole, arguing that we use these textual indicators and analogies to reconstruct character, making use of patterns of 'repetition, similarity, contrast, and implication' to do so. The definition of character lies in 'the more or less unified construct' (p. 39) formed by the resulting generalizations.[18] This runs in line with Martin Price's view of character as 'all verbal surface at one level . . . all implication and suggestion of human life on another'.[19]

My analysis of the tutor text will however modify Rimmon-Kenan's model in attempting to re-establish the connections between 'character' and her or his socio-historical context which, I suggest, she underplays. I do this in two ways. First (as I will explain more fully later) I will introduce short digressions to punctuate the application of Rimmon-Kenan's 'grid'. These are intended to site the represented subject in relation to those wider social and historical frames which both condition our understanding of – and are, in their turn, implied within – the literary text. In doing this I suggest that the traits which emerge as a result of the type of analysis Rimmon-Kenan suggests cannot be divorced from the social reality which helps to form them.

This tactic is, as it sounds, a rather intrusive one. More methodologically consistent is my second ploy which is to re-work some of the implications of Rimmon-Kenan's system to somewhat different conclusions. For, first, her definition of character as 'more or less unified construct' contains within it the possibility of fragmentation as well as unity (though this is not one which she pursues). As I examine character in *The Sun Also Rises* in the light of her model it becomes clear that the 'characters' central to this text are in fact not coherent but self-divided, less unified rather than more. Secondly, Rimmon-Kenan's model operates on the principle of character difference. I will show in my final section how the use of analogy as a pointer to character leads to a discovery of sameness which threatens the whole notion (of difference) on which character theory is based. Self-division and similarity run alongside one another in this text. Both, as I finally suggest, are to be explained by reference to the issue of social and historical change; both suggest a questioning of that notion of autonomous individuality which so many critics and teachers still take for granted. Rimmon Kenan's model, my suggestion is, despite its pragmatic strengths and undoubted usefulness, does not go as far as it might to recognize the disjointed nature of the fictional subject, its location within larger formative frames. I place rather more stress on the slippery nature of identity than she does.

II

Character as subordinate to action?

> What is character but the determination of incident?
> What is incident but the illustration of character?
>
> (Henry James)[20]

Both formalist and structuralist critics argue for the placing of individual texts in a system which governs all narrative, looking for the general laws by which this system operates.[21] Their refusal to discuss character in terms of psychological depth stems from this stress on the system, not the subject. And they reject any approach to literature (and 'character' within that literature) as 'realistic' representation in favour of one which sees narratives as artificial constructs, subject to formal analysis. Their attempt to construct a 'narrative grammar' leads to a concentration on character as participant in the narrative *action* (grammar being verb centred), not as 'psychological essence', a mistaken notion to their minds. Their analyses have as their basis 'strictly . . . what characters DO in a story, not . . . what they ARE – by some outside pyschological measure'.[22]

Thus we might analyze a single sequence from Hemingway's novel to show how a character's actions take on narrative significance:

> The bull who killed Vicente Girones was named Bocanegra, was Number 118 of the bull-breeding establishment of Sanchez Taberno, and was killed by Pedro Romero as the third bull of that same afternoon. His ear was cut by popular acclamation and given to Pedro Romero, who, in turn, gave it to Brett, who wrapped it in a handkerchief belonging to myself, and left both ear and handkerchief, along with a number of Muratti cigarette-stubs, shoved far back in the drawer of the bed-table that stood beside her bed in the Hotel Montoya, in Pamplona (p. 199).

Characters act in a text within different spheres. In this passage the role and function of character[23] is constructed in relation to two particular spheres which I term *Inside* and

Outside the Bullring, and which I see existing in fundamental opposition. This opposition is central to the text and is often revealingly transgressed.[24] Within the ring Romero's role is that of heroic performer and community avenger. In the sequence of events describing his actions there he fulfils role requirement, his defined task is successfully completed. I am using here a modified form of Claude Bremond's approach to textual sequences. Bremond analyses such sequences in terms of the way they affect a narrative situation, lead either to improvement or deterioration.[25] Referring to the three stages of an event sequence as Bremond describes them, it is evident that, in the ring, Romero has:

(a) *a task to accomplish*: the killing of Bocanegra.
(b) *the process of accomplishing this task* (steps taken): these are, unusually, described at a later textual point when his technique and skill in bullfighting on this occasion are detailed.
(c) *the accomplished task*: here completed successfully; the killing of the bull.

When we embed this sequence in an overlapping one, however, the parameters dividing bullring interior and exterior are revealingly breached. For Romero's role as heroic performer works much better inside the ring than without. Outside it, this 'boy' (p. 163) may still behave, according to Jake's lights, in an exemplary manner. The event-sequences in which he figures however (the fight with Cohn, for example) are far more difficult to assess in terms of whether they end in the improvement or deterioration of the narrative situation. Here, for example, what begins in the ring and ends outside it must be read ambiguously; as Romero fills that role of suitor which he shares with Jake, Robert, and Mike. His task to accomplish is to win the love of Brett. The steps he takes to accomplish this task are to exercise his skills as bullfighter for her benefit, to give her the ear which symbolizes both his skill and the act of community vengeance performed.[26] Whether Romero succeeds in his accomplished task is ambiguous. Brett accepts the ear, thus in terms of the particular sequence success would seem implied. Her consequent actions, though – outside the ring, and described in the chain of subsidiary clauses which bring the passage juddering to a halt – suggest deterioration. She fails to value or to retain the token given her. Romero's role as both suitor and heroic performer is questioned when the barriers of the bullring are crossed.

Jake's actions and the role he plays in this sequence also offer information about his character. Jake's role is one recurrently associated with him: that of spectator. We see Romero perform through his eyes. Just looking, Jake, whose sexuality is in-valid, vicariously consumes those skills which in the symbolic arena before him translate Romero into what the Davidsons call 'an icon of essential masculinity'.[27] Jake here, as in other spheres, associates himself with passivity rather than activity: not 'the handkerchief I gave her' but 'the handkerchief belonging to myself'. He has however acted, handed this handkerchief over, and a second and vital role emerges from his activity in the sequence: that of *facilitator*, easing the exchange between Romero and Brett, again a role which is repeated textually. If we wish to detail that part of the narrative sequence which, however minimally, involves him, it could be done in the following way:

> *task to accomplish* : facilitate exchange of ear from Romero
> to Brett
> *steps taken* : giving handkerchief
> *task accomplished* : successfully

His role as middleman, which he performs at the cost of his own emotional interests (in his role as suitor), emerges clearly in such an analysis.

I have given this brief example of analysis of a short sequence of textual events, to illustrate how character can be subordinated to textual sequence, to action; how function (significant action) can be categorized in terms of roles. My analysis confirms James' fusion of character and action. It would be however a limitation, a mistake, to subordinate, as some formalist critics do, the one to the other, for to view the character in terms of action, of plot function, is potentially to deny that character complexity. So Chatman argues that a plot-centred approach:

ignore[s] the shift in interest in a sophisticated reading-public, from 'what happens' to 'whom does it happen to?' Indeed, fiction of the twentieth century by the Woolfs and the Prousts clearly discounts the importance of 'What happens'.[28]

Narratives can, in fact, as Todorov recognizes,[29] be either plot-centred or character-centred (psychological). Barthes in *S/Z* separates off the semic code from the proairetic, though both can overlap. While the proairetic code deals with the sphere of action, it is the semic code which involves 'the struggle to name', the building up of the complexity of a character's entire 'personality':

if we are told that Sarrasine had '*one of those strong wills that know no obstacle,*' what are we to read? *will, energy, obstinacy, stubbornness*, etc?[30]

III

Action as subordinate to character

Rimmon-Kenan's model in *Narrative Fiction* argues for a similar flexible critical approach to the question of function and character. She subordinates the one to the other when she focuses on characterization as her theme, claiming – sensibly – that 'it is legitimate to subordinate action to character when the latter is the focus of our study' (p. 36), and vice versa. In discussing character, she therefore takes action as just one of that network of indicators which, scattered through the text, reveal the attributes or traits invested in, and which together constitute, particular characters. I now wish to describe and apply this network to *The Sun Also Rises*.

Rimmon-Kenan opens her discussion of characterization, though, by distinguishing between direct definition of character, where a trait is named, and indirect presentation, which 'does not mention the trait but displays and exemplifies it in various ways, leaving to the reader the task of inferring the quality they imply' (p. 60). *Direct definition of character* is the explicit attribution of character traits, such as we associate with the authoritative narrator of the nineteenth-century novel. So James' narrator in *Washington Square* (1880) describes Mrs Sloper as 'amiable, graceful, accomplished, elegant'.[31] By and large, such a means of character definition is by-passed as both too static and reductive for twentieth-century needs:

> in the present day, when suggestiveness and indeter-
> minacy are preferred to closure and definitiveness and
> when emphasis is put on the active role of the reader,
> the explicitness and guiding capacity of direct definition
> are often considered drawbacks rather than advantages
> (p. 61).

Direct definition of character can only 'count' according to Rimmon-Kenan if it comes from the most authoritative textual voice. Such a statement however needs qualification as, in first person texts, even the most authoritative voice can be thoroughly unreliable (see my first chapter). So when Jake directly defines Robert's as a 'nice, boyish, sort of cheerful-ness that had never been trained out of him' (p. 45), we need to be aware that Jake's descriptions of Robert are generally informed by what David Wyatt calls 'gratuitous bile'.[32] The voice through which direct definition passes can be heavily distorting, and any 'reading' of character on such a basis should be very tentative.

The modern novel relies far more heavily on *indirect presentation of character*. In suggesting a number of different ways in which character traits are indicated, Rimmon-Kenan offers a helpful method of systematizing the area. The categorizations she suggests provide a pragmatic and rewarding way of buil-ding up combinations of character attributes around which our final 'struggle to name' can range. The first in the series of indicators which she lays out is, in fact, that of *action*. In doing so, she acknowledges its centrality in terms of character construction. She divides action into two sorts – one-time, and habitual or repeated. She associates one-time actions with 'the dynamic aspect of the character, often playing a part in a turning point in the narrative' (p. 61), while habitual or repetitious actions illustrate the more constant and static sides of character. In terms of its strong impact on the course of the narrative, traits revealed by one-time actions can, she claims, be more significant than those revealed by normal routine actions. She divides both types of action into classes; acts of commission, acts of omission, and contemplated acts. These correspond in turn to actions performed by a character, those which should be performed but are not, and planned or intended actions which remain unfulfilled. So, to schematize this material:

$$
\text{ACTION}
\begin{cases}
\text{one time} & \text{dynamic aspect (narrative} \\
& \text{turning point)} \\
\text{or} \\
\text{habitual} & \text{constant, static aspect}
\end{cases}
\begin{cases}
\text{acts of commission} \\
\text{omission,} \\
\text{contemplated acts}
\end{cases}
$$

I wish to illustrate this type of indirect presentation of character by examining Jake's character in the novel. I will then, in the interests of economy, variation, and cross-reference, move between Brett and Jake at will in illustrating the other types of indirect presentation of character. As Jake is 'the voice of authority'[33] in this narrative, and as the gaps between his expression, intention, and performance are ones I wish initially to foreground, the first section on action will be out of balance with the rest of my units. My presentation is of necessity selective; its intention, though is to lay out Rimmon-Kenan's 'grid' as it might be applied to any character, or set of characters, in texts in which 'characters are still recuperable as humanistic and explicable'.[34] I start with the field of action.

Jake's one time actions

(a) *picking up Georgette, the prostitute*

Jake offers two explanations for this act, and its continuation, his taking her to the dancing club:

> I had picked her up because of a vague sentimental idea that it would be nice to eat with some one. It was a long

time since I had dined with a *poule*, and I had forgotten
how dull it could be (p. 16).

'What possessed you to bring her?'
'I don't know, I just brought her.'
'You're getting damned romantic.'
'No, bored.' (p. 23)

The incident in itself indicates the bohemian quality of Jake's
life and of life in the Quarter. Its matter-of-fact presentation
masks its radical content. Many American readers must have
been taken aback by the lack of social and moral boundaries,
the relaxed codes of behaviour, that Jake's casual pick-up
implied.[35] More importantly, it introduces us to the two modes
of discourse associated with Jake: the sentimental/romantic
and the cynical. The incompatibility of these two modes,
these two parts of his 'character', will be central to the text.
This is not a turning point in the narrative: its positioning
so close to the narrative's start precludes this. The action
does however illustrate Jake's dynamic aspects in ambiguous
terms. He acts but appears to regret it almost immediately;
involvement is followed by retreat as he abandons Georgette
in the dancing club, leaving her a fifty franc note as payment
for her time and trouble. Patterns of involvement and retreat
mark Jake throughout the text (indicated character trait,
solitariness/sociability), and connect with that impotence to
which reference is so briefly made in his conversation with
Georgette after he has 'put her hand away' (p. 15) in the taxi.
His ironic reticence at this point alerts the reader to another
central trait, one which can be categorized as an habitual act
of omission. This is Jake's evasiveness, marked by a 'strategy
of deferral',[36] his refusal to reveal the full meaning of things
either to his interlocutor or to the reader:

'What's the matter with you, anyway?'
'I got hurt in the war,' I said.
'Oh, that dirty war.'
We would probably have gone on and discussed the war
and agreed that it was in reality a calamity for civilization,
and perhaps would have been better avoided. I was bored
enough (p. 17).

(b) *Jake's attempt to hit Cohn, after being called a 'pimp'*

This connects up with a previous contemplated act when Jake's anger surfaces, directed against the gays in the dancing club:

> . . . The wavy blond one answered: 'Don't you worry, dear.' And with them was Brett.
> I was very angry. Somehow they always made me angry. I know they are supposed to be amusing, and you should be tolerant, but I wanted to swing on one, any one, anything to shatter that superior, simpering composure. Instead, I walked down the street and had a beer at the bar at the next Bal (p. 20).

Again 'narrative subterfuge'[37] is involved, subterfuge given away by the positioning of the 'And with them was Brett'. This, her first appearance in the novel, is presented by Jake almost as an afterthought. He tacks her on to the end of his description of the homosexuals ('with them was Brett. She looked very lovely and she was very much with them'). This deceit, a drawing of the reader's attention away from what is of central importance, is then repeated in the reason he gives for his contemplated action. His anger at the homosexuals is not just because of their 'superior, simpering composure'; that 'somehow' which qualifies 'they always made me angry' suggesting a source of irritation impossible to define. The source is only too clearly at hand. Brett, whom Jake loves, is 'very much with' those who lack the desire, though not the potential, to sexually fulfil her. He has the desire, though no longer that potential. If their homosexuality defines his manhood (his conventional sexual preference marking theirs as aberrant), nonetheless Brett's choice of their company is a sharp reminder of his own sexual lack (absence of 'manhood') which has led to his solitude. His anger indicates a sexual and emotional frustration which is directed at those who adopt 'fraudulent' heterosexual roles in relation to the woman he loves, and at his deep recognition of his and their 'fundamental equivalence' – the disguised nature of their shared 'masculine absence[s]'.[38]

What is important for my purposes is Jake's public control

of his emotions here (trait: self-control). Jake later attempts
to deflate Cohn's romanticization of Brett Ashley through a
laconic and cynical realism:

> 'She seems to be absolutely fine and straight . . . I shouldn't
> wonder if I were in love with her.'
> 'She's a drunk,' I said. 'She's in love with Mike Campbell,
> and she's going to marry him. He's going to be rich as hell
> some day' (p. 38).

Cohn's response is to stand up to defend her good name from
'insult'. To his 'You've got to take that back', Jake replies, 'Oh,
cut out the prep-school stuff.' Implicit in his decision not to
'swing on one' of the homosexuals is this realization that it
would be 'prep-school stuff', an adolescent gesture out of all
keeping with his imposed 'hard-boiled' stoic code, a gesture
directly related to his emotional concern for Brett.

His one-time action of hitting out at Cohn, 'I swung
at him and he ducked' (p. 191), takes on significance in
the light of the contrast with the earlier contemplated act.
It is a textual turning point in that it is the only time Jake
publicly loses control of those emotions that are so tightly
reined in. As a gesture, it reveals Jake's similarity to Cohn,
even though he predicates his whole narrative (fraudulently)
on the basis of their difference. For Cohn will immediately
mimic Jake's action by hitting out at Romero, doing 'battle
for his lady love' (p. 178) and her honour (he wants 'to
make an honest woman of her . . . was crying and telling
her how much he loved her . . . Damned touching scene',
pp. 201–2).

Jake's action is similarly adolescent, similarly romantic
in its implication. He too is fighting for his lady love's good
name, for if he is a 'pimp' (p. 190) then she is a prostitute.
He acts against the requirements of his own hard-boiled
code – one which operates on irony and understatement,
objective distance rather than subjective engagement – in
doing so. His essential similarity to the romantic Cohn is
suggested also in his post-fight sensations which remind him
of how 'I felt once coming home from an out-of-town football
game' (p. 192) in the course of which he had been kicked on
the head. This is one of the few textual references to Jake's

pre-war past. The analogy between this incident and Cohn's earlier statement that, if he could do anything he wanted, 'I think I'd rather play football again with what I know about handling myself, now' suggests that *both* men may, in fact, be cases of 'arrested development' (p. 44). Jake is trapped in a hopeless romantic attachment which parallels, in its 'uncanny pattern of repetition beyond his control', his feelings after the fight. Such a sense of entrapment is continually denied by his self-presentation: Jake's apparently 'frank and simple' prose style, narrative, conceals a story which as David Wyatt points out does not quite hold together.[39]

Habitual actions

The stress on repetition in *The Sun Also Rises* is particularly strong. So strong, in fact, that I suggest that it is in the conflict between various types of repetition that the major turning points of this text occur. Rimmon-Kenan's scheme will need some modification here to meet what is, in Hemingway's novel, a textual emphasis on circularity and on self-division. These repetitions occur in a large number of areas. My treatment is, throughout, selective.

(a) *Walking, riding and watching*

Jake spends much of his time in motion reporting on what he sees as he walks, or as he rides in taxis, trains, buses, and cars. This repeated activity apparently characterizes him as a type of *flâneur*.

I here introduce my first digression. Rimmon-Kenan's model is a very useful one. A shortcoming is, however, its tendency to suggest that 'character' exists in some way apart from social formation, to lift 'character' above the world of history in which is is inevitably anchored. I will introduce three brief sequences which I will signal by means of asterisks (Jake as *flâneur?*, Rates of exchange, Costume and gender role) into my text. Their purpose is to connect elements of characterization as they emerge from Rimmon-Kenan's scheme back to the socio-historical frame which exists within, and extends beyond, the written text. It is social reality which gives the subject his or her meaning. Rimmon-Kenan appears to sidestep this fact.

*Jake as flâneur?

Henry James (to whom Jake is textually compared) used a version of this label to describe himself: 'afternoons in the streets, walking, strolling, *flânant*, prying, staring, lingering at book stalls and shopwindows'.[40] Jake is not quite the idle, sauntering, man about town that the name denotes; when Bill accuses him of spending all his time 'talking, not working . . . You hang around cafés', Jake counters with 'It sounds like a swell life . . . When do I work?' (p. 115). His work, though, is textually downplayed. And Jake certainly bears resemblance to the *flâneur*, as Walter Benjamin describes him. Benjamin, writing on Baudelaire, stresses the *flâneur*'s 'gaze', his position on 'the threshold, of the city as of the bourgeois class. Neither has yet engulfed him; in neither is he at home. He seeks refuge in the crowd'. Jake is a journalist, one who has learnt from the *flâneur* to move 'among the crowd' with 'skill and ease'.[41] Jake is on the threshold of Parisian life, partly because of his status as expatriate. He knows Paris, yet is distanced from its routinized work, 'men . . . working on the car-tracks by the light of acetylene flares' (p. 25). He associates with writers and has a lifestyle which uncomfortably bridges bohemian and bourgeois. He walks, rides, and watches, taking in all around him; the traffic signals, the 'electric signs', 'the 'crowd going by' (p. 14). He is both within and without the city's life: idly looking at what is to be seen.

Jake, though, is not an artist (as is, for Benjamin, the *flâneur*); is not excited by what he sees. He may share something of the *flâneur*'s qualities, but he seems a type of burnt-out case, receiving no *frisson* from what he comes across. This can be linked to the fact that his status as leisured observer is severely undercut by the 'shocks and collisions' which occur as he moves through 'the traffic of a big city'.[42] Repeated sequences of leisured looking which suggest Jake may have the aesthetic eye and sense of autonomy of the *flâneur*, are counter-posed to the repeated metropolitan experience of crowdedness,

and of the sudden jolt which suggests that Jake's self-determination is sharply at question. The 'red and green stop-and-
go traffic-signal' (p. 14), the nightclub where 'it was so crowded we could barely move . . . We were caught in the jam'
(p. 62), the taxi where 'we jolted close together' (p. 25); all
carry such an implication. Habitual actions ('I walked', 'I
stopped and read', 'I sat . . . watching') are thus counterposed
to, contradicted by, repeated references to the frame which
conditions Jake's movements, which affects any notion of individual autonomy on his part.

Baudelaire's move away from the position of *flâneur* is
signalled, for Benjamin, in his submission to the shocks of
urban life as he hurries 'across the boulevard, and amidst
this moving chaos in which death comes galloping at you
from all sides at once'. The metaphor of 'death . . . galloping . . . from all sides' is more applicable to war than it is
to city life. Baudelaire's 'impotent rage'[43] transfers itself with
exact appropriateness to Jake Barnes whose 'experience of
shock' is comprised of war experience, of the jolting impact on
the self of outside forces, here textually symbolized by urban
parallels – the policeman's baton and abrupt traffic movement.
Rimmon-Kenan's categories must always be read in context,
I would suggest: the location of the subject in relation to the
conditions of her, or his, existence must never be subsumed
by a focus on character alone. Both Jake and Brett cannot be
explained outside their determining context, without regard
to their various wounds (physical, emotional, psychological)
caused by the war; without regard to the modernized urban
environment which initially surrounds them and which dislocates in analogous ways.

(b) *Brett and Jake: a circular routine*

'Oh, darling,' Brett said, 'I'm so miserable.'
I had that feeling of going through something that has
all happened before . . .
'Want to go?'
I had the feeling as in a nightmare of it all being
something repeated, something I had been through and
that now I must go through again (p. 64).

The taxi scenes which frame Brett and Jake's textual
relationship are just two examples of the whole series
of repetitious actions in the text centering around Jake's
interactions with Brett. The to-ings and fro-ings of their
relationship operate on several levels. In terms of physical
contact, Jake's emotional attraction for Brett and hers for him
lead both recurrently to seek physical contact with the other
(implied trait; desire, passion). The first time this occurs, in
the taxi as 'we jolted close together', commences a sequence
of episodes in which both parties are associated with the same
habitual action. Their emotional need for one another triggers
physical contact; their physical contact triggers a renewed
realization of the hopelessness of their position, where full
emotional satisfaction can only be concomitant with that sexual satisfaction which is unrealizable (implied trait, impotence
– sexual and emotional). The nightmarish sense of repetition
without resolution (character trait, irresolution) that ensues is
heavily figured when they first kiss:

> . . . I kissed her. Our lips were tight together and then she
> turned away and pressed against the corner of the seat, as
> far away as she could get. Her head was down.
> 'Don't touch me,' she said. 'Please don't touch me.'
> 'What's the matter?'
> 'I can't stand it.'
> 'Oh, Brett.'
> 'You mustn't. You must know. I can't stand it, that's all.
> Oh, darling, please understand!'
> 'Don't you love me?'
> 'Love you? I simply turn all to jelly when you touch me.'
> 'Isn't there anything we can do about it?' (pp. 25–6)

When the reprise occurs at the end of the first part
of the book, mutual physical contact is again broken by
Brett, the circularity of the routine by this point textually
established around the contemplated act of living together,
even marriage. When the Count suggests the latter, both
Jake and Brett's quick dismissals of the notion point to
their emotional dissimulation, Brett closing off the subject
to public discussion in a change of conversational direction
which echoes her discomfiture:

'Why don't you get married, you two?'
'We want to lead our own lives,' I said.
'We have our careers,' Brett said. 'Come on. Let's get out of this.' (p. 61)

Jake's repetitions and lack of emotional equilibrium are evident in the way his 'there's not a damn thing we could do' (p. 26) swiftly modulates to 'Couldn't we live together, Brett? Couldn't we just live together?' (p. 55); his 'We'd better keep away from each other' (p. 26) to 'I love you so much' (p. 54). These patterns of physical and emotional advance and retreat suggest the highly unstable nature of both Jake and Brett's emotional state in the first part of the novel where such habitual actions are concentrated.

This physical contact is reduced dramatically in the rest of the novel ('we walked arm in arm', 'Brett put her hand in my arm') though the professions of love, the language of love ('Oh, darling . . . Please stay by me and see me through this') remain (pp. 182–4). Brett's habitual action of taking off with a man, in this case with Robert Cohn to San Sebastian, opens Book Two. And though a full knowledge of this situation is deferred, this, together with Mike's presence, apparently marks the change in her and Jake's relationship. Focus shifts from Brett's physical relationship with him to that with Cohn, Mike, and Romero; those 'bedroom scenes' (p. 13) implied if not described. Only at the novel's end does a repetition of the type of contact established in Book One occur, Brett pressed against Jake as the taxi slows suddenly. This contact takes place between Brett's final words, 'Oh, Jake . . . we could have had such a damned good time together', and his reply, ' "Yes." I said, "Isn't it pretty to think so?" ' (p. 247). The question arises here as to the relation between words and action. Is the habitual action (the making of physical contact), even if it is caused from without, a signal that their relationship and feelings for one another remain constant throughout the text, to be re-established once other 'suitors' are absent; or do the words used suggest a new turn to this relationship? The final implications of this must remain uncertain.[44] Jake's use of the word 'pretty' in this final scene slips between the ironic and the sentimental. Such a slippage is in perfect fit with the division within Jake as a subject as revealed by the text as a whole.

(c) *Jake as facilitator*

Similar self-division is evidenced in examination of the way Jake acts to facilitate Brett's relations with other men, and Romero in particular. This constitutes a second area of habitual action associated with their relationship. For Jake is unable to refuse Brett anything. His love is depicted in terms of emotional weakness not of emotional strength. His connection with her carries heavy costs; his status as *aficionado* surrendered by his compliance to her requirements. In introducing Romero to Brett at her request, he indirectly threatens Romero's career as a bullfighter; is cut by Montoya as a result. Since Montoya's valuation of Jake is intimately connected with his own self-valuation, the importance of the incident should not be underestimated.

This facilitating action is soon repeated when, relying on Jake's love for her, Brett gets him to further her connection with Romero. Her question, 'Do you still love me, Jake?' is directly linked to her feelings for Romero, 'Because I'm a goner . . . I'm mad about the Romero boy'. Jake asks, 'What do you want me to do?' and Brett replies, 'Come on . . . Let's go and find him'. The pick-up is then made, with Jake only too aware of his role in the exchange; Brett coming with one man, leaving with another. Because of the understatement and evasiveness which mark Jake's narration throughout, his feelings remain undefined. He says, though, that 'It was not pleasant' as the 'hard-eyed people at the bull-fighter table watched me go'. And his self-conscious awareness of his role is clear when Romero looks at Jake to make sure that he is reading the signals right: 'It was a final look to ask if it were understood. It was understood all right' (pp. 183–7). The character traits indicated here include self-disgust, instability, the possession of a contradictory value scheme.

(d) *Jake as aficionado*

This novel deals strongly in repetitious actions. These, I suggest, rather than one-time actions, constitute the textual turning points. For, concerned with the illustration of Jake's self-division, the text opposes one set of habitual actions to another. In the tension which results, one aspect of Jake's

character (romanticism, emotional dependency) clashes dynam-
ically with another (desire for measured rituals, for secure
meaning, as represented by his *aficion*).

A central crux in the narrative is thus revealingly highlighted. For Jake's dedication to, and understanding of, bullfighting as a skill and as a sport has conditioned another
series of habitual actions revealed in the text. His trip to
Spain to see the bullfights is a yearly ritual, his reading of
the bullfight papers a regular routine. His narrative functions
as an 'instruction manual'[45] as he describes the finer points
of the subject. He has passed the 'sort of oral spiritual examination' (p. 132) which identifies him as an *aficionado*. This is
his yearly pilgrimage which parallels that of the Catholics
('snappers') whose journey to Lourdes coincides with his to
Bayonne. As Michael S. Reynolds comments, 'If ever a man
needed a miraculous cure, it is Jake'.[46] His trips to church
(habitual action) are all unsatisfying however: his religion
does not sustain him, his prayers intruded on by more secular
matters. Jake's *aficion*, his love of the bullfight and his following of its routines – the buying of the seats, the watching
of the unloading of the bulls and their running, the attendance
at the fight – are his substitute for the rituals of the church.
Mystery (a 'shocking but really very deep secret', p. 131),
brotherhood, and blood all help to give this ritual its meaning.

When Jake's actions as an *aficionado* clash with his actions
as one who facilitates Brett's affairs, the result is – for him –
disastrous. He breaks his *aficionado*'s code in setting Romero up
for potential ruin. In doing so, he is no longer part of the male
solidarity of *aficionados*: no more for him the 'embarrassed putting the hand on the shoulder, or a "Buen hombre"' (p. 132).
Montoya never comes near him again. Though the bullfighting
code is open to strong critique in the novel, nonetheless it
has provided Jake with a central element of meaning in a
life where the traditional props are gone, or do not seem to
work.[47] As one side of Jake meets another though, this prop
splinters to nothing. And as the text draws to an end Jake is
left only with self-hatred as he recognizes where his habitual
actions have led him:

That seemed to handle it. That was it. Send a girl off with
one man. Introduce her to another to go off with him. Now

go and bring her back. And sign the wire with love. That was it all right. I went in to lunch (p. 239).

All that is left to sustain him is food, and of course, drink; for drinking is another habitual action in the novel. But the six bottles of wine drunk, mostly by Jake, in the text's final sequence suggest the habit is, on this occasion at least, subject to deliberate excess: such excess a measure of his unhappiness, his impotence, his anger; of his emotional 'bankruptcy' at the narrative's end.

** Rates of exchange

Financial metaphors load *The Sun Also Rises*. To lay another text, that constituted by Hemingway's *Letters*, against this one is to see how Hemingway's own expatriate status led him to place emphasis on the worth of the dollar. He was employed as a newspaperman in Paris but his financial wellbeing, and certainly that of the other expatriate writers in residence in Paris in these years, depended on the strong value of American currency in post-war Europe. 'Wherever Hemingway looked in 1925, he saw dollar signs', writes Reynolds, 'Everything was for sale, its price clearly marked'.[48] When he returned to Paris after the war, his early letters home were filled with details of the cost of living in terms of exchange rates:

> *Two can get a high grade dinner* [at the Restaurant of the Pre aux Clercs], *with wine, a la carte for 12 francs. We breakfast around. Usually average about 2.50 F. Think things are even cheaper than when you all were here.*

> *Living is very cheap. Hotel room is 12 francs and there are 12.61 to the paper one. A meal for two hits a male about 12–14 francs – about 50 cents apiece. Wine is 60 centimes. Good Pinard. I get rum for 14 francs a bottle. Vive la France.*

The economics of life abroad so favoured American travellers and residents that in Germany he would write, 'Because the

mark keeps dropping we have more money than when we started two weeks ago and if we stayed long enough could doubtless live on nothing. Economics is a wonderful thing'.[49]
The cost of living preoccupies Jake too in *The Sun Also Rises*. The careful checking of his current balance against his bank statement (p. 30) introduces a concern for economics which runs through the novel (habitual action: spending money and emotional energy; counting the costs): 'We . . . hired [a car] . . . for four hundred francs . . . we . . . had a beer . . . It was only sixteen francs apiece for Bill and me, with ten per cent added for the service' (p. 91). Bill Gorton, too, speaks of 'exchange of values' when he is drunk and suggests buying a 'nice stuffed dog' in the taxidermist's he and Jake pass. A running joke develops around the idea:

'Mean everything in the world to you after you bought it. Simple exchange of values. You give them money. They give you a stuffed dog . . .'
'How'd you feel that way about dogs so sudden?'
'Always felt that way about dogs. Always been a great lover of stuffed animals.'
We stopped and had a drink (pp. 72–3).

Bill also introduces the 'utilization' catchphrase – 'Let us utilize the fowls of the air. Let us utilize the product of the vine' (p. 122) – which Harris and Jake then take up: 'You know this [wine] does utilize well' (p. 129). Utilization stresses the *functional* value of an object; its instrumentality rather than its form. Barthes refers to the concept in discussing Dutch still-life painting:

the object is never alone, and never privileged; it is merely there, among many others, painted between one function and another, participating in the disorder of the movements which have picked it up, put it down – in a word *utilized*. There are objects wherever you look, on the tables, the walls, the floor: pots, pitchers overturned, a clutter of baskets, a bunch of vegetables, a brace of game, milk pans, oyster shells, glasses, cradles. All this is man's space; in it he measures himself and determines his humanity.[50]

Bill and Jake measure their space in accord with the functional objects of a leg of chicken, a bottle of wine. Their space is generally however very empty. There is a lack there to which Barthes' listing of the wide range of domestic details filling the still-life points. The province of 'man's space' seems shrunken in this text. Jake and Bill derive 'functional value' from 'stubborn matter' where they can but, in the world of Hemingway's expatriates, humanity is determined in a very narrow area: of food and drink alone.

Elsewhere matter seems closed off, separated from man. It has value in monetary terms only (the exchange value of that absolutely useless stuffed dog). In the Paris shop windows exchange value eclipses intrinsic value: we see what Benjamim calls 'the enthronement of merchandise, with the aura of amusement surrounding it'.[51] Jake and Bill are caught between a world of consumerism (a product of the 'new wave of capitalism')[52] where the use value of objects dissipates, and a more traditional world where objects function as a measurement of man's humanity. Their failure to fit in this latter sphere, the narrowness of the sustaining framework to their lives, is suggested by the equally narrow range of things called on for 'utilization'. Suggestions of discontinuity and inconsequentiality are inherent in the domiciliary absences of the novel.

Exchange value at a financial level is metaphorically related to emotional exchange throughout the novel, and Jake's ironic retreat after the Fiesta to the realm of monetary exchange only, is a measure of his final emotional dislocation and alienation. In France everything is 'on such a clear financial basis', human exchange can be reduced to the cash nexus. He overtips one waiter − 'the waiter liked me. He appreciated my valuable qualities. He would be glad to see me back'. He only tips the porter at the station at the basic rate 'because I did not think I would ever see him again' (p. 233). This retreat to cash values where 'loyal' friendship can be commodified is Jake's response to all the emotional payments which have fallen due during the 'explosion' of the Fiesta; the complications of life in Spain where Jake's 'values' have collapsed in on themselves, where friendship (for Brett) works against friendship (for Montoya), where Jake is left psychologically and emotionally bankrupt: both accounts drained completely. Mike's running out of funds and the funny looks it brings ('Bill's face sort of changed' p. 229) financially parallels Jake's emotional state. Jake's move to negotiate the human world on a financial basis is, in turn, a measure of his own emotional exhaustion.

IV

Indicators of character: speech and external appearance

Having looked in some detail at how Jake's actions display and exemplify traits of his character, I now wish to take up the remaining indirect indicators of character as categorized by Rimmon-Kenan. In the case of the next two areas – speech and external appearance – I wish to focus mainly on Brett as my exemplar.

Speech

A character's speech, whether in conversation or as a silent activity of the mind, can be indicative of a trait or traits both through its content and through its form (p. 63).

Speech content can clearly indicate character traits, thus 'antisemitism' is marked in the way the majority of the characters discuss Robert Cohn. A character's comments, both about self and others, help to 'characterize' both.[53] Brett's description of the count as 'quite one of us' (p. 32), stressing his qualities of understatement, his insistence on 'the values' (on learning to live 'decorously and well' through experience), is a self-referential one. Again, in line with the patterns both of contrast and similarity operating in the text, Brett's statement is open to question, particularly in the light of those actions which reveal the dynamic aspects of both Brett and Jake's character. For the habitual nature of the count's actions suggests that he lives by a fixed code that they, in fact, are still struggling to attain. A character's speech content must thus be carefully cross-referenced against other character indicators before given firm validity.

Brett's speech content at the novel's end, 'I feel rather good, you know. I feel rather set up . . . it makes one feel rather good deciding not to be a bitch . . . It's sort of what we have instead of God', taken in juxtaposition with her one-time action 'shaking and crying' (pp. 243–5), can be read to suggest acute emotional distress, and an accompanying 'coming to maturity' on her part. Linda Wagner writes that:

> She has thought of someone else – Romero – and she continues thinking of Mike, and always of Jake. Stanley Edgar Hyman suggests, 'The key action of the book is Brett's renunciation of Romero for the boy's own good, the first truly unselfish act of her life'.[54]

Such a reading, however, based on Brett's own self-characterization, I would consider very provisional in a novel marked by what Docherty would call 'narrative hesitancy': where the writer asserts 'nothing in his . . . own name', where all the words belong 'to another than the author'.[55] The Davidsons, in fact, stress that this novel – and this episode in it – resonate ambiguity and undecidability:

> the code of self-fulfilling romantic love is every bit as undercut in the novel as the code of heroic solitary selfhood. And neither can the two codes inhabit the same novel. Thus Brett's most triumphant moment by virtue of one code, 'I'm thirty-four, you know. I'm not going to be one of these bitches that ruins children' is also, not coincidentally, her greatest defeat by virtue of the other. The code for a woman . . . is, it seems, as arbitrary, inconsistent and contradictory as the code for a man.[56]

Rimmon-Kenan also notes how speech-acts provide 'a common means of characterization' where there is a clear difference between the narrator's style of speech and a character's. A style of speech, she comments, 'may be indicative of origin, dwelling place, social class, or profession' (p. 64). Brett's origin and class are clearly indicated by her style. Her mode of speech signals her as upper-class English: 'It was rather a knock his being ashamed of me' (p. 242). The repetitive 'give a chap a drink', 'give a chap a brandy and soda', together with her repetitive actions (wrinkling up the corners of her eyes) suggest that she is stuck in fixed, perhaps sterile, routines.[57] The formulaic nature of her speech suggests that, like Jake, her 'sense of option' is constricted.[58] Her speech then reveals more than just her social aspects. Her throwaway style – sentences which are incomplete – evidence a distrust of language which she also shares with Jake (her 'Talking's all bilge' corresponding to his 'You'll lose it if you talk about it'). This distrust is not just a class trait: 'The English spoken language – the upper classes, anyway', according to Jake, 'must have fewer words than the Eskimo' (p. 149). It also suggests a shared stance concerning the relationship between language and authenticity, a tightlipped minimalist verbal style which is to be counterposed to Cohn's sloppy romanticism.[59] Depth of feeling in the case of both Brett and Jake usually bears direct obverse correlation to the number of words used to express or suggest it.

External appearance

Traditionally, and particularly in the nineteenth-century novel, character traits were related to physiognomy: 'blue eyes', for example, signified honesty. While this kind of signalling is rare in the modern novel, character traits can be inferred through those elements of a person's appearances which are self-chosen, i.e. hairstyle, clothes, etc. This area of indirect definition is of particular interest in *The Sun Also Rises* where it raises the question of gender role which is so crucial to the text as a whole. For just as Brett refers to herself in speech by a term which normally denotes masculinity ('give a chap a drink') so her hair and clothes signal her relation to those 'female cross-dresser[s]'[60] who were seen in the post-war years, and in its literature, to pose such a challenge to existing gender conventions and the balance of sexual power. Jake first describes Brett in terms of her clothes, her hair and her body:

> Brett was damned good-looking. She wore a slipover jersey sweater and a tweed skirt, and her hair was brushed back like a boy's. She started all that. She was built with curves like the hull of a racing yacht, and you missed none of it with that wool jersey (p. 22).

'Women's clothing' Sandra M. Gilbert asserts, 'is more closely connected with the pressures and oppressions of gender'[61] than is that of the male. Here, Jake's description of the wool jersey and its accentuation of Brett's bodily curves typifies what Annette Kuhn sees as male ways of looking, a 'spectator's gaze' which lingers on the female body as representation of masculine desire. Brett's status as object of male desire is somewhat modified by the alienation effect created by her assumption of a boy's hairstyle and, later, by the masculine insignia she wears: 'her man's felt hat' (p. 28); the same headgear – 'a Basque beret' (p. 134) – as Mike. Repeated stress on such insignia, her copying of male styles, signals her status as at least partial cross-dresser.

Kuhn describes cross-dressing as:

> a mode of performance in which – through play on a disjunction between clothes and body – the socially constructed nature of sexual difference is foregrounded and even subjected to comment: what appears natural . . . reveals itself as artifice.[62]

Brett characterizes herself as unconventional, even daring, by her mode of dressing, as signalled by the reaction of the Spanish women to her. Certainly, in adopting it, she questions conservative and hierarchical ways of seeing womanhood and woman's role. Any reading of Brett as cross-dresser must fully recognize the partial nature of such a guise, must recognize too the contradictions in her self-presentation. However, such an approach does revealingly open up the area of gender representation in this text.

*** Costume and gender role

In *The Sun Also Rises* gender roles have lost all stability. In his description of Brett, Jake evidences all the signs of masculine desire. His way of looking at her insistently foregrounds her sexuality. Notions of sexual difference, however, were particularly unstable at exactly this historical period. Sandra M. Gilbert pinpoints the First World War as particularly significant in increasing a 'male sexual anxiety',[62] which has – she claims – its literary results in the misogynistic and sexually conservative texts of male modernist writers (Eliot, Lawrence, Joyce). I would argue that, while sharing similar concerns, Hemingway's novel is far more open-ended; indeed drastically upsets those hierarchies of sexual stereotyping which some of his male contemporaries are so firmly engaged in re-establishing.

Caroll Smith-Rosenberg, using Barthes, shows how the conventional social order is constructed through a 'male sexual discourse'. This discourse fuses the biological and the sociological; natural sexual difference with established gender conventions and the social roles associated with them. Feminist modernists challenged such a discourse, arguing that such gender conventions (which represented man in terms of mind, woman of body; man in terms of power and ambition, woman of purity, weakness, and nurturance) were in no way 'natural', but artificial and man-made constructions. The male modernists on the other hand, Smith-Rosenberg asserts, pursued strategies which affirmed this 'bourgeois social order':

> What is bourgeois becomes 'natural', all else 'unnatural'. Male modernists, by fusing gender and genitals, by insisting that to repudiate gender conventions was to war against nature, had . . . construct[ed] a classic bourgeois myth. They had clothed gender distinctions specific to late nineteenth-century industrial countries in the unchangeability of human biology.[64]

In *The Sun Also Rises*, the closure placed on discussion of gender convention by such means is removed, together with the bond that fuses Jake's gender to his genitals. To root 'gender distinction in genital difference' with the penis as 'prime *insignia* of maleness'[65] becomes difficult when the penis has been destroyed. For just as genital difference is compromised by Jake's war wound, so questions of gender distinction also blur in the text. Sandra M. Gilbert compares male experience in the First World War to Victorian female experience in terms of the emasculation, loss of autonomy, which mutually resulted: the 'Jake Barneses of the early twentieth century were locked up like Victorian girls in the trenches of No Man's Land'.[66] Despite the inaccuracy concerning Barnes' war experience and the hyperbolic quality of the metaphor, to compare Jake to a Victorian girl does bear further consideration. Sexually damaged as a result of the war, Wendy Martin suggests further that his stoic attitude, developed in the knowledge of his own vulnerability, is:

> in many respects a startling echo of the Victorian adage to 'suffer and be still' that was directed to women who felt help-less to meet the demands of their sacrificial role.

Martin also parallels that female hysteria associated with Victorian womanhood with the shell-shock marking 'the disequilibrium of the war-weary man of the lost generation', and of which Jake's insomnia is a sign. The one (hysteria) she sees as 'a response to excessive domestic *confinement*'; the other (shell-shock) to 'excessive *exposure*'. Both, though, have similar symptoms of which exhaustion, confusion and paralysis are examples. Jake's passivity and privacy (his retreat to his bed-room is similar to Nick's retreat to his tent in 'The Big Two Hearted River') are qualities which Martin associates with 'the housebound Victorian nurturer'.[67]

All these things point to a real fluidity concerning gender role in the novel. Georgette makes the first sexual advance on Jake, not vice versa. Brett visits his bedroom at half-past four in the morning, after he has retreated there alone with 'a rotten headache'. The count brings him a bunch of roses. Jake is the one who cries. Gender role and sexual identity are also questioned in the bullfighting metaphors that run through the novel, where Robert and Jake – despite the former's phallic potency – take the role of steers and, by analogy, Brett takes the role of bull, prime sexual force in the textual scheme of gender-relations. The sexual codes in *The Sun Also Rises* are wild. The polarizations which 'normally' constitute a firm structure of gender difference – what constitutes a male role/a female role – are subverted throughout the text. And this illustrates both a deep uncertainty about the conventions of a patriarchal culture, and Hemingway's refusal to reassert the patterns of 'male mastery'[68] in the manner of other male modernist writers after the war.[69]

Brett, as her association with cross-dressing suggests, challenges and disrupts the hierarchies of a traditional

patriarchal culture as well as those firm notions of female
identity which accompany the 'culturally taken-for-granted
dualities of male/female and masculine/feminine'. Annette
Kuhn points out the firm connection between mode of dress,
gender identity, and selfhood, and suggests that 'clothing as
performance threatens to undercut the ideological fixity of the
human subject'.[70] In her cross-dressing, Brett challenges traditional definitions of what a woman's role is, and thus of what
her identity – as socially given (what is 'womanly') – consists.
Susan Gubar speaks of the cross-dresser as a kind of 'heroine
of misrule' whose 'cross-dressing becomes a way of ad-dressing
and re-dressing the inequities of culturally-defined categories
of masculinity and femininity'.[71]

Brett must be seen as a modified version of such a
'heroine': she is inconsistent in the challenge she poses
to gender conventions. However, that she does re-dress the
boundaries of these roles is clear. She assumes equality in
the public sphere; does not, as Wendy Martin points out,
recognize areas previously defined as 'off-limits' (p. 68) to
women, the bars and the bullfight in particular. Her sexual
freedom and autonomy mark her resistance to patriarchal
control. And 'traditional theories of sexuality . . . based on
male sexual drive and female receptivity' (p. 70) are turned
upside down in her behaviour, her role as the novel's source
of sexual vitality and power. Her behaviour, despite her title,
is dramatically 'unladylike'. As 'performer' she steals attention
in all contexts. Her smoking, excessive drinking, her 'social
and sexual energy' (p. 70) and daring, knock topsy-turvy
traditional definitions of female roles.

At the same time however, and paradoxically, Brett confirms those roles. Like Jake, she is a self-divided figure. Jake's
donning of a traditional male role in his ('masterful') organization of the fishing trip and Pamplona expedition cuts against
his ('feminine') passivity in other areas. Brett's adoption of
elements of male dress and appearance certainly suggests the
loosening of 'the ideological fixity of the human subject' in
that the behaviour which goes with it breaks the boundaries
of the traditional feminine self. However, she too is defined by
her very incoherence as a subject. Brett's self-division appears
in the gap between man's felt hat and sleeveless black evening

dress. Her autonomy and independence are countered by her assumption of traditional female role of nurturer – 'she loves looking after people' (p. 203) – and of dependency – 'COULD YOU COME...AM RATHER IN TROUBLE' (p. 238). As Wendy Martin points out, 'she has not yet redefined the traditional relationships of sex and money', dependent as she is on men to pick up the bills that her pleasures produce. Martin calls Brett's role 'awkward and contradictory', caught as she is between playing at wife, mistress, and free woman.[72]

Alternatively, one might say that the contradictions of her role and character imply a rejection of the very notion of the coherent self. Examining the costume changes that occur in female modernist texts, Gilbert claims such imagery as 'radically revisionary' in its suggestion that 'no one, male or female, can or should be confined to a uni-form, a single form or self'.[73] Hemingway accepts the divisions of self that modern life produces, and expresses them in his novel. The stress his narrator undergoes in the face of such self-division is perhaps implicitly suggested when he takes temporary refuge in San Sebastian and notes that 'Everything was fresh and cool and damp in the early morning. Nurses in uniform and in peasant costume walked under the trees with children' (p. 237). Uniforms and costumes imply a blurring of individuality, but more importantly for Jake, they imply certainty and security. He knows how to interpret these costumes; as signs of a more traditional and stable social order where gender roles, social hierarchies, all exist in their 'proper' (i.e. traditional) place. As in all Hemingway novels, however, such certainties do not last.

V

Indicators of character: environment and reinforcement by analogy

I wish now to discuss the final area of indirect presentation of character as Rimmon-Kenan categorizes it, environment, and then look at her additional classification, reinforcement of character by analogy.

Environment

A character's physical surrounding (room, house, street, town) as well as his human environment (family, social class) are often used as a trait-connoting metonymies (p. 66).

The connecting links between character and environment can be most clearly seen in the nineteenth-century novel. Madame Merle in *The Portrait of a Lady* says, 'we're each of us made up of some cluster of appurtenances. What shall we call our "self"? Where does it begin? Where does it end?', and descriptions of physical environment, Osmond's villa, for example, are most obviously indicative of character.[74] In *The Sun Also Rises* the absence of thick description to which I have already referred in my discussion of 'utilization' is connected to the lack of historical referent concerning character. Jake's background and family history remain a textual lacuna, the emphasis not on the 'cluster of appurtenances' which 'express' him, but on the public space and rented rooms where he is located. James' emphasis on personal space on which the decorative signature of the owner has been applied is lacking here, and that lack provides evidence of a failure of the construction of identity on traditional lines (as part of a family, belonging to and sited in a particular personal space, with a particular conditioning background). Jake's Paris bedroom contains to our knowledge only a lamp, a bed and a big armoire with a mirror. The minimalism of such description denotes the lack of deep connections in the lives of those portrayed: they are, in Madame Merle's terms, human beings removed from their expressive shell.

Benjamin's discussion of the shock-effects of modern city life is again relevant here, though I would – as previously – foreground the shock of the war as analogous to, but much more extreme than, that of the city. For narrative time only starts in this text with the war: life previous to it is as if it had never been. Benjamin describes the gambler (a type of idler) as a mirror image of the worker, and associates each with that quality of futility, emptiness, incompletion and exact repetition, which marks modern urban life. He asserts that the participants of the realms both of gambling and work 'live their

lives as automatons . . . resemble Bergson's fictitious characters who have completely *liquidated their memories*' (my stress).
Their time is 'time in hell, the province of those who are not
allowed to complete anything they have started'. Only in the
realm of ritual does Benjamin see a step out of such a crisis
('breakdown').[75]

In the tradition and ceremonial of the Fiesta, Jake and
his crowd attempt temporary connection with the kind of
meaningful continuity which offers the fulfilment not available elsewhere. They are, however, not part of the Spanish
community, cannot share its rituals. Bill refers to the Fiesta as
'wonderful nightmare', not quite the 'repeated . . . nightmare'
of Jake's relationship with Brett in Paris, but an event nonetheless which provides no escape from the repetitions which
mark the lives of the characters generally. Their futilities
and incompletions are, rather, speeded up under the Fiesta
conditions. The liquidation of memory in this text, the loss
of meaningful personal history and expressive environmental
location which follows, result primarily from the shock of the
war. Its metaphorical consequence is time spent in hell. As
Hemingway wrote 'it . . . is such a hell of a sad story . . . and
the only instruction is how people go to hell'.[76]

Reinforcement by analogy

Rimmon-Kenan also categorizes the construction of characterization under the heading 'Reinforcement by Analogy'.
She distinguishes between character indicators as previously
discussed, and those analogies which, rather, reinforce characterization. The 'characterizing capacity' of analogy, she writes,
'depends on the prior establishment, by other means, of the
traits on which it is based'. As example, she offers a dreary
landscape which does not imply a character's pessimism, but
'may enhance a reader's perception of this trait once it has
been revealed' by other means (action, speech, etc.). Analogy
operates then where causal connections no longer strongly
operate.

Rimmon-Kenan admits some cross-over exists here with
her prior categorizations, but marks their differences in
terms of the diminishing links between cause and effect as
she proceeds through them. From action and speech which

'convey character-traits through a cause and effect relation', the areas of external appearance and environment are seen rather as being marked by 'a relation of spatial contiguity'. This contiguity, a relationship of contact or close proximity, can also, though, be causally linked. Thus, Brett's man's felt hat both connotes her unconventionality and also results from it. Contiguous relations are not so time-bound as those in the earlier categories. In analogy the relations of contiguity are much weaker: the cause and effect relationship absent or 'extremely weak'. Analogy 'may emphasize either the similarity or the contrast between the two elements compared, and it may be either explicitly stated in the text or implicitly left for the reader to discover'.[77] Rimmon-Kenan sub-divides 'Reinforcement by Analogy' into three sections:

(a) *Analogous names*

Names can parallel characters' traits though no causal relationship is usually apparent. Thus the semantic connection between Daisy in *The Great Gatsby* and the flower of that name is clear. In this text such analogies are not foregrounded, though Brett's name, which might easily be taken as masculine, does reinforce readings of her character which stress the slippage of gender role.[78]

(b) *Analogous landscape*

Unlike furnishings, houses, etc. (environment), landscape is independent of man thus causal relations (rooms decorated with lace denoting an artistic or 'feminine' sensibility) do not normally pertain. Analogies between landscape and character traits can operate on principles of similarity or contrast, thus in Rimmon-Kenan's example Catherine and Heathcliff in Emily Brontë's *Wuthering Heights* (1847) are 'similar to the wilderness in which they live' (p. 69). The relations between landscape and character in this novel can be divided into four elements – Paris, Pamplona, San Sebastian, the Spanish countryside. I tentatively depart from Rimmon-Kenan here in placing the towns in this category (which I would rename analogous places) rather than in that of environment (indication of character). I do this hesitantly, but my reasons are two-fold. First, I cannot see that Rimmon-Kenan's distinction between town and country – the one placed under 'environment', the other under 'analogous landscape' – is operable in terms of this text. And secondly, to distinguish between the reinforcement and establishment of characterization can be difficult, the gap between the two narrow. If anything, it seems to me that the Spanish countryside and its presentation here helps to establish Jake's character (and that of others); the other main locations to reinforce character. The blurring of boundary lines here suggests a certain overlap in Rimmon-Kenan's categories that may be unavoidable.

Jake lacks psychological or emotional stability. His subjection to, and relief from, stress is placed in analogous correspondence to the four main settings in which he is sited. The move from Paris to Pamplona to San Sebastian parallels the tension–explosion–recuperation patternings associated with Jake as he is subjected to emotional and mental pressure. His uncertainty and instability is presented in relation to the locations in which he is sited.

Thus, Paris is initially associated with Jake as locked into certain routines and transactions which gain their ease at the cost of a certain emotional indifference. Focus is directed to Paris as a space of public entertainment, where sensual satisfaction is gained through food, drink, observation and walking. Jake's deepening unease, though, is revealed by Brett's presence here. His private torment spills over into this public space as feelings of 'nightmare' occur in the crowded nightclub, Zelli's.

Pamplona is placed in analogous correspondence to Jake's loss of self-control, his explosion into violence, his drunkenness, his self-divisions, which climax at the same time as the Fiesta. Stress is placed on the constant noise in Pamplona at Fiesta time; the pounding drums, the 'close, crowded hum' (p. 161) of the café. The sense of dislocation, of the collapse of any notion of the stable self, is suggested by the comparisons with war: the rocket announcing the Fiesta produces a 'ball of smoke [that] hung in the sky like a shrapnel burst' (p. 153). A sense of alienation is strong –

'Where are the foreigners?' Robert Cohn asked.
'We're the foreigners,' Bill said (p. 154).

– and religious and community rituals are exclusive, rather than the opposite. A growing sense of unreality and of impending violence accompanies the bursting of the Fiesta into life: 'At noon of Sunday, the 6th of July, the Fiesta exploded' (p. 152). With this explosion, the tensions, emotional conflicts of the characters also come to a climax. The Fiesta's end ('the Fiesta was finished . . . The Fiesta was over') is paralleled by emotional exhaustion, depression, and sense of an ending, which hangs heavily over Jake: 'The three of us sat at the table, and it seemed as though about six people were missing' (p. 224).

Recuperation is paralleled by the San Sebastian setting. Spain is left behind and with it not only the turmoil of the Fiesta, but also the positive values offered by a contact with the land and its values: 'The car was powdered with dust . . . It seemed the last thing that connected me with Spain and the fiesta' (p. 232). Jake's emotional recovery is aided by immersion into a dull daily routine:

> After I was dressed and had paid for the bath-cabin, I walked back to the hotel. The bicycle-racers had left several copies of *L'Auto* around, and I gathered them up in the reading-room . . . and sat in an easy chair in the sun . . . (p. 238)

Repeated deep-diving, with the implications of cleansing and recovery, occurs as Jake steadies himself after his display of personal vulnerability in Spain. His routine is again interrupted by Brett.

These analogies and their tripartite division suggests the shifting nature of Jake's presentation. Any notion of a coherent and unified self is difficult to endorse where a loss of self-control, the fractured nature of a self torn by conflicting demands, lies at the text's centre; where the different settings parallel different facets of a character's composition, with little development necessarily suggested. For recuperation leads to renewed involvement with the source of emotional strain, rather than recovery.

The Spanish landscape is analogous with a type of serenity and deep security – an emotional and psychological unity – which Jake associates with, and to a small degree, recovers in that setting. 'The earth abideth forever': so runs the quotation from Ecclesiastes which prefaces Jake's story. And it is in the Spanish soil, and the rural community which has its firm base there, that the utopian – and regressive – element of Jake's personality finds expression. The stress on community is strong here, evidenced both in the bus-trip Jake takes, and in the community ritual of Girones' funeral. Such an emphasis on community and on religious belief is in favourable contrast to Jake's general lack of such connection. The Spanish landscape – 'a field of grain going right up to the walls and shifting in the wind' (p. 93) – suggests the continuity of natural process, and the involvement of a peasant community with those processes.

The whole notion of ritual, the Fiesta as originally a pagan celebration, endorses this sense of continuity and coherence. Jake's appreciation of that Spanish landscape which Cohn misses completely ('I turned around. Robert Cohn was asleep, but Bill . . . nodded his head', p. 93) and his appreciation of the community suggests his deep desire for – and temporary recapture of – that ease and stability which contrasts so strongly with the liquidation of his own past, his own lack of stable relationships, the loss of a sense of place, which are generally dominant. The fishing-trip provides an idyllic time-out within this landscape. It is an occasion when romance and religion (A. E. W. Mason and Roncevaux), both attractive under other circumstances, can be rejected ('It isn't the same as fishing', p. 128) in favour of a utopian retreat into all-male company in a natural setting. Perfect moments, though, never last. Cohn's telegram calls Jake back to Brett. Also in the fishing-trip there is an early hint of the fragility of Jake's codes. He fishes with worms and does not even feel the fish he catches take the bait. Bill's 'lazy bum!' (p. 121) is a signal to the reader that Jake is not quite as committed to the 'correct behaviour' associated with his sport as he might first seem to be.

(c) *Analogy between characters*

> When two characters are presented in similar circum-
> stances, the similarity or contrast between their behaviour
> emphasizes traits characteristic of both.[79]

As I argued in my section on actions, Jake's denigratory

attitude to Robert Cohn masks their strong similarity in terms of character traits. A fundamental equivalence marks their behaviour towards Brett. Cohn is textually revealed as Jake's alter ego despite Jake's insistence on their difference. This similarity is unwittingly confirmed by David Wyatt who speaks of Jake as follows:

> Jake's irony is to be granted the comparative immortality of a 'steer'. He drifts onward in a life promising no final climax. By insisting upon the analogy between the tragedies of the ring and the ironies of the café ('It's no life being a steer'), Hemingway again confounds anxieties over death and sex. *The Sun Also Rises* can be read as the story of an impotent animal submitted to repeated gorings.

Wyatt's application of a phrase which is directed at Cohn as a keystone of his analysis of Jake suggests the strong analogy between them. Romero, in contrast, can be read in terms of trait differences with Jake. His potency, bravery, skill and control in the ring (all of which add up, for Jake, to a version of heroic behaviour) is contrasted to the absence of these qualities in Jake in his arena, that of café life. Again, the breachings of the fixed lines between ring and café tends to make such initially simple contrasts more questionable as the text continues.[80]

VI

The instability of character

Rimmon-Kenan's scheme for approaching character is in general sound and useful, especially when taken in conjunction with the stress James Garvey lays on character development or change, and its relation to 'temporal orientation'.[81] Such an orientation which would mark when in a text character attributes change, and how suddenly or gradually such changes occur, could be usefully linked to my earlier examination of elementary textual sequences and the patterns of improvement or deterioration there realized.

Where I particularly wish to modify and extend her scheme, however, is in two related areas. Her stress on character as an independent unit of narrative grammar downplays, as I have suggested, the symbiotic relationship between the human subject and the social and historical context which contributes so vitally to its formation. As one way of re-establishing such a balance, I have introduced brief disquisitions to show how the conclusions drawn from a use of Rimmon-Kenan's model might be related to the larger systems of cultural meaning which locate the text and the characters in it. Another way of attaining a similar end, though, is to lay more stress on the *instability* of character than she does. She recognizes that the different types of traits suggested by character indicators may 'cause the reader to hesitate among various labels' (p. 70), and speaks of 'a unity in diversity' as the possible nature of the final construct. Her approach, though, stresses 'cohesion' (p. 40) and implies culmination with 'the more or less unified construct called character' (p. 39).

I wish to emphasize rather how her method, as applied to this text, reveals that character is not a unity, is rather divided, disjointed, 'slippery', difficult to pin down firmly and finally. This is not to invalidate the previous stages of my argument. Jake, Brett, etc., can be defined according to their various character traits. It is, however, to recognize that attempts to establish separate 'identities' must take on board the fragility of this term. Such fragility does not operate only in terms of the division within characters but also in terms of the connections between them. If a subject is marked out by the way she or he differs from another, her or his position in a social framework always means that other markers will be working to obliterate this difference. If our use of the term 'identity' suggests something discrete, clear cut, and stable, then the lack of confidence both in the internal coherence of the subject and in the distinction between subjects evident in Hemingway's text (and in much modern writing) causes us to question our use of this term.

Rimmon-Kenan's discussion of similarity and difference, briefly raised in her section 'analogy between characters', can, first, be revealingly extended. Chatman says that 'the "meaning" of a character I take to be the set of personal traits that delineate him, set him apart from the others, make him memorable to us'.[82] Joel Weinsheimer in his anti-mimetic approach to Jane Austen's *Emma* (1816) sees a 'tendency towards *undifferentiation*' (my stress) occurring when close attention is paid to these 'marks in a book' which constitute character. I do not wish to follow his theoretical model; its implication extends, however, beyond the limits he sets himself.

For Weinsheimer suggests that if we examine a text as a completely closed system, we will discover that 'the hard clear lines which . . . differentiate one character from another tend to dissolve'. I would suggest that in *The Sun Also Rises* if we examine character on the basis of speech, traits and role, even if we do not follow his strict semiotic approach, similar overlappings occur; 'that the boundaries separating one character from another will be inexact and fuzzy'.[83] My suggestion is that Rimmon-Kenan's category of 'analogy between characters' fails to take full account of the way that similarity can lead to slippage – a loss of an unbreachable notion of discrete individual identity.

In terms of speech patternings, for example, it becomes difficult to tell certain characters apart: their idiolects merge. As a social group, Jake and his crowd communicate via a type of language which – in its use of shared conventions, coded terminology ('one of us'), catch phrases, and stylistic nuance – asserts their membership of a particular closed community. When Bill and Jake speak, the individuality of their voices tend to blur – 'Utilize a little, brother . . . ', 'Here . . . utilize a little of this' (p. 122) – just as Brett, Jake and Mike's voices tend to overlap in the following:

'It made me damned well sick . . . '
'Damned noble of you . . . '
'Come on . . . Do buck up. You've got to go through with this thing now' (p. 143).

A kind of echolalia comes to inhabit the text as one character repeats the other, as their voices merge; become indistinguishable. Even Montoya is pulled into such routines:

'Well, how did you like the bulls?' he asked.
'Good. They were nice bulls.'
'They're all right' – Montoya shook his head – 'but they're not too good.'

'What didn't you like about them?'
'I don't know. They just didn't give me the feeling that they were so good.'
'I know what you mean.'
'They're all right.'
'Yes. They're all right.'
'How did your friends like them?'
'Fine.'
'Good,' Montoya said. (pp. 144–5)[84]

Such lack of differentiation between characters becomes pronounced when we look more closely at those traits or characteristics which are named in, or can be inferred from, the text. 'A single complex of characteristics', Weinsheimer says, 'applies to an indefinite number of characters'.[85] If Brett's definition of Mike with which I started this chapter is almost inseparable in both form and content from Bill's description of Cohn, then Bill's characterization of Jake raises similar problems. 'You're an expatriate', Bill says:

'You've lost touch with the soil. You get precious. Fake European standards have ruined you. You drink yourself to death. You become obsessed by sex. You spend all your time talking, not working. You are an expatriate, see? You hang round cafés' (p. 115).

This is the most extended description of Jake in the text, and even despite its note of flippant reductionism, it is worth noting that it fails to distinguish him in any way from his 'crowd'. The very use of that term, in fact, is a denial of the notion of difference. Jake is 'blind, unforgivingly jealous' (p. 99) of Cohn, presumably the exact emotion which leads Mike to bait Cohn, Cohn to pummel Romero. Brett's a 'goner' (p. 183) about the Romero boy; Jake, Mike, Cohn, Romero, are 'goners' about Brett. Jake and his crowd are characterized on the one hand as hard-boiled stoics, ironic, living by a certain code of values. On the other, they are seen as sentimental ('I . . . turn all to jelly when you touch me', p. 26, 'I'm fonder of you than anybody on earth', p. 116), unable to stick to the required code (Mike not being able to pay for the drinks; Brett going off without explanation or farewell

– 'Bad thing to do ... She shouldn't have done it', p. 223),
and emotionally weak – Jake, Cohn, Brett, all at one point or
another give way to tears. Traits are duplicated to the extent
that characterization can be applied fairly indiscriminately
to Jake's crowd and, modifying Weinsheimer, 'shifts among
them with as much ease as the pronoun him/her'. Romero
can be seen in terms of 'the positive photographic image' of
Jake's negative. As Weinsheimer says 'once [a] characteristic
is perceived as wandering among a number of characters, it
becomes detachable from any'. In terms of role (or action) I
have earlier suggested how, in opposite ways, both Romero
and Cohn stand in as 'vicarious other' for Jake, as 'surrogate
selves'.[86]

The thrust of Rimmon-Kenan's argument, as most studies
of characterization, focuses on character as difference. What
I would suggest Weinsheimer opens up is the critically
destabilizing notion of character as similarity, a powerful
textual thrust which radically undercuts and questions the
notion of the sovereign self. Such an undercutting is, of
course, thoroughly appropriate to Hemingway's text, where
all characters can be read as variation on a type ('You are
all a lost generation'). But it also connects up with Catherine
Belsey's argument that 'at times of crisis in the social
formation ... confidence in the ideology of subjectivity is
eroded'.[87]

For if the characters in the novel tend, when taken
together, to blur into one another, when taken separately they
tend to show signs of deep self-division. Notions of character
as unified construct tend to explode in one's face in this text
as I have tried to show in the course of my argument thus far.
Such an explosion evidences deep uncertainty concerning the
very coherence of the subject. Barthes describes our attempt
to discover character traits in terms of a metonymic skid:

> to read is to struggle to name, to subject the sentences of
> the text to a semantic transformation. This transformation
> is erratic; it consists in hesitating among several names: if
> we are told that Sarrasine had *'one of those strong wills that
> know no obstacle'*, what are we to read? *will, energy, obstinacy
> stubbornness*, etc.? The connotator refers not so much to a
> name as to a synonymic complex whose common nucleus

we sense even while the discourse is leading us toward
other possibilities, toward other related signifieds: thus,
reading is absorbed in a kind of metonymic skid, each
synonym adding to its neighbor some new trait, some new
departure: The old man who was first connoted as *fragile*
is soon said to be '*of glass*': an image containing signifieds
of rigidity, immobility, and dry, cutting frangibility. This
expansion is the very movement of meaning: the meaning
skids, recovers itself, and advances simultaneously.[88]

Such skidding meaning suggests the difficulty of fixing a
centre; defining a character as a unity. As I have examined
some of the indicators of character in *The Sun Also Rises*, this is
exactly what has happened. Even the metonymic skid breaks
down, as neighbouring traits are on occasion separated by
vast abysses: Jake's weak-willed romanticism polarized with
his hard-boiled qualities; Brett's brash daring at odds with
her tendency to rely on patriarchal figures. Such divisions
within the subject relate here to the impact of change,
modernization, war. In Brett, 'the Victorian faith in sexual
polarity'[89] does battle with the ideology of autonomy and
liberation associated with the New Woman of the 1920s.
Jake is likewise decentred as a result of the tensions between
romantic and religious conceptualizations inherited from a
nineteenth-century world, and that secular irony produced by
the sudden collapse and discrediting of such norms. The vital
thing to note here is that character is composed of a number
of subject positions – in Catherine Belsey's terms:

> The individual consciousness . . . can no longer be seen as
> the origin of meaning, knowledge and action . . . 'Identity',
> subjectivity, is . . . a matrix of subject–positions, which may
> be inconsistent or even in contradiction with one another.[90]

The notion of autonomous individuality is a myth. We are
constructed as subjects by the ideological formations in which
we are located, whose languages we learn. Jake takes up a
series of recognized subject positions in this text (as 'man',
'invalid', 'aficionado', 'romantic', 'ironist', 'expatriate', 'newspaperman', 'catholic', etc.), a series of 'languages' which position him. The lack of coherence that results is paradigmatic

of deep rifts and tensions apparent in any subject. When Jake hears Bill singing 'Give them Irony and Give them Pity. Oh, give them Irony. When they're feeling [shitty]. Just a little irony. Just a little pity' (p. 114), neither man recognizes the incompatibility of the two poles. The modes of irony and romance are equally incompatible as David Wyatt points out in his comments on *A Farewell to Arms* (1929).[91] It is just such incompatibilities within Jake and Brett's 'selves' that Hemingway's novel reveals.

4
The Dynamics of Reading:
A Lost Lady

' . . . the reader plays the part of a prince to the
sleeping beauty'[1]

Literary texts are not self-sufficient objects: they 'do not
exist on bookshelves . . . For literature to happen, the reader
is quite as vital as the author'.[2] From the moment a text
opens the reader is engaged – as Wolfgang Iser, one of the
foremost of 'reader-response' critics, puts it – in a 'process of
building and cancelling expectations'.[3] Terry Eagleton wittily
exemplifies something of this process by referring to the first
two sentences of John Updike's novel, *Couples* (1968): ' "What
did you make of the new couple?" The Hanemas, Piet and
Angela, were undressing'. He illustrates the kind of inferences
we make when we read:

> We may infer, for example, that the 'couple' referred to
> is a man and woman, though there is nothing so far to tell
> us that they are not two women or two tiger cubs . . . The
> phrase 'The Hanemas', we imagine, is probably in grammati-
> cal apposition to the phrase 'Piet and Angela', to indicate
> that this is their surname, which provides a significant
> piece of information for their being married. But we cannot
> rule out the possibility that there is some group of people
> called the Hanemas in addition to Piet and Angela, perhaps
> a whole tribe of them, and that they are all undressing
> together in some immense hall. The fact that Piet and
> Angela may share the same surname does not confirm that

they are husband and wife: they may be a particularly liberated or incestuous brother and sister, father and daughter
or mother and son . . . Most readers will by now probably
have assumed that Piet and Angela Hanema are a married
couple undressing together in their bedroom after some
event, perhaps a party, at which a new married couple was
present, but none of this is actually said.[4]

Such readers – basing their assumptions both on the conventions for reading a specific literary mode (realism) and on the
characteristic plot situations to be found in Updike novels –
would, of course, be correct. None of it, to repeat, is said.

There are many distinct types of current reader-response
theory. Despite differences in approach, though, what they
have in common is a breaking down of a traditional critical
hierarchy in which the 'prime mover of all meanings and
emotions' is the text itself, a text then explicated by the
'disinterested critic' for that 'lowly reader' who is the passive
recipient of such mediations. A 'swerve to the reader'[5] has
taken place in this type of theory, producing critical statements of the following type:

'It is in the reader that the text comes to life'

(Wolfgang Iser, p. 19)

'Texts are lazy machineries that ask someone [the reader]
to do part of their job'

(Umberto Eco)[6]

Stanley Fish stresses 'the *activity* of reading', the italicized
word pointing to 'where the action is – the active and
activating consciousness of the reader'.[7]

This focus on the importance of the reader's role will be my
jumping off point for an examination of Willa Cather's novel,
A Lost Lady (1923). I want initially to follow the model proposed
in Wolfgang Iser's works (most especially *The Act of Reading*,
1976) to show the kind of work the reader does, the dynamic
relationship between her or him and the text. Iser's laying out
of a method for treating the text from a readerly position is
one which I find very useful. My unease with such a model
is prompted mainly by Iser's stress on textual stability, the

way the signals structured within the text lead us as readers towards some type of final synthesis or 'gestalt'. This failed to explain my own *change* of 'gestalt': the fact that when I first taught *A Lost Lady* some fifteen years ago, I interpreted it in a completely different way than I do now. Then I taught it as a novel 'about' the American frontier; now I read the novel in terms of its concern with the female 'subject'.

As I proceed, therefore, I will highlight both the usefulness and shortcomings of Iser's approach. His stress on the extent to which the literary text structures the reading process will be countered at a later stage of my chapter. Using Steven Mailloux's *Interpretive Conventions* (1982) as my model, I will there argue that texts are also actively 'written' by readers according to the type of reading conventions that apply in their particular historical community. Iser's assumption of textual stability is thrown in doubt by such a stance. Such an assumption will, in the following chapter on Barthes' *S/Z*, be again subjected to question, but from a very different angle. In that chapter too, though, I wish to hold on to Mailloux's argument that to accept a text's indeterminacies is not to close off interpretive activity and to use it – as I do in the present chapter – as the basis for some critical mapmaking of my own.

This however is to run considerably ahead of myself. My reconstruction of the reader's role with regard to Cather's text is fraught with difficulties. I am not after all the lowly reader referred to above, but a male academic mediating all I can! As a starting point for my analysis, then, I must acknowledge my particular reading position; one who is a male reader and teacher, who constructs his own conception of the meaning of the text in responding as an individual to its potential. The 'gestalt' (a key term for Iser, taken from psychological discourse) or 'configurative meaning' of the text must, in Iser's terms:

> inevitably be coloured by our own characteristic selection process. For it is not given by the text itself; it arises from the meeting between the written text and the individual mind of the reader with its own particular history of experience, its own consciousness, its own outlook.[8]

As I respond, as Iser would put it, to the text's 'potential meaning',[9] it is my outlook, my history of experience, which colours my reading. I construct my reading on such a basis; and will return later to the problems which such a tactic raises.[10]

Another difficulty, however, in terms of my reconstruction of the reader's role, is suggested by the use of that word 'reconstruct'. As Stanley Fish points out, a commentary on the process of reading can never coincide with the initial experience of that reading.[11] Iser speaks of the way in which we gather meaning in a 'snowballing process' (p. 67) as we read. I have, in fact, already made my snowball, constructed my version of the text. In now trying to show how this occurred, I am constructing retrospectively a model of the way the reader works, with all the kinds of synthesizing and editing which comes with such a backward glance (in this perhaps I mirror the narrator of *A Lost Lady*, also 'reading' Marian Forrester retrospectively). If such a reconstruction cannot re-create the initial reading experience, it can suggest the kind of operations and processes occurring as we read: their usefulness in showing how a text can be approached as a 'potential effect that is realized in the reading process' (Iser, p. ix).

'The written utterance', Iser writes, 'continually transcends the margins of the printed page' (p. 55). When readers interact with any text 'a dynamic process of self-correction' (p. 67) occurs, as they make conjectures, formulate hypotheses, which must then be constantly modified as they continue to read. Such an approach stresses 'the nature of reading as a *temporal process*' (my stress).[12] It constitutes a move away from a more traditional type of criticism which tends to concentrate only on a final reading of the literary text and focuses on 'the aesthetic experience of the artistic whole'. Instead, it foregrounds what Steven Mailloux calls 'the author's rhetoric of entanglement, a rhetoric resulting in sequential responses from the reader' (p. 90). Mailloux lists the reading responses to which such a 'temporal model of reading' calls attention:

> making and revising judgements, solving mysteries and puzzles, experiencing attitudes, taking on and rejecting perspectives, discovering sequential structures of similarity and contrast, formulating questions and answers, making and correcting mistakes (pp. 70–1).

Such a type of reading does not reject final holistic interpretations, but rather first gives close attention to 'the series of interpretations and effects leading up to that final synthesis' (p. 71).

One way of constructing such a model of reading is to detail the use of primary effects and recency effects in a text. For we can see here the process by which the text *unfolds*: the way our reading activity works. The information we are presented with first in any narrative (primary effect) tends to influence us strongly: 'information and attitudes presented at an early stage of the text tend to encourage [us] to interpret everything in their light'.[13] Our first view of Marian Forrester in *A Lost Lady* sets up a strong impression of domestic harmony and perfection. She is described as follows, standing in the doorway of 'the Forrester place':

> She was always there, just outside the front door, to welcome their visitors . . . If she happened to be in the kitchen, helping her Bohemiann cccook, she came out in her apron, waving a buttery iron spoon, or shook cherry-stained fingers at the new arrival. She never stopped to pin up a lock; she was attractive in dishabille, and she knew it . . . In [Cyrus Dalzell's] eyes, and in the eyes of the admiring middle-aged men who visited there, whatever Mrs Forrester chose to do was 'lady-like' because she did it. They could not imagine her in any dress or situation in which she would not be charming.[14]

Primary effects produced in this passage include the equation between Mrs Forrester's actions and the 'lady-like', and her definition in terms of her marital role as Mrs Forrester. This dependent status is reinforced by the fact that this description follows an earlier paragraph which begins significantly, 'To approach Captain Forrester's property . . .'. Also of note here are her measuring of her own attractiveness in terms of her effect on male eyes, and – perhaps overwhelmingly – the domestic nature of her appearance sited in relation to the front door with kitchen and cherry jam/cherry pie in background evidence.

But a primary effect is often modified, as we are led to alter our initial interpretation of a textual segment by information later presented. This is the recency effect, which 'encourages the reader to assimilate all previous information

to the item presented last'.[15] [In William Goldman's *Magic*
(1976), our initial reading of the dialogue between the narrator who commences the novel (Fats) and the magician Corky
Withers is transformed when we realize later in the novel that
Fats is, in fact, a ventriloquist's dummy, owned and operated
by Corky!]. The recency effects in *A Lost Lady* do not operate
to disorientating effect. The first impression of Mrs Forrester
has, however, to be modified as her over-indulgence in alcohol,
her relationship with Ellinger, and Niel's judgement of her as
a 'common woman' (p. 173), are made textually evident. Our
reaction to such recency effects are not, though, simple. For
the primary effect – together with the related effect of nostalgia
and loss produced by a retrospective and involved narrator
– lingers throughout the text, whatever new information is
presented.

This omniscient narrator is a somewhat mysterious figure
in the novel. It is not Niel who is, as Ellen Moers suggests,
the 'remembering narrator'[16] of *A Lost Lady*. We do not know
who, nor of what sex, is s/he who presents Mrs Forrester to
us here. Our lack of readerly knowledge about the narrator
constitutes an information gap in the text. Such a recognition
can be seen in terms of Iser's view of the text as a response-
inviting structure: what Fish calls its 'kinetic'[17] nature. For
the sequential mode of reading which a focus on a narrative's
primary and recency effects provides (the relationship of part
to part in a literary work as well as part to whole) is one which
indeed draws attention to the way in which we, as readers, are
constantly negotiating, filling in, or failing to fill in, textual
gaps of this and more obvious kinds as we proceed through
it. Rimmon-Kenan explains:

> How to make a bagel? First you take a hole . . . And how
> to make a narrative text? In exactly the same way. Holes or
> gaps are so central in narrative fiction because the materials
> the text provides for the reconstruction of a world (or a story)
> are insufficient for saturation. No matter how detailed the
> presentation is, further questions can always be asked; gaps
> always remain open (p. 127).

Through our filling in of the 'inevitable omissions' in any
narrative text that story 'will gain its dynamism'.[18] Henry

James' story *In the Cage* (1898) provides a perfect paradigm of such a process. The young lady telegraphist, whose perspective is dominant, tries to 'read' the relationship between Lady Bradeen and Captain Everard. Her source material is composed of the telegrams they send, telegrams of the following type:

> Everard, Hôtel Brighton, Paris. Only understand and believe. 22nd to 26th, and certainly 8th and 9th. Perhaps others. Come. Mary.

Telegrams are, of course, the most condensed forms of communication. What is more, the young lady never receives the answers to these messages; they are sent to another office. She has to try and construct meaning by reading metaphorically between the lines; filling in the gaps between the words, filling in also the missing answers between telegrams. She also tries to construct the meaning of Bradeen and Everard's relationship from her position 'in framed and wired confinement',[19] caged off from their lives by the wires of the post office in which she works. Again she fills in massive gaps on the basis of what little she sees of their lives, and it is not surprising that her reading is both partial and largely inaccurate. As readers we are put in the same position as the young lady, seeing Everard and Bradeen through her eyes, trying to fill in with her a text which is full of holes.

To a lesser extent, this is what we do whenever we read; try and fill in, make sense of, textual gaps, some of which deny our attempts to do so. A simple example of the kind of gaps found in *A Lost Lady* which can be filled is in Chapter Five. During a sleigh-ride, Ellinger and Marian make explicit the nature of their relationship:

> 'You won't let me write you love letters. You say it's risky . . . '
> 'Be careful, Frank. My rings! You hurt me!'
> 'Then why didn't you take them off? You used to' (p. 61).

The tone of Marian's voice changes ('he knew the change'). She tells Frank to stop, and he sees a thicket with a dry watercourse behind leading into the bluffs: ' "Sit still," he said, "while I take out the horses" ' (p. 62). What occurs at this point is a textual gap, suspended 'connectability'.[20] The abrupt juxtaposition – in terms both of chronology and sentence content – between the conclusion of the above textual segment and the beginning of the next, 'When the blue shadows of approaching dusk . . . ', calls for readerly activity. Such activity is minimal here; we re-connect the two segments with ease. First, there is a common framework[21] to both sections, both in terms of location and evidence of physical intimacy between Frank and Marian. The taking off of rings on one side of the gap, Marian's 'clinging' to Ellinger, 'a faint, soft smile on her lips' (pp. 62–3), on the other, allows us to fill the empty textual space with both ease and certainty. Secondly, the above details are well-worn ones in what Umberto Eco calls our 'encyclopedia of narrativity' (what we expect when we read a narrative: our own reference to and knowledge of other texts), clear markers to the fulfilment of illicit sexual passion. Such 'already recorded narrative situations (intertextual frames)'[22] tell us exactly what is omitted here.

What Iser calls the *determinate meaning* (p. 196) is then explicit. It is, however, noteworthy that a direct presentation of sex remains almost entirely absent from the text. This central absence might be explained by the fact that too explicit a depiction of Marian's sexuality would affect the primary effect of delightful domesticity too radically, or would tilt the fragile balance between sexual self-expression (nature) and fidelity to the institution of marriage (culture) too far in the former direction. The unease of the latter balance has been suggested by the incompatibility of the nature–culture poles in the metaphor describing Marian in the first chapter as 'scudding . . . like a hare . . . and stubbornly clinging to the crimson parasol . . . ' (p. 7). Were Cather's reader to be shown Marian's sexual activities in fuller detail, would the reaction be similar to Niel's, who the first time he actually sees direct sexuality expressed – Ivy Peters putting 'both hands around [Marian] . . . meeting over her breast' – judges Marian a 'common woman' (p. 173) and departs never to see her again? Cather's retaining of readerly sympathy for her central protagonist may be at stake here. This seems unlikely: readerly susceptibilities are not normally that delicate. Cather is more probably following the literary conventions of romantic fiction, avoiding an explicit presentation of adultery by using what Ellen Moers refers to as the 'tricks of the cautious novelist's trade'.[23] In using Adolph Blum, however, as sympathetic focalizer, Cather certainly counters any sense of strong moral condemnation on the readerly part.

Another type of textual gap, and one which produces much greater readerly activity, is suggested by Niel's reactions when he sees, as described above, Marian and Ivy Peters together. Niel's sexual interest in Mrs Forrester is never mentioned in the text, yet it is central to it. This is one of the major textual absences. How do we become aware of this interest when it is never made explicit? First, I would suggest – again in line with a temporal model of reading – that we discover 'sequential structures of similarity and contrast' as we move from one textual segment to the next. Wolfgang Iser uses the term 'reciprocal spotlighting' (p. 114) to explain how the reader's 'wandering viewpoint' leads to the accumulation of 'views and combinations' as the text passes in front of him or her as an 'ever-expanding network of connections' (p. 116). One reading moment illuminates other such moments as connections are established in the reader's mind. When Mrs Forrester – in the sleigh with Ellinger – takes off her rings, she releases her sexual vitality with that symbolic gesture. She escapes her confined and defined role as ornamental addition to the Captain's 'unornamented phrases' (p. 50).

Meaning begins to gather meaning in the kind of snow-balling process Iser describes, as we feed this incident back into (spotlight reciprocally) the textual repertoire already processed. Mrs Forrester has previously taken off 'her glittering rings' to tend the injured twelve year old Niel, who lies on her 'white bed' watching Marian's 'white throat rising and falling so quickly . . . inside the lace ruffle of her dress'. When we read of this incident early on in the text, the images that we, as readers, build in our minds are, I would suggest, images of comfort, security, innocent protectiveness: 'Oh, how sweet, how sweet she smelled!' (pp. 23–4). We build up such images in textual sequence, but when we try and develop them as we read on, certain 'contradictions and contrasts' (Iser, p. 148) will become apparent. So, as we glance backwards on our prior readerly constructions, the signifying gesture of taking off the rings – clearly associated with sexuality and escape from marital bonds in the Ellinger scene – radically affects our first reading of the earlier incident; this we reconstruct in terms of stirrings of sexuality in the pre-adolescent Niel.

Niel's sexual interest in Marian is never made explicit. But it is suggested not only in the manner above described but also in relation to our previously noted encyclopedia of narrativity, our intertextual frames. The way Niel chooses to describe Mrs Forrester fits clearly into codes of sexual desire long established in what Roland Barthes would call the book of romantic fiction: 'Her mouth which could say so much without words', 'those beautiful eyes'. Such descriptions are matched by Niel's words elsewhere. He shows no recognition, though, of the sexual freight they carry: 'You seem always the same to me . . . Lovely. Just lovely'. The clothes, too, that Niel recalls her wearing – the 'swirl of foamy white petticoats', the 'Japanese dressing-gown' – also are coded in terms of exotic sexuality.

The impact such impressions have made on Niel become apparent to the reader when Forrester leaves his wife on business. Niel wakes before dawn the following day to the sound of a local steam-engine: 'the sound of escaping steam' awoke him, the feeling that 'dawn would soon be flaming gloriously . . . ' intense in him. He immediately goes over to the Forresters' land in a scene suffused with lubricity, 'heavy, bowed grasses' splashing him, the marsh flowers 'globed with dew'. The wild rose petals are in this description – focalized through Niel – stained with a 'burning rose-colour . . . so intense that it cannot possibly last . . . must fade, like ecstasy'. He picks these roses to make 'a bouquet for a lovely lady; a bouquet gathered off the cheeks of morning' (pp. 81–2). All these details, in terms of the intertextual frames to which we relate them, speak of but one thing: sexual passion. When Niel then hears Ellinger's laugh behind Mrs Forrester's window (his role as 'eaves dropper' is a repeated one in the narrative), his let-down is all the more intense. He throws the wild roses into a 'mudhole' trampled by cattle. Niel's motivation is presented as entirely innocent. The reader, however, takes into account both the language used and the narrative line – young man rises at dawn to place a bunch of wild roses outside the bedroom window of an attractive wife of a much older man absent on a business trip. In terms of our repertoire of intertextual knowledge, this scenario – 'young bachelor courts attractive young wife' – is what Eco would call an 'overcoded'[24] narrative situation.

As readers, we use the technique of reciprocal spot-lighting and our knowledge of intertextual frames to note the inconsistencies between Niel's own self-presentation as distanced moral judge and commentator, and a sub-text which suggests his sexual passion. This latter part of Niel's make-up we construct *out of the text's silences*. And such a construction leads us on to one of the central elements of Wolfgang Iser's theory: the way in which each reader produces a *'gestalt'* (a 'consistent interpretation', p. 119) not directly offered by or in the text. The reader is given a number of perspectives in the novel, 'different layers of consciousness' which switch about as s/he reads. Again, the notion of the gap becomes impor-tant: it emerges in what these various represented positions exclude. Only the reader can fill in the absences Iser points to when he describes how 'contrasts and discrepancies within the perspective of the characters give rise to the missing links' (p. 199) in the text. The reader 'sets the work in motion, and so sets [her or his individual] self in motion, too' (p. 21) by taking on board the various perspectives offered within the text. S/he assesses the various value systems represented by such perspectives, works out their separate strengths and weaknesses, gradually refining and broadening her or his attitudes, until finally ending up at 'a transcendental vantage point from which [s/he] can see through all the positions that have been formulated' (p. 99).

The reader transforms the positions textually represented into a 'determinate meaning' and produces a final synthesis, 'a definitive frame of reference by which to judge the events of the narrative' (p. 205). This comes out of an awareness not just of the various strengths and weaknesses of the positions revealed in the text, but also of what these various positions exclude. The final synthesis, or 'gestalt', is central for Iser to the reader's role and constitutes the very core of her or his activity. Such determinate meaning is nowhere given in the text.

Iser's stress on our individual readerly syntheses and his use of the word 'transcendental' here, sits rather uneasily with the earlier focus on reading as a dynamic process. It is not, however, inconsistent. There is an end to the reader's textual journey. The text still escapes the margins of the printed page for Iser, in so far as each readerly construction of meaning depends on which particular elements are grouped together in works overloaded with possibilities; in so far as each production of meaning resulting from the examination of such groupings will be a departure from what is actually written in the text. Undoubtedly, however, this stress on final realization cuts somewhat against the apparently flexible nature of a mode of criticism which places so much attention on our transaction with the text in its sequential immediacy. As Eagleton says:

> The doctrine of the . . . closed text surreptitiously under-lie[s] the apparent open-endedness of much reception theory . . . the 'openness' of the work is something which is to be gradually eliminated, as the reader comes to construct a working hypothesis which can account for and render mutually coherent the greatest number of the work's elements (pp. 80–1).

Our working hypothesis in *A Lost Lady* is constructed on the basis of an examination of the various perspectives represented in the novel. Of these, Niel's is of utmost significance. For the illustrated gap between what Niel says and what his words and actions reveal points to certain problems concerning his perspective, his value system. It is Niel through whom we predominantly see the lives of the Forresters; indeed, the final sections of the text are focalized entirely through him. His values though are suspect, thus the validity of his judgements questionable.

The reader constructs 'the meaning of the text on a question-and-answer basis' (p. 228), and one central question here is 'what is deformed about Niel's world view?' Iser suggests a crumbling set of norms (framework for social action) is indicated by surface signs of 'failure and deformation' (p. 227). These signs are readily apparent in Niel's case. His value system is that of a nineteenth-century genteel traditionalist. Undemocratic in his values, references to 'commonplace people' with their 'ruffianly manners' (p. 67)

contrast with his celebration of the 'elegant . . . fashion-
able . . . distinguished' (p. 37). His conscious admiration for
Mrs Forrester (unconsciously, it is erotically charged) is mainly
based on her role in the Victorian patriarchal family. Captain
Forrester is a 'massive man' textually associated with granite,
mountains, stone: 'it was as [his] wife that she most interested
Niel . . . in her relation to her husband that he most admired
her' (p. 74). Niel believes in good taste and aesthetic ideals.[25]
His mind is both backward-looking and idealistic, preferring
the 'dreamers' of 'The Old West . . . great-hearted adventur-
ers who were unpractical to the point of magnificence' (p. 104)
to a present generation of greedy and corrupt materialists.
Though he is to become a city-dweller and an architect,
he is not a modern man. His thoroughgoing nostalgia and
traditionalism is nowhere better illustrated than in his 'final
break' with Marian Forrester, who – after her husband's death
– is now involved with Ivy Peters. His judgement is revealing,
especially in terms of the implicit view of gender relationships
it suggests:

> It was what he most held against Mrs Forrester; that
> she was not willing to immolate herself, like the widow
> of all these great men, and die with the pioneer period
> to which she belonged; that she preferred life on any
> terms . . . Niel . . . went away with weary contempt for her
> in his heart (p. 172).

Niel suggests here that, on the Captain's death, he would
have liked to make a funeral pyre of Forrester's heavy walnut
furniture, and encourage Marian to jump on top of the blazing
pile! Her staying on as widow in 'his' (the Captain's) house
would, however, have been 'immolation' enough to satisfy him.

Niel's 'deformation' is suggested by his unadmitted sexual
attraction for Marian Forrester. He can only deal with Marian
as the Captain's wife and cannot, even after the latter's death,
step outside a rigidly nostalgic and patriarchal value system
which stultifies. The strongest picture I have of Niel is when
he cuts the telephone wire with a pair of 'big shears' when Mrs
Forrester speaks with passionate anger to Ellinger on hearing
of his marriage. 'For once he had been quick enough; he had
saved her' (p. 134). He adopts the role of Victorian patriarch

here, denying her the choice of speaking her deepest feelings. His motives are good – to save Marian and her husband from public gossip – but whether he has the right to deny her expression in this way is another matter. His protective stance is an example of the way Mrs Forrester is infantilized in the novel: her husband's way of addressing her as 'Maidy' is another. In this case, her full expression of a 'quivering passion' causes Niel literally *to cut off her voice*. His action, unusual for one whose passivity is a dominant characteristic, is significantly associated with an attempt to retain the status quo, to deny that which is disruptive.

Niel's world view is under great strain from within. His genteel separation of admiration from sexuality; his understanding of the male role as patriarchal protector; the gap between consciousness and action revealed in him; his ideological commitment to the old order; all limit his position as reliable focalizer here. He denies his own sexual identity; his erotic feelings for Marian can never surface. Even though when he penultimately glimpses Marian – a 'ship without ballast' (p. 154) since the Captain's death – he still feels 'the right man could save her' (p. 169), he will not propose himself for this role. And this, despite her promptings. He is described variously as 'a little cold' with a 'critical habit of mind', 'a trifle stiff', 'stiff – so . . . superior . . . a snob', and this suggests his failure (rather like Miles Coverdale in Hawthorne's *The Blithedale Romance*, 1852) to fully involve himself in the dramas around him. This is his deformation – never, to paraphrase James' description of Lambert Strether, to have lived all he could. A note of loss and regret permeates Niel's focalization. A proleptic intrusion in Chapter Six reads significantly, 'when he was dull, *dull and tired of everything*, he used to think that if he could hear that long-lost lady laugh again, he could be gay' (p. 67). He remembers her eyes 'in her best days' as promising 'a wild delight that *he had not found in life* (my emphasis, p. 174). Such markers alert the reader to the deficiencies of Niel's value system.

What alternative value systems are we offered in the text if Niel's (whose norms dominate, orient the reader in the text) are accepted as in some measure deformed? Because Niel's focalization is textually dominant, squeezes out that of the narrator, the reader finds her or his 'mirror image'[26] in him. The signals noted above suggest, however, that we should be rather careful about sharing Niel's reading of this 'lost lady'. His centrality to the text, though, makes a step back from his values – and perhaps also from our 'own governing norms of orientation' (Iser, p. 187)[27] – a difficult one. However, there are other perspectives offered by the text. The collision of Niel's value system with Ivy Peters', and what we can construct of Marian's own, provides us with a position from which 'determinate meaning' can emerge.[28]

Ivy Peters is soon dealt with. He is presented, both by the narrator and by Niel, as the deeply unpleasant representative of modernization, equated in the text with an immoral materialism. His first appearance with his 'narrow beady eyes', the absent eyelids giving 'his pupils the fixed, unblinking hardness of a snake's or a lizard's' (pp. 16–7), and his first action – slitting the woodpecker's eyes – let us know at once how Ivy is to be judged. Our readerly role is minimal in terms of constructing this character: the 'guiding capacity of direct definition'[29] is imposed on us here in a way totally absent elsewhere in the book. Ivy is the figure of the mod-ern – as Niel and the narrator envisage it. His motivations are apparent from his actions. Associated directly with the 'changes' which have occurred in Sweet Water, it is he who has 'drained the old marsh', destroying in the name of eco-nomic pragmatism what Captain Forrester has preserved in the interest of aesthetic beauty. His materialism with its 'petty economies' is opposed by Niel to 'the space, the colour, the princely carelessness of the pioneer' (pp. 104–5). Ivy cheats Indians,[30] is 'unprincipled', but his are the methods – as Mrs Forrester puts it – that 'work nowadays' (p. 123). If Daniel Forrester represents the 'pioneer period' which Niel idealizes, Ivy is the representative of the new whom he hates. Such is Ivy's one-dimensional presentation in the text, that the reader has little option but to participate in that dislike. His value scheme is presented as deeply flawed.

Marian Forrester is a much more interesting case. The reader is encouraged from an early point in the novel to 'read' Mrs Forrester through male eyes (how Niel sees her; the picture of domesticity she presents to Dalzell, etc.). Such a strong primary effect can only be countered by a reader who, in filling in the missing links of the text, finds evidence of the limitations of such a view. Such a reader ends up questioning that patriarchal system which conditions the position of Marian in the novel. Cather builds such resistance into her text by setting the value schemes which are represented in it against one another; by implicitly suggesting the inadequacy of each (even Marian's own).

For Marian Forrester – so the title at any rate suggests – is the novel's major character. What, then, can we construct of her perspective, her value scheme? This is a problematic question, since the narrative presents Marian from without, rather than from within: no direct access is allowed to her thoughts, no interiority. This is what gives the quality of 'opacity' to her depiction. We can, however, note that Niel's view of her is – especially early in the text – balanced by other perspectives (notably, that of Adolph Blum in the sleigh-ride scene). We can also note that, as readers, we are given information, through dialogue and action, which allows us to build some tentative picture of her world scheme, her value system. This allows us both access to her identity as defined by others, and projected insight into that identity as understood, and as constructed, by herself.

Niel, as we have seen, cannot handle anything but an idealized version of Marian. He carefully limits her identity to that of Captain Forrester's wife. Had she died with him, Niel's problem of knowing how to treat her in a changed role would have been avoided. After the captain's death, her refinements are now practised on 'heavy lads'; consequently she has been written off as 'Merry Widow' in the town's eyes. Niel, at this point, still feels that 'the right man could save her', but the words appear just textually prior to his sight of Ivy with his hands over her breast. The reader, making the connection that is not explicit textually, reconstructs the scene in terms of Niel's hands, not Ivy's. But such a reconstruction must be cancelled as soon as floated, because of Niel's stiffness and prim scrupulousness (we remember the 'monastic cleanliness and severity', p. 29, of his rooms), his inability to treat her as anything other than the Captain's wife.

Indeed, this is how her identity is defined throughout the text. I find difficulty calling her Marian, as it is as Mrs Forrester she is known almost solidly through the novel. In the last chapter, for example, the name Mrs

Forrester appears eight times, 'Daniel Forrester's widow' once, 'Daniel Forrester's wife' once, and then – finally, and on her gravestone – the name 'Marian Forrester Collins'; her given name doubly outweighed by the adopted names of her two husbands. Otherwise, the name 'Maidy' is used four times (on each occasion by the Captain), 'Marian' five times textually; twice though in the context of the Ellinger relationship, twice in the context of her pre-nuptial days. Concerning the latter, it is noticeable that Marian scarcely has, in this text, a pre-marital identity. From this period, we are given a brief narrative of her disastrous first engagement and the consequent mountain trip. These facts are, though, used only to provide a context for the romance with Captain Forrester. Aside from this, we are given the briefest of details (learning to swim) of her Californian girlhood.

It is as Mrs Forrester, then, that she is textually confined. We are told that the Captain, a 'commanding figure' (p. 44), had long planned to build a house at Sweet Water, 'dig my well . . . plant my grove . . . build a house that my friends could come to, with a wife like Mrs Forrester to make it attractive to them' (p. 49). The description is noteworthy first in the link between possessiveness and property suggested by that litany of 'my's'. Secondly, we see in it that 'a wife' is given the role of ornament, to set off and enhance the property. And thirdly, in talking about Mrs Forrester, the Captain raises the ghost of a first wife: an invalid who died prior to his meeting Marian. The knowledge, introduced at this textual point, that there have been two Mrs Forresters, suddenly blurs even the clear lines of Mrs Forrester's *marital* identity to this textual point.

The notion of wife as ornamentation connects up with the role of jewelry in this text. Both Niel and the Captain like to see Marian wear a certain pair of earrings. Niel admires their aesthetic effect, likes 'to see the firelight sparkle' on them. The Captain's pleasure comes 'because they had been his mother's. It gratified him to have his wife wear jewels; it meant something to him. She never left off her beautiful rings unless she was in the kitchen' (p. 36) – or unless, the reader can add, from a later and more cynical position of textual knowledge, she was making love to Ellinger. What, though, is this never defined 'something' that the wearing of the jewels meant to

Forrester? This can, I suggest, be deduced from the way in which we read a text synchronically, to use Steven Mailloux's synchronic–diachronic polarity. I will focus on this reading dimension, and return to this point, in due course.

I would suggest for the moment, however, that Mrs Forrester's value scheme is one in which she accepts her role as wifely ornamentation to the Captain's life (and this, in one sense, explains for us the epithet 'lost'). Her 'world structure'[31] (her model of coherence, frame used to order and contain her perception of reality) is one in which the female identity depends on a strong male support. Her identity is composed of her marital role, as Mrs Forrester, and she – as well as others – accepts such definition. This is, given the lack of interiority, a speculative reading projected into the text's silence over Marian's motivations and thoughts, but on the basis of the textual words and actions we are given such a 'finalized hypothesis'[32] appears to hold water.

For Marian defines women in terms of their appearance in male eyes. Asking Niel whether Boston women smoke with the men after dinner she comments, 'women can't be attractive if they do everything that men do' (p. 111). Her own status as ornament to the Captain's life, dependent on him for her very identity, is suggested by the fact that when her role as marital dependent on a strong male figure is lost, her world-structure falls apart. Mrs Forrester goes 'quite . . . to pieces' when the Captain's stroke deprives him of power and authority, her role as ornament radically affected by the loss of his powerful physical and economic base. She is now in charge and, as such, 'drudged in the kitchen, slept, half-dressed, in one of the chambers upstairs, kept herself going on black coffee and brandy. All the bars were down. She had ceased to care about anything' (p. 139). Niel steps in to take temporary control, and Marian – able to rest – becomes 'in command of herself again'. The implication is, though, that such self-command depends on the presence of a male authority figure to sustain it. This, after all, is the way her nineteenth-century world has worked. It has been the pattern of her life since the age of nineteen, when Captain Forrester – heart pumping and muscles straining – carried her broken-legged body down the Sierras, with her knowledge that 'he would never drop me' (p. 168).[33]

Once Forrester dies, her stability and sense of direction

founder. Niel describes her as having 'become another woman', without the Captain rudderless, 'driven hither and thither
by every wind' (p. 154). Ivy Peters now becomes the dominant
figure in her life (and controller of her economic affairs) almost,
so it seems, for want of any alternative: 'You are still younger
than Ivy, – and better looking!' (p. 156) she prompts Niel, who
can only react coldly. She recaptures something of her old
manner and vivacity at the dinner party she holds for Niel,
Ivy and the local boys. Niel here sees evidence that, despite
the cloddishness of the company, 'she was still her indomitable
self, going through her old part', but that 'only the stage-hands
were left to listen to her' (p. 169).

The stage metaphor is appropriate, for this 'indomitable
self' is in fact an adopted role, a 'self' constituted around
the necessary presence of male authority which then collapses
when no such presence is available. Such an identity is
constrained both from within and without, for it must be constructed within the allowed norms of the cultural environment.
Marian loses social respectability, and thus a social identity
– is 'sadly broken' (p. 174) so Niel hears – when her name is
linked, outside the bounds of marital respectability, with Ivy
Peters. Such respectability, and with it a reconstruction of the
'broken' self, only returns with Marian's re-marriage, and the
accompanying newly acquired wealth in Buenos Ayres, where
she is described as being '*a good deal made up* (my stress) . . . like
most of the women down there' (pp. 176–7).

The former phrase resonates. Marian constructs her identity
to fit her world picture: one in which neither social function
nor sense of self-identity is available for her outside the
limits of the marital framework. Re-adjustment to fit the
role of spouse of the 'cranky old Englishman' allows her
finally a secure role and situation ('things turned out well'
for her). The dominant irony, of course, is that both outside
the marital frame – and within it – Marian is 'lost'. Her identity is constructed to fit the role allowed her in a patriarchal
culture (Mrs Forrester, Mrs Collins) rather than to giving full
and free expression to that 'power to live' (p. 124) with which
she is associated.

We are, then, offered at least three textual perspectives
in *A Lost Lady*. Marian has, in Carolyn Heilbrun's words,
'internalized the male view' of herself, 'accepted it as the

"truth"'.[34] Her value system is in accord with that patriarchal culture to which she never quite comfortably acquiesces. Her role is related to two other perspectives: Niel with his nostalgia and conservative idealism; Ivy Peters and his aggressive materialism. What is clear is that none of these positions offers an admirable model for conduct. And this again – according to Iser – is where our individual readerly role becomes so central and vital. For we focus on what the represented textual positions exclude. We transform these 'interacting positions . . . into a determinate meaning', but this textual meaning is constructed out of human possibilities suggested by the very insufficiencies of those textually presented: 'the aesthetic object – which is the whole spectrum of human nature – begins to arise out of what is adumbrated by the negated possibilities' (p. 200).

The reader thus constructs the meaning of the text. When we fix our attention on these positions, try to construct a satisfactory value system from them, their mutual insufficiencies are clear. We are given a ruthless materialism on one hand, a nostalgic idealism on the other. The third position represented is Marian as victim and product of a social world constructed on a patriarchal model. Her vitality is stifled by the inability of this world to provide opportunity to fully express it, either within or without the marital frame.

Marian, like the reader, is caught between unsatisfactory value systems: a fact suggested (as far as her limited position goes) by the text's central metaphor of the blinded female bird corkscrewing its 'wild and desperate' way to the perch it recognized, and 'as if it had learned something by its bruises . . . pecked and crept its way along the branch and disappeared into its . . . hole' (p. 20). This place of safety is a place of darkness, the only place where this winged creature – blinded by a cruel male figure[35] – can find security, the place from which she has first emerged. The metaphoric fit is loose, but the connecting links ('reciprocal spotlighting') are made when Niel, on his return from college, catches Marian up in his arms from the hammock in which she lies: 'How light and alive she was! like a bird caught in a net. If only he could rescue her . . . She showed no impatience to be released . . .' (p. 109). Niel, paradoxically, is both imprisoner and potential rescuer here. That elegant wildness that he recognizes in her suggests how inextricably what is seen in the novel as her natural vitality has become bound up with her cultural role; and his acceptance of Victorian social norms means that he (both timid and conventional) will be unable to release that 'power to live' which is her mark. He is no rescuer; more sinister, his earlier attempts to put that bird out of its blinded misery only end in self-injury. Marian too fits the metaphor, blind in the sense that no clear alternative is envisaged by her outside the limits of the marital role in which she is first seen. She corkscrews about wildly when such a secure position is removed, but creeps gratefully into such a resting place when renewed opportunity arises.

Given the various perspectives offered in *A Lost Lady*, how then do we as individual readers assemble the text? How do we actively synthesize this collection of 'constantly shifting viewpoints' (Iser, p. 97) to reach a final 'transcendental vantage point from which [we] can see through all the positions that have been formulated' (p. 99)?[36] As we read – and the plot structure confirms this – the faults in all characters' world views become apparent. *Our* norms (and this for Iser is also vital) are also challenged as we both recognize Niel's patriarchal values and abandon any idea of him as discerning moral commentator. We have to step 'back from [our] own governing norms of orientation' (p. 187); reassess our own ways of 'reading' or – in the case of female readers – 'being' women, as Cather guides us to take an 'unfamiliar view' (p. 130) of the world she describes; as we measure the perspectives being portrayed against the norms we take for granted.

Such a reassessment of ways of reading (or being) a woman may in fact be implicit in a further value scheme apparent in the novel: that of the narrator. The anonymous nature and lack of determinate sexuality of this narrator, and the way as focalizing presence s/he fades from the text's foreground, makes such a scheme, however, difficult to pin down. We might, though, consider the large information gap concerning this figure exactly as a way of suggesting her or his perspective. Obviously nostalgic ('even she, alas! grew older', p. 8) this narrator may – in withholding sexual identity – be implying some kind of move beyond those value systems offered in the text, suggesting the possibility of transcending the man–woman antithesis and finding a space beyond gender

from which one can write and see. The use of such a narrator
might, alternatively, be related to Cather's lesbianism: an
adoption of a 'neutral' persona in order 'to express safely
her emotional and erotic feelings for other women'.[37] This
gap must remain, I think, unfilled through a very lack of
further information: the questions raised here are, however,
fundamental. This is another textual perspective viewing
Marian's story of 'loss' retrospectively, and such a point of
view cannot be discounted.

What 'transcendental viewpoint' (p. 98) do we adopt in
reading *A Lost Lady*? Our own position becomes characterized
by 'a blank which has relatively clear outlines' (Iser, p. 217).
Seeing what the three main textual perspectives exclude, and
picking up hints from the narrator's silences, we construct a
subjective position which centres on the need for a new constitution of female identity beyond that shaped by a patriarchal
culture, and a related need to recognize and alter the pressures
resulting from a society in which (to quote Charlotte Perkins
Gilman) 'the economic status of the human female is relative
to the sex-relation'.[38]

Added to this, we recognize a need to reassess our ways of
'reading' or 'being' women in a culture where, to paraphrase
Carolyn Heilbrun, women have been seen only as men choose
to see them; where this male world has imposed such a view
on women themselves.[39] Finally, and more generally, we
re-affirm the need to come to terms with modernization
without losing contact with traditional values. None of these
possibilities are allowed by the textual viewpoints themselves:
the text becomes an 'enabling structure' to determine personal
meaning. Thus, though I have used the convention of speaking
for my reader throughout my analysis ('we recognize . . . ' etc.),
my awareness that I will not speak for all readers remains. In
reconstructing my production of textual meaning, I recognize
that such a reading will not necessarily be shared. For centrally
– although certainly, in Iser's view, any reading is structured
by the text ('the meaning of the text is prestructured by the
signs given in the text', p. 141) – the reading of each individual
will subjectively differ, due to the 'overdetermined' nature, the
'indeterminacy' of a literary text. He stresses the '*layer upon
layer* of significance' (my stress) in a text,[40] the 'multiplicity
of [its] interconnecting perspectives' (p. 118). Other readings

will subjectively differ from mine, other readers plot their individual ways through a text: all these readings are, however, 'intersubjectively accessible' (p. 124) as we are all using the same textual structure as our base.

My reading, then, of *A Lost Lady* conforms to Iser's pattern. I have stressed primarily the way in which reading is a temporal act: caught in the 'strategies of entanglement'[41] which go to make up the literary text, we build patternings and consistencies as we proceed, by a 'reciprocal spotlighting' procedure. To explicate such a procedure is a new and useful departure from traditional critical stress on the text taken as an organic whole. Secondly, I have shown how in Iser's model a 'holistic'[42] reading is finally constructed: working our readerly way through the different perspectives portrayed in the text, we sift and order as we go, building up specific meanings which go *beyond* those directly portrayed within the text.

In coming to these conclusions, however, some of the difficulties of Iser's critical model have become apparent. He sees the text as 'a structured indicator to guide the imagination of the reader',[43] asking us to respond in certain ways to it. But he also allows for the individual readerly imagination powerful activity in the way it works – and is potentially affected – as it negotiates a text which is overdetermined; as the reader's world view adjusts itself to, and measures itself against, those presented in the text. 'The self' he writes 'that begins reading a book may not be quite the same as the one which finishes it'. The text's overdetermination, however, means that other readers will form different gestalts. It is so full of gaps that many different ways can be found to fill them. Its 'semantic potential'[44] is so rich as to be inexhaustible: thus 'every text is potentially capable of many different realizations and no reading can exhaust the text's full potential which is always infinitely richer than any of its realizations'.[45] How far, then, is my reading individual to me; how far a product of signals already built into the text?

The move from controlling text to interpretive reader is the weak point here. The stable text guides us, but all our readings of it will be different. The author's intentions direct us, but our own specific cultural and historical position contributes to our reading. The incompatibilities suggested here are spotlighted by Elizabeth Freund. She points out that, looking at this one way, 'everything depends ultimately on the author's stable text which supplies all that the interpreter requires'; from another, 'the author's text is deprived of all authority, and any textual "fact" such as a blank will be the product of a certain reading strategy, so that all is supplied by the reader'. In short: 'the compromise formation whereby the text instructs and the reader constructs breaks down under critical scrutiny' (p. 147).

Iser's model does reveal useful tactics to be used in a sequential processing of the text; does suggest some of the ways in which patterns of meaning are built up. It is, however, suspect on two counts in its stress on the stable and controlling text which gives triggers to which we react and which has 'conditions already structured in [it]' (p. 50) which we fulfil. First, the whole project of deconstructionist criticism has been to show that a text is not a stable thing. Language is subject to ceaseless slippings and slidings, all structures lack stability: 'there is something in *writing itself* which finally evades all systems and logics. There is a continual flickering, spilling and defusing of meaning – what Derrida calls "dissemination"'.[46] Iser's division of the text into fixed 'stars' joined by variable lines[47] (authorial guides to interpretation; free space between, in which we use our readerly imagination) collapses when seen from this position. Secondly, not only is the text itself unstable, but the readers who approach that text bring to it their own very different set of expectations/framing contexts which vitally affects their readerly role. As Roland Barthes says in *S/Z*, a book to which I return in my next chapter: 'this "I" which approaches the text is already itself a plurality of other texts, of codes which are infinite . . . '.[48]

Once we start framing our reading in such a way, the whole process of reader-response becomes rather more open and fluid than Iser suggests. Terry Eagleton rightly echoes Barthes when he says that 'the reader does not come to the text as a kind of cultural virgin'.[49] Indeed, the way in which our own different frames of reference radically affect our readings of a text is comically highlighted in David Lodge's *Small World* (1984), where the Japanese Akira Sakazaki is engaged in translating Ronald Frobisher's *Could Try Harder*. Sakazaki's knowledge of British mores is not that of cultural virgin, but neither is he as fully initiated as Lodge's (British) reader. His translation of Frobisher, one of a 'new generation' of 'Angry Young Men', presents certain problems to the puzzled Japanese: 'p. 107, 3 down. "Bugger me, but I feel like some faggots tonight". Does Ernie mean that he feels a sudden desire for homosexual intercourse? If so, why does he mention this to his wife?'[50] So, too, Umberto Eco in *The Role of the Reader* (1979) suggests the way in which different types of cultural awareness can greatly affect our readerly role when he writes:

> It is possible to be smart enough to interpret the relationship between Nero Wolfe and Archie Goodwin as the umpteenth variation of the Oedipus myth without destroying Rex Stout's narrative universe. It is possible to be stupid enough to read Kafka's *Trial* as a trivial criminal novel, but at this point the text collapses – it has been burned out, just as a 'joint' is burned out to produce a private euphoric state.[51]

It is possible in both the above examples partially to cope with the problem of such variant readings by drawing on such controlling concepts as Stanley Fish's notion of the 'informed' reader,[52] or Iser's pluralistic model of intersubjective accessibility. The issue of framing contexts remains, however, a central one in any discussion of how we read.

Steven Mailloux in his valuable book *Interpretive Conventions: The Reader in the Study of American Literature* (1982), suggests one way around the difficulties raised above. For he shifts our terms of reference away from the text and its guiding capacities, and on to the kind of interpretive work we as readers do in our 'concretization' (p. 166) of it. In doing this, he builds on Stanley Fish's work on 'interpretive communities', the 'bundle of straategies or norms of interpretation that we hold in common and which regulate the way we think and perceive'.[53] I wish to recap Mailloux's discussion as a way of suggesting both the strengths and limitations of my reading of *A Lost Lady* to this point. First, his division of reading activity into two different dimensions – synchronic and diachronic – exposes the limitations of any approach which focuses too closely on reader-text interaction to the exclusion of those controlling cultural frames we have been discussing. By 'diachronic' we mean the way we read a text sequentially: the way we respond to it in exactly the kind of 'reciprocal spotlighting', 'theme-and-horizon' way described earlier in this chapter. A diachronic reading stresses 'the temporal aspect of reading' (p.90); our movement through a text, the way we relate one part to another as we proceed. This Mailloux sees as vital to the reading process. However, he places such activity in the context not of authorial intention (the author's guiding hand . . .) but of our readerly expectations. For diachronic reading goes alongside 'synchronic' reading – its 'convention-based aspect' (p. 91) – a focus not on ongoing textual development, but an 'atemporal' stress on all those various frames *outside* the immediate text which affect the way we read. Such a division has already been suggested when I earlier introduced Eco's notion of an 'encyclopedia of narrativity', the way our knowledge of other texts conditions our present reading. This is one element of our synchronic textual reading. We make sense of a text by relating it to a frame, the network of texts of which it is a part. Iser would not deny this, though he does not see the full implications of it in terms of readerly differences.

Mailloux, however, places critical stress on one particular frame outside the text which conditions our reception of it: the (synchronic) interpretive reading conventions – the conventional frame we place *around* literature – which affects our readerly processing of it. This constitutes a step away from the subjective free-flow implicit in my discussion of readerly difference, the way in which each reader brings her or his own framing contexts to a work. For Mailloux, 'the successful act of framing is communal, not individual' (p. 136). He suggests that a discussion of literature normally takes place within a particular type of community:

> historical communities that fill the category of 'literature' can be whole societies, but more often are societal groups based on economic organization (for example, the network of authors, publishers, periodical editors, and book reviewers), social rank (for instance, intelligentsia and governing classes), or institutions and professional position (such as English professor [or undergraduate student]) (p. 138).

It is as members of such communities that we give shared meaning to literary texts; such membership conditions our reception of them. We read them in the context of certain mutual expectations – the frameworks by which our particular historical community of 'literature' readers make sense of such texts. In other words, the conventions which operate in a particular historical reading community crucially affect how we receive a text. So, for instance, Mailloux shows how Herman Melville's *Moby Dick* (1851) met criticism in contemporary British reviews because the 'British preoccupation with literary conventions' (p. 175) led to real frustration with Melville's refusal in it to stick to the limits of a single genre. This, in turn, led to its negative evaluation.

Centrally, Mailloux stresses the need to recognize that reading conventions can change 'from culture to culture, from period to period' (p. 136). Depending on our cultural concerns (what is occurring in one specific historical community) our framings of the literary text change. Interpretive conventions are not static. Framings of *A Lost Lady* have depended on the ways of making sense of literary texts generally within a particular culture at a particular time. Thus, given the 'traditional conventions' (p. 151) of American literary practice, it is not surprising to see interpretations of the text emphasizing Niel's role (young man's initiation theme) or focusing on the loss of the old West (geographical change as locus of American cultural identity). Edward and Lillian Bloom's 1962 study of Cather, for example, treats Marian as a kind of cipher in a novel which is read as a 'parable descriptive of the frontier's downfall'. Mrs Forrester, they say, 'is genuinely tragic because she drifts away from the felicitous spirit of the pioneer and is absorbed into the new evil order promulgated by men like Ivy Peters'.[54] In such a reading, Captain Forrester becomes the hero, he who represents the Old West. Mrs Forrester becomes nothing more than a reflection of first his, then Ivy's, values. It is the loss of the West, not the loss of Mrs Forrester that really 'counts'.

Eagleton writes that 'all [literary] responses are deeply imbricated with the kind of social and historical individuals we are' (p. 89). The way we now frame and interpret American literary texts has been profoundly affected by the ideological impact of feminism. Jonathan Culler illustrates in *On Deconstruction* how, until recently, male gender inflected textual readings were taken for granted – indeed, shared even by the women whose best political, cultural and personal interests were negated by such a reading.[55] So, Niel and Captain Forrester tend to overwhelm Marian in earlier readings of *A Lost Lady*; so, as Nina Baym shows, Nathaniel Hawthorne's *The Scarlet Letter* (1850) which – exceptionally, in terms of the American literary canon – portrays 'a fully developed woman of sexual age', only enters that canon 'by virtue of strenuous critical revisions of the text that remove Hester Prynne from the centre of the novel and make her subordinate to Arthur Dimmesdale'.[56] Present readings focus much more insistently on the figure of Hester herself.

The ways in which we interpret texts, then, depends on the changing nature of our cultural and historical concerns: a reading of Twain's *A Connecticut Yankee in King Arthur's Court* (1889) as an anti-imperalist text, for example, would not have been readily accepted on the novel's first appearance. My point here is that my previous reading of the Cather text is directly affected by the kind of interpretive strategies prevalent in the critical community to which I belong. I wish to repeat Mailloux's important quote here: 'The successful act of framing [a text] is communal, not individual'. This harks back to Iser's notion of intersubjective accessibility, but changes the stress from the diachronic to the synchronic. As we read, not only do we play off one element of the text against another to make our own readerly sense of it, but we undertake this activity in the context of the reading conventions which we share with the particular community in which we fit.

Thus while we can continue to accept Iser's basic premise, that we pick our readerly way through an overdetermined text (one richly dense in layered meanings), we need to look again at his view of the way we also move from one textual perspective to another. The stability Iser assumes to be a textual given – our readerly move from the hero's perspective to that of a minor character, for example – is in fact missing. In Mailloux's words:

Whether the hero's perspective cancels a minor character's or vice versa is always an *interpretation* (my stress) and never the textual given that Iser assumes. Any particular perspective arrangement is a construct varying according to an ongoing critical interpretation . . . Of course, I can go even further and say that not only is the negative relation between the hero and a minor character an interpretive construct but so is the 'fact' that a certain character is designated 'the hero' and another only a 'minor character' . . . *It's interpretation all the way down* (my stress, p. 198).

Because my reading of *A Lost Lady* is framed by a present cultural concern with a re-defining of the literary canon (in a direction away from male exclusivity), I interpret the text from this foundation. My construction of Marian's character is a sequential reading carried out within such an interpretive frame; the textual signals I responded to, a product of my position in a particular reading community. My making of her the central protagonist of the text also stems from such a base. It would be quite possible to interpret the text as one in which Niel is the hero, or the Captain.

Steven Mailloux categorically states 'texts do not cause interpretation, interpretations constitute texts' (p. 197). I would not go this far. Iser's notion of intersubjective accessibility still counts. While *A Lost Lady* can be interpreted in many different ways, it cannot be interpreted as, say, a rewriting of *War and Peace*. The text constrains the critic, as well as being subject to her or his interpretive position. However, we undoubtedly shape our reading of a text ('write' that text, if you like)[57] according to the interpretive conventions we bring to bear on it; find our own 'stars' in the text to suit our own reading needs. It would be possible to 'write' *A Lost Lady* as a *bildungsroman* (Niel's education into the world), as elegiac pastoral (loss of the Old West, the frontier spirit), as ironic modernist text (focusing on failures emerging from Niel's consciousness-action divide), as proto-feminist novel (my reading), as love-story (Niel's buried love for Marian), or as indeterminate text (where, as shown earlier, images of entrapment and freedom, nature and artifice, outsider and insider, collide head-on in a spiralling and self-defeating manner). Each reader concretizes and constitutes the novel according to the conventions s/he operates as s/he reads.

Pragmatically, then, we read and make sense of what we read by bringing to the text ways of framing it. My cultural and historical siting as a reader strongly affects the way I have been able to use Iser's model of the reading activity to make what I consider an 'acceptable and approximating translation'[58] of Cather's text. First, I bring to the text that 'interpretive convention' shared by the community of critics and readers of which I am a part. I construct my textual meanings (and accept those of others) out of the need to re-read American literature – and particularly women's writing in that domain – in the light of both the near complete exclusion of less powerful (in terms of public voice) ethnic and gender groups from the canon; in the light, too, of feminist re-readings of that literary history. This way of creating meaning is licensed by the group of which I am a part; is – I would suggest – right at the top of the 'hierarchy of reading conventions' (Mailloux, p. 136) operating in my particular historical community.

Other ways of siting the novel are obviously available – as modernist text, western text, 1920s text, text of male initiation, and so on. Iser's description of the way we create textual meaning remains valid for these approaches. The theme-and-horizon operation would, however, alter in accord with the particular interpretive convention applied. And the success of such framings' accessibility would depend on what ways of making sense of literary texts were licensed – what status they held – in the reading community at any particular historical moment. In this text – as I suspect happens often – I had several interpretive approaches which suggested themselves to me as I first read the text. In synthesizing, though, reaching a final (retrospective) 'reading', these were played off against one another for my determinate meaning to emerge. An interpretation in the light of the 'western' theme would have meant the downgrading of Mrs Forrester's centrality, and was thus subordinated to my own. An interpretation in the light of a modernist frame was readily and consistently available, but again, in terms of my present hierarchy of critical concern, remained subsidiary, though contributory, to my final reading.

The reading was also affected by the framing textual network I brought to the novel, part of which I share perhaps with all other readers of that novel; part with few. This network, which included my reading of modernist texts generally, of women's writing such as Kate Chopin's

The Awakening (1899) and Charlotte Perkins Gilman's *The Yellow Wallpaper* (1892), of other texts by Cather, helps add a subjective note to that (communal) interpretive frame I have placed around the novel. One brief example, which informs my final interpretation, relates to my earlier comments about what exactly Mrs Forrester's wearing of jewels means to her husband. A synchronic approach tries to site this detail in relation to an intertextual context: we are constructing Daniel Forrester's value scheme, not just from other textual detail, but also from our framing knowledge of nineteenth-century norms. In *The Theory of the Leisure Class* (1899) the American sociologist, Thorstein Veblen — 'the best critic of America that America has produced'[59] — examines exactly these norms, suggests the meaning we, as readers, are trying to flesh out. He sees the institution of marriage as evolving from a situation where women were useful as 'trophies' (p. 34), visible results of the success of powerful men. Their 'ownership-marriage' of the women they seized illustrated lastingly their 'prowess' and their 'mastery'. Veblen uses an anthropologic frame to comment ironically on the American present throughout his text.

He then speaks of 'emulation' (p.35) generally. One's possession and consumption of wealth is both a sign of success and a way of showing one's status. Leisure becomes a mark of 'pecuniary strength and therefore of superior force' (p. 43). In a contemporary world, though, 'leisure and a conspicuous consumption of goods' (p. 70) are delegated to wives and children: their wastefulness shows the male head of the household's 'ability to pay' (p. 71). The wife's status as chattel remains, for — to Veblen — 'the habitual rendering of vicarious leisure and consumption is the abiding mark of the unfree servant' (p. 69). Expensive dress is another way of showing 'social worth': for again, it 'should make plain to all observers that the wearer is not engaged in . . . productive labor' (p. 120). The wearing of the corset also thus signifies: like the gentleman's walking stick, a sign that the owner or wearer is exempt from 'any employment that is directly and immediately of any human use' (p. 121).

Veblen — in his ironic mode — relates the wearing of the corset to the whole field of economics: 'in economic theory, substantially a mutilation, undergone for the purpose of lowering the subject's vitality and rendering her permanently and obviously unfit for work' (p. 121). So, on a lesser scale, signify the earrings. I would suggest that the wearing of the earrings constitutes – in terms of Veblen's argument – a twofold sign, both of Marian's unfitness for work and of her 'mutilation', and also of the wealth (and thus status) of the Captain, who has the ability to adorn his wife in such a manner. Captain Forrester sees – if unconsciously – hung on his wife a mark of his own status, power and wealth. The earrings elaborately insist on Marian's idleness and confirm that 'in the modern civilized scheme of life the woman is still, in theory, the economic dependent of the man – that, perhaps in a highly idealized sense, she is still the man's chattel' (p. 127). This underlies, I would suggest, the 'meaning' that Mrs Forrester's jewelry has for her husband. If so, the final comment made on their relationship before his death has a double edged ring: Niel 'felt that the Captain knew his wife better even than she knew herself; and that, knowing her, he – to use one of his own expressions – valued her' (p. 143).

'Reading has a history' in Culler's words.[60] The intertextual network with which I synchronically frame the text (of which the Veblen is one small example) belongs just to this reader (the exact combination of texts I have read which help place and explicate this novel). The network connects up with those of others, all positioned within a particular shared literary community. Intersubjective comprehensibility is spurred as other readers are led to read Veblen – or Gilman perhaps – thus endorsing the interpretive conventions that they, in turn, bring to the novel. When we read, then, we are faced with a potentially daunting task: to make meanings from a dense network of words, phrases, symbols, characters, view-points, plot structures, all of which connect with one another in potentially multiple ways. In practice, though, we make sense of a text according to our knowledge of the frames in which to site it, and according to the types of interpretive strategies we operate as we work our way through it. Our 'horizons of expectations' lead us to concretize the text as we read; entangled in a text which we never see whole until the last page, we construct and put aside meanings as we go, thoroughly implicated in, and giving form to, the novels that we paradoxically both consume and produce.

5

The Portrait of a Lady and *The House of Mirth*: A Barthesian Reading

I

> We know now that the text is not a line of words releasing a single 'theological' meaning (the 'message' of the Author – God) but a multi-dimensional space in which a variety of writings, none of them original, blend and clash. The text is a tissue of quotations drawn from the innumerable centres of culture.
>
> (Roland Barthes)[1]

Roland Barthes' work, and especially *S/Z: An Essay*, challenges the whole premise of what we conventionally call *Realism*. Realism as a literary mode disguises the conditions of its production. Appearing to accurately reflect the world of external reality, a realist text reads like a seamless and thus apparently 'natural' whole. We note as readers, as Barthes points out, 'only the smooth surface, imperceptibly soldered by the movement of sentences, the flowing discourse of narration, the " naaturalness" of ordinary language'.[2] Attention is diverted in realist literature away from the instabilities of language and reference. Language, rather, gives here a seemingly transparent representation of a solid world. All stress is placed on referent: word becomes a 'translucent window . . . neutral and colourless'[3] onto world.

162

To suggest briefly how this process works, we might compare the title of Henry James' realist novel *The Portrait of a Lady* (1881) with that of a novel which operates in a different literary mode, Thomas Pynchon's *The Crying of Lot 49* (1966). James' title is unambiguous. Solidly framed, this will be, in the dictionary definition of portrait, 'a representation made from life' of one particular 'vivid individual',[4] Isabel Archer. In the case of Pynchon, the reader immediately faces problems with the meaning of language which were not apparent in James' title. How do we interpret, pin down, that rather disconcerting title, *The Crying of Lot 49?* The immediate reference, not how-ever discovered until the *end* of the text, is to an auction and the 'crying of the lots' therein. Initially, though, to borrow a term from the novel, the reader is left 'unfurrowed'[5] as s/he tries to work out what the phrase signifies. Words here are resistant rather than transparent and we are immediately faced with the possibility of a number of meanings. The crying of one's lot could refer to lamentation concerning one's destiny, a reading of the title which certainly might apply to the text as a whole. What though do we then do with the numeral '49' left over, supplementary? There are references in the novel to the Californian goldrush of 1849. Is this relevant? or does the number carry occult connotations? It is a multiple of seven 'the most mysterious and uncanny of numbers' which 'occurs frequently in the Bible . . . especially in the Book of Revelation, which abounds in sets of 7'.[6] It is also the Pentecostal number. This seems relevant, too, in a text at whose conclusion the reader, like the main protagonist, is left awaiting final revelation.[7]

In Barthes' terms, Pynchon's novel would in this respect be a more 'writerly' text than James' 'readerly' one. Realist literature for him fits the latter category. It is a form of 'classic writing that complies with our expectations'[8] and such compliance Barthes sees as its essence. Such 'readerly' texts encourage a sterile and passive consumption on the part of the reader. 'Everything holds together' (p. 156) in them: smooth surface resists active access to, and opening up of the text by, the reader. Writing about *Strong Poison*, a TV adaptation of a Lord Peter Wimsey narrative, John Naughton described the series as having 'a smooth and polished look, like an expensive coffin . . . The costumes are perfect, as is the Lagonda'.[9] The metaphor used here would exactly fit Barthes' conception of the readerly.

The 'writerly' text, on the other hand, encourages the reader to act as *producer* of meaning. The classic text can be seen as a 'stable object' with a 'hierarchy of textual "levels" '[10] with the reader clearly signposted in the direction of the relative significance of these levels. The literary work is thus contained within an 'ideology of totality' (p. 15) which Barthes connects up with what he sees as 'the closure system of the West' (pp. 7–8). The 'writerly' text is, on the other hand, both open and 'plural'. It is Barthes' ideal, and as such 'we would have a hard time finding it in a bookstore' (pp. 5–6), though the modernist novel would certainly come closer to representing its possibilities than the realist text. The 'writerly' text allows the reader a vast amount of play and pleasure (both central terms for Barthes). It is a text which is open-ended, with a multiplicity of networks and entrances 'none of which can be authoritatively declared to be the main one' (p. 5). 'Meaning proliferates' (p. 8) in such a text, and the reader 'writes' the text as s/he reads it, playfully tracing and articulating meanings which are released as she or he, immersed previously in other texts and other codes, engages in 'collision/collusion'[11] with the textual network at hand. In Terence Hawkes' terms, the writerly is that literature which:

> invites us self-consciously to read it, to 'join in' and be aware of the interrelationship of the writing and reading, and which accordingly offers us the joys of co-operation and co-authorship.[12]

This stress on co-authorship sites Barthes at the far end of the spectrum from Iser in terms of reader response theory, one of the contexts in which he must be read. Iser's notion of fixed textual 'stars' which guide our readerly activities, explodes in *S/Z* where every textual fragment becomes a star equal in status to all those innumerable others which compose the text's metaphoric galaxy. Though, like Mailloux, Barthes emphasizes the way we 'write' our own texts, his stress is not on our final communal readings (Mailloux's 'holistic interpretation'),[13] but rather on our open-ended personal negotiation of each of its small sections. The final framing of the text is subordinated (indeed subject to critique) in favour of a playful interaction with it. Barthes focuses on all the various frames which have a part in creating reader/text collusion. While Mailloux does not argue with this, his own critical concern lies in one particular framing direction; how as literary and cultural community we receive and interpret a text. My own chapter tries to provide something of a bridge between the two critics. While illustrating the playful indeterminacy of Barthes' stance, I show how we can gather certain threads from that weave of meanings to be discovered in/elicited from our readerly meeting with the texts, which do contribute to that redefining and recontextualizing of a literary tradition referred to in my last chapter. I finally arrest the unbounded free-play of Barthes' model to trace the particular determinate critical lines I wish to pursue.

The movement away from any notion of unitary centres and fixed meanings for which Barthes calls may seem, in theory, puzzling. It is, though, to be seen illustrated in *S/Z* where Barthes takes *Sarrasine* (1830), a realist text by Balzac, and shows how there are many entrances even to a text like this with its apparently very limited, 'parsimonious' (p. 14) plurality. He cuts against traditional unitary forms of criticism by refusing to look for any overall, 'singular, theological meaning' (p. 11) in the text, rather ceaselessly breaking it up into small units (or lexias), '*manhandling* the text, *interrupting* it' (p. 15),[14] showing both how the 'reality effects' of the text are produced and how multiple these effects can be seen to be – once any individual textual section is unravelled, *decomposed*.

In doing this, Barthes show how realism as a literary mode is based on a fraud. He shows how a text's 'reality effects' are created by the use of certain *codes* and conventions which both author and reader share. He unravels the way meaning is produced in *Sarrasine* by illustrating how the apparently seamless textual surface, one which seems to 'naturally' depict and reflect the world it describes, is in fact composed of a network and overlapping of codes:

> Truth is . . . found to have no real status in the literary text. Far from ordering and creating literature from without, Barthes shows truth to be a mirage produced by one of his five codes.[15]

These codes work as signals to the reader, tying in with her or his prior expectations and knowledge of cultural and literary systems. 'The code' he writes:

> is a perspective of quotations, a mirage of structures; we know only its departures and returns; the units which have resulted from it (those we inventory) are themselves, always, ventures out of the text, the mark, the sign of a virtual digression toward the remainder of a catalogue (*The Kidnapping* refers to every kidnapping ever written); they are so many fragments of something that has always been *already* read, seen, done, experienced; the code is the wake of that *already*. Referring to what has been written, i.e., to the Book (of culture, of life, of life as culture), it makes the text into a prospectus of this Book. Or again: each code is one of the forces that can take over the text (of which the text is the network), one of the voices out of which the text is woven. Alongside each utterance, one might say that off-stage voices can be heard: they are the codes: in their interweaving, these voices (whose origin is 'lost' in the vast perspective of the *already-written*) de-originate the utterance: the convergence of the voices (of the codes) becomes *writing*, a stereographic space where the five codes, the five voices, intersect (pp. 20–1).

This approach to literature sees the essence of writing in multiplicity: the text as saturated with overlapping voices from an inherited tradition; what Vincent Leitch calls 'the greater archival Book'.[16] Barthes thus sees the activity of reading not in terms of treating the Author 'as source and arbiter of meaning',[17] but rather puts the reader in a central role as s/he finds access to a text, 'a network with a thousand entrances' (p. 12), and starts tracing back some of those layerings of codes and conventions which constitute both text and self. In *S/Z*:

> Barthes dallies with the codes. He works with them only up to a point. They function economically in the process of *structuration*: they aid the reading activity. But they are not allowed to build structure. The ludic motion of the reading, not the law of the tale, is Barthes' game. He wants to produce, to write, to disseminate the text, not

consume it, not determine it, not close it. No matter how plural the text, whether triumphantly or parsimoniously so, the interpretive ideal orients reading toward triumphant dissemination. Excess of meaning rather than truth is the goal.[18]

Taking *Sarrasine* as his exemplar, Barthes literally cuts the text to bits. 'We shall . . . star the text', he explains, 'separating, in the manner of a minor earthquake, the blocks of signification of which reading grasps only the smooth surface' (p. 13). The smooth surface of Balzac's story is broken up into 561 lexias which Barthes then discusses in terms of the overlapping and interweaving of the codes he finds there. And he uses asterisks, italics, abbreviations as he writes, thus jumping in his turn right away from the unfissured discourse of accepted critical practice. The five codes he uses as organizing base, codes which are in no way seen as exclusive, run as follows.

Proairetic or narrative code: The code of actions which Barthes abbreviates as ACT. Actions, he asserts, 'can fall into various sequences which should be indicated merely by listing them, since the proairetic sequence is never more than the result of an artifice of reading: whoever reads the text amasses certain data under some generic titles for action (*stroll, murder, rendez-vous*), and this title embodies the sequence' (p. 19). Barthes stresses that this code has its basis in the empirical rather than the rational: we name these sequences once we have read them, seen where they are leading and thus how they can be entitled. However we do have certain well-worn models of narrative sequences – the declaration of love, the seduction, and the murder, for example – which enable us provisionally to name these sequences (according to the 'logic of the . . . already-read')[19] as we proceed.

Semic code: Abbreviated as SEM., this is the code of character. Barthes takes Balzac's description of Sarrasine's having 'one of those strong wills that brook no obstacle', and places it under 'SEM. Obstinacy' (p. 96). The seme is 'the connotative signifier referred to in the lexia' (p. 17). The reader links these connotations 'to a character (or a place or an object)' until they can be grouped in order to make generalizations about that character, place, or object. To Barthes, they are 'flickers of meaning', dispersed and unstable like 'motes of dust' (p. 19) appearing throughout the text. The proper name (Isabel Archer, Sarrasine) in particular 'acts as a magnetic field for the semes' (p. 67). The reader again has in mind certain 'cultural stereotypes (models of personality, for example)'[20] as s/he reads. Thus, according to the romantic code, Sarrasine's ugliness connotes genius; 'SEM. Genius' (p. 103) consequently appears when we are textually informed of this ugliness. Our knowledge of these stereotypes allows us to cluster attributes around character (or place, etc.).

Hermeneutic code: Abbreviated as HER. This code operates around the formulation and final disclosure of an enigma. The reader's 'familiar model of coherence' here (precisely what Barthes means by a 'code') is that on which all fictional narratives are based: keep the reader in suspense and asking questions. 'The text's very existence depends on maintaining the phase of the "not yet fully known or intelligible" for as long as possible'.[21] So immediately we have the title *Sarrasine* we enter the hermeneutic sphere. '*What is Sarrasine?* A noun? A name? A thing? A man? A woman?' (p. 17). The hermeneutic code operates by raising mysteries to be subsequently resolved, often after a series of what Barthes defines as delays, partial answers, snares ('deliberate evasion of the truth') and equivocations, all of which help 'to *arrest* the enigma, to keep it open' (pp. 75–6) until the conclusion of a particular textual sequence. In terms of familiar models of coherence we know (in a British cultural context) when we pick up a green Penguin paperback book that the hermeneutic code in operation will conform to the 'Whodunnit' in which the central enigma will normally remain unresolved until the final chapter.

Cultural code: Abbreviated as REF. (reference code): 'the numerous codes of knowledge or wisdom to which the text continually refers' (p. 18). This body of knowledge can be 'physical, physiological, medical, psychological, literary, historical, etc.' (p. 20). A reference to Minerva springing from the head of Jove is thus categorized 'REF. Mythology' (p. 49)

in *S/Z*. It is the area of the *'already-written'* (p. 21) to which
we are here directed: a whole cultural heritage available at
our readerly fingertips. Writing of Balzac's line concerning
'daydreams which overtake even the shallowest of men, in the
midst of the most tumultuous parties', Barthes suggests we
are close to 'what might easily be a real proverb: "*Tumultuous
parties: deep daydreams*". The statement is made in a collective
and anonymous voice originating in traditional human experience. Thus, the unit has been formed by a gnomic code', so
'REF. Gnomic code' (p. 18).

Late in his text, Barthes devotes one of his ninety-three
divagations (micro-essays written on topics suggested by his
reading of certain specific lexias) to this code, which he also
calls 'The Voice of Science'. It is worth quoting this in some
detail, as again he convincingly makes his point about the
deceptive nature of realism as literary mode. In no sense
reflecting 'life as it is' such a text instead reflects 'life as it has
been constructed under a particular set of cultural codes'. He
speaks of the many references to the cultural codes in *Sarrasine*,
'citations . . . extracted from a body of knowledge, from an
anonymous Book whose best model is doubtless the School
Manual'. This anonymous Book is composed of a series of
Histories (of Literature, of Art, of Europe), of Handbooks (an
Outline of Practical Medicine; a Treatise on Psychology), all
of which are 'accessible to a diligent student in the classical
bourgeois educational system' as a source of wisdom. And
this wisdom is now 'remobilized' in Balzac's text. Such source
material also includes 'an anthology of maxims and proverbs
about life, death, suffering, love, women, ages of man, etc.'.
Barthes speaks of all these materials as follows:

> Although entirely derived from books, these codes, by a
> swivel characteristic of bourgeois ideology, which turns cul-
> ture into nature, appear to establish reality, 'Life'. 'Life'
> then, in the classic text, becomes a nauseating mixture of
> common opinions, a smothering layer of received ideas . . .
> it is in these cultural codes that what is outmoded in Balzac
> . . . is concentrated . . . a fatal condition of Replete Litera-
> ture, mortally stalked by the army of stereotypes it contains
> (pp. 205–6).

This is one of Barthes' clearest statements on the way realist texts work: the production of 'naturalness' in them.

Symbolic code: Abbreviated as SYM. Barthes associates this code with a series of antitheses – life and death, male and female – which in Hawkes' words 'ultimately generates the dominant figure in the carpet'.[22] Certain central oppositions come to dominate the symbolic patternings of the text, as the move outwards from 'textual details to symbolic interpretations'[23] occurs. And Barthes is particularly interested here in the *Transgressive*, that figure which *joins* two antithetical terms, which cuts a 'passage through the wall of the Antithesis' (p. 27). An example of this is when, in *Sarrasine*, physical contact occurs between castrato and young woman. There is, to Barthes, an 'explosive shock' here as old meets young, female meets male, animate meets inanimate. The resulting 'paroxysm of transgression' (p. 65), breaching of symbolic poles, resonates through the entire text.

In *S/Z*, Barthes traces the interweavings of these codes which 'frequently heard simultaneously . . . endow the text with a kind of plural quality (the text is actually polyphonic)' (p. 30). Barthes' method is one which defamiliarizes. In showing how 'realist' literature is *constructed* from a set of culturally accepted codes, he makes our use of the equation 'realism equals "life-like" or "natural"' henceforth impossible. Barthes writes in both a tricky and highly sophisticated manner and Vincent Leitch, quite rightly to my mind, calls *S/Z* 'quite simply . . . one of the most celebrated masterworks of contemporary criticism'.[24]

While not attempting to match Barthes' literary pyrotechnics, I wish to show how any reader can use his '*step-by-step* method' (p. 12) to approach and interrupt a text, and in doing so separate it off from that 'ideology of totality' which Barthes so distrusts, opening up productive meanings which move in the direction of pluralism rather than attempting to nail the text down to any one fixed meaning. As exemplar, I wish to take just the opening passages from Henry James' *The Portrait of a Lady* (1881) and Edith Wharton's *The House of Mirth* (1905) and subject them to a Barthesian analysis. My particular intention here is to take two realist texts, both concerned with a central female protagonist, one written by a man and one by a woman – a woman, moreover, who has been seen as a 'lesser version' of that same male writer. For to compare her stories and novels with those of James is, one critic has remarked, to help 'define the scope of both: her not inconsiderable talent is dwarfed by his'.[25] Such shrinkage is reflected in their respective places in the American literary canon. In taking as my principle the Bakhtinian one of culture being composed of a number of voices in conflict, I wish to see what differences start emerging in laying one text against another, exposing the codes by which they operate. In doing this, I hope to show not just the interweaving of codes which compose each separate text, but also the productive exchange occurring between texts which makes any notion of a previously established literary hierarchy seem both limited and limiting. I will follow Barthes' practice in terms of textual layout, re-citing each unit of text before commenting on it; stopping at various points to make more extended comments on particular issues in my 'divagations'.

II

(1) *The Portrait of a Lady* * The title introduces us to the narrative and immediately raises questions. Who is this lady? (HER. Enigma 1). Enigma firmly answered by authoritative (authoritarian) narrator on p. 99: 'our heroine'. Her status has, in fact, already been textually revealed in James' *Preface* written for the 1908 *New York Edition* of the novel. ** REF. Code of Authors. An introduction to a literary text written some quarter of a century after its first publication: James retrospectively frames his work as indeed he frames his 'lady' within that work. The right to rewrite, supplement the text. *** REF. Code of Art. The Portrait, something static and framed. How then is the narrative (dynamic by definition) brought into being ('My . . . desire . . . to place my treasure right', preface, p. x)? Placing his 'treasure' in context (that of Europe, of the other characters) allows the narrative to proceed: 'they [Touchett, Osmond, Merle, etc.] were the numbered pieces of my puzzle'. The differences between narrative art and portraiture are here suggested, as is a further enigma. **** HER.

Enigma 2: 'Well, what will she *do*? (p. xiv). ***** SEM. Refinement; to be a lady is to be an 'object of chivalrous devotion'. The distance and 'difference between feudal society and bourgeois society, index and sign' (Barthes, p. 40) is suggested in the use of this term. That woman who rules over subjects and to whom obedience is due, the lady of feudal society, is here replaced by a different type of 'lady': the term here merely designates 'manners, habits and sentiment'. The 'meaningful regime of the old society' (Barthes) gives way to that which indicates wealth. Nobility gives way to fortune. 'The signs are wild', in Barthes' terminology, as the 'consecration of origin' is replaced by an indicator (wealth) which anyone can come to possess. The 'bourgeois sign' money replaces the feudal index. The confusion of realms between index and sign is suggested in the presentation of Countess Gemini. Her title is the product only of her financial coin (p. 280). Her social coin, though, is valueless; her 'circulation' restricted due to the mismanagement of her 'improprieties' (p. 279). One definition of 'lady' clashes directly with another.

DIVAGATION I.   THE PORTRAIT
(Divagations to be signalled from henceforth by Roman numerals)

The 'pictorial code' (p. 55), as Barthes calls it, is pre-eminent in realist literature, and he himself includes a divagation on exactly this subject. Ralph, speaking of Isabel's unexpected entry on to the scene of his life as an 'entertainment of a high order' overtly refers to this code, compares her arrival to 'suddenly . . . receiv[ing] a Titian, by the post, to hang on my wall' (p. 63). Isabel is here related to a prior 'depicted copy of the real'.

Is the Titian Ralph has in mind (REF. Psychology. Décor expressive of desire) *Sacred and Profane Love*: on the left 'a richly dressed female figure with jewels at her waist and flowers in her lap, who represents the love of wordly things'; to her right '*amor celestis* untrammeled by earthly possessions, holds the burning lamp of Divine Love'?[26] If so, the argument between Merle and Isabel concerning the former's 'great respect for *things* . . . one's garments . . . are . . . expressive' and Isabel's response that 'nothing that belongs to me is any measure of me' (p. 201), would suggest a replication of such a model. The analogy between Ralph's face and a 'lighted lantern' (p. 337) would put his love in the category of 'sacred', rather than 'profane'. Or is there erotic wish fulfilment implicit here? A reference to *The Three Ages of Man*? In the right foreground young nude male in the peak of physical condition, his genitals covered by a thin piece of material (Ralph has to protect his 'sensitive organ' p. 40, too: his peakiness results from those damaged lungs which cause him to winter abroad), looks passionately at the clothed girl, pipes in hand, who evidently shares his desire. In right foreground, sleeping babies and a cherub; in right mid-distance an old man, eyes and head downcast, holding two skulls. As Ralph says, he should be in love with Isabel 'if certain things were different' (p. 181). Is Ralph's real status encoded in the figure of the old man, nearing the end of his life, in contact with death; his erotic ideal in that of the young curly-haired lover?

This is speculation. Other Titians may be in Ralph's mind. It is though the reference to a prior model that is vital here. Immediately 'the portrait' is mentioned, the reader is drawn into a web of replications: no coincidence that the two most recent Penguin editions of the novel have Robert Henri and Edmund Tarbell portraits on their front covers. Isabel Archer's portrait like that of the old man in *Sarrasine*, 'copies a painted model. (SYM. Replication of Bodies)', all those portraits of 'ladies' available for our spectatorial consumption: the whole history of elegant women's portraiture.

Barthes examines the relation between realist literature and that pictorial code it has as its base. Using his terms we can see Isabel as positioned within 'the empty frame which the realistic author always carries with him' (p. 54): Let me show you *this* picture, *this* view. Isabel, this framed object, is then removed from the frame to be described through language: one code (realistic literature) refers to another code (portraiture) which in turn refers to framed, and partial *copy* of one view of reality (this is the Isabel *I* see, *I* paint). This process of piling 'code upon code' is realism. For Barthes it 'copies what is already a copy' (p. 55).

Isabel's portrait, then, is the 'replication of a model set forth by that code of the arts' (Code of Portraiture). The woman copies the painting; her beauty is referred to a pictorial cultural

code. 'The origin of the desire is the . . . painting' (p. 33). In
the realist novel, this portrait is built up through language.
Those semes (lady: grace, dignity, etc.) and references (Titian)
which attach themselves to Isabel are amassed as we read
until 'an image of movement, an image of life' is produced:
the portrait. Barthes points once more to the codes through
which literary meaning is produced. Our reading of Isabel's
portrait is – to transfer Barthes' words to this context – 'a
cubist reading: the meanings are cubes [blocks of meaning],
piled up, altered, juxtaposed, and yet feeding on each other,
whose shift produces the entire space of a painting' (p. 61).
Isabel is not, then, 'pre-existent' in any way: standing there
complete before the reader. Rather, as we respond to those
codes (semic and referential) which bear connotations of grace,
beauty, etc., so our 'picture' of her is produced.

(2) *Under certain circumstances there are few hours in life more agreeable
than the hour dedicated to the ceremony known as afternoon tea.* * ACT.
Afternoon tea: I: the discourse gives an overall name to what
it will proceed to detail. ** REF. Englishness. This code is
enchained to a covert literary code (Pope, Jane Austen, etc.).
Afternoon tea is seen as epitome of English social life (***
SEM. Agreeable)[27] and this secular activity is filtered through
theological discourse – L. caerimonia, religious worship (****
REF. The Book of Religious Practice) – to suggest the ritualistic
and fixed nature of the code governing bourgeois activity.
***** HER. Enigma 3: What are these *certain circumstances*
that make this *ceremony* so *agreeable*? An implicit answer is
contained within the discourse: those arising from wealth,
leisure. See Thorstein Veblen's *The Theory of the Leisure Class*
(1899): 'the signature of one's pecuniary strength should be
written in characters which he who runs may read'.[28] Signs
of pecuniary strength abound in this first paragraph of the
novel: this sign system can be easily read by even the most
casual of readers ('he who runs').

II. EQUIVOCATION: DOUBLE UNDERSTANDING

How is the reader to receive the information contained
in this second lexia. Ironically or not? Is the *ceremony* of
afternoon tea subject to narrative celebration here, or does the

hyperbolic language, the use of religious discourse, connote irony concerning the fixed and thus sterile nature of English social institutions? Equivocation 'results from two voices, received on an equal basis': the reader 'must be imagined as being divided into . . . two zones of listening' (p. 145). Barthes describes literatures as 'arts of "noise"' explaining that such *double understandings* and 'countercommunications' imbue, in varying density, all classic ('polysemic') writing. He states revealingly, 'the reader is an accomplice, not of this or that character, but of the discourse itself insofar as it plays on the division of reception, the impurity of communication: the discourse, and not one or another of its characters, is the only *positive* hero of the story' (p. 145).

(3) *There are circumstances in which, whether you partake of the tea or not – some people of course never do –* * ACT. 'To narrate': I: to receive the story. Narrator addresses reader. Whilst *you* can substitute generically for *one*, it at the same time encourages reader to situate her/himself within, as well as without, textual frame, and so encourages a reading of the scene as 'natural', unmediated. ** SYM: Wealth and leisure as opposed to what? Poverty? Industry? The text remains silent on the specificity of what is here *Excluded*.

III.   ABSENT BASE

It is possible to begin to fill this vacuum (what is excluded) by reference to Henrietta Stackpole and Caspar Goodwood (REF. Americanness. Hard work ethic allowing little or no time for 'waste' of time, or money). The referential codes which govern the text, however, limit themselves largely to the province of high bourgeois cultural forms: what is absent is their proletarian or industrial manifestation. Descriptions of London life are confined to Winchester Square, the British Museum, the Abbey, the Tower, the National Gallery, Ralph's club, etc. This is a tourist's London, the London of the gentility, that of a cultural élite. The poor, when mentioned, are referred to in terms of their *exclusion* from this context: 'two small children from a neighbouring slum . . . poked their faces between the rusty rails of the enclosure' (p. 144), that enclosure being the Winchester Square gardens in which Isabel and Ralph sit.

Ralph apologizes for the fact 'that there wasn't a creature in town'. Henrietta sharply reminds him:

> There's no one here, of course, but three or four millions of people. What is it you call them – the lower-middle class? They're only the population of London, and that's of no consequence (p. 138).

Overtly 'of no consequence' to the narrative, this class, however, and the context of industrialization and modernization in which they must be located, is the largely absent pole in the Leisure/Work, Wealth/Penury, symbolic antitheses of the text. Notions of economic exchange and trade (see, too, the functioning of the related symbolic code: SYM. Aesthetic versus Commercial: an opposition whose *transgression* is one of major import to the text) are both recurrent and important. The hierarchic scale of socio-economic levels, one of the networks around which the narrative is constructed, have as *covert* base that 'ugliness and obscurity' which 'reality' is for those at the lower end of that spectrum; the different representations of exchange value suggested by the young lady of James' *In the Cage* (1898) who, in the first weeks of her job as telegraphist:

> had often gasped at the sums people were willing to pay for the stuff they transmitted – the 'much love's, the 'awful' regrets, the compliments and wonderments and vain, vague gestures that cost the price of a new pair of boots.[29]

Edith Wharton in her novel will make such a covert base overt.

(4) *the situation is in itself delightful. Those that I have in mind in beginning to unfold this simple history* * ACT. 'To narrate': 2: to start to tell the story. ** REF. Code of Authors. Use of self-depreciation: Her story is complex; anything but 'simple'.

(5) *offered an admirable setting to an innocent pastime. The implements of the little feast had been disposed upon the lawn of an old English country house in what I should call the perfect middle of a splendid summer afternoon.* * ACT. Afternoon tea: 2: nomination of context, initial detailing of immediate scene. ** SEM. Innocence and perfection. Both the *ceremony* and the setting

bear utopian connotations. REF. Book of Literature: Genesis. Gardencourt, despite its (transgressive) deaths, is presented as Edenic. As location, it is opposed in particular to Osmond's villa with its 'massively crossbarred' (p. 227) windows; to that symbolic 'house of darkness . . . of dumbness . . . of suffocation' (p. 429) in which Isabel is to be imprisoned – thus SYM. Gardencourt/Osmond's house antithesis.[30] As we notice here, codes overlap and at times blend: 'the five codes create a kind of network, a *topos* through which the entire text passes (or rather, in passing, becomes text)'.[31] *** REF. Book of Religious Practice: *feast*. As with *ceremony* above, secular and theological discourse conjoin; the words signify in both spheres. **** SYM. Nature/Culture antithesis. The *lawn* itself is a place of transgression where the supposed 'irreducibility' of the Antithesis is breached. In this 'tamed' setting, the *implements* of the tea *ceremony* (with its rigid cultural formalities) will be plied. Isabel will finally flee from this transgressive sphere, and the utopian connotations associated with it (the place where nature/culture difference is effaced) at the text's conclusion. This flight is a direct response to Goodwood's kiss.

IV. GREEN LAWN: WHITE LIGHTNING

It is on these green lawns that Isabel receives Goodwood's 'kiss . . . like white lightning', darts away to the door which may lead back to Osmond's house of suffocation. The mutilating force of sexuality (SEM. mutilation) intrudes on Edenic landscape. The metaphor used to describe the kiss suggests transgressive touch: male sexuality as, in Habegger's words, 'an aggressive act of possession that seeks to deprive the woman of her independence and stamp her with the man's own identity'.[32] SEM. Sexual fear. Whose metaphor is this? Whose voice expresses this fear? The narrator's? Or Isabel, the focalizer's? Voices dissolve the one into the other here. Sexuality is certainly a central absence in this text. Madame Merle informs Rosier and the reader that Isabel 'had a poor little boy, who died two years ago, six months after his birth' (p. 361). This is the only reference, bar the mutilating kiss, to the breaching of Isabel's self-containment; to childbirth and the breaking of mother-child bond which must have been traumatic. Why is this presented through a focalizer several times

removed from the immediate event? The dis-ease regarding
sexuality in the text is suggested by the brevity of its mention,
the traumatic nature of its results.

(6) *Part of the afternoon had waned, but much of it was left, and
what was left was of the finest and rarest quality. Real dusk would
not arrive for many hours; but the flood of summer light had begun to
ebb, the air had grown mellow, the shadows were long upon the smooth,
dense turf. They lengthened slowly, however, and the scene expressed that
sense of leisure still to come which is perhaps the chief source of one's
enjoyment of such a scene at such an hour. From five o'clock to eight
is on certain occasions a little eternity; but on such an occasion as this
the interval could be only an eternity of pleasure.* * SEM. The time
and the place (*the scene*) combine to form special associations
of pleasure and contentment. ** SYM. The paradox contained
in the phrase *little eternity* suggests the tension between the utopian and static (the effect of timelessness) and the timebound
(shadows lengthening) attached to this whole symbolic locale,
Gardencourt. Its utopian connotations are threatened not just
by the intrusion of sexuality (see last divagation) but also by
death (Ralph's; his father's).

(7) *The persons concerned in it were taking their pleasure quietly,
and they were not of the sex which is supposed to furnish the regular
votaries of the ceremony I have mentioned.* * ACT. Afternoon tea.
3: Initial detailing of participants. ** REF. Defect in code
governing bourgeois ritual. *** HER. Enigma 4. Who are
these persons? A question soon to be resolved. Enigma 5.
Where are the women?

V.   WHO WILL BE MOTHER?

In the stereotype of that English cultural institution, the
taking of afternoon tea, the major *votaries of the ceremony*
are traditionally female, figures of domesticity and comfort.
Here the absence of the mother raises questions concerning
traditional gender roles in a patriarchal society that recur
throughout the text.[33] Mrs Touchett – the woman who should
be 'high priestess' of the opening tableau – has removed
herself from patriarchal control. The 'collection of semes'
(p. 191) that compose her person (Barthes sees 'character as

Proper Name: the semic raw material . . . *fills* the name with adjectives') come to include: obstinate, independent, solitary, unimaginative, stiff, firm, honest, narrow-minded. Her denial of traditional gender roles, her cutting of traditional familial bondings, thus appears to bear mainly negative connotations.

A contest for sexual supremacy, a questioning of gender roles, runs throughout the text (SYM: Male/Female antithesis) and it is to be noted that Mr Touchett, Ralph, and even Osmond, who 'house-keeps', collects 'old curtains and crucifixes' (p. 255), have traits which must be categorized under SEM. Femininity.[34] It is to be noted too that Isabel's purchasing power enables her to modify the patriarchal system. Her 'fortune' gives her the opportunity to pick and choose among the goods on the marriage market; she becomes 'serious' (p. 210) when she acquires the 'power' this money brings her.[35] Among the familiar 'commodities of the age of advertisement' (pp. 246–7) – at least in the expatriate world which the text explores – is the young American girl with money who, as Merle *advertises* to Osmond, is available and 'on the market'. Isabel's wealth, though, gives her a stake in the exchange: what will she find worth the spending of her money? The irony, of course, is that she purchases commodification, becomes (she is talking about her mind here, but the quote can be read synecdochally) 'a pretty piece of property for a proprietor [Osmond] already far-reaching' (p. 432).

The male/female antithesis is being continually breached in this text. Though marriage is sited at the centre of the bourgeois social network, and will safely contain even the seemingly autonomous Henrietta at the text's conclusion, deep unease about the institution (and concerning gender roles generally) is revealed in the novel. Isabel metaphorically sites herself revealingly in saying she is not afraid of men, 'I'm as used to them as the cook to the butcher-boys' (p.245). Traditional female role (cook) carries connotations here of authority and power, but her dismissive reference to those seen principally as antagonists carries its own unrecognized assumption of their capacity for violence, harm, 'butchery'. Sexuality, Power, Economics, Gender Roles: the text is deeply questioning on these issues. And to come back to the title of my divagation, 'Who will be Mother?' Not Isabel; her child dies. Not Merle; she is 'awfully careful' never to 'betray herself'

(p. 547) as the mother of the Pansy who doesn't even like her (p. 545). Countess Gemini has 'no children; she had lost three within a year of their birth' (p. 280). As for Mrs Touchett, Ralph – though of course he *is* her son – often says to himself that 'his father . . . was the more motherly; his mother, on the other hand, was paternal, and even . . . gubernatorial' (p. 37). The male/female antithesis provides one very complex and interesting site of entry to this text.

(8) *The shadows on the perfect lawn were straight and angular*; * REF. Pictorial code. Framed view of reality. 'Blocks of meaning' being 'piled up' to construct a representation of a landscape painting with figures foregrounded. Gradual depiction of the elements in the frame; a gradual sharpening of focus. Shift in spatial juxtapositions from large masses (afternoon light) to small, highlighted, detail: *large cup*.

(9) *they were the shadows of an old man sitting in a deep wicker-chair near the low table on which the tea had been served, and of two younger men strolling to and fro, in desultory talk, in front of him.* * HER. What is the relation between the men? Why is one static, the others strolling? To be quickly answered. ** SEM. Leisured; there is no hurry anywhere here – this is stressed by the whole description so far. *** REF. Pictorial code: it is the *shadows* which are described: use of delay in reaching the human centre of composition. **** ACT. To stroll. 1.

(10) *The old man had his cup in his hand; it was an unusually large cup, of a different pattern from the rest of the set and painted in brilliant colours.* * ACT. Afternoon tea. 4. Process of taking it. ** REF. Defect in code governing bourgeois ritual. Why has the old man not got a similar cup to the others? According to this code all the pieces in the tea-set should be similar; this rich note of colour is disjunctive. SYM. Patriarchal power, 'father's cup', and/or REF. Americanness. As an alien he does not mind disrupting ritual; is not strictly governed by codes of English culture. This introduces *** SYM. American/European antithesis. Another symbolic entry point to the text, though – as here, where small eccentric gesture is largely contained by its framing context – this antithesis resists easy

polarizations. All the major characters (bar Warburton) are American. Osmond who looks like 'a demoralized prince in exile' (p. 244) is really only 'a vague, unexplained American' (p. 249). Mrs Touchett is described by Countess Gemini as 'an old Florentine . . . Her face is very much like some faces in the early pictures' (p. 258) (REF. History of European Art) but both women again are Americans. 'American' does, however, come to mean *empty of meaning*, at least in those last examples, meaning being defined in terms of European models and images alone.

VI.   INDEX, SIGN, MONEY: A BRIEF ADDENDUM

We will soon discover the old man to be a banker; one of the younger men to be a Lord. Warburton is a nobleman: in Barthes' terms his textual presence is *index* of 'the meaningful regime of the old society' despite his own awareness of an anachronistic status. Touchett, however, is a banker. His function is symbolic; his sign is money. In the text to come, the sign – not the index – will predominate. The sign has, unlike the index, no origin: no fixed nature. 'In the sign . . . the two elements [nobility and wealth] *interchange*, signified and signifier revolving in an endless process: what is bought can be sold' (p. 40). Buying and selling directly affect status and position in the free flowing bourgeois world of this text.

(11) *He disposed of its contents with much circumspection, holding it for a long time close to his chin, with his face turned to the house.* * SEM. Caution; Sense of Ownership. This riverfront house with its distinguished history has 'passed into the careful keeping of [this] shrewd American banker' (p. 6). He has used his wealth to buy into what was once a traditional and hierarchical world (see previous divagation). This, once a house where 'the great Elizabeth' had stayed overnight, still conveys the sense of 'well-ordered privacy in the centre of a "property"' (p. 54). This privacy/property has now been purchased at 'bargain' price (p. 6) by a representative of the world of commerce, not of the aristocracy: a banker, and one who is moreover quite alien to the world of English traditionalism. ** SYM. American/European antithesis and its transgression.

(12) *His companions had either finished their tea or were indifferent to their privilege; they smoked cigarettes as they continued to stroll.* * ACT. To stroll. 2. ** SEM. Leisure, Privilege. *** REF. Book of Popular Wisdom. If cigarette smoking carries here connotations of pleasure, idleness, male companionship, its dangers should not go unrecognized. *What a Young Woman Ought to Know* (1898) will quote Dr Pidduch on:

> the hysteria, the hypochondriasis, the consumption, the dwarfish deformities, the suffering lives and early deaths of inveterate smokers [which] bear ample testimony to the feebleness of constitution which they have inherited.[36]

Given that Ralph – one of the strollers – has a very feeble constitution, and almost died once before of that 'advanced stage of pulmonary disorder' (p. 182) from which he suffers, one can retrospectively note of him, SEM. Indifference to physical needs; lack of care of physical self.

(13) *One of them, from time to time, as he passed, looked with a certain attention at the elder man, who, unconscious of observation,* * HER. What is the relation between the two men? Why does one regard the other with a certain attention? We will shortly learn the bond is that of father and son, and that Mr Touchett is dying (SYM. Edenic/Timebound). ** SEM. Illness. Protectiveness. Ralph plays a maternal role here, adopting in his turn his father's 'motherly' stance in the latter's time of need. Both men are however 'lame ducks' (p. 9). *** SYM. Male/Female antithesis; weakness/strength antithesis.

(14) *rested his eyes upon the rich red front of his dwelling.* * SEM. Wealth, possessiveness. 'What a sense of property!' (p. 41) Ralph says in describing his mother's attitude to her niece. The wider application of this phrase suggests another point of recurrent entry into this text.

VII. WHO OWNS WHOM?

'She's my niece; she's not his', Ralph's mother says of Isabel. Ralph, too, shares this proprietorial sense. He wishes 'to put money in her purse' (p. 183) to allow Isabel to meet her imagination's requirements. She is described as being something in the nature of a business investment for Ralph. Mrs Touchett notes that he talks 'as if she were a yard of calico' (p. 44). He speaks of 'risk' and 'calculation' (p. 186). He is playing the market, investing in Isabel (without her knowledge) to buy himself 'amusement' (p. 184). His profit comes in different forms than his father's but he is still a banker's son, looking for a good return from his investment.

In fact, loss not profit results. His investment results in his own 'ruin' as well as Isabel's. For Isabel exchanges her fortune (an ambiguous signifier, this) for Osmond's hand in marriage; spends out on his 'connoisseurship' (p. 262), his 'adorable taste' (p. 242), his 'wilful renunciation' of the vulgar in favour of the 'curious and precious' (pp. 265 and 263). She fails completely to realize, though, that he is a dealer in the commercial as well as the aesthetic sense of the word; that he is buying too. His 'profit' (p. 239) in the exchange is both commercial and aesthetic (these are inextricably bound one to the other in the bourgeois world; the word 'precious' cuts for him both ways): 'seventy thousand pounds . . . *en écus bien comptés*' (p. 243) as well as another 'figure', Isabel herself, to place 'in his collection of choice objects' (p. 304) alongside his 'autograph of Michelangelo' (p. 275). In not seeing this central fact, Isabel, who has the wealth to buy at liberty in the world's market, finds herself instead well and truly 'sold'; another of those 'fine pieces' which Osmond annexes.

(15) *The house that rose beyond the lawn was a structure to repay such consideration and was the most characteristic object in the peculiarly English picture I have attempted to sketch.* * ACT. To narrate: 3: to complete initial description. Narration here described by analogy to the painterly. ** REF. Code of Art. Pictures of English landscape, English teatimes, English country houses. Sterile: 'a nauseating mixture of common opinions, a smothering layer of received ideas' (Barthes, p. 206). Fixed conceptions of a series of genres, *characteristic*, *peculiarly English*, here signed, sealed, delivered, framed. It is what is *uncharacteristic* in this picture which prevents it entering completely the realm of the 'already written', the already painted.

*

What becomes evident in employing a Barthesian approach to *decompose* the text, to show how its 'reality effects' are created, is how plural the number of entrances are, how vast the number of networks, even in a supposedly 'readerly' text. Such an approach moves away from an *authoritative* declaration concerning any single determinable textual meaning and rather opens up a way of reading non-hierarchically. 'Literature' becomes not the voice of any single truth but rather becomes 'intentional cacography' (p. 9), composed of a *chain* of systems, a *proliferation* of layerings, allowing many meanings to emerge.

III

I wish now, somewhat formulaically, to examine the title and first paragraph of *The House of Mirth* (1905) in a similar manner to that used in approaching *The Portrait of a Lady*. This will provide a way of comparing the types of layerings that appear in the two novels, and will be useful as a way of enquiring whether there are differing intersections to the codes which compose them; whether the types of code patterings which recur within them move in separate directions. Both texts – though a quarter of a century separates them – explore the construction of femininity, the way the female subject is called into being in relation to what Mary Schriber calls 'the culture's horizon of expectations'.[37] The fact that one is written by a woman writer who did not share membership of the dominant patriarchal grouping would lead me to expect that, even within the limits of my exploration of the texts, crucial distinctions in approach, in the siting of the heroine in relation to the symbolic codes which operate, will emerge. My brief analysis will, I believe, point towards both the differences and the similarities of the two texts.

(1) *The House of Mirth* * Book titles, like other textual components, are designed to key into a reader's prior knowledge and expectations. Here, Wharton refers to Ecclesiastes (REF.

Biblical Code) – 'The heart of the wise is in the house of mourning; but the heart of fools is in the house of mirth'. The novel may then be seen in terms both of the insubstantiality of all human activities (the general tenor of Ecclesiastes)[38] and in more immediate terms of Wharton's satiric denunciation of a particular society 'of irresponsible pleasure-seekers'.[39]

However the title operates on another level, too, connecting with the type of abstract and allegorical model used earlier by Dickens in *Bleak House* (1853), later by Galsworthy in *The Inn of Tranquillity* (1912). James tended to use titles which referred more directly to his protagonists and which drew attention to their representative status: *The Europeans* (1878), *The Bostonians*, (1886), etc. Is the house of Wharton's title to be located in the text (as in Hawthorne's *House of the Seven Gables*, 1851)? What does the *mirth* signify? HER. Enigma 1. Relation of novel's title to its content? For Lily Bart, central protagonist, her very identity depends on the organic relationship between self and environmental background: she 'could not figure herself as anywhere but in a drawing-room, diffusing elegance as a flower sheds perfume' (p. 100). The houses she graces differ in décor and status. Initially, she is seen at Bellomont with its 'deer-hound and two or three spaniels doz[ing] luxuriously . . . on the crimson carpet' (p. 25). As in James, décor signifies wealth and status (or lack of it) throughout the narrative. This is true of realist novels generally which 'naturalize meaning' (Barthes, p. 23) by close attention to the details and furnishings of its bourgeois world, thus depending for their effects on the solidity and 'solidarity' of their represented world.[40]

Lily has no *house* of her own. Her aunt's house, her temporary base, 'in its state of unnatural immaculateness and order, was as dreary as a tomb' (pp. 99–100), its funereal discomforts a reflection of its inhabitant's glacial attitude to life. Lily herself is located in a succession of different drawing-rooms, different houses, which reflect her own decline in social status. Unlike Isabel Archer, whose marital status gives her a home and 'customary place' (p. 366), however uncomfortable, to which she may choose to return at the novel's end, Lily drifts between houses, 'through layers of social strata, none of which provides a foothold, a place to put down roots'.[41] At the narrative's end there is a particularly swift move from the gaudy tastelessness of the Emporium Hotel, where as companion to

Mrs Hatch, Lily finds herself in a world 'over-heated, over-upholstered, and over-fitted with mechanical appliances for the gratification of fantastic requirements' (p. 274), to the boarding house with its 'blistered brown stone front', 'muddy vestibule' (p. 293) and lingering smells, in which she spends her final days.

The increasing sense of impermanency and poverty revealed in these location shifts clearly suggests an ironical element to the title. Irony, as Barthes points out, is a mark of the readerly not the writerly text. It is heavily applied in both James and Wharton, and 'acts as a signpost' (p. 44) which potentially destroys textual multivalence.[42] *Mirth* is apparent in the narrative but it is often forced and – as in its biblical source, and in *Sarrasine* – used as 'a substitute for the cry'. Lily laughs at Trenor's jokes since that is 'required' (p. 86) of her in her financially dependent status. Her friends are highly amused at Evie Van Osburgh's engagement to Gryce, so soon after the latter's interest in Lily, reacting with 'the zest of surprising destiny in the act of playing a practical joke' (p. 98). Most revealingly, when Lily's father reveals his bankruptcy, it is when she is asking if she can order more lilies-of-the-valley for the dinner table: 'suddenly he looked at his daughter and laughed' (p. 32). Laughter here is a cry which, to use Barthes' words, 'breaches the wall of the Antithesis, removes from the coin the duality of reverse and obverse; erases the paradigmatic slash mark' (p. 49) which here 'reasonably' separates wealth and poverty, life and death. Mirth leads in the direction of the abolition of meaning, the fall from material 'grace' (SYM. Material/Moral antithesis) – signals the 'practical joke' to be textually played at Lily's expense: as she suffers in the narrative her unreasonable destiny.

(2) *Selden paused in surprise.* * REF. Typology of Nomenclature. Selden is male. By cultural convention, identification by surname alone applies only to the male gender. ** SYM. Male/Female antithesis. Such a mode of identification discourages intimacy. Connotations of emotional reserve are implicit. Of Selden, Diana Trilling says he 'moves toward Lily from behind a cruel shield of emotional self-protection'.[43] *** HER. Who is Selden? What is his status in the narrative? Why his surprise?

(3) *In the afternoon rush of the Grand Central Station* * SEM.
New York. Locus of *modernization*. One of those 'dynamic
new landscape[s]' which Marshall Berman associates with
nineteenth-century modernity:

> a landscape of steam engines, automatic factories, rail-
> roads, vast new industrial zones; of teeming cities that have
> grown overnight, often with dreadful human consequences;
> of daily newspapers, telegraphs, telephones . . . of an ever-
> expanding world market embracing all . . . [44]

Grand Central Station immediately connotes the machine,
the crowd, the very conditions of modern life: connotations
which are entirely different from that London imaged as
cultural museum in *The Portrait of a Lady*. Issues of adaptation
and survival in a modernized environment will foreground
themselves here in a way unforeseen or avoided in the
earlier text. Lily will move from a position where, like Lady
Skiddaw, she can make an occasional 'dip into "the street"',
essentially Isabel Archer's position too, to one where as 'a
bread-winner' (p. 297), 'a worker among workers' (p. 301), she
has to negotiate these streets in an entirely different way.
Her failure to do so relates to a turn of the century use of
Darwinian discourse. REF. The Book of Evolution: 'Inherited
tendencies had combined with early training to make her the
highly specialized product she was: an organism as helpless
out of its narrow range as the sea-anemone torn from the
rock' (p. 301).

(4) *his eyes had been refreshed by the sight of Miss Lily Bart.*
* ACT. 1. Social engagement (the taking of tea) between
Selden and Lily: initial encounter. ** HER. Who is Lily
Bart? What is her relationship with Selden? *** SEM. Marital
status: with that *Miss,* marriageability is announced as a subject at the commencement of the text. The reader will soon
be asking what Lily has got to *barter*? Her 'little gold purse'
is 'almost empty' (p. 27). It is her face which is her potential
fortune:

> She remembered how her mother, after they had lost
> their money, used to say to her with a kind of fierce

vindictiveness: 'But you'll get it all back – you'll get it all back, with your face' (p. 28).

**** SYM. Male/Female antithesis. In a patriarchal culture, women (and especially penniless women) are defined in terms of their relationship to men, in terms of what Elaine Millard calls their 'degree of desirability'.[45] The problems and insufficiencies of such forms of female definition have led to the creation of a woman's literature, the landscape of which is, in Elaine Showalter's phrase, 'strewn with dead female bodies'.[46] ***** REF. Book of Flowers and Women. Women constructed as vulnerable and fragile. Lilies are associated, according to Cynthia Griffin Wolff, with the 'rarefied virtue' of womanhood in 'Art Nouveau', the style 'synonymous with decorative elegance' in Edith Wharton's America.[47] (REF. Code of Art). The use of such identifying motifs suggests deep confusions concerning the relationship between art, nature and social reality.

I. ENGAGED IN THE TANGLE

If Lily is imaged as 'hot-house' bloom (p. 150), she is also, we have seen, imaged as sea-anemone. Metaphoric slip accompanies the disruption of the garden or conservatory/ (sea) wilderness antithesis as Lily's 'protected' status is removed. Both images, though, carry connotations of vulnerability. What is the rock from which, in this latter environment, she is torn? (REF. Code of Aquatic Biology). Money? A male partner? Social respectability? In fact, all three combine to form Patriarchy (SYM. Male/Female antithesis): a society in which 'to be lady-like' is *de rigueur* to share the sea-anemone's qualities; attractive but many-tentacled and devouring, dependent for life on the stable rock to which it clings.

Henrietta Stackpole in *The Portrait of a Lady* may be, as Judith Fryer asserts, more 'a vehicle for humour than . . . a model for what a truly liberated woman ought to be'.[48] James does, however, give a sense of a number of 'options open to women' through his use of 'female satellite figures'[49]; not only Henrietta, but also Mrs Touchett and Madame Merle. Such

options are reduced in Wharton. Mrs Peniston has wealth, but
her life seems frozen. Gerty Farish is a career woman (a social
worker) but Lily is not bred for these working conditions; this
is not a 'climate she could breathe in' (p. 26). Gerty, moreover,
is judged unmarriageable by Lily (p. 7) and certainly does not
fulfil standard definitions of the lady-like, with her 'mean and
shabby surroundings', 'the squalid compromises of poverty'
(p. 26) with which she is linked.

Wharton's version of sexual difference in this novel is far
more constrictive than James'. Isabel Archer's 'free expansion'
(p. 51) is that of one who is 'at large, not confined by the
conditions, not engaged in the tangle' (p. x). Judith Fryer talks
of her 'complete independence'.[50] Only when she chooses to
enter the Machiavellian province (p. 259) of Osmond does full
entanglement occur.[51] Darwin, not Machiavelli, is Wharton's
model to explain the female fate. Lily is caught within the
web of larger forces from childhood on. Wharton stresses her
'whole training and habit of mind' (p. 278), the fact that she
(and Selden) are 'victim of [their] environment' (p. 152). Her
identity is much more strongly constituted than is Isabel's by
the social world of which she is a part, a world in which men
have the real power as source of monetary supply. James' sport
with the socio-sexual norm in giving Isabel the freedoms he
does are brought back into focus by Wharton's fuller stress
on the social conditions which form the female 'self'.

II. THE DIVIDED SELF

There is some one I must say goodbye to. Oh, not *you*
– we are sure to see each other again – but the Lily Bart
you knew. I have kept her with me all this time, but now
we are going to part, and I have brought her back to you
– I am going to leave her here. When I go out presently
she will not go with me. I shall like to think that she has
stayed with you – and she'll be no trouble, she'll take up
no room (p. 309).

Lily, in fact, finds herself unable to thus cast off one
of her two selves, but the price of such an inability is
death. Annette Kolodny speaks of 'the amputation of Self

from Self'[52] as a recurrent concern in women's fiction. And a feminist criticism, one of many kinds of criticism which can in Barthes' terms 'make its voice heard, which is the hearing of one of the voices of the text' (p. 15) is certainly applicable here. Lily lives, according to the codes of 'the civilization which had produced her' (p. 7), codes which emerge in two different forms.

The dominant cultural requirement of femininity is as ornamental commodity, one placed in a particular market, that of marriage. As Selden comments, 'there must be plenty of capital on the lookout for such an investment' (p. 12). Lily recognizes the need to adapt herself to fit the requirements of this role. And thus she offers a certain 'version' of herself – pious, non-smoking, non-gambling – to convince Percy Gryce that she could be for him 'the one possession in which he took sufficient pride to spend money' (p. 49). She keeps herself 'fresh and exquisite and amusing' as the 'tax' she has to pay for living '*on* the rich' (p. 266), as outlay on the prospect of becoming (through marriage) one of them. Lily's very 'identity' is paradoxically constructed on a cultural definition of womanhood as what one might call *empty space* (REF. Code of Sexual Stereotype). It is constituted by outward appearances, surfaces, 'the external finish of life' (p. 25). Cynthia Griffin Wolff describes this 'pernicious form of femininity':

> Who am I? I am the sum of the impressions I have made upon other people; I am only what others think of me; I am valuable only insofar as I can please others. This is femininity as the art of 'being'.[53]

It is Lily's physical beauty that makes her valuable in this social world. She ornaments it as fine surface. Selden, we are told, 'watched her hand, *polished as a bit of old ivory*, with its slender pink nails, and the sapphire bracelet slipping over her wrist' (my stress, p. 7). Lily is formed by, and acts according to, a social discourse which is, in Barthes' term, 'murderous' (p. 148). Unable to sustain it, her death will finally result.

Lily is unable to sustain such an 'identity' exactly because of its murderousness. For the clear suggestion is that if she uses her 'plastic possibilities' (p. 237) to negotiate her way to a stable position inside the 'charmed circle' (p. 50) of upper-class American life, fully enters this 'inner Paradise' (p. 240) in the only way available to her, through marriage, then her symbolic death will occur. For to marry is to exchange fluidity for fixed identity (as wife, as trinket, or social ornament); a rigid and life-denying crystallization of 'self'. The charmed circle she would join reeks of death (SEM. death-like).

If Lily were to marry Gryce, use her charms to enter this circle, 'bridal spoils' (p. 89) would result, but she would be spoiled in turn. Would she become one of those women she sees 'buried under their jewelry' (p. 176): an ornament collapsing under the weight of further ornamentation? Certainly, to adapt herself to Gryce's desires would be life-denying: to do so, as Lily realizes, 'on the bare chance that he might ultimately decide to do her the honour of boring her for life' (p. 25). The sterility of Gryce's world is symbolically suggested by the fact that his book collection is carefully enclosed and protected. The pleasures of these texts, which Barthes would celebrate, are not available to ready access. Rather the books are placed in 'a fire-proof annex that looked like a mausoleum' (p. 22). The world to which Lily – as socially constructed ornament – seeks entry shares this mausoleum-like quality: her aunt's drawing room resembles 'a well-kept family vault, in which the last corpse had just been decently deposited' (p. 224).

Lily's sense of her own value however is directed towards such a world, for this is the context framing her. She displays herself in its shop window despite her ability to see that its social interactions create what the narrator calls 'human automata' (p. 52). When Selden asks 'Isn't marriage your vocation? Isn't it what you're all brought up for?' she can only reluctantly answer, 'What else is there?' (p. 9).

Her construction of self according to the values of this social world is, however, (partially) challenged by Selden. For her 'free spirit' (p. 64), the very sense of plasticity and consequently possibility associated with her, resists the sense of confinement which an ornamental role carries with it. Selden projects another version of femininity, one which releases Lily from this prior sense of constriction: from her view of her beauty as an 'asset' (p. 34) which must be capitalized on due to her marginal economic status.[54] His talk of a 'republic of the spirit' (p. 68) based on 'personal freedom' is remarkably abstract, but opens the possibility of a different construction of social and gender relations.

This imaginary republic is one where 'social bonding' does not mean 'physical bondage'[55]; where questions of financial worth are, apparently, replaced by those of moral worth. It represents a 'world outside the cage' (p. 54) to Lily: the thought of it lifts her 'into a finer air' (p. 73). He gives her another value scheme round which to construct an alternative sense of herself. This value scheme it is which will lead her finally to refuse to indulge in morally deplorable tactics for purposes of social and economic advancement; will lead to her feeling that she has saved herself from 'inner destitution' even be it at the cost of 'material poverty' (p. 318).

Such apparent moral triumph is however undercut, as Cynthia Griffin Wolff so clearly shows, by the fact that Lily suffers from exactly that inner destitution she seeks to avoid. For this, the 'second' version of Lily's self, is also of an 'entirely dependent nature'. She replaces the dominant society's 'definition of her as a beautiful object' (p. 110) with Selden's, seeing 'the world (herself in particular) through *his* eyes',[56] identifying 'with his values and his artistic standards' (p. 123). And Selden would have Lily behave in a way he himself – with his 'contradictory' (p. 120) attitudes, 'the illogical self-deception of his narrowly virtuous position' (p. 123) – never dreams of doing. He defines femininity in a different way from other voices in the novel, as a 'flawless, absolutely constant embodiment of virtue' (p. 129). But his definition is one arising only from a different type of cultural code – that of the 'connoisseur' who views woman as 'moral-aesthetic object'(p. 125) – and bears no relation to practical possibility in the world presented.

His 'republic' is a fraud as revealed by his own moral compromises, his material ease. Only Lily falls for it, finding herself as a result caught between versions of self, *both* of which are imposed on her from without; hollow at the very centre. In Wolff's words, Lily's 'sense of "self" is confirmed only when she elicits reactions from others; and when she is alone (and she increasingly fears loneliness), her inner emptiness becomes terrifying, unbearable. The symptoms of this depersonalization are found throughout the novel' (p. 128). This hollowness is what constitutes her womanhood. The impossibility for Lily of reconciling her two contradictory 'selves' leads inexorably to her destiny.

(5) *It was a Monday in early September, and he was returning to his work from a hurried dip into the country*; * SYM. Town/Country antithesis and, in metonymic relation, two other antitheses, work/leisure and work/home. 'Work' primarily signals masculinity in this text (at least as it is part of the lives of the upper social world). Men provide the means for both leisure and security in a realm (home) from which they are largely absent. So Lily's 'neutral-tinted' father is a shadowy figure, who filled for her 'an intermediate space between the butler and the man who came to wind the clocks' (p. 29). Once he fails in his role as provider of resources, 'to his wife he no longer counted: he had become extinct when he ceased to fulfil his purpose' (p. 33). REF. The Book of Evolution, and role differentiations contained within it: hunter, gatherer/child minder, *house*keeper. Thus SYM. Male/Female antithesis also. In taking paid employment, Lily will transgress these class-based symbolic barriers through economic necessity. She thus becomes, in Barthes' terms, a *scandal* in abolishing the separating limits which constitute the 'pertinence' (*S/Z*, p. 65) of upper class distinctiveness in the text. In transgressing these barriers, she is consigned to the (social) 'rubbish heap' (p. 308), all distinctions lost, yearning 'for that other luxurious world' (p. 301) now denied her.

(6) *but what was Miss Bart doing in town at that season?* * ACT. Lily's activities. 1. Her presence in town. These activities will provide the focus of textual interest throughout. ** HER. The text explicitly asks a question that it will quickly answer. No snares here. The snare lies in *** SEM. Wealth. Lily as one of the wealthy classes who spend late summer 'out of town'. This is misleading as the reader soon discovers. Lily has to 'calculate and contrive' (p. 48) to maintain this appearance.

(7) *If she had appeared to be catching a train, he might have inferred that he had come on her in the act of transition between one and another of the country-houses which disputed her presence after the close of the Newport season*; * ACT. Lily's activities. 2. Speculation concerning her present siting. ** SEM. Wealth. Popularity. *** REF.

Popular wisdom. Newport, architecturally noteworthy for its 'monuments of pecuniary power'. Summer holiday place for wealthy businessmen and their families: 'an opportunity for escaping the summer heat of other places, for bathing, for boating, for riding and driving, and for many sorts of more or less expensive riot'.[57] Voice of narrator absorbs internal focalization of character: *If she had . . . he might have inferred.*

(8) *but her desultory air perplexed him.* * HER. Why such an *air?* ** SEM. wavering, unsteadiness. Though local in connotative power, this description might be seen to look forward to the 'decentraliz[ing]' (p. 151) of Lily's life which occurs in the text as a whole.

(9) *She stood apart from the crowd, letting it drift by her to the platform or the street,* * SYM. This introduces one of the most persistent paradigmatic oppositions in the text: Wealth/Poverty antithesis.

III. THE CENTRIFUGAL DANCE

Wealth and poverty are seen in antithetical terms at the text's commencement. Lily stands *apart from the crowd*; does not 'know a soul in town' though she is surrounded by a 'throng' of 'sallow-faced girls in preposterous hats, and flat-chested women struggling with paper bundles and palm-leaf fans' (pp. 4–5). Even in this early passage is the female subject fixed in terms of her relation to the money economy. The focalization is Selden's male gaze, one which links the common to the sexually undesirable.

Lily as subject is, as we have seen, one who sees herself 'as an object to be judged by others'.[58] Her subjectivity is also constituted (and the two are of course related) in relation to her position within the social formation. This seems firm; social divisions appear to have cast iron boundaries at the novel's start. Selden sees her almost as a member of a separate race from 'the herd of her sex' (p. 5) in the opening passage.

Lily recognizes the relationship between the world of wealth and that of poverty; that 'such existences as hers were pedestalled on foundations of obscure humanity' (p. 150). This comes home to her in concrete terms when she visits Gerty Farish's Girls' Club and recognizes how the girls' 'eager reachings for pleasure' echo her own. She receives as a result 'one of those sudden shocks of pity that sometimes decentralize a life' (p. 151). This is a transgressive moment when wealth and poverty touch.

The connection between the decentering of the subject and the recognition of the relations between social groups is crucial here, for these relations are not static. This breaching of the wealth/poverty antithesis looks forward to Lily's own unfixing as a subject. She moves from 'the artificially created atmosphere' of a 'hothouse filled with tropical flowers' to a 'dreary limbo of dinginess'; the 'shriek of the "elevated" and the tumult of trams and waggons' (p. 289) now her defining and confining context rather than the artificially protected environment in which as 'orchid' (p. 150) she previously blossomed (REF. Typology of Flowers and Women. The protectors are those to whom her decorative qualities have appeal).

Lily's own disruption of the wealth/poverty antithesis is, in Barthes' term, 'outrageous' in that it reveals the whole instability of social and economic boundaries in a world in which the 'contrasts' between the various circles had seemed so 'dramatic' and so 'natural' (p. 150). Her sharp social slippage, consequent recognition of life not as firmly structured within comforting (for her) layers of social difference, but as 'wild centrifugal dance' (p. 139), is symptomatic of an unacknowledged blurring of boundaries which is evident in the social world of the novel as a whole. For this is a world, as in James' *Portrait*, where sign has replaced index. Money is collapsing traditional class boundaries. The stress on the elaborate codes of the leisured world in which Lily initially moves is based on the very finest of distinctions. It is a world which sets up its own value system, placing the index of *worth* in the smallest of details: 'I think it was odd, their serving melons before the *consommé*; a wedding breakfast should always begin with *consommé*'; 'the only restaurant in Europe where they can cook peas' (p. 107, 185). The stress on such distinctions, though, cannot hide the fact that this 'aristocratic' world has no real prop on which to rest, that worth is finally not to be judged in terms of such distinctions but of money (the bourgeois sign). For Wall Street and Fifth Avenue are now indissolubly connected (p. 240) and he who has power in the money market (Rosedale) will also rise in the social one.

Prior rules of social exchange, based around member-ship of 'the class of old New Yorkers' (p. 37), collapse as Rosedale, self-made and Jewish, embarks on a revision of the boundary-lines of this society. The novel reveals, though, that the 'aristocratic' index in America is illusory, and has always, it is implicitly suggested, been contaminated by the sign of the dollar. The difference between Rosedale and the present 'lords of the only world' (p. 50) Lily cared for are minimal. Gryce's wealth is inherited; comes from his father's invention of 'a patent device for excluding fresh air from hotels' (p. 22). If Rosedale's moneymaking activities reflect a move from industrial to speculative activity, such a move is not major, and his example is followed swiftly by the members of the society he wishes to join; it is his 'tips' which result in 'big rise[s]' all round (p. 86) which Trenor describes. In fact, Rosedale's 'shoppy manner' (p. 81) merely makes explicit what is already covert in a textual world where the shop-window metaphor recurs. He is just more blatant about what he wants to buy, and the cash available to do so, and Lily finally appreciates at least the related honesty of his approach.

Barthes describes 'Parisian Gold' as 'money . . . withdrawn from the consecration of origin' (p. 40). Here the lines sepa-rating old money, belonging to the progeny of the 'industrious stock of early New York' (p. 37), and new are difficult to draw. Any categorization in terms of aristocratic and bourgeois tends, in this American context, to collapse in on itself. It is, however, clear that Lily's aunt's 'copy-book axioms' (p. 9; REF. Code of Moral Convention), which one might associate with what Barthes calls a 'moral heredity' (p. 40) based on the possession of 'old money', bear no relevance to the fluid society (morally and economically) in which Lily moves.

Considerable slippage thus exists in terms of both the material and the moral economies of the text. This world which appears so stable is based on very shaky foundations. Lily's role as what Barthes would call a type of mediating figure (p. 27) – her beauty 'the last asset in [her family's] fortunes' (p. 34), 'worthy' in terms of charm and manners,

though not of cash – is to provide the means for such
instability to be revealed. It is through her, too, that the gap
between the material and the moral economies of the text are
revealed. For Bertha Dorset uses her 'social credit' based on
an 'impregnable bank balance' to purchase Lily's own 'social
non-existence' (p. 261). Her behaviour, though, is immoral –
deceitful, aggressive, and manipulative. Indeed, the possibility
of moral worth is placed in symbolic antithesis to the power of
money. Narrative patterns develop at the text's end which have
sentimental recourse to the Code of Christian Ethics (REF.
The Holy Family: The 'blessedness' of poverty). Lily has at
this point a 'vision of the solidarity of life' which is opposed
to the 'rootless' and 'shifting' (p. 319) business it has come to
seem to her. This solidarity, which contains 'mysterious links
of kinship to all the mighty sum of human striving', is found
in Nellie Struther's kitchen, where connotations of warmth,
tenderness, motherhood, and husbandly support coalesce. The
brevity and intrusiveness of these lexias suggest this recourse
to the moral possibilities latent in working-class existence is
a very frail element in the web of narrative hermeneutics, of
cultural and symbolic codes (here SYM. Antithesis working
class/leisure class; moral life/material life) of which the text is
constructed, and the frailty of such an element is endorsed by
the earlier textual use of Mrs Haffen.

(10) *and wearing an air of irresolution which might, as he surmised, be
the mask of a very definite purpose. It struck him at once that she was
waiting for some one, but he hardly knew why the idea arrested him.*
* SEM. Irresolute/purposeful. The paradoxical nature of the
narrative here suggests the problems Selden (the focalizer at
this point) will have in assessing Lily's motives and behaviour
throughout the narrative. In fact, he consistently misinterprets
her: even the reconciliation and penitence which occur on her
death (REF. Code of Amorous Typology: the reluctant and
'fastidious' lover, p. 329) are self-deceit. For as Cynthia Griffin
Wolff points out:

Wharton measures the insufficiency of Selden's understanding of Lily by constructing her novel so that he
never does know that Lily possessed Bertha's letters to him,
never does know that she destroyed them when she might

have saved herself by using them: the very nature of this fictional world defines the mawkishness of his sorrow at her death.[59]

(11) *There was nothing new about Lily Bart, yet he could never see her without a faint movement of interest: it was characteristic of her that she always roused speculation, that her simplest acts seemed the result of far-reaching intentions.* * SEM. Enigmatic, interesting (Lily); interested (Selden). This relationship between spectatorial observer and enigmatic subject will persist through the text. Though Selden's role will change as he wavers between detachment and subjective emotional 'engagement' with Lily, she will continue to retain for him her enigmatic qualities. He constructs explanations of her actions but even at the text's conclusion these are tentative: 'That was all he knew – all he could hope to unravel of the story' (p. 329). The reader can unravel more: the narrative's use of Lily's focalization allows consistent access to her motivations and speculations. These are denied Selden.

IV. THE AROUSAL OF SPECULATION

Sexual and financial discourse coalesce here. *Speculate*: from the Latin *speculari*, to watch, spy from watchtower. See too *specere*, 'to look'; and *speculum*, 'mirror' and 'male instrument for the further penetration of the woman'.[60] What will happen to Lily cannot be separated out from the process of 'buying and selling for gain'. Who will invest what in her? What will their sexual/emotional/social profit be? Trenor invests time and money in her. Her reluctance to pay in sexual/emotional kind leads him to protest: 'the man who pays for the dinner is generally allowed to have a seat at table'. REF. Proverbial wisdom of the ages. In this case, the relationship between male economic ascendancy and related cultural expectations of subordinated and submissive femininity is clearly evident. This protest acknowledges in its use of metaphor the financial basis of Trenor's amorous demands, as does his additional response to her defensiveness: 'you . . . thought you could turn me inside out, and chuck me in the gutter like an empty purse' (p. 145). The discourse of the novel explores the contagious relationship between economics and sexuality. Charlotte Perkins Gilman's statement in *Women and Economics* (1898) duplicates this discourse:

> We are . . . the only animal species in which the sex-relation is also an economic relation. With us an entire sex lives in a relation of economic dependence upon the other sex, and the economic relation is combined with the sex-relation. The economic status of the human female is relative to the sex-relation.[61]

IV

My use of Barthes to approach *The Portrait of a Lady* and *The House of Mirth* has meant that only a fragment of each text has been closely treated. In modifying his model and using such fragments to give access to the text-to-come, I have attempted to show the larger resonances of his method. Barthes' way of reading allows the reader to gain access to some of the ways in which the 'realist' novel is constructed; to break down the apparently 'natural' establishment of reality in, the seamlessness of, such a text to reveal its highly artificial principles of construction. In such a text the 'already written' is, as Barthes shows, continually cited (p. 33) to produce effects of solid and already accepted meaningfulness. The 'tableaux vivants', for example, provide a central set-piece to *The House of Mirth*. Here, Lily impersonates a picture: 'Reynolds's "Mrs Lloyd" '.[62] The audience gasps at this three-dimensional impersonation of two-dimensional painting which, in turn, replicates three dimensional 'original'. Lily's citation of this 'old picture', however, then leads further backwards, for Art is the 'code underlying all beauty' (Barthes, p. 33).

Selden sees Lily, in replacing 'the phantom of [Reynolds's] dead beauty by the beams of her living grace' as catching 'for a moment a note of that *eternal* harmony of which her beauty was a part' (pp. 134–5, my stress). 'Beauty' in Barthes' words, can only assert itself 'in the form of a citation' (p. 33). Similarly the realist novel is composed of endless 'citations' to other texts, to a multitude of codes and voices all 'woven into the text' (p.9). The partial unweaving of these voices, in accordance with the reader's own cultural siting, transforms for Barthes his or her role from passive recipient of meaning to active producer of it.

I have here attempted to move in the direction of such a production; *decomposing* the texts to allow 'threads of [plural] meanings' (p. 12) to emerge. These threads intersect and interact. The codes 'mobilized' extend, in Barthes' terms, '*as far as the eye can reach*' (pp. 5–6). The discovery of multivalence rather than univocality becomes the critical intention.

Barthes, while resisting any demand for 'metameaning' (any one ultimate and authoritative reading of the text) does however allow for the reconnection of 'certain sequences which might have become lost in the unraveling of the tutor text' (p. 14). Due to my working limits, I have been making some of these reconnections as I have proceeded. I have also been generally framing my reading by placing heavy reliance on one of the codes which constitutes me as a critic (REF. Code of Critical Practice: Feminist Criticism).

The re-thinking concerning gender roles taking place in the contemporary academic 'interpretive community', to recall Mailloux, has obviously influenced my drawing of strands of meaning from these texts. I slant my text in a similar way to that in which Barthes does his (deconstruction of bourgeois values). I hope I do this neither at the expense of Barthes' playfulness, nor totally at the expense of those other meanings which have been seen to circulate and spill out of my reading of the (fragments of the) two novels. Finally, though, my reading does not share the aim of 'triumphant dissemination' which is Barthes' critical ideal. There are certain strands of meaning I see as more important (for my critical purposes at least) than others. His approach I find enormously liberating and stimulating. My gathering stress on the social underpinnings of the American novel leads me, however, to conclude with an unapologetic anti-Barthesian move towards a summing up and connective statement concerning the two texts with particular reference to their treatment of gender difference, a perfectly logical (if totalizing) step in regard to novels in which issues of power/economics/sexuality are recurrent. At this concluding stage, I wish to signal my critical difference from Barthes by discussing just one major (shared) textual issue, rather than many. I will make reference to parts of the text not yet subject to analysis when it suits my needs to do so.

Both sequences, it is clear, use signifiers ('fortune', 'speculate') which waver ambiguously. Characters in both 'persistently confound the language of love and money'.[63] The stress on *rates of exchange* within and between those two realms (who is worth what?) endorses their mutual status as novels working, at one level, in a bourgeois tradition.[64] So, too, does their concern with the relationship between the 'autonomy' of the individual subject and forms of social engagement which threaten to reduce that subject's status. It is, though, in their response to this issue that James and Wharton differ.

The Portrait of a Lady retains Isabel as a type of gold standard: her subjectivity gives the novel its meaning. Though her project of self-development is open to strong critique – her concept of 'free expansion' (p. 51) is an empty one exactly because of its free-floating nature [65] – nonetheless it is her individual consciousness and its workings, her ability to learn from her experience, to retain mental independence despite the constraints which come to surround her, which help to give Isabel what James calls 'the high attributes of a Subject' (p. xi). If she becomes unwittingly an object of exchange, a commodity, her final position is, nonetheless, that of one who fully knows and understands just what freedoms she lacks as a result of her immersion in the world of social interaction; whose *essence* remains uncontaminated by such immersion (SEM. Imaginative, sensitive, morally resolute). Such knowledge, such subjectivity, strongly counteracts the reification to which she has been subjected.[66]

Isabel's qualities are *special* ones. She stands out even among the other *exceptional* women in James' text. James, moreover, carves out a highly foreign, thus interesting, territory in which to place her (SEM. Expatriate. Wealth. *Outside* the normal social order). In doing so, he makes what he calls his 'female fry' (p. xi) of novelistic interest. Wharton does not, as Mary Schriber points out, 'stand apart from [her] heroine' in the way that James does. The latter accepts Isabel's 'beautiful difficulties' as the artist's challenge.[67] He writes of Isabel in terms of 'a class [of "frail vessels"] difficult, in the individual case, to make a centre of interest' (p. xi).

Wharton writes *against* James in seeing no such difficulty in making a woman's everyday experience in a patriarchal culture a centre of interest. Neither does she make Lily exceptional in the way that James makes Isabel. For though both women are intelligent, good-looking, and (initially) single, Lily, unlike Isabel, is measured against the conditioning circumstances of conventional female life from the very start of Wharton's text, as it relies on a cultural code (Book of Darwin/Evolution) which stresses issues of survival and adaptation in relation to environment. Lily is thus seen more as *object* than as subject; is thoroughly conditioned by these norms – what it means to be, and what is expected of, a woman in an American leisure class environment (REF. Stereotyped code of sexual difference). What Madame Merle calls 'the whole envelope of circumstances' (p. 201) press on Lily from the first: in Isabel's case, it is an envelope that only takes material form as the narrative progresses; one which threatens, but fails to destroy, her subjectivity.

Both proairetic and semic codes operate differently in the two novels. Isabel constructs meaning for herself, at the same time as meaning is being constructed by others on the site of her femininity. Lily, 'never seen as competent adult woman',[68] seeks a definition of self in the eyes of others. She cannot be the novel's gold standard, not only because of her lack of financial worth, but also because the very coin of her personality is counterfeit, a construction of others' expectation. Her definition of self is reflected from male eyes: as ornament, as 'moral-aesthetic object', as child.[69] Such a meaning is self-divisive and self-destructive; leads to her suicide and ruin. If Isabel, in marrying Osmond, makes the wrong choice, Lily, in Wharton's novel, has no choice – is defined, confined, and destroyed *because* of her womanhood. In Mary Schriber's terms:

> Wharton imagines more fully and deeply than her male counterpart the consequences of the culture's ideology of woman. The pursuit of marriage and the conventions that test and mature James' Isabel Archer ruin . . . Lily Bart.[70]

Wharton's novel is, then, far bleaker in terms of its presentation of female identity and cultural convention. The novel ends with:

Wharton's camera focus[ing] our attention on a dead woman in a bare room, destroyed by a culture that has taught her to experience herself only as a beautiful object to be appreciated – or bought – by men.[71]

Though both James and Wharton make use of the same symbolic codes, and site their meanings around them, Wharton, writing from a female position, places her subject in a much more constricting cultural context, puts greater emphasis on this subject's self-divisions. In terms of the male/female antithesis, and the struggle for ascendancy it encodes, the scales are still moving in *Portrait*; we do not know where they will rest. Isabel's battle with Osmond is not yet over. In *The House of Mirth* all movement stops, scales weighted in heavy and conclusive favour of patriarchy, with Lily's death. Lily is bound by the gender expectations of her culture much more firmly than is Isabel. Wharton's stress is far more intensely focused than is James' on 'the psychological distortions, the self-alienation, that a woman suffers when she accepts the status of idealized object'.[72]

6

The Clash of Language:
Bakhtin and *Huckleberry Finn*

I

Issues of language and of voice are raised at the very start of Mark Twain's *The Adventures of Huckleberry Finn* (1885). For the first voice which speaks to the reader is that of the posited author's [1] deputy, G. G., Chief of Ordnance:

> Persons attempting to find a motive in this narrative will be prosecuted; persons attempting to find a moral in it will be banished; persons attempting to find a plot in it will be shot.
>
> BY ORDER OF THE AUTHOR
per G. G., CHIEF OF ORDNANCE.[2]

This surrogate voice[3] is of course comic, parodying the voice of officialdom ('trespassers will be prosecuted'). Bourgeois values in their most fundamental form, the owning of private property, are already subject to parodic attack here; the novel being treated as though it were the author's possession alone. A note of repression and of violence however is also present, introduced with the references to banishment and shooting. Chief of Ordnance is he who is responsible for military supplies, for implements of war, and the main implement of war in the novel is language. Different voices, different discourses, battle it out for authority, for power, throughout the text. Languages which are unacceptable will be suppressed, by force if necessary. Such potential suppression is rehearsed in comic form when Huck and Jim discuss people who talk French:

> '*No*, Jim; you couldn't understand a word they said –
> not a single word.'
> 'Well, now, I be ding-busted! How do dat come?'
> 'I don't know; but it's so. I got some of their jabber
> out of a book. 'Spose a man was to come to you and
> say *Polly-voo-franzy* – what would you think?'
> 'I wouldn't think nuff'n; I'd take en bust him over de head.
> Dat is, if he warn't white. I wouldn't 'low no nigger to call
> me dat' (p. 135).

G. G. however, Chief of Ordnance, represents the posited author, and this authorial voice is capitalized. It is the voice of forceful (guns at his command) authority, attempting to control the responses of those of inferior status, a potentially undisciplined and undiscriminating audience. You must not, the voice says through its subordinate (ranks, levels, hierarchies, thus being signalled as important from the start) respond to my text in the following ways. Comedy, however, instantly undermines authority here. This, for Mikhail Bakhtin, the Soviet critic whose theory I shall be explicating in this chapter, is its function: 'it is precisely laughter that . . . destroys any hierarchical distance'.[4] For that authoritarian 'NOTICE' is also that which, together with the name Mark Twain on the title page, first signals the novel's comic aspects. The words of this 'author' cannot be taken seriously. His voice is untrustworthy. For a narrative without a plot is a contradiction in terms. The notion of shooting the (invisible) reader is comic hyperbole, an authoritarian yet ridiculous threat to destroy the process of author-reader communication by which the novel form operates. For how could the reader's 'attempt' to approach the text ever be known by this capitalized 'AUTHOR'?

Apart from a brief note referring to the 'number' of dialects 'painstakingly' used in the novel, this is the last time the authorial voice is directly heard in the text. Already, however, a number of important concerns have been placed on Twain's novelistic agenda. Reference has been made to the variety of speech types which will interact in the novel. Comedy has been introduced to undercut the author[itarian] voice: he who would seek to control our responses in so absurd and perverse a manner. The whole question of voice, its authority, weaponry at its command, trustworthiness, and relation to other voices, has been swiftly and incisively introduced. Indeed, it is the way in which voices clash in a novel, and the related issues of power and authority, which are prime subjects of Bakhtin's interest. The military metaphors he uses (ideologies 'battle it out in the arena of the utterance', p. 431) suggest the connections to be made with Twain's writing practice.

II

The novel can be defined as a diversity of social speech types . . . and a diversity of individual voices, artistically organized (p. 262).

Bakhtin's formulation might sound like merely a variant on Genette's work on speech representation and voice (see my chapter on Fitzgerald). My reason, however, for concluding my study of critical models with Bakhtin is that, unlike Genette, he presents language as the site of 'opposition and struggle', a conflict which, for him, lies at the very 'heart of existence'.[5] And this conflict is social and historical ('socio-ideological', p. 273) in nature. In his view 'any single national language' is composed of a series of different 'languages' internally stratified into a series of complex and overlapping levels:

into social dialects, characteristic group behaviour, professional jargons, generic languages, languages of generations and age groups, tendentious languages, languages of the authorities, of various circles and of passing fashions, languages that serve the specific sociopolitical purposes of the day, even of the hour . . . (pp. 262–3).

Language, then, is a register of social and historical diversity, of 'power relations and hierarchies' in any given culture.

Bakhtin's examination of voice and speech type thus leads away from the ahistorical frame in which Genette's criticism is posited, and which I have been attempting to modify in the early sections of this study. It seeks instead to locate literature firmly in its historical and social context. His criticism also replaces Barthes' stress on playful indeterminacy in *S/Z*. While Barthes' method does feed back into both cultural and social history, his very stress on play, plurality and incompletion means that principles/practices of 'dispersal and fragmentation'[6] operate to the detriment of that firm stress on speech diversity and social struggle in which Bakhtin's theory is rooted.

Despite difficulties in discovering the exact range of his authorship,[7] Bakhtin has become an increasingly important influence in Western literary thought. I intend to place my main stress on his concept of the novel as an open-ended form – 'a living mix of varied and opposing voices' (p. 49) – in which a number of types of speech (and belief systems) carry out an unresolved battle with one another. I will, however, also attempt to use his arguments both to briefly site Twain's novel in relation to the literary culture of his period, and in relation to the larger social and historical context in which it was produced. The issues of race, class, and gender which have emerged as of increasing importance as this study has progressed, are particularly open to Bakhtinian analysis. Russell Reising, in fact, sees his work as providing 'the basis for a new appreciation of the heterogeneity of American literature' as it pushes us 'toward a greater understanding of the social and ideological implication of language'.[8] Some of these implications will become evident both here and in my final chapter.

Bakhtin's view of the novel relates closely to his view of language as a site of conflict. For it is the novel which for him best 'represent[s] all the social and ideological voices of its era' (p. 411). When he talks of the novel as a diversity of 'social speech types' he is insisting on the fact that language does not, and cannot, exist in a vacuum. Any speech, any use of language, reflects the belief system and value judgements of the person using it. Language reveals a person's social and cultural role, according to her or his membership of – and use of the language of – different regional, social, ethnic and professional groups; whether she or he is in authority or opposed to it. The 'indispensable prerequisite' for the novel as a genre is, according to Bakhtin, 'this internal stratification present in every language *at any given moment of its historical existence* (p. 263, my stress).

Bakhtin uses the term *heteroglossia* to describe this effect, the 'plurality of discourse' produced by 'the interweaving of different registers in the text of the novel'.[9] 'Authentic novelistic prose', for Bakhtin, is that in which a 'multiplicity of social voices' (pp. 263–4), all found pressing on one another, are realized within the context of the novel form. He describes 'the prose art' as presuming 'a deliberate feeling for the historical and social concreteness of living discourse, as well as its relativity, a feeling for its participation in historical becoming and in social struggle' (p. 331). The style of a novel cannot, Bakhtin insists, be examined independently of the social and historical voices it sounds. Such voices are 'ideologically saturated' (p. 274); they represent a social position, a way of viewing the world, and are in tense relationship – in terms of 'social significance' – with the other voices to be heard in any novel. Style, then, becomes something which has little to do with the individuality of any given author, the 'unity (and uniqueness)' (p. 264) of the language she or he uses. Rather, it is the way in which that author juxtaposes those voices available. The *dialogue*, a key term for Bakhtin, that occurs between different discourses – and the points of view, belief systems, social stances they represent – within a novel, is for Bakhtin what makes the genre so flexible. He sees it as the one literary form in 'living contact with unfinished, still evolving contemporary reality (the openended present)' (p. 7).

Bakhtin, however, is not just concerned with the individual text in his writing, and the plurality of discourses within it. He is also interested in the text's position in relation to other texts being produced within a given social and literary environment. Literary texts are always engaged in dialogue with other literary texts. The totality of the cultural conversation, to paraphrase Bakhtin, is made up when all these texts (and the voices they contain) are set alongside one another in a multi-layered whole.

Again, the idea of conflict is central here. Bakhtin makes a fundamental distinction between *centripetal* and *centrifugal* forces in his criticism, and this is of relevance both to the internal workings of a text, and to its position within the general cultural conversation. The centripetal he sees as the (unhealthy) tendency towards 'ideological unification'. Such a tendency is expressed in the way a culture and a language always works in the direction of the establishment of 'socio-political and cultural centralization' (p. 271). This movement is in the direction of a closed system: the attempt to establish an officially recognized 'unitary' or 'monoglossic' language, a recognized cultural voice or literary language which goes hand in hand with an officially recognized set of national values.

In dynamic tension with this Bakhtin sets the centrifugal. He presents, on the one hand, the movement towards monoglossia, the 'closed-off' (p. 67) unitary language which represents a unified and centralized verbal-ideological world; on the other, the forces of disunification and decentralization (the centrifugal), 'endlessly developing new forms which parody, criticize and generally undermine the pretensions of the ambitions towards a unitary language'.[10] This model of language is 'almost Manichean' in its sense of conflict and struggle at the centre of existence;[11] it is strongly dynamic in its version of language 'in which "centripetal" forces seek to unify and homogenize it against "centrifugal" forces which seek to pull it apart. These opposed pressures or tendencies keep language mobile just as they are responsible for its transformations'.[12]

The one word 'white' as used both in the novel, and in the pre-civil war South as a whole, might be seen as a site of such verbal struggle. Centripetal tendencies led to a use of this word in the context of a 'canonization' (p. 271) of a particular ideological system: 'white' as one who is a member of the ruling caste. This Southern world is divided by colour, and in such a context white has only one meaning: she or he who is superior. Jim defines Huck as 'white genlman' (p. 172) to his fellow slaves, thus endorsing the centripetal tendencies of the word. To be white means, in Pap Finn's terms, to be a 'man' rather than to be a 'nigger' (p. 78). The fact that it is Pap who makes such a distinction suggests, though, how 'the centrifugal forces of language carry on their uninterrupted work' (p. 272). For 'white' does not have one unified meaning. There are different types of white ranging from 'aristocracy' (p. 164) to 'mighty ornery lot' (p. 201), from the 'gentleman' to those like Pap who 'warn't no more quality than a mud-cat' (p. 164).

The ideological system built on the notion of 'white' as unitary concept is destabilized by such social distinctions. The potential 'transformations' associated with the centrifugal are suggested by Huck's description of Jim as 'white inside' (p. 349) at the novel's end; by Twain's description of Roxy, in *Pudd'nhead Wilson*, as 'white as anybody'[13] despite the fact that she is 'black' by social definition, by reason of her ancestry. Bakhtin's stress on the materiality of language is central here; the way in which 'every concrete utterance of a speaking subject serves as a point where centrifugal as well as centripetal forces are brought to bear. The processes of centralization and decentralization, of unification and disunification, intersect in the utterance' (p. 272).

In his favouring of the centrifugal, Bakhtin asserts his commitment to social diversity and change rather than to the hierarchical. A culture is not, to him, something fixed, rigid, and ordered – either in terms of the established positions of those within it, or of the dominant voices which speak for it. He emphasizes, rather, its multilanguaged aspects, assigning qualities of health and vitality to those ongoing forces of decentralization and disunification which the authorities and ruling classes of any society would try to deny. The notion of heteroglossia or variety, diversity, the pluralistic (as set strongly against the idea of any absolute authority) again becomes significant.

In America in the 1880s, this opposition between the centripetal and centrifugal can be clearly seen working in the field of literary culture. By and large associated with the East Coast, with Boston in particular, this culture and the literary language which expressed it ('the oral and written language of a dominant social group', p. 290) was undoubtedly, as Alan Trachtenberg illustrates in *The Incorporation of America*, both genteel and hierarchic.[14] Twain, in writing *Huckleberry Finn*, opposed and thus deprivileged this official voice. Completely shattering the accepted boundaries of literary language in his America, the tendencies of the novel are strongly centrifugal. The vernacular voice (that of the common people) is placed, after that initial brief 'authorial' statement, in charge of the text (channelled through the first person narrator). In giving such full voice to an unofficial folk discourse, Twain forced his intended audience to engage 'with another language as a deeply important part of its own culture'.[15] This argument is one which operates at the level of literary politics, and the cultural assumptions that lie behind them. At an internal level – whether Huck's unofficial language can challenge, overturn, the official languages which surround him – we are faced, as will be seen later, with quite another matter.

In terms of Twain's challenge to a 'unitary' literary culture, the centrifugal tendencies of his writing, it is noticeable that *The Dial*, one of America's major literary periodicals, would completely ignore *Huckleberry Finn* on its publication. In fact the only reference to Twain in the year following the novel's publication is in the form of an advertisement for the self-pasting scrap book that he had patented. The wording of one of the quotations used within the advertisement is of real interest, in so far as it suggests Twain's antagonistic position to any notion of a monoglossic cultural voice: 'No library' it reads 'is complete without a copy of the Bible, Shakespeare, and Mark Twain's Scrap Book'.[16] Official hierarchies are undercut here. The mentioning of a Scrap Book on equal terms with the Bible and Shakespeare clearly dislocates the latter's status as sacred cultural texts. Such dislocations occur within Twain's novel too. For *The Dial*'s promulgation of a literary canon based on English models needs to be set against the laughter which occurs in *Huckleberry Finn* at the expense of what Bakhtin would call the 'ennobled' (p. 384) literary word. *The Dial* worries about 'how best to introduce pupils in our high schools and academies to the English classics . . . a burning question which ought to have the attention of all thoughtful teachers'; has lead articles on the like of Kit Marlowe, 'the most illustrious of all the contemporaries of Shakespeare . . . the father of the English drama'.[17] This kind of reverence gives way to ridicule in *Huckleberry Finn* with the duke's version of Hamlet's 'sublime' soliloquy which ends:

But soft you, the fair Ophelia:
Ope not thy ponderous and marble jaws,
But get thee to a nunnery – go! (p. 199)

Here, the ennobled word (Shakespeare) is completely garbled and so becomes ridiculous. The piety with which Shakespeare's drama was greeted by America's literary establishment becomes a source for comic effect. The sense of high seriousness associated with a strictly hierarchical literary order is replaced by an authorial guffaw.[18]

Such comic effects suggest the carnivalistic element in *The Adventures of Huckleberry Finn*. For *carnivalization* is another of Bakhtin's key terms. It is the model of carnival festivity 'transposed into the language of literature':[19] life here is turned upside down as conventional hierarchical barriers are removed. The reasons for Bakhtin's attractions to carnival are, I think, obvious, and emerge clearly in his studies of Dostoevsky and Rabelais. Carnival (and carnivalization) relate to the ideological thrust of his general arguments: his preference for 'low' languages over 'high', realized in literary terms in the comic overturning of official systems of life and thought by an unofficial folk culture and the energies with which it is associated.

Any talk of 'folk energies' in *Huckleberry Finn* is, as I will show later, subject to major reservation. There is, nonetheless, clear use of carnivalization in the novel. Carnival is associated with masquerade, an upsetting of the firm structures and the strict rankings of the 'official' life by an assumption of masks, false identities, which blur any boundaries between high and low: decentre authoritative 'systems of life and thought'.[20] The notion of masquerade is central to Twain's novel, and is given fullest realization in the circus performer episode.[21] For Huck himself, however, such shape shiftings, identity maskings, contain none of the joyful qualities of carnival – they are merely survival techniques in a world where hierarchical orderings are not seen as subject to overthrow. The king and the duke, however, come much closer to the carnivalesque. Their masquerades are so effective that their true identities remain masked. Brook Thomas points out how Twain manipulates the reader in this respect:

> the king and the duke ask the townpeople [in the Peter Wilks episode] to call them Harvey and William. We, however, refuse to call them Harvey and William because they are merely playing the role of heirs. Yet we call them

the king and the duke, even though they are neither king nor duke. How many roles exist behind these roles we will never know.[22]

These masquerades are also much more disruptive to the established order than Huck's. For carnival is associated with 'parodying doubles', and both in their language (as seen in their use of garbled Shakespeare and, more generally, of 'high' rhetorical forms), and in the very roles they play – aristocrats, clergymen, classical actors – the king and the duke fulfil this function.

In both its use of location and in its comic aspects *Huckleberry Finn* fits Bakhtin's notion of carnivalized text. In carnival, the public square is the place where normal hierarchies are suspended as the festival runs its course. It becomes a zone of 'free and familiar contact' (p. 123) between all types of people. In literary terms, carnivalization calls for a plot centred around 'meeting and contact-points for heterogeneous people' (p. 128). Twain's use of the picaresque form with its use of chance meetings between a variety of social types, with the river rather than the road as central determination of action, provides such a 'carnival square significance' (p. 128). Again, though, the actual potential for suspension, or reversal, of hierarchical relations in such locations is highly qualified.

The same is true of the novel's humour. Carnivalization is primarily associated with laughter: a laughter 'directed toward something higher – toward a shift of authorities and truths' (p. 127). What results is the relativizing 'of all structure and order, of all authority and all (hierarchical) position' (p. 124). Twain's text operates at two levels. He certainly makes use of a carnival base in using a (picaresque) form which allows Huck to rub shoulders with all strands of Southwestern culture, and by using humour to undercut the hierarchic values of that culture. He moreover turns an established literary order topsy turvey in his own carnivalistic overthrow of 'respectable' modes of discourse (exemplified by Shakespeare in my earlier example) in favour of the folk energies contained in Huck's vernacular voice. However, such a carnival sense of the world is radically dissipated in terms of its actual effect within the represented world of the novel. The king and the duke may disrupt official hierarchies as parodying doubles, but there is no sense of 'communal performance' (p. 138) (the very essence of carnival) in such parody. They do not wish to overturn the language and structure of officialdom on behalf of 'the folk'; merely to bend these forms to their own private and selfish benefit.

The very issue of folk energies on which the whole carnivalistic notion rests, becomes in fact a highly disturbing one in a novelistic world where the majority of the ordinary people are portrayed as foolish, gullible, animalistic ('squirming and scrouging', p. 206), cowardly yet cruel. Huck's own more vital folk-energies always work on the margins of, and are finally contained by, the world of socio-hierarchical inequality – law, prohibition, and restriction – which determines 'the structure . . . of ordinary, that is noncarnival, life' (p. 122). The measure of the communal in his performance is intensely limited.

However muted the sense of carnivalization might be, it cannot be discounted in the novel. Laughter, the decentering of authority, that source of 'folk energy' contained in Huck's 'indecorous' presence and voice, all manifest such a presence. And carnivalized literature in its 'interweaving' of 'disparate styles and registers'[23] encourages and increases the heteroglossic effect in the novel. So in *Huckleberry Finn* the carnivalesque features run alongside and blend with that stress on linguistic 'variety and conflict', on 'multiple worlds of discourse',[24] which exerts such 'centrifugal' pressure on the text. For it is a novel in which all kinds of intersecting voices are heard, where 'official' voices are subject to contest, to potential overthrow, from many different directions. And it is the *dialogization* between these intersecting voices which, for Bakhtin, creates the novel's most interesting effects.

Dialogization is a vital term in Bakhtin's literary theory, and is central to his conception of the novel form. Most straightforwardly, it can be defined as 'one point of view opposed to another, one evaluation opposed to another, one accent opposed to another' (p. 314). It is the novel's 'profound speech diversity' (p. 315), its ability to lay a series of autonomous voices ('the speech of another in another's language') alongside and against each other, that constitutes its 'determining factor'. Such a stratification of linguistic (and 'socio-ideological') zones is what allows the entry of heteroglossia into the novelistic text. It is in the setting of these zones in oppositional relation to one another that dialogization occurs.

So, in *Huckleberry Finn*, Twain uses Huck's voice (and language) to dialogize all those who seek to gain, or retain, 'authority' in the text: those whose forms of language are thus associated with the 'centripetal' tendency. Crucially, dialogization depends on the conscious *awareness* of linguistic and social conflict. This is where the role of the author emerges in all its importance. For it is novelistic dialogue which 'push[es] to the limit the mutual nonunderstanding represented by people *who speak in different languages*' (p. 356). The novelist 'ventriloquates' (p. 299) such dialogue, presenting all the different languages to be found in the text from a 'third party position' which the reader can then share. For Bakhtin, 'a word, discourse, language or culture undergoes "dialogization" when it becomes relativized, de-privileged, aware of competing definitions for the same things'.[25]

Thus, when Twain 'ventriloquates' Huck's voice, it is to set it against all the other ventriloquated voices in the novel. Huck's own awareness of this linguistic relativism is often nil. When he describes the widow's behaviour at table – 'you couldn't go right to eating, but you had to wait for the widow to tuck down her head and grumble a little over the victuals, though there warn't really anything the matter with them' (p. 50) – he is not aware that his word 'grumble' is in competition (both linguistically and ideologically) with the word(s) the widow would have used, 'say grace' or 'pray'. The humour emerges precisely because of our knowledge, and Huck's ignorance, of the de-privileging of discourse which is occurring as the widow's word for a formal ritual, part of the day to day fabric of her Christian respectability, is set against Huck's puzzled and pragmatic description of her activity. Huck's inability to 'read instinctively . . . cultural signs'[26] is what is at stake here. But what is also implicitly at stake is the whole meaning of Christianity as it relates to everyday action and experience. Here, as so often in Twain, what initially merely encourages readerly laughter at Huck's naiveté will later connect up with, switch into, a more serious argument about the relationship between Christianity and racist ideology in the pre- and post-war South.[27]

In incorporating such dialogization into his novel, Twain presents a whole series of different languages in their 'socio-ideological' typicality, so as to show their relativity to one another. He fulfils the authorial function as Bakhtin describes it, making 'use of this verbal give-and-take, this dialogue of languages at every point in his work, in order that he himself might remain as it were neutral with regard to language, a third party in a quarrel between two people (although he might be a *biased* third party)' (p. 314). And if Twain himself dialogizes expected literary horizons in his use of the vernacular narrative voice, he also foregrounds such issues within the text, most obviously in the dialogization between Huck's language and that of Tom Sawyer, on whose 'style' so much textual stress is laid.

For Tom's speech (and world view) is invaded by, often composed of, the language of fantasy and romance literature. To him, relying as he does on such literary 'authorities', hogs are to be called 'ingots', turnips and other garden produce 'julery', when his gang embark on their 'robberies'. Twain again uses Huck's naiveté, this time to question *Tom's* potentially monoglossic discourse. Huck's response to Tom's talk of 'genies', to be called up by rubbing a tin lamp, is typical: 'then I reckoned I would see if there was anything in it. I got an old tin lamp . . . and went out in the woods and rubbed and rubbed till I sweat like an Injun . . . but it warn't no use, none of the genies come. So then I judged that all that stuff was only just one of Tom Sawyer's lies' (p. 64). Here Huck directly dialogizes Tom's discourse, rejecting its validity. It is the ventriloquating author, though, who – as Michael Davitt Bell shows – places Huck's vernacular against Tom's book-learnt language to create a much deeper dialogic effect. Phrases like 'sweat like an Injun' and 'all that stuff' are set against Tom's talk of 'enchantment', transformation, and power, with the result that 'the romantic discourse by which "Tom Sawyer's lies" claim to legitimize themselves'[28] is inevitably deflated.

'Lies' seems a strong word to use to describe Tom's construction of play worlds. Again, the reader is being prepared for the shift to a deeper thematic level, which occurs in the novel's final stages, when the boundary lines between the playful and the serious disturbingly blur. A brief example of Huck's words, regarding Tom and his response to Jim in the concluding section of the novel, shows how they are dialogized by Twain to serve such deeper authorial purposes. Huck's statement, when the narrative is effectively concluded, 'Tom give Jim forty dollars for being prisoner for us so patient' (p. 368), contains no overt value judgement of Tom's actions. The words are framed, though, within an earlier verbal context of Huck's use of the phrase 'forty dirty dollars' to describe the money received by the king and the duke for re-selling Jim into slavery; framed, too, in the context of Tom's knowledge that Miss Watson 'set [Jim] free in her will' prior to the whole tormenting 'evasion' routine. Huck's statement comes then to carry – from the ventriloquating author – a clear moral condemnation of Tom's actions.

In the examples I have given so far of the dialogization which occurs between Huck's language and the widow's, Huck's and Tom's, I have noted the quality of naiveté with which Huck is associated. Bakhtin's comment that 'the coupling of incomprehension with comprehension, of stupidity, simplicity, and naiveté with intellect' is a common feature of much novelistic prose is directly relevant here:

> Stupidity (incomprehension) in the novel is always polemical: it interacts dialogically with an intelligence (a lofty pseudo intelligence) . . . whose mask it tears away . . . at its heart always lies a polemical failure . . . to understand generally accepted, canonized, inveterately false languages with their lofty label for things and events (p. 403).

When Bakhtin speaks of the 'radical character' of a naive narrator who completely fails to understand the usual ways of looking at the world, he could have had Huck Finn in mind. Bakhtin uses the word *estrangement* (his closeness to Russian Formalist conceptions of 'defamiliarization' is obvious here)[29] to suggest what happens when a fixed way of looking at and speaking about the world meets a narrator who is uncomprehendingly naive; who 'by his very uncomprehending presence . . . makes strange the world of social conventionality' (p. 404).

As Huck's naiveté comes in contact with more conventional ways (in terms of Southern historical and ideological norms) of viewing the world, exactly such dialogical interaction occurs. The Grangerfords, for example, are Southern ' "quality" . . . the ruling patricians and affluent Whites'. Huck's description of the family takes nothing for granted; he has no pre-conceived version of their values or mode of life. His description therefore exposes for the reader exactly their 'stagy charm'.[30] He notices the chips in the crockery fruit in the basket on the Grangerford's table where the white chalk showed through: fruit 'much redder and yellower and prettier' (p. 159) than the real article. Similarly, he describes the verbal politeness of this mannered world, the boys' bowing to their parents every morning and toasting them with 'Our duty to you, sir, and madam' (p. 165); a mode of formality and gentility stripped of its supposed meaning by Huck's careful description of the feud, with its brutal murder committed for little reason. Huck's innocent questions about the nature of the feud:

> 'What was the trouble about, Buck? – land?'
> 'I reckon maybe – I don't know.'
> 'Well, who done the shooting? – was it a Grangerford or Shepherdson?'
> 'Laws, how do *I* know? it was so long ago.' (pp. 167–8)

tears the mask from the Southern aristocratic 'style': that concern with manners and elaborate language and behaviour. For the Grangerfords deal in abstractions. The feud is something vague (Buck cannot explain it) and has meaning for this aristocratic 'clan' in so far as it can be associated with concepts of honour and correct behaviour rather than their opposite, cowardice. So when Bud, for instance, is about to be killed, 'he stopped and faced around so as to have the bullet holes in front, you know' (p. 168). The Grangerford's 'lofty label' for things, a 'feud', is here dialogized by having Huck focus on the actual 'shooting' involved, how 'sick' he feels when he sees Buck shot and finds the 'two bodies laying in the edge of the water' (p. 175). From a third person position we see the feud, when described through the eyes of one who fails to understand this 'canonized' term, to be butchery pure and simple.

And, again in terms of literary language, the occasion

provides opportunity for a dialogization of sentimental pathos. The comic style depends on the 'stratification of literary language', and the consequent intersection of 'different linguistic planes' (p. 311). Huck's words, in running up against Emmeline Grangerford's art (verse and paintings), reveal its malicious inadequacy to reality. Huck is a type of innocent abroad, and his naive description of Emmeline and her poetry comically reveals both the morbidness of her imagination and the falseness of the emotion on which her 'verse' rests. As always we laugh in two directions, both at Huck and with him. When he calls Emmeline's crayon picture with the six arms 'too spidery' (p. 161), we laugh with him in that the word he chooses provides a way of denting the exaggerated nature of the discourse Emmeline adopts (with picture titles like 'Shall I Never See Thee More Alas'). We laugh at him in his failure to see the implications of his own remarks: he remains naively impressed by both paintings and doggerel verse.

Emmeline's pathos-charged discourse is shown to lack all felt emotion and discrimination though. There is no proportion to her artistic world: everything is very black like that spider, and it lacks all selectivity – 'Every time a man died, or a woman died, or a child died, she would be on hand with her "tribute" before he was cold' (p. 162). Its lack of discrimination is to be seen in the fact that the death of a bird ('I Shall Never Hear Thy Sweet Chirrup More Alas') is given as much time and attention as any human victim of her art. Huck's failure – despite his acceptance of their artistic value – to fully appreciate her paintings, his inability to 'sweat out a verse' in her manner, is 'polemical'. The false conventionality of her art is dialogized by Huck's restrained language as *he* responds, shortly afterwards, to the death of a child (Buck). His words are commonplace; his treatment of the event depends on reticence and understatement. His language provides genuine expression of feeling and effect which provides strong contrast with Emmeline's literary 'sentimentering': 'I ain't agoing to tell *all* that happened – it would make me sick again if I was to do that. I wished I hadn't ever come ashore that night, to see such things. I ain't ever going to get shut of them – lots of times I dream about them' (p. 175).[31]

III

Bakhtin insists that verbal discourse is a 'social phenomenon' (p. 259). Words are selected from a 'tension-filled environment' (p. 276) and are 'shot through' with different accents and value judgements. For him, an examination of style is not a matter of studying an utterance or sentence in isolation (a 'stretch of speech between two periods of silence or potential silence') in a text. It is, rather, a matter of placing that utterance in its specific social and historical context, of studying 'the transfers and switchings of languages and voices; their dialogical interrelationships' (p. 50):

> The living utterance, having taken meaning and shape at a particular historical moment in a socially specific environment, cannot fail to brush up against thousands of living dialogic threads, woven by socio-ideological consciousness around the given object of an utterance; it cannot fail to become an active participant in social dialogue (p. 276).

For a clear example of such 'social dialogue' I wish to step outside Twain's text for the moment to refer to *Narrative of the Life of Frederick Douglass, an American Slave*, a non-fictional account of Douglass' experiences as a slave published in 1845, the approximate dating of the events of Twain's novel. Douglass, like Jim, describes his escape from slavery, writing of his plans to do so as follows:

> In coming to a fixed determination to run away, we did more than Patrick Henry, when he resolved upon liberty or death. With us it was a doubtful liberty at most, and almost certain death if we failed. For my part, I should prefer death to hopeless bondage'.[32]

Here Douglass dialogizes the official language of American revolutionary politics. The sentence has to be read both in the context of what it meant to be a slave in the 1830s, and what it meant to be an American in the revolutionary period. It is noticeable here that Douglass does not write in the black vernacular. This is because, in Gates' words, 'to become subjects, as it were, black ex-slaves had to demonstrate their language-using capacity before they could become social and historical entities'.[33] It was ironically Douglass' 'articulate mastery'[34] of the written forms of the dominant culture that gave him his existence for, and allowed dialogue with, that white audience to whom he primarily spoke.

What is of more immediate importance for my argument is how Douglass' words deliberately brush up against that 'living dialogic thread' represented by Henry's utterance; how, by switching that utterance to a different historical context and speaking it in a different (black) voice, a 'social dialogue' is actively engaged. For Douglass uses a cultural image ('we did more than Patrick Henry') which is calculated to appeal to the ideological values of the dominant (white) society, but transforms it to his own ends. Douglass' utterance both contains Henry's words and argues with them, illustrating how, for black Americans in the 1830s and 40s, Henry's clear cut and romantic distinction between colonial oppression and the freedom of the individual must be re-examined, recontextualized in the frame of the doubtful liberty/hopeless bondage/death axis which formed the real conditions of choice in the lives of slaves. Oppressed is now oppressor: the irony rings clear as the particular historical moments of the two dialogic strands brush up against, and relativize, one another.

The 'transfers and switchings of languages and voices' are equally apparent in *Huckleberry Finn*, where words are 'shot through' with different accents and value judgements. Twain, not subject to the same socio-ideological constraint as Douglass and writing after the slavery issue has been resolved, at least at an 'official' level, uses the black vernacular as one of the multiple 'languages' of the novel. Jim's mode of discourse is that of the slave: he who is of lowest status in this particular social and cultural environment (the pre-Civil War South). When he says 'We's safe, Huck, we's safe! Jump up and crack yo' heels, dat's de good ole Cairo at las', I jis knows it!' (p. 146), the accent and value judgements are his, together with the social group he represents, alone. For what he actually means is 'I's safe', safe meaning here safe from capture, safe to make his way to the 'freedom' of the Northern States.

Exactly how 'doubtful' such 'liberty' would in fact be, is spelled out in Douglass' text. For no one else in the

novel does the word 'safe' have this meaning. For Huck,
safe means on the raft, 'free and easy and comfortable',
'free and *safe*' (p. 176, my stress), away from everything
'self-alienating, laborious: Civilization, Writing, Authority,
clocks, tight clothes, hard chairs'.[35] When Jim says 'we's
safe' he speaks a different language to Huck, just as when
Huck uses the word 'free' he speaks a different language to
Jim. Huck's already 'safe', as far as he can ever be, when
Jim cries out with such joy. The same words here contain
very different value judgements. I will return to this sense
of difference between Huck and Jim later.

Dialogism, as becomes clear from such examples, depends
on the siting of an utterance in relation to its 'particular historical moment', its 'socially specific environment'. 'At any
given time, at any given place, there will be a set of conditions – social, historical, meteorological, physiological – that
will ensure a word offered in that place and at that time will
have a meaning different than it would have under any other
conditions'.[36] Meaning itself, in short, depends on the social,
historical (etc.) conditions in which acts of language occur. So,
in *Huckleberry Finn*, social and geographical location and the
kinds of dialogue layered against each other in such locations
strongly affect the meanings which emerge. For Twain places
Huck and Jim's socially powerless voices in relation to the
more strongly authoritative and powerful voices which compose the riverbank world of Southwestern society. The way
in which Jim's position as a slave conditions his utterance in
this location is clear, his language thoroughly subordinated
to that strongly repressive master language which treats him
(and his fellow slaves) more as manipulable objects than as
human subjects.

The context of the master-slave relationship is one which
validates Jim's voice in its comic and non-threatening aspects
only. His 'funny, familiar slave talk'[37] ('Dog my cats ef I didn''
hear sumf'n' etc., p. 53) is the only kind of talk available to
him within the context of a society where any note of black
self-assertion is taboo and punishable by harsh physical inju-
ry. Huck's servant at the Grangerfords practises the evasions
which are part and parcel of black utterance in a slave-holding
society when he says to Huck 'if you'll come down into de
swamp, I'll show you a whole stack o' water-mocassins' (p. 170)

instead of just telling him of Jim's presence there. Evasions, passivities ('Jim . . . allowed we was white folks and knowed better than him', p. 321), silences, are the defining features of black discourse in a slave-holding society which, in its monoglossic absolutism, brooks no argument at all from this particular subordinated group.

Huck, self-defined as 'ignorant and . . . low-down and ornery' (p. 61), only rarely takes open issue with the various authority figures around him. However his voice carries the narrative. His language is thus able, as Jim's is not (due to the limitations *Twain* places on it), to interact with those other languages it meets. Huck, speaking as one who lacks all status in this riverbank world save that of being white, struggles with and often reveals as inadequate the words of those who are socially, or in terms of age, more powerful than he in the small town societies he moves through. This struggle is marked by his testing out of the language of the authorities (of this particular time and place) against which he brushes, to see if it can internally persuade him.[38] As we have seen, he is not always persuaded by Tom's words, by Widow Douglas' or Miss Watson's. Moses has been 'dead a considerable long time' (p. 50) so he loses interest in the meaning of his story. When the preacher at the camp-meeting goes through his routine, '*a-a-men! glory, glory hallelujah!*' and the rest, he remains unmoved by it; does not echo the 'shouting and crying' (p. 193) from the crowd. As a general rule, he remains unpersuaded by the words of the authority figures he meets.

However, and this is crucial, the very speech Huck himself uses is partly composed by the language of that 'Civilization . . . Authority' he would seek to escape. He might dent the 'norm language',[39] temporarily avoid its control, as he checks off the words it uses against what he sees, feels and experiences: as, for example, he re-defines respectability in terms of the 'dismal, regular and decent' (p. 49). But to test out all the words we use would be an impossible task. As Bakhtin stresses so importantly, our language is not our own. In everyday speech 'of all words uttered . . . no less than half belong to someone else' (p.339). We constantly use the speech of another. Prior discourse – that associated with 'a past that is . . . hierarchically higher', a discourse which is 'religious, political, moral' (p. 342) – invades our language at every turn.

The preacher's voice at the camp-meeting, for example, is profoundly unoriginal. He merely transmits an inherited religious discourse: 'come with a contrite heart! . . the door of heaven stands open – oh, enter in and be at rest!'. When Tom's gang decide not to begin its activities on a Sunday because 'all the boys said it would be wicked to do it' (p. 59) they share the discourse and values (the conventional pieties) of the larger society of which they are a part. Another's word constantly intrudes into one's own.

Twain dialogizes Huck's language with the various political, religious and moral discourses represented in the novel. It is the use of his voice which allows us to recognize the gap between Miss Watson's Christian discourse and her selling of Jim for eight hundred dollars away from his wife and children. It is the use of his voice, too, which allows the ironic counterposing of Jim's humanity and the denial of his natural rights with the animalistic crowd struggling to glimpse the dying Boggs and asserting their 'rights' to get the chance to do so (again, it is Twain's ventriloquatings which allow such dialogization to occur; Huck himself remains unconscious of his voice's effect).

But Twain also dialogizes the different elements which compose the flow of Huck's own voice, one of which is his use of that prior authoritative discourse which has contributed to his formation as social being. For the words of Authority constantly press down on him; his own language is partially moulded by such words. So influenced is he by 'the word of . . . adults and of teachers etc.' (Bakhtin, p. 342) that he is unable ever adequately to counter their effect. This is evident, for example, when Huck says of Jim, after he has stayed with the wounded Tom at the cost of his own freedom, 'I knowed he was white inside'. This sentence cuts two ways. First, given the behaviour of such as Pap, the king and the duke, the Grangerfords etc., the words carry a powerful ironic thrust of which Huck himself is unaware. And second, and vitally here, it shows Huck as absolutely caught within the language and (racist) ideology of that culture which has helped mould him. Huck's inability finally to 'subvert [the] control' of the 'prestige language'[40] is evident, as I will show, even on the raft, on the river, that different location and social context where Huck and Jim's voices are able to take on a very different quality:

where the meanings which emerge from their utterances can take on quite different resonances because of the altered set of conditions in which they are spoken.

IV

Neither Huck nor Jim's speech is single-voiced. Bakhtin points out that dialogical relationships are not just a matter of those between 'language styles, social dialects, and so forth', but that they can also 'permeate inside the utterance, even inside the individual word, as long as two voices collide within it dialogically'.[41] Thus both man and boy speak quite differently when alone together on that raft, than when in a 'riverbank' situation. Their voices are not consistent, unified. Their interaction on the raft occurs at one remove from the laws, customs, regulations, dominant voices, of Southwestern culture. 'Every word' Bakhtin says 'is directed toward an *answer*' (p. 280). The answers Huck expects of Jim in this context (and vice versa) are not the same as those they expect on shore, or in the company of the king and the duke. In both these situations their voices modify according to the demands of the particular type of cultural conversation they are engaged in. On shore they are subject to far more constraints, have to negotiate the strong and dominant utterances of others which immediately press on them. On the raft, when Jim and Huck are together, that sense of social and linguistic domination eases off. The plurality of voices, battles between 'points of view, value judgements' (p. 315) which for Bakhtin compose the novel, temporarily quiet – though, as I will show, cannot entirely disappear – as we are left with just two individuals, both from the lowest end of the social spectrum, in communication with one another. We are here down to the barest form of social bonding, for, to Bakhtin, two voices are 'the minimum for life, the minimum for existence'.[42]

Different meanings emerge in this situation, as these two voices make contact with and cut across one another in a different type of linguistic interaction from that possible on the riverbank. Huck's vernacular language ('the excluded language of the vulnerable, the ignorant, the innocent')[43] functions in another manner here, for it is not subject to the immediate repressive authority of his social superiors (or those, such as the king and the duke, who mimic such authoritativeness for their own ends). The religious, political and moral categorizations of the dominant society drop away in the discourse produced in a new social situation; a language where Huck can respond to Jim just as he finds him (in this particular context) rather than in terms of prior authoritarian models. Huck's recognition that Jim 'had a good heart in him and was a good man' (p. 362) is a recognition validated by the experience of their community of two, by all that happens on their journey; one which cuts completely against that dominant voice of Southern culture which would first categorize Jim as 'other', as black, as property – a good slave perhaps but certainly not a good man. It is his pragmatic experience in a largely one-to-one context with Jim which enables Huck to temporarily cast off both the words and the requirements of officialdom. Alone on the raft, the sense of social and linguistic battle which Bakhtin associates with 'authentic novelistic prose' (p. 264) would seem, on first inspection, to disappear. In this location, between the two members of this social unit, a clear sense of democratic equality exists which is nowhere realized in the riverbank world. Twain here makes use of the 'idyll' form.[44]

Bakhtin speaks of the idyll in terms of its restoration of 'folkloric time' (p. 224). Clark and Holquist comment on the way he 'consistently idealizes the folk as untamable, rebellious, and regenerative force that will destroy the status quo'; on the way he sees, 'newer and finer worlds' consequently rising from the ashes of the old order.[45] Such a conception is implicit, if considerably muted, in the presentation of Huck and Jim on the raft. For here, to apply Bakhtin's words to Twain's novel, 'the healthy "natural" functions of human nature are fulfilled' in a way unsanctioned by the 'reigning ideology' (p. 162). It is clear, however, that in overall terms, Twain is far more pessimistic about such overturnings of the 'authorities' by a folk culture than is Bakhtin, with his revolutionary ideals. For the 'folk voice' in *Huckleberry Finn* contains a strain which is selfish and depraved. Pap's voice, for example, is demotic (of the common folk), but certainly not democratic. His grotesque caricature of the notion of political 'rights' as they relate to matters of race provides 'the reader's first extended introduction to the ideology of white supremacy'[46] in the novel. His is a corrupt version of the folk voice, one which parasitically leans on the 'official' language available to it.

The folk voice, however, does find positive expression on the raft, though the fragility and temporariness of such expression, and the limitations of the sense of 'community' involved, is clear. In this context Huck and Jim can talk to each other freely, on an equal basis. Jim can criticize Huck for his thoughtlessness, when he tricks Jim after the separation of raft and canoe in the fog. Huck can apologize for his actions. Both responses would have been impossible in the different setting and social context of the riverbank towns. On the raft 'a just and loving community based on the dignity' of each participant comes into being. This is, in Joyce Rowe's words, 'that redemptive American community which the shore has betrayed'.[47]

The idyll restores folkloric time. It limits itself, to draw on and modify Bakhtin's statement, to but few of the 'basic realities' (p. 225) of life: food, leisure, stages of growth, love. In the idyll, human life is 'conjoined with' the life of nature in 'the unity of their rhythm, the common language used to describe phenomena of nature and the events of human life' (p. 226). So, when Huck describes life on board the raft, the days 'slid along', he and Jim 'slide into' the river; 'the whole world was asleep', Huck and Jim 'kind of lazy along, and by-and-by lazy off to sleep'; the days and nights 'swim by', 'we . . . had a swim'; 'not a sound, anywheres', Huck and Jim silently listen 'to the stillness' (pp. 177–8). Life in the heart of nature is here opposed to the complications and upsets of life in a larger society. In the idyll 'all temporal boundaries are blurred and the rhythm of human life is in harmony with the rhythm of nature' (p. 229). Bakhtin, in writing this, might have been taking *Huckleberry Finn* as his model.[48]

However, these 'idyllic' aspects of Huck and Jim's raft journey cannot be thoroughgoing. For the society of two on the raft is always sited in relation to the larger society in whose interstices it functions. And if Huck and Jim's voices and world views temporarily merge on the raft ('free again...all by ourselves on the big river and nobody to bother us', p. 273), the sense of conflict between them, resulting and hanging over from their respective positions in that larger world, can never entirely recede. For both speak with overlapping languages; one the product of their interrelationship on the raft, the other the product of their positioning in the world of Southwestern culture as a whole. Neither language can remain discrete of the other. Twain will not let his reader forget that Jim and Huck do not fully share a language. Racial difference, and the implications of such difference in the pre-war South, cannot be forgotten even on the raft. The authentic human relations shown to exist between Huck and Jim (such relations are based, for Bakhtin, on the family model) are in tension with a different set of relations based on conflict rather than idyll. Dialogical interaction occurs even within this small social unit: meaning emerges from the way Jim and Huck's languages not only blend, but also struggle with one another.[49]

To see the raft journey as idyll, as I have described it, is only half the story. As a place where love and affection can be expressed between black man and white boy ('I's mighty glad to get you back agin, honey', p. 176), the raft does provide a context where Huck and Jim's relationship can exist outside the province of the larger community's norms, where a language can be used in quite a different way than it can be within that community. It is a place where both man and boy can share a sense of mutual freedom from the various societal constraints that press on them. This sense of joint identity is clear in the way their discourses tend to overlap, the way they include the other as part of their utterance, even when – on closer readerly examination – this might be inappropriate. Thus Huck says 'They're after us' (p. 117) when he and Jim flee from Jackson's island; Jim says 'We's safe' (p. 146) when he thinks Cairo has been reached.

If Huck and Jim's discourses overlap, however, they also differ – are dialogized one with the other. Bakhtin notes that 'every discourse has its own selfish and biased proprietor . . . *Who* speaks and under what conditions he speaks: this is what determines the word's actual meaning' (p. 401). Huck's language is that of ill-educated white boy, his social position weak. He is, however, in a position of authority and power in the novel in one crucial respect: it is he who speaks, he who narrates the tale as 'biased proprietor'.

In *Of Huck and Alice: Humorous Writing in American Literature*, Neil Schmitz suggests how Huck's discourse conflicts with, and at times silences, Jim's. The conditions under which Huck speaks on the raft are those of one who has managed to escape all the discourses of mastery imposed on him as 'cramped up' (p. 49) victim of shore life. Everyone in that former context is trying to teach Huck something. Pap replaces the widow's (and the school's) reading lesson with one of his own, that when it comes to authority he comes first. He asks Huck the meaning of a picture he finds in his room, and when Huck replies ' "It's something they give me for learning my lessons good". He tore it up, and says – "I'll give you something better – I'll give you a cowhide" ' (p. 70).

Huck speaks on the raft as one who has escaped all such lessons, all constraint both physical (Pap's 'hick'ry') and mental. He speaks, too, as one who is now 'free and easy and comfortable'. These words are shot through with a certain specific set of meanings, the product of his situation now in comparison to that former one. He is 'comfortable' because he can lazy about, 'laying off comfortable all day, smoking and fishing, and no books nor study' (p. 75). He is 'free' of Pap's violence, Tom's games he cannot quite make sense of, of a hierarchical and repressive society. He is 'easy' since he has no firm plans for the future. On the raft, desire is no longer displaced. The language (and values) of riverbank society which have particularly adversely affected Huck are challenged by his stress on drift, nakedness, ease, rather than decency, regularity, respectability, and school. The conditions of Huck's speaking define the meaning of his words: 'the raft is for Huck the end of his journey, the place where his "free and easy" river world is regained'.[50]

Huck's discourse, though, dialogically interacts with Jim's. Their languages, and world views, are not the same. The conditions of Jim's speaking are those of one who has escaped from slavery. He speaks now in a different way than he has formerly, as owned slave. On the raft, Jim is no longer in that position of 'crouching servility'[51] most acceptable to the slave owner and his (in Jim's case, her) community. On the raft, Jim speaks his mind and does so, in Schmitz's words, 'as a determined and clear headed adult' (p. 103). His words and their meanings stem precisely from his socio-historical position as a runaway slave, who wants to go North, save money, buy his wife out of slavery, then his children, 'and if their master wouldn't sell them, they'd get an Ab'litionist to go and steal them' (p. 146). Freedom for him means something very different than it does for Huck. For Jim it means, to borrow Frederick Douglass' words, to 'clear himself of the chains and fetters of slavery' (p. 138). On the raft, he speaks these needs, gives utterance to a position ideologically separate from Huck's. His notion of 'freedom' is in fact, as Laurence B. Holland points out, actually 'antithetical' to Huck's, 'his longing to escape from slavery and enter *into* the civilization that chafes Huck'.[52]

Huck's language and Jim's are in conflict; Jim's words and plans cut against Huck's. He wants to get off the raft not stay on it, while to Huck, the *meaning* of the raft – freedom, safety, ease, 'home' (p. 176) – is conditional on Jim's presence (he gets 'sort of lonesome', p. 91, very swiftly when he is by himself on Jackson's Island). When Huck is faced with Jim's words running off in a different direction than his own ('He said . . . he'd be a free man the minute he seen . . . Cairo'), he immediately slips back into the language of the dominant culture, for this is his way of retaining some kind of control of the situation. He talks about Jim as '[Miss Watson's] nigger', one who has run off from 'his rightful owner' (p. 145).

In the *Narrative of Frederick Douglass*, Douglass' master tells his wife it is both unlawful and unsafe to teach a slave to read: 'If you give a nigger an inch he will take an ell' (p. 78). Douglass sees the 'white man's power to enslave the black man' residing in this refusal: for if a slave can read, he becomes 'discontented', 'unmanageable'. Douglass learns to read and write, and in so doing, gives himself the power to enter the arena of written discourse, enter his voice in the argument regarding race in America. Jim, however, is illiterate. He has to depend on Huck (ironically, given his writerly voice by the Widow Douglas, school, etc.) for his voice to be heard. And at this point in the narrative, Huck tries to shut off that voice. He reacts to Jim's escape plans in a way sanctioned by the slaveholding culture of his region, with racist slur. He, in fact, repeats the words of Douglass' master, 'It was according to the old saying, "give a nigger an inch and he'll take an ell" '[53] (p. 146). Schmitz suggests Huck is here reacting exasperatedly to Jim ruining his narrative, disrupting his script. He resorts to words taken from the racist ideology of his larger culture as a means of denying the validity of, and needs revealed in,

Jim's words. He takes over the prestige language as a way of gaining power over Jim; reducing him to a stereotype who can, if he will not easily go along with Huck's words, Huck's plot, be simply handed back to his 'owners'. Thus are Huck and Jim's voices dialogized.

Huck's language is not coherent, though. He is double-voiced, for two conversations occur at once – one with the Jim who contextualizes himself, and is in turn contextualized by Huck, in the framework of the socio-geographical world around them; the other with that (same) Jim with whom he shares the community of two on the river. His attempt to put Jim's voice out of hearing by using that denigratory 'nigger'[54] fails immediately Jim uses a second discourse, one which reminds him that their relationship also exists beyond the boundaries of the larger community's norms. For within their small community, these norms have already been overturned: they have identified with one another, talked easily together, accepted each other lovingly. When Huck has the chance to 'tell on' Jim when he takes the canoe to see if they have reached Cairo, Jim's calls of the 'you's de bes' fren' Jim's ever had' (p. 146) type, remind Huck that the term 'nigger', in Schmitz's words, cannot contain 'the fullness of Jim's humanity' (p. 118). They remind him of the dialogue they have entered into on the raft. He therefore drops his use of the official discourse, steps back from the site of their conflict, reasserts the 'idyllic' qualities of their relationship; what they share, rather than how they differ.

For the discourse Huck 'inherits' from his larger society is one he cannot quite bring himself to use in this situation. When, in the canoe, Huck meets two men in a skiff and is about to tell them about Jim, he finds that 'the words wouldn't come' when they ask whether the man on Huck's raft is 'white or black' (p. 147). The prestige language which 'defines' Jim as runaway 'nigger' clashes with that language of equality and kinship which belongs to the idyll, and which is wholly the product of Huck's social interrelationship with Jim on the river. So, when he does respond to the men's question, he identifies Jim both as equal ('he's white') and as kin ('it's pap'), and switches to a form of discourse quite other than that associated with 'officialdom'.

And this double-edged quality of Huck's voice continues

to sound in the novel, and to be dialogized by Twain, even after the source of immediate conflict between Huck and Jim is removed. For Huck's double-voicedness is not just a product of the differences between his and Jim's respective expectations and positions on the raft itself. Indeed these potentially disruptive differences are removed from the foreground of the novel as the plot turns, Cairo is discovered passed by, and the raft temporarily abandoned after the steamboat collision. Once refloated, moreover, the raft will be dominated by the king and the duke who turn it 'into an image of the civilization with its discontents on shore'.[55] Huck and Jim's words (and needs) are both subject, in this altered context, to suppression. The fact is, however, that Huck's utterances inevitably contain traces of their prior social context. For his language has been formed by his engagement in two (irreconcilable) communities, both on and off the raft. His language, and identity, is thus composed of *two different languages* which inextricably combine in the one stream of discourse. So in the famous incident in Chapter 31, when Huck is deciding how to act in relation to the re-enslaved Jim, he acts positively (tears up his letter, goes 'to work and steal Jim out of slavery again') but he cannot fully justify that act to himself. For the monoglossic discourse of the 'religious, political, moral' authorities forms part and parcel of his own speech. He cannot avoid this prior discourse which is always a part of his voice; a part of his very being.

Facing once more the problem of Jim's status as slave, after the king and the duke's selling of him, Huck immediately – as it were – re-enters a conversation which has never fully been interrupted with that slave-holding society of which he is a part. And in entering this conversation, he re-assumes immediately, slips straight into, the language of those particular authorities; the social language, verbal and ideological point of view, which he has himself appropriated as part of what Bakhtin would call his own 'ideological becoming' (p. 341). Thus he speaks of Jim as a piece of property whose possession is endorsed by the word of God: 'here was the plain hand of Providence slapping me in the face and letting me know my wickedness was being watched all the time from up there in heaven, whilst I was stealing a poor old woman's nigger . . . ' (p. 281).

Huck does however recognize that this discourse is no

longer quite persuasive, talks of 'playing double . . . trying
to make my mouth *say* I would do the right thing' (p. 282).
It is here that Bakhtin's notion of 'the word in language'
as 'half someone else's' is made explicit, as Huck speaks
the language which has been taught him, tries to make his
mouth *say* the words the dominant culture has given him to
use concerning the slave. Huck almost recognizes here his own
double voicedness; there is scarcely a step from playing double
to saying double. Two languages both operate, both strive for
dominance within him; the 'host'[56] language of the authorities
which has helped form him, and that language which has
emerged during and out of the conversation with Jim on the
raft – that of equality and friendship, one rooted in pragmatic
experience, of doing and acting. It is this language which, having written the letter which makes him feel 'all washed clean
of sin', he shifts into, as he metaphorically lays out another
part of himself, another side of the language available to him:
'I see Jim before me . . . and we a floating along, talking, and
singing, and laughing . . . I'd see him standing my watch on
top of his'n . . . ' (p. 283). The latter language, celebrating 'an
affirmation of a friendship among equals'[57] wins out (in terms
of the way Huck will act) in the contest of both language and
values that is occurring, and leads to Huck's famous decision
to tear up the letter and '*go* to hell'.

And here of course lies the rub. For in terms of his
use of language (and the moral and religious assumptions it
contains) Huck cannot overthrow the monoglossic discourse
which has formed (part of) him. He is caught within its
terms, its judgements, even as he decides to act in a
way which counters its commands. For he immediately
re-engages his conversation with his larger (authoritative)
society, and condemns himself to hell and damnation, using
its words, seeing his action through its eyes. Huck cannot
finally avoid the control of the prestige language. It forms
part of his identity; he judges himself by its standards. All he
can do is move uneasily between the two (uncomplementary)
discourses which compose him. The lack of ease involved in
such movement is stunningly brought home to the reader
soon after this point, when Aunt Sally asks Huck if anyone
was hurt in the supposed steamboat cylinder head blow
out, and he answers, 'No'm. Killed a nigger' (p. 291). The

language of care, concern and equality that has developed in the community of two on the river cannot find any bridge, form of connection, to the language and value schemes of that racist, slave-holding society of which he is a speaking part.

V

Every quotidian utterance . . . is like a 'password' known only to those who belong to the same social horizon.[58]

The language which has developed out of Huck and Jim's relationship on the raft, which belongs to that particular social horizon, is put under threat as a result of plot development. For once Jim is enslaved again, this language can no longer freely function. Huck can plan to steal Jim out of slavery again, but, caught in the language and ideological system of the dominant culture, he sees this act as criminal and immoral rather than as socially transforming. Moreover, the very notion of stealing Jim out of slavery has come to have negative connotations, for as Holland points out:

> Jim's enslavement, and the process of liberation offered in the book – Jim in chains in the cabin, Jim disguised as King Lear or a sick Arab aboard the raft, Jim chained on the raft pretending to be a recaptured runaway – both make a scapegoat of Jim and are virtual mirror images of each other. Liberation dissolves into enslavement and they come close, without actually doing so, to cancelling each other out.[59]

Both Huck and Jim have become, from the point of the running down of the raft onwards, increasingly subject to the monoglossic discourse of others. Jim's voice, indeed, has been more or less silenced from the time the raft passes Cairo, at least in all but its more passive aspects. The determined, clear-headed adult in him has been swiftly killed off as his social position changes, as he becomes once more subject to voices of authority which suppress his speech almost entirely ('Jim said it was so; and the king told him to shut up', p. 274).

He is painted blue by the king and the duke: as that 'sick Arab', 'he didn't only look like he was dead, he looked considerable more than that'. And though he is finally 'freed', the meaning of that particular word still remains in doubt. For his situation is of one eleven hundred miles away from home, without wife and children, alone, 'all but forgotten by Huck', Tom's forty dollars in his pocket, but nothing else.[60] His position, too, is to be put into the context of the position and status of the free black in the South in the 1840s; where Frederick Douglass, for example, can report of Talbot County, Maryland, 'that killing a slave, *or any colored person* (my italicising) . . . is not treated as a crime, either by the courts or the community' (p. 68).

Huck retains narrative control of the text, and will literally have its last word: 'THE END. YOURS TRULY, HUCK FINN.' Yet he, too, increasingly finds himself in the position of a socially subjected person, his language too weak to oppose those dominant voices which take over the raft, take over his and Jim's lives. That element of his voice which has emerged – hesitantly and sporadically – to find positive expression within the context of that community of two on the raft, is muted to greater and greater extent. First, Huck subjects himself to the king and the duke: the duke 'said we ought to bow, when we spoke to him, and say "Your Grace", or "My Lord" . . . and one of us ought to wait on him at dinner . . . Well, that was all easy, so we done it . . . I learnt that the best way to get along with this kind of people is to let them have their own way' (pp. 183–6). And though Huck recognizes their parasitic use of authoritative discourse as corrupt, he has no way of overthrowing it. He can escape their influence – in telling Mary Jane 'they was beats and bummers' (p. 255) he thinks 'to be free again' (p. 273) to resume the relationship with Jim on the raft. But such a resumption is of the briefest. Their voices on the raft are monoglossic. They act and speak tyrannically, 'lording it' over Huck and Jim who fall silent as a result. The king and the duke are finally tarred and feathered, run out of town by the Pikesville inhabitants (their cover finally blown by Jim, who thus uses his voice to get some revenge for the way they have abused him). But all that then happens is that Huck finds himself in another subordinated position, now caught, again with Jim, in the persuasive 'idiocy of Tom's script' (Schmitz, p. 121).

For when Huck has made his decision 'to go to hell' in rescuing Jim, the unease of his discourse, the lack of complementarity between its several parts, has become manifest even to him ('trying to make my mouth say . . . '). Bakhtin says of the hero in Dostoevsky that he 'never for an instance coincides with himself'.[61] A similar loss of 'the unity of the "I" '[62] is evident in Huck as I have just shown him. At the end of the novel, it is Aunt Polly who has to tell of Huck 'who I was, and what' (p. 366). Jim's question earlier 'Is I *me*, or who *is* I?' (p. 141) raises questions of identity which run right through the text. It is noticeable just how quickly Huck slips into Tom Sawyer's role. Significantly, he uses a variation of the phrase to describe this role which he has used earlier to describe being on the raft – 'Being Tom Sawyer was easy and comfortable' (p. 294) – though the 'free' has now been noticeably dropped.

In becoming a double to Tom Sawyer,[63] going along with his words, his plans, in the evasion routine, Huck can rest easy within society, is not confronted with the painful separations in his own 'self'. He can take a secondary role, merge himself in Tom's monoglossic voice, while at the same time carrying out his plan to free Jim. If Huck's single discourse has two (and more) incompatible voices, if on the riverbank he is generally more at ease with a passive rather than active role, such a merging can well be explained. Only when he learns that Tom has been 'playing' with both him and Jim (he knows Jim is officially 'free'), only after Tom pays Jim off for 'lost time' like any other wage-slave in the context of that rapidly industrializing America in which Twain writes, does Huck separate his voice off from Tom's. Tom's inability to consider Jim in any other way than as puppet to his own monologic discourse is one Huck has finally to reject.

VI

In *Huckleberry Finn* the centripetal and the centrifugal, the forces of linguistic and socio-ideological centralization and decentralization, are held in tension as nowhere else in Twain's work. The forces of centralization operate effectively in so far as the two main discourses introduced with the potential to overthrow official forms of language and meaning – Huck and Jim's – both end up effectively silenced. Jim's relationship with Huck on the raft can, to a degree, escape the limits of class and ethnic distinction that predominate in the surrounding society. Though it is Huck's voice that, as a norm, contains Jim's, it is noticeable that he speaks for them both as a unit: 'we hung up our . . . lantern, and judged that we was free and safe once more' (p. 176). Such a breaking of limits is, however, constantly challenged by that official language and its values which press on and infect the speech of both man and boy at every turn. Jim's voice as independent, self-determining black man is shown, too, as fragile in the extreme;[64] is silenced almost as soon as heard, limited in expression to two or three short speeches – taboo to a racist society that retains its authority and power by continual suppression of such a voice. When the doctor describes Jim's giving up of his own freedom to nurse Tom, it is not as that 'good man' of Huck's earlier description, but as one who 'ain't a bad nigger', one who is 'worth a thousand dollars' (pp. 360–1).

Jim's human value is judged finally in the dehumanizing terms of economic exchange, his worth as property rather than as one with his own voice, his own stake in the social exchange. And though 'free' at the novel's end, Jim's voice will, the suggestion is, continue to be suppressed and subordinate to the 'official' language. Such a suggestion is of course confirmed when we dialogize Tom's 'Turn [Jim] loose! he ain't no slave; he's as free as any cretur that walks this earth!' (p. 365) with Martin Luther King's March on Washington speech (August, 1963) where the prospect of being 'Free at last!', free of racism and prejudice, is still one that lies in the future ('I have a dream . . . ').[65] 'Freedom', in its fullest sense, still has not arrived for the black man or woman, even a century after the time of the novel's events.

Huck does manage to dent elements of the official language throughout the novel, though he is not always aware of the impact of what he says. He is, however, finally bound by its words, its value scheme, at least as long as he is positioned in close relation to that culture which has helped to mould him. His vernacular voice can, as it stands on the margins of that culture, develop other conversations (with Jim, with the reader) in which such official forms of language are challenged and overthrown, but not until the end of the novel when Huck 'light[s] out for the Territory' is there any suggestion that such an overthrow can be anything more than temporary. Such an overthrow is, moreover, never fully recognized by Huck; only by the reader as the result of the dialogization of voices by which Twain composes his novel. Huck has the final word in the novel, but the implications of those last words are, in Bakhtinian terms, bleak. In retreat from those authorities – Tom, Miss Watson, those who hold power in Southwestern society and endorse its particular kind of Christianity, its 'peculiar institution' of slavery; authorities whose language and values one part of him cannot help but share – he will remove himself from the province (social and geographical context) of their influence. In doing so, lighting out 'ahead of the rest', Huck chooses to end all dialogue with those around him; stands silent, voiceless, asocial. And to be asocial is, for Bakhtin, not to exist. The monoglossic languages of Southwestern culture are thus left both powerful and triumphant.

However, looked at from another point of view, *Huckleberry Finn* can be viewed in terms of what Bakhtin would call a *polyphonic* novel, one in which centrifugal forces (decentralizing and disunifying) operate strongly. Bakhtin makes a distinction between the heteroglossic and the polyphonic which must be briefly shown. The novel form is heteroglossic by nature of its interweaving of various stratifications of languages and belief systems. Polyphony, celebrated by Bakhtin in his work on Dostoevsky, is where this plurality of voices is embraced and welcomed into the novel; where all kinds of languages and world views are accorded equal status by the novelist. Bakhtin describes such an effect in Dostoevsky as 'a plurality of independent and unmerged voices and consciousnesses, a genuine polyphony of fully valid voices . . . a plurality of consciousnesses, with equal rights and each with its own world'.[66] As McHale points out: 'It is important to distinguish between the formal and stylistic heteroglossia of a text and its ideological polyphony, for heteroglossic texts are not inevitably polyphonic'.[67] Thus, Eliot in *The Waste Land* (1922), as Murray shows, is undoubtedly heteroglossic in terms of all the layers of language introduced, but is monologic, rather than polyphonic, in his 'attempts to bind together the disparate voices and explicitly to counter the centrifugal social and cultural forces of the time'.[68]

Huckleberry Finn might appear a strange novel to propose as polyphonic. After all, it is Huck's voice which monologically controls the text: and if he reports the direct speech of others, he just as often *merges* their voices with his own, reporting their words indirectly. What for me gives this novel polyphonic qualities is, first of all, the way that Twain, like Dostoevsky, produces 'a polygeneric text; that is, a mixture of nineteenth century non-canonic literary genres with canonic motifs of the "great" literary tradition going as far back as the Renaissance'.[69] As Harold Beaver points out, the novel is based on at least four models, 'the picaresque, the epistolary, the autobiographical, and the adventure story'.[70] The narrative process is fragmented as Twain moves between these forms and those of fugitive slave novel, 'ideological drama', 'low brow "escape" fiction', 'historical novel', 'panegyric', etc.[71] These extraordinary shifts allow an *'accumulation* of several, *different* points of view'[72] to occur as we move between a number of controlling perspectives – Miss Watson's, Pap's, Tom's, Jim's, the king and the duke's, etc. – all contained within Huck's single narrative.

Secondly, it is the balance between the social powerlessness of Huck's voice, and its narrative authority over those more powerful other voices presented through it, which creates polyphony. For the 'multiplicity of social voices' channelled through Huck – all those internal stratifications of language as they exist at a particular moment of Southwestern history – finally silence his and Jim's voice more or less completely in terms of social interaction. Huck lays out all those voices for us to hear in both their power, their typicality, and their interweavings. If these languages tend to silence Huck socially, they cannot of course do so formally, in terms of his narrative authority. In this role, his voice is used by Twain to dialogize all these other voices; used to apply a lever to all the languages of the various types of authority represented here. This he was never to find a way of doing again. He ventriloquates, with Huck as his instrument, the competing voices of Southwestern culture at this social and historical moment, sets them in relation to one another in terms of their mutual struggle for domination. It is Huck's own voice which then is made to effectively challenge, tear the mask from these languages, even while that voice cannot escape their influence, and is indeed finally silenced by them. In the orchestrated balance between narrative voice and the discourses channelled through it – the power of the latter within the represented world of the novel; of the former in representing this world – Twain ensures that the various languages of the text resist integration, unification; that centrifugal pressures never cease operating within it. 'The polyphonic novel as a whole is thoroughly dialogical':[73] this statement precisely describes *Huckleberry Finn*.

Such centrifugal pressure also operates in terms of another aspect of Twain's use of the novel form itself, one which Bakhtin sees as an 'ever-developing' genre (p. 6). For he enters into dialogue, polemically interacts with, the literary models available to him at the end of the nineteenth century. In his introduction of a first person narrator who uses the vernacular, he dialogizes and disrupts all previous accepted conventions concerning the nature of novelistic discourse in America. Introducing a black voice into the literary mainstream, and registering its appearances and disappearances as it responds to, and briefly avoids, the pressure of a dominant discourse, he further questions any notion of a common value system, a unitary literary language. If, for Bakhtin, society consists of a plurality of voices in dialogue, then in the use of a distinctive black voice, in the use of Huck's vernacular, Twain points the way to the seeing of American literature as a clash of voices – ethnic, class, regional, gendered – which cuts against the grain of any notion of a fixed, stable and unitary literary canon. We can, I think, now safely extend Bakhtin's words 'the novel must represent all the social and ideological voices of its era' (p. 411) to rephrase it, 'a nation's literature must represent all the social and ideological voices of its particular eras'.

One last point remains to be made. The whole basis of Bakhtin's theory rests on the need to be aware of the way in which 'particular meanings are triggered off, and others suppressed, by the actual historical situation of each individual utterance'.[74] This calls attention to the need to examine the historical situation of the text's production as well as of those voices located in it. To pose the issue differently, if Huck wonders with Aunt Sally 'what on earth did [Tom] want to set [Jim] free for, seeing he was already free?' (p. 365) so we, as readers, wonder what on earth did Twain want to write a novel about slavery for, when slavery had been abolished two decades prior to his writing. Of which social and historical situation is Twain's authorial discourse a product? This question calls for extended treatment. Here I do no more than suggest the beginnings of an answer. C. Van Woodward's work illustrates the course of race relations in the South after the Civil War. He shows how a phase of Southern history began in 1877:

> inaugurated by the withdrawal of federal troops from the South, the abandonment of the Negro as a ward of the nation, the giving up of the attempt to guarantee the freed man his civil and political equality, and the acquiescence of the rest of the country in the South's demand that the whole problem be left to the disposition of the dominant Southern white people.[75]

Steven Mailloux valuably sites the novel, focusing on 'the ideological rhetoric of the text and the way its arguments relate to political quarrels of the 1880s';[76] sees Twain then as entering in dialogue with the other forms of cultural discourse around him. He shows, in line with Van Woodward, how America had turned its 'rhetorical attention' away from race relations by 1877; how 'by 1885 the ideological rhetoric of white supremacy . . . dominated Southern politics and eventually became institutionalized in state laws regulating relations between the white and black races' (p. 110). *Huckleberry Finn* can be seen as taking part in the re-opened debate on the race issue, 'a highly charged and polarized argument . . . about the ideology of white supremacy' (p. 112) which consequently occurred. Rather than rehearsing the stages of Mailloux's arguments, I wish only to stress the fact that the novel is socially and ideologically accented towards the 'dialogizing background' of its era, Twain finishing it in 1883, 'the year . . . the Supreme Court declared the Civil Rights Act unconstitutional'.[77] Bakhtin points out that 'every age re-accentuates in its own way the works of its most immediate past' (p. 421). The ability of Twain's text to spur such re-accentuation is a measure of the importance of the social and ideological issues it confronts. To conclude with Laurence Holland's words:

> The flukish fact of Jim's legal freedom, and the failure of his world to flesh it out with the family, the opportunities, and the community that would give it meaning, define with haunting and painful relevance, and with absurd precision, the problem of setting a free Negro free, which is the pressing problem, in all its extensions, in post-Civil War America and more recent decades.[78]

7

A Medley of Voices: Zora Neale Hurston's *Their Eyes Were Watching God*

'Ah got to say a piece of litery [literary] fust to git mah wind on'.[1]

I

My final chapter takes the form of a brief implementation of all that has gone before. It is Bakhtinian in the sense that it consists of a medley of most of those voices thus far introduced; a chapter constructed out of 'a polyphony of voices, where each remains distinct and yet every voice is posited in relation to every other'.[2] As the narrator of this critical text, I thus find myself in the position of Dostoevsky's narrators as viewed by Bakhtin. Lacking a 'single [and unified] authorial consciousness',[3] I converse with my 'characters' (the critics I have chosen to explicate in this study), and so become 'a plurality of centers of consciousness irreducible to a common denominator'.[4]

My conclusion, however, is not quite as open-ended as such a notion of a medley of co-existing critical voices might imply. For if my narration here is composed of a number of interpretive positions 'counterpointing' one another (all voices made simultaneous), then my own position as narrator and focalizer – my own relation to the critical stories I tell – remains vital. I constitute the voices which compose my text in a certain form, and even while I recognize the fragility and impermanence of such a holding operation (the voices I bring together constantly threaten to fly off in their own different directions, follow a different narrative path than that into which I provisionally co-opt them), my narration offers my particular 'point of intersection'[5] between these critical voices, the texts I approach, and the reader for whom I write. It is my critical plot, if you like, which gives a conditional coherence to the various voices (non-exclusive interpretive positions) which I have attempted to record here.

There is one critical approach I choose to omit in this final chapter: that dealing with issues of narration, speech representation, and focalization. This reflects the fact that, as became apparent in my last chapter, the first two of these subjects are, to some extent, subsumed by a Bakhtinian analysis concerning stratifications of language in the novel and their relation to social and historical conditions of existence. My decision then is one which was taken in order to avoid unnecessary repetition. The subjects of narration and focalization are not however completely ignored: some reference will be made to them in my discussion of other critical areas.

So the organization of my final chapter. I take up again here the critical theories I have introduced earlier, but in piece-meal form. This is partly because of the obvious limitations of space. But it is also because I wish to direct the critical voices to a certain provisional end. My choice of a final text, Zora Neale Hurston's *Their Eyes Were Watching God* (1937) suggests that end, one in line with Bakhtin's undercutting of the oppositional distinction between 'low' literature and 'high' literature; his decentering of both official values and official language. For Hurston, one of the most important black women writers in America in the first half of this century, has been excluded until very recently from an American literary canon which had come to be defined not just, in Nina Baym's terms, as 'essentially male', but also as essentially white.[6] My handling of my critical sources is directed in this final chapter to what I see as political ends: to join those other voices calling for a widening of the canon; calling in Bakhtinian terms for a reading of American literature which represents 'all the social and ideological voices'[7] of an era, which recognizes that a culture, like a novel, may – indeed, must – be read polyphonically: as a multiplicity of regional, social, ethnic, professional, and gendered voices, all in dialogue with one another. Like Henry Louis Gates Jr., I see such renegotiations and re-workings of the canon as a source of excitement; a source of a genuine democratization of American literary history. Gates speaks specifically of black literature, and his optimism is qualified. His scope can, I think, be widened to take in other voices; his optimism more fully endorsed:

> the 'non-canonical' critic can barely contain her or his elation at the faint hope that the republic of 'literature' is experiencing alterations which can, at last, enable it to accommodate even those citizens historically disenfranchised by the critic's version of the 'grandfather clause'.[8]

Hurston is such a citizen. This chapter joins with such full length studies as Robert F. Hemenway's *Zora Neale Hurston* (1977) and Karla F. C. Holloway's *The Character of the Word: The Texts of Zora Neale Hurston* (1987) to recuperate her voice in the public and political world of American literary history.

II

Time and *Their Eyes Were Watching God*

> 'Ah know exactly what Ah got to tell yuh, but it's hard to know where to start at'.[9]

Clock time and internal time (the time of consciousness) are juxtaposed in *Their Eyes Were Watching God* in a way paradigmatic of the modernist novel. That clock and calendar 'time' which 'makes everything old' and which marks off Janie's development from birth to middle-age (she is 'around forty' when she first starts going out with Tea Cake) is set against Janie's ability to span its entire duration in a single act of consciousness (internal time): 'Janie saw her life like a great tree in leaf with the things suffered, things enjoyed, things done and undone. Dawn and doom was in the branches' (p. 20). This typical modernist strategy of juxtaposing the act of memory, the condition of consciousness, with the passing of time measured by external, public criteria, is one introduced to frame Janie's story. The organic metaphor of the beginning, however, with its heavy sense of a final ending ('doom') is replaced with a much more open-ended finale:

> Janie . . . sat down. Combing road-dust out of her hair. Thinking.
> The day of the gun, and the bloody body, and the courthouse came and commenced to sing a sobbing sigh out of every corner in the room; out of each and every chair and thing. Commenced to sing, commenced to sob and sigh, singing and sobbing. Then Tea Cake came prancing around her where she was and the song of the sigh flew out of the window and lit in the top of the pine trees. Tea Cake, with the sun for a shawl. Of course he wasn't dead. He could never be dead until she herself had finished feeling and thinking. The kiss of his memory made pictures of love and light against the wall. Here was peace. She pulled in her horizon like a great fish-net. Pulled it from around the waist of the world and draped it over her shoulder. So much of life in its meshes! She called in her soul to come and see (pp. 285–6).

Metaphors of human control have replaced the organic metaphors of the beginning of the novel. The recapturing of experience through consciousness is associated with a life-giving energy stemming from the recovery of images of 'love and light' from the past. A bridge is formed between abstract memory and tangible physical (erotic) presence with the phrase 'the kiss of his memory'. It is not 'doom' we end up with but 'so much of life' in this highly romantic hymn to consciousness. For Janie's mind is that which pulls in 'her horizon'. As Barbara Johnson points out, horizon acts as both 'the net and the fish'[10] in this metaphor. Time is caught in the meshes of this net (Janie's past) as well as space (horizon metaphorically compressed into that bedroom where Janie sits). The effect is similar to Lily Briscoe's 'vision' of Mrs Ramsay in *To The Lighthouse*.[11] Internal time ('feeling and thinking') triumphs over clock time at the end of the novel. The image of the dead Tea Cake with teeth buried in Janie's arm is replaced by that of him 'prancing around her ... with the sun for a shawl'. Doom gives way before imaginative transcendence. As Janie has told her story, recovered her past, so too she achieves the ability to celebrate memory and feeling even in the face of the inevitable decay and defeat that time has thus far brought her.

When we come to try to pick out the *temporal references* that are contained in *Their Eyes Were Watching God*, what is immediately apparent is the lack of textual specificity in relation to the world of public history. Reference is made in Janie's grandmother's story to the Civil War and end of slavery, but apart from that the main events of a public nature in the novel are the incorporating of Eatonville as independent black community and the hurricane and flood which occur near the narrative's end. The grandmother's narrative allows us to chronologically locate the novel in approximate terms. Janie must have been born around about 1882; the narrative thus bringing us up to about 1922.[12] No dates, however, are mentioned in the novel, and historical referents are both rare and unhelpful. The actual incorporation of Eatonville for example occurred in 1886, thus has been shifted to fit Hurston's fictional needs. So, too, have the details of that hurricane which she experienced in Nassau in the Bahamas in 1929.[13] Hurston is concerned in this novel both with ethnicity and gender. Such concerns are, however, not strongly sited in terms of exact historical location.

The one exception to this generalization, as we have seen, comes in relation to Janie's grandmother. This significantly provides the sole firm base for dating the events of the narrative. When we examine temporal *order* in this novel, we find a fairly uncomplicated relationship between story time and text time.[14] A rough schematization of the novel – naming the linear sequence of events (text time) alphabetically; numbering the chronological position of these events in relation to a reconstituted story time – gives us the following movement:

A3   Time of first narrative beginning 'Ships at a distance', pp. 9–19.

B2   Mixed homodiegetic analepsis (a retrospective sequence starting before and then joining the time of the first narrative, which is part of the main story line) pp. 20–283 ("Ah ain't never seen mah papa . . . Now that she was home . . . ").

C1   An external (outside the time of the first narrative) and heterodiegetic analeptic sequence. This narrative whose reach centres on the experience of the grandmother (thus heterodiegetic – a shift away from the main protagonist) and runs back to the time of her birth, continues from page 31 ('Ah was born back due in slavery') to page 37.

The whole novel then, despite the presence of other brief analeptic sequences, follows the pattern A3 [B2 (C1) B2] A3, a pattern whose regularity is only modified by the placing of the C1 sequence at a very early stage in terms of text time.

The significant thing to note concerning these temporal orderings is that Janie's grandmother's narrative not only provides our basis for dating the events of the entire novel, it is also its genesis; the originating event – in terms of story time – described in the narrative. Janie's story, in other words, looks back to that variety of slave narrative which is (at least part of) her grandmother's story. Despite the affection he shows her, Janie's grandmother's owner makes 'a spit cup' (p. 37) out of her. She has no voice in her sexual destiny: as owner and master he has complete authority over her. Her story illustrates precisely the 'economics of slavery' as Houston Baker describes them:

> the owner's sexual gratification (forcefully achieved) was also his profit. The children resulting from such a violation followed the enslaved condition of their mother, becoming property. 'Succeeding generations' . . . translated as 'added commodities' for a master's store. The Civil War putatively ended such a commercial lineage.[15]

Though Nanny's flight to the swamp and the Confederate surrender at Richmond lead to the removal of her mistress' threat to sell her child, nonetheless it is against this whole sequence that Janie's story must be placed. Janie is the literal product (one generation removed) of this slave narrative. The colour of her skin – she is a mulatta with a 'coffee-and-cream complexion' (p. 208); looks 'white folkish' (p. 215) – conditions the response of the fellow members of her community to her, and in part defines her 'identity'. Whiteness is associated with 'divinity' by Mrs Turner. Tea Cake's slapping of Janie only has public significance as a sign of his authority over her because of her skin colour (as Sop-de-Bottom says, 'you can't make no mark on . . . dese ol' rusty black women', p. 219). Janie's earlier association with royalty by Joe and by the voice of Eatonville[16] again establishes both the way in which the values of the Afro–American community have been conditioned by the standards of the dominant ethnic group; also establishes class (within this community) as well as race as one of the narrative's central issues.

Janie's grandmother's notion of success, of standing on 'high ground' (p. 32), however, relates not to skin colour but to economics. Her 'text' is that to avoid being a 'work-ox and a brood-sow' all her life, a black woman needs protection. Janie's feathers will not get crumpled if she has economic security, 'big protection'. This is her version of how 'colored women' can sit on high. She conflates too, in Baker's terms, 'the securing of property with effective expression. Having been denied a say in her own fate because she was *property*, she assumes that *only* property enables expression' (p. 57). Though Janie rejects Nanny's text, her 'freedom feeling' (p. 139) is in fact dependent on her economic status after Joe's death.

Work becomes play for Janie on the 'muck' only because of the cushion this financial security gives her. This is nowhere explicitly recognized, but is implicit both in the difference between Janie and Tea Cake and some of the other families who come to the muck – 'People ugly from ignorance and broken from being poor' (p. 196) – and in the relations between white and black worlds even now slavery has been abolished, where economic power is still directly related to personal mastery and political authority. This is the point both of the Palm Beach episode and the trial scene. Janie can only live her way *because* she 'done lived Grandma's way' (p. 171). However much these economic facts of life are muted in this text and in its presentation of Afro–American culture, the fact that they can never be entirely forgotten undeniably conditions our reception of Janie's narrative. *The analeptic sequence concerning Nanny's slavery provides the very basis for a full understanding of the entire narrative.* Only in the context of slavery can the present conditions of Afro-American existence be understood.

A discussion of that category of narrative temporality which Genette entitles *duration* (the relations between story time and textual linearity) in relation to *Their Eyes Were Watching God* need only be brief. For by and large Hurston gains her acceleration and deceleration effects in this narrative – her changes in narrative pace – through what Genette would describe as conventional means. The novel commences with a rare example of 'the absolute slowness of descriptive pause'[17] where story time is at a complete standstill, while the text unfolds with the following sequence:

Ships at a distance have every man's wish on board. For some they come in with the tide. For others they sail forever on the horizon, never out of sight, never landing until the Watcher turns his eyes away in resignation, his dreams mocked to death by Time. That is the life of men. Now, women forget all those things they don't want to remember, and remember everything they don't want to forget. The dream is the truth. Then they act and do things accordingly.

This is panchronic and panoramic focalization, the classic version of an extradiegetic narrator who is omniscient. Here a pause occurs before the story's movement begins, while gender differentiation is signalled as a subject for textual enquiry. So, too, as Hurston traces and amends Frederick Douglass' 'apostrophe to the moving multitude of ships'[18] on Chesapeake Bay in his *Narrative*, are modes of black literary production. This sequence provides both a philosophical frame to the story of Janie's life, and an artistic frame to Hurston's writing of it.

Otherwise, however, the narrative moves forward through the use of ellipsis, summary and scene, with all the emphasis on the latter. The narration of Janie's childhood years proceeds through a mélange of summary and ellipsis. The resulting speed is explained when we learn, through Janie's focalization, that 'her conscious life' (p. 23) had not commenced until she was sixteen years old. This statement is, in fact, challenged by the two brief scenes that she chooses to illuminate this childhood. I will focus on the first, one of those classic recognition scenes which recur as a primary distinguishing feature of black literature.[19] Here, Janie realizes her difference from those around her – that her colour constitutes her otherness. A photograph is taken of her when she is about six years old, in the company of the white children with whom she plays:

> when we looked at de picture and everybody got pointed out there wasn't nobody left except a real dark little girl with long hair standing by Eleanor. Dat's where Ah wuz s'posed to be, but Ah couldn't recognize dat dark chile as me. So Ah ast, 'where is me? Ah don't see me?' . . . Everybody laughed . . . (p. 21).

Janie's recognition here – 'Aw, aw! Ah'm colored!' – is obviously central to the development of her conscious life. Thus, the slowing down of pace at this point. It is her introduction to the state of 'double-consciousness' which W. E. DuBois saw as basic to the black condition in America, 'this sense of always looking at one's self through the eyes of others, of measuring one's soul by the tape of a world that looks on in amused contempt and pity'.[20] Here, Janie measures her face by the tape of the (white) world. Such a recognition of difference, which carries with it the knowledge of the co-presence of two separate standards of self-measurement (one according to white criteria, the other according to black), prepares the reader for the trial scene near the novel's conclusion, where the stress on the way in which white eyes regard and define Janie cuts right across the previous sense of identity which she has established for herself within the black community. Identity is a fragile and incoherent thing in a racially divided society. The move from summary to scene at this point of the narrative carries with it heavy thematic implication. By and large, though, this is a traditional novel in terms of the techniques Hurston uses to affect its pace. Summary is the 'connective tissue'[21] that holds its various scenes together.

In terms of those *frequency* effects which help give the narrative its rhythms, I wish only to mention the repetition which frames the narrative. Janie's statement that she has

now returned from 'de big convention of livin'' (p. 18) at
the start of the novel is repeated, though using a different
metaphor, in one of her final phrases, 'Ah done been tuh de
horizon and back' (p. 284). This repetition (telling twice what
happened once) is a way of stressing the circular patternings
of the novel. Change – Janie's personal growth – takes place
in the context of what becomes a circular movement: from
Eatonville to the horizon and back again. Robert Stepto
associates black literature with the paradigm of the ascent
narrative and associates the move from forms of slavery to
forms of freedom with the geographical move from South to
North.[22] Black women's literature fits into the former pattern
(the female character 'part of an evolutionary spiral, moving
from victimization to consciousness'),[23] but may perhaps be
identified with a different narrative structure in terms of
the protagonist's return to her home community (see also
Toni Morrison's *Sula*, 1974, and Alice Walker's *The Color
Purple*, 1983). Accumulation and growth in such narratives
are measured against the boundaries of a known and constant
communal base, rather than in an existentialist vacuum (the
Invisible Man's underground hole), or in a context of constant
social and political change.

III

Character construction

As a modernist text, *Their Eyes Were Watching God* operates
through indirect presentation of character. In this section
I will briefly illustrate some of the ways in which Janie's
character is constructed in the novel, using the categories
introduced in my chapter on *The Sun Also Rises*.

Action

Rimmon-Kenan sees one-time (or non-routine) actions as
particularly significant in the construction of character, since
they often 'evoke the dynamic aspect of the character, often
playing a part in a turning point in the narrative' (p. 61).
In this novel, I would focus on four particular illustrations

of such action: Janie's telling of her story to Pheoby, her marriages,[24] her verbal attack on Joe, her shooting of Tea Cake. Again due to the constraints of space in this chapter, I will confine my comments only to the first and last of these one-time actions. They will, it is to be hoped, provide a base for further exploration of these areas on the reader's part.

Janie's telling of her story to Pheoby's 'hungry listening' (p. 23), her own narrative act, is crucial to her self-definition. Anne Goodwyn Jones writes that 'to have a voice is to have a self',[25] and Janie's move from private thought to public self-expression in itself constitutes a defining of her identity. Silenced by Joe – 'mah wife don't know nothin' 'bout no speech-makin' . . . She's uh woman and her place is in de home' (p. 69) – her thoughts and feelings remain repressed, locked inside herself, unexpressed. The consequence of this is a form of self-division: 'Things packed up and put away in parts of her heart where [Jody] could never find them . . . She had an inside and an outside now and suddenly she knew how not to mix them' (pp. 112–3). Janie's refusal to finally submit to Joe and that 'bow-down command' (p. 75) associated with him, the freeing of her voice in the relationship with Tea Cake, make this novel into that 'ascent narrative' previously mentioned.

Janie's ability to tell her story, a story which is presumably to be made public through Pheoby ('mah tongue is in mah friend's mouf'), runs alongside both her overcoming of this particular form of self-division – in the form of a public expression of her innermost feelings – and her acquisition of knowledge both about herself and the world: 'It's uh known fact, Pheoby . . . Two things everybody's got tuh do fuh theyselves. They got tuh go tuh God, and they got tuh find out about livin' fuh theyselves' (p. 285). Janie has found out about living for herself. She finds the pulpit to preach her grandmother's text 'about colored women sittin' on high' (p. 32) on her back porch, her congregation represented by her best friend Pheoby, who in turn represents the reader. Her ability to tell this story represents a narrative turning point, in that it marks the full finding of Janie's voice, her ability literally to *express herself* (my stress).

Janie's shooting of Tea Cake, who attacks her with murderous intent while suffering from rabies, is also a significant turning point in the narrative. The melodramatic nature of this incident sits uneasily in what Susan Willis calls 'this otherwise very modernist text', and Hemenway calls it 'poorly plotted'.[26] The jarring nature of this extraordinary scene does call attention, I would suggest, to certain (aesthetic) difficulties in terms of plot resolution which connect up with certain unresolved (indeed contradictory) ideological tensions in the novel. Such tensions can be examined in relation to the construction of Janie's character in the text as it relates to her marital role and extends beyond it.

For it is the marriage with Tea Cake that allows Janie the fullest expression of her personality; at least in the context of the three heterosexual relationships around which the centre of the narrative organizes itself: 'He could be a bee to a blossom — a pear tree blossom in the spring. He seemed to be crushing scent out of the world with his footsteps. Crushing aromatic herbs with every step he took. Spices hung about him. He was a glance from God' (p. 161). The passivity and voicelessness that Joe required of her in her (largely ornamental) role of Mrs Mayor ('Here he was just pouring honour all over her'), an identity imposed from without, are put to one side in the relationship with Tea Cake. Indeed, this relationship is presented in seemingly idyllic terms in the 'utopian'[27] space of 'de muck'. Tea Cake offers, it is implied, a rediscovery of that spirit of heterosexual play she had lost in the marriage with Joe: once more she can be 'petal-open' on the 'daisy-field' (p. 111) of the marital bed. With Tea Cake, Janie is given equal participation in areas previously denied to her. Their 'love game' (p. 171) consists, after its initial stumblings, of Janie 'partak[ing] wid everything' (p. 186) he does. They shoot together, dance, sing, laugh, even work together. As Tea Cake says, 'we ain't got nothin' tuh do but do our work and come home and love' (p. 199). Here Janie is given equal voice to the male members of the community, getting 'so she could tell big stories herself' (p. 200). It is with Tea Cake that Janie learns a new 'language' (p. 173) of living, appears to express herself most fully. 'God snatched me out de fire through you', Janie tells him, 'And Ah loves yuh and feel glad' (p. 267).

How then can his violent death at Janie's hands, as he literally sinks his teeth into her in a spirit of absolute

fiendishness, be explained? Why should idyll turn to tragedy,
soul mate to enemy, in such a way? After shooting Tea Cake
in self-defence:

> he crashed forward in her arms. She was trying
> to hover him as he closed his teeth in the flesh of her
> forearm. They came down heavily like that. Janie struggled
> to a sitting position and pried the dead Tea Cake's teeth
> from her arm (p. 273).

Susan Willis points out that unless we want to 'accuse Hurston
of literary overkill' we need to read this episode in a 'figural
way' (p. 51). I suggest that even if we read it figurally, this is
still literary overkill as Hurston looks to develop two aspects
of Janie's character which cannot be satisfactorily contained
by her narrative.

And the clue to this figural reading is perhaps implicit in
an earlier incident when Janie watches her sleeping husband:
she 'looked down on him and felt a *self-crushing* love' (p. 192, my
emphasis). However fulfilling a heterosexual love relationship
might be, its fulfilment comes at the expense of other possible
manifestations of selfhood. For the self is multiple,[28] and the
marriage with Tea Cake satisfies but one part of that self.
Janie lives 'through' Tea Cake in their relationship. Though
she participates equally in his life, it is still a union based
on a patriarchal model. He takes the decisions; she follows
where he leads. When Tea Cake dies, Janie 'thanked him
wordlessly for giving her the chance for loving service'
(p. 273). Self-expression in this relationship, portrayed as the
best potentially realizable in heterosexual terms, goes hand
in glove with a form of self-extinction. And, significantly, the
final picture of Tea Cake, affected by the paranoia that comes
with hydrophobia, is a mirror image of an earlier picture of Joe,
who sees Janie as his property, whose intense jealousy (Tea
Cake's suspicion here is directed at Mrs Turner's brother) is
accompanied by a display of authority and control. Tea Cake
and Janie's relationship cannot escape models of patriarchal
domination. He still sees himself in the role of provider, even
slaps Janie 'around a bit to show he was boss' (p. 218).

Read in this frame, Janie's shooting of the maddened
Tea Cake can be seen as a symbolic move by which

Hurston asserts the possibility of a different type of female self-expression, a realization of a further element of Janie's multiple self, outside the context of heterosexual relations. This possibility is reinforced by Janie's words 'Ah jus' loves dis freedom' (p. 143) when she is earlier placed outside such a context with Joe's death (killed 'in a sense'[29] by Janie's profound insult). It is also reinforced by the very structure of the book, where the three heterosexual relationships are contained by a different type of 'sisterly' relationship, in which another side of the self can be displayed as Janie tells Pheoby her story, tells of the need 'Tuh find out about livin' . . . tuh *go* there tuh *know* there' (p. 285) which can only finally be done alone. Susan Willis sees the significance of the one-time action of the shooting in extreme terms, claiming that Hurston here makes clear that 'women cannot hope to have themselves fully realized in their husbands. When Janie shoots the maddened Tea Cake, she not only saves her own life, she also steps outside of the male-defined circuit of exchange'. The action is, she asserts, a 'radical response to potential domination', a 'symbolic claim [on Janie's part] for her own time and space' (p. 51).

I would modify such a reading to see the melodramatic nature of this incident (and the 'forcing' of the plot which results) as evidence of unresolved strain in so far as the whole issue of sexual politics in the novel is concerned. One side of Janie's self is 'fully realized' in her husband. Her self crushing love allows her soul to crawl 'out from its hiding place'. The price of such satisfaction is a denial of certain aspects of the self and an acceptance of patriarchal behaviour patterns. The killing of Tea Cake by Janie's own hand and the framing focus on that sisterly relationship between Janie and Pheoby suggests an alternative version of self outside these constraints. Their mutual incompatibility is suggested by the violent nature of that narrative rupture which leads Janie from one form of being to another. The confusion about sexual politics involved is suggested in Pheoby's final response to Janie's self-expressive narrative: 'Lawd! . . . Ah done growed ten feet higher from jus' listenin' tuh you, Janie. Ah ain't satisfied with mahself no mo''. This is not, however, a prelude to stepping outside the 'male-defined circuit of exchange'. Far from it! It rather serves as preamble to quite a different type of statement, 'Ah means tuh make Sam take me fishin' wid him after this' (p. 284).

To present the self as different, depending on the nature of its framing contexts, is however to suggest its multiplicity. This notion of the self as composed of variant facets of the personality, illuminated in different contexts and circumstances, is reinforced when we focus on the indirect presentation of character through environment in this novel, and on the use of analogous names. Restricting my discussion to these few areas of character presentation is not, though, to suggest that an examination of those other areas outlined in Chapter Three might not be of equal worth. It reflects rather the selective nature of this final chapter.

The relationship of environment to character depends on the way in which 'a character's physical surrounding (room, house, street, town) as well as his human environment (family, social class) are also often used as trait-connoting metonymies' (Rimmon-Kenan, p. 66). This area is a particularly rich one in *Their Eyes Were Watching God*. Different sides of Janie's character are illustrated as she moves from one environment to another. Her uncomfortable fit in the social hierarchies of the Eatonville world is made evident in her words to Pheoby: 'Jody classed me off . . . When Ah wasn't in de store he wanted me tuh jes sit wid folded hands and sit dere. And Ah'd sit dere wid de walls creepin' up on me and squeezin' all de life outa me' (p. 169). Her character is temporarily shaped by this environment. Janie becomes a divided self, as inner needs conflict with social (and marital) demands. Her forced fit in the environment of Joe's store, as Joe's wife, is clear in her consideration of her work in this context as 'such a waste of life and time' (p. 86). It is also clear in her assertion of the values of laughter and play in the face of Joe, who models his life on the values adopted from the (white) dominant capitalist mode; who, disturbingly, creates an environment for her to live in which mirrors the sense of unbridgeable difference (in terms of class and status, if not of race) that was apparent in the pre-Civil War South:

The rest of the town looked like servant's quarters surrounding the 'big house' . . . And look at the way he painted it – a gloaty, sparkly white. The kind of

promenading white that the houses of Bishop Whipple,
W. B. Jackson and the Vanderpools wore (p. 75).

The differences in Janie's environment (as measured by
her childhood and her three marriages), between 'de Muck'
and Palm Beach, between family life and family histories,
provide a crucial point of comparison for the measuring of
Janie's changing and developing self.

I will focus, however, on one particular set of environmental contexts which provide access to a depiction of
Janie's multi-faceted character. For the novel can be seen
as structured around two different sets of locational shifts.
On the one hand, Janie's movements are traced according to
precise geographical locale. The novel opens with Janie going
back to Eatonville. It then returns to trace Janie's moves from
West Florida where she spent her girlhood and time of her
first marriage, to Eatonville, Jacksonville, the Everglades ('de
Muck'), and thence to Palm Beach. From here, a return movement occurs, back to the muck, and finally back to Eatonville
again. On the other hand, we have a different type of spatial
structure in operation, one suggested in the references made
to the horizon, and to 'porches beside the road' down which
Janie comes in Chapter One. This structure can be represented
in terms of menonymic connection, as follows:

bedroom – parlour/kitchen – doorstep/porch – road – horizon
back porch

I signal the back porch as an environment which exists (and
which symbolically suggests an area of consciousness) apart
from, to one side of, those which are dominant in the reconstituted story time of Janie's narrative up to the point of Tea
Cake's death. All these other environments are shared by both
male and female (though significantly not by black and white).
The back porch symbolizes, I would suggest in line with prior
arguments, an alternative space where another side of Janie
can be given expression, an area – in Mari McCarty's words
– outside the 'cramped confines of patriarchal space'.[30]

To follow through this argument, I would see the bedroom as representing the 'spirit of marriage', the territory
of heterosexual play which she initially haas with Jody and

rediscovers with Tea Cake. The parlour (or kitchen in the cabin on the muck) is the place where 'company came to visit' (p. 111), one remove from the intimacy of the bedroom, a sphere associated primarily with the two-person relationship which composes domesticity, marriage, but one which provides an area of contact with the larger social group.[31] Janie expresses herself differently in each of these contexts. The porch-doorstep is the absolute middle ground in terms of the private-public polarity that is represented in this syntagmatic (and metaphorical) chain: the point of intersection and of fullest interaction between the community and the domestic world. Janie cannot express herself in public or domestic environments in the relationship with Joe. Joe's speech in the street before the store, to celebrate the bringing of the first public light to Eatonville, with both its biblical resonance and its Promethean ring, illustrate clearly the sense of patriarchal authority with which he is linked:

Us poor weak humans can't do nothin' tuh hurry [the sun] up nor to slow it down. All we can do, if we want any light after de settin' or befo' de risin', is tuh make some light ourselves. . . . De first street lamp in uh colored town. Lift yo' eyes and gaze on it. And when Ah touch de match tuh dat lamp-wick let de light penetrate inside of yuh, and let it shine, let it shine, let it shine (p. 73).

Janie feels unnatural (p. 74) in her relationship with Jody. This is precisely because traditional gender roles, which he asserts, require silence and passivity on her part. This becomes her identity, both in public and in private; the mask she is forced to wear before the world (and before Joe). Janie is consequently silenced in the intersecting area, the porch; not allowed to join in the 'lying', the game playing.

Tea Cake, though, acknowledges her right to equal access and pleasure in this area. She is, as it were, a different 'self' in this relationship, not muted, stifled, but 'glowing inside' as he plays checkers with her there: 'Somebody wanted her to play. Somebody thought it natural for her to play' (p. 146). The changing sense of self which results is confirmed in the scenes which occur in the doorway before her and Tea Cake's house on the muck (the equivalent to the porch, with all notion of hierarchy removed). Janie is here given equal voice to the male members of the group. Human environment (the different type of marriage) and spatial environment here interact in giving access to Janie's sense of her changing self.

The road and the horizon are the areas of public interaction which Janie negotiates in her quest for change and exploration of both self and the world (repeated action: looking to the horizon). Janie's journey comes full circle, and her movement between the different links of this 'environmental' chain is summarized and concertina-ed in one of the last things Janie says: 'Ah done been tuh de horizon and back and now Ah kin set heah in mah house and live by comparisons. Dis house ain't so absent of things lak it used tuh be befo' Tea Cake come along. It's full uh thoughts, 'specially dat bedroom' (p. 284).

The back porch, though, stands to one side of this chain. It is a related area, which Pheoby reaches through 'the intimate gate' (p. 14), but one which is only associated in this text with a single gender. Here two women can talk freely. Here the community voice, which though composed of both male and female elements is associated with a specifically patriarchal order ('Mouth-Almighty', 'lords of sounds'), drops away; where we are left with an image that represents a different type of communication, a different type of self-expression, available. Susan Willis' vision of the utopian possibilities of this relationship, I would rather see in the context of the notion of multiple selfhood which I have been developing: the idea that different sides of the personality can express themselves according to the particular social conditions at hand; that Janie's identity must be seen both in the context of the bedroom (with Tea Cake) *and* the back porch (with Pheoby). The fact that the back porch exists to one side of those spatial networks developed in the main part of the novel suggests again that the aspect of personality revealed in this setting cannot be easily integrated with aspects expressed elsewhere. Willis glosses over such difficulties when she writes:

> The image of Janie and Pheoby captures the spirit and hope for some new community based on sisterhood. This is not to suggest that in killing Tea Cake Janie has put an end to her heterosexuality. Rather, Janie has learned that

although women must be with men and for men, they must also be with women and for women. Pheoby brings to the sisterhood her care of Janie's fatigued body; Janie supplies the lessons she has learned (p. 52).

The notion of multiple, many-faceted selfhood which I think is evidenced in this narrative, can be reinforced by a brief reference to the notion of analogous names; names used to suggest the nature of a particular character. The only scene I wish to focus on here is that in Janie's childhood. Kimberly W. Benston tells the story of Malcolm X's 'heated debate with a prominent black academic' when, at the point of impasse:

> Malcolm paused briefly, then queried his antagonist: 'Brother Professor, do you know what they call a black man with a Ph D ?' 'No. What?' came the reply, to which Malcolm answered simply: 'Nigger'.[32]

Thus, to follow through the argument, does a master society reductively label the black man, depriving him of any sense of his individual identity (his name and social position), naming him instead as indistinguishable 'other'. So when Janie and Tea Cake briefly move from the Afro-American world which dominates the text to the larger world which must always be seen as bracketing it (the black community is as marginal in American culture as the black writer), our awareness of the 'viciously segregated'[33] nature of this world is partly evidenced by the complete denial of black identity: ' "Hello, there, Jim", the tallest [white man with a rifle] called out, "We been lookin' fuh you." "Mah name ain't no Jim," Tea Cake said watchfully' (p. 251).

Janie has been given the name of Alphabet as a small child ''cause so many people had done named me different names' (p. 21). In part, this might be seen as a denial of an illegitimate black child's identity by the world, both black and white, within which she moves. Another way of looking at the use of this name is to see Alphabet (Janie) in Houston Baker's phrase as 'embodying within herself the possibility of all names'.[34] To celebrate the black female self is also to celebrate the 'play on possibilities' which constitutes the interaction between subject and world. To play on possibility is to be aware of all the different versions of the self which can be expressed: in alphabetical terms, one can be whatever letter one chooses, Z (or) A – to pun on, and transfer the significance to, Hurston's own name – depending on the circumstances at hand. That name 'Alphabet' suggests exactly such a play of possibility, that sense of fluid development, associated with the character of Janie throughout this narrative.

IV

Reader response

Wolfgang Iser and Steven Mailloux both stress the reading process as one of constant interaction between text and reader; how one reading moment illuminates the next. They focus on the way we continually make and revise judgements as we negotiate the text, formulate then modify conjectures and hypotheses as we engage in the activity of reading. It is the 'nature of reading as a temporal process' to which attention is drawn, the way in which meaning is constructed by the reader as he or she responds sequentially to segments of the text and their relation to one another. This replaces a more traditional critical focus on the text as complete entity subject to 'holistic' reading. How the reader interacts with the text in a 'dynamic process of self-correction'[35] is foregrounded, at the (initial) expense of any notion of a final synthesis.

Brief illustration of the types of interaction which occur when reading *Their Eyes Were Watching God* can first be given by noting the use of primary and recency effects in the novel. The information we are first given in a text (primary effect) tends to have a strong influence on the reader. In Janie's case the 'primary effect', I would argue, is complicated by the narrative structure. For the information and attitudes presented early on in the text are filtered through three different focalizations – those of the narrator, the Eatonville community, and Janie herself.[36] The way we are shunted from one focalization to the next; are in fact guided as readers towards Janie's own authenticating voice, all in the context of the narrative's opening frame – means that our original impression of Janie is held in suspension until all three voices have been heard from. We are, I would suggest, given an unusual kind of primary effect, which consists of three versions of Janie being laid side by side. This is what provides the first strong readerly influence.

This might seem self-contradictory. Initial information, even if it is all in the one introductory chapter, is not after all presented to the reader simultaneously. My 'side by side' metaphor seems misleading when (the very point of my opening remarks) one sequence in fact *follows* the other. However Hurston, I think, brilliantly causes the reader to suspend her or his response to Janie; signals that we, as readers, are to be given a number of perspectives before such an initial step may be taken. She does this by giving us a first view of Janie, from the position of the extradiegetic (framing) narrator, which largely jams any readerly reaction to her: 'So the beginning of this was a woman and she had come back from burying the dead. Not the dead of sick and ailing with friends at the pillow and the feet. She had come back from the sodden and the bloated; the sudden dead, their eyes flung wide open in judgment' (p. 9). The brevity of this passage, its rather odd rhetorical effects, its lack of contextualization, leaves the reader perplexed. The relation of the conjunction 'so' to the prior paragraph is at this point unclear; its 'continuative force' (o.e.d.) not as yet subject to ready explanation. What, too, is 'this' the beginning of? The lack of any designated noun referent here leads the meaning of the pronoun to hang somewhat ambiguously. The emphasis of the passage is on untimely death, death presumably by drowning. But it stands in a narrative vacuum: what precedes it and what follows fail to offer any light on the nature of the event to which it refers. And why should the eyes of the dead be flung open in judgement? A question further complicated by the mention of 'the Watcher' in the first paragraph of the novel and by its title. We ask, with no hope of an immediate answer, who is watching whom? Who is judge and what or whom is being judged?[37] The first depiction of Janie, therefore, suggests she has lived through some tragedy, but is otherwise enigmatic, resists the readerly desire to fill in the details of this yet unnamed woman.

Interpretation of Janie is thus signalled as subject to delay. A second view of her is now presented as she is seen through the eyes and words of 'the people' as they

sit on 'their porches beside the road' and respond to her
(re-)appearance. This view differs so widely from the first as
to deny the possibility of synthesis; the questions it raises
almost entirely different in kind from its predecessor. It is
this narrative technique – leading us from an initial view
of Janie to a different vantage point, jamming any first
interpretation of her – which prompts us to hold back first
impressions until the whole sequence of focalizations which
centre on her complete themselves within this narrative unit
(the opening chapter).

And what we are now offered as this chapter develops
are two conflicting versions of Janie – one from without
(the community), one from within. I see this as the strong
primary effect which conditions our attitude to, and developing impression of, Janie throughout the text. For she is
presented from a double perspective: what is expected of
her in terms of womanly behaviour (the 'conventional images
and expectations of womanhood'[38]) and her self-definition of
womanliness. First, the reader is given a view of Janie from
without – a swirl of voices (words 'walking without masters',
p. 10) representative of the black community of Eatonville. The
sense of such a community voice is given by the unusual tactic
of placing the direct speech of a number of people within a single set of quotation marks. The community voice judges Janie
according to conventional standards. Her wearing of overalls
signifies accordingly a downgrading in terms of wealth, social
status and elegance. Such a judgement is seen entirely fitting
her breaking of the frames of behaviour sanctioned by a
patriarchal social order. The strong suggestion is that Janie's
breach of the conventions as to how a wealthy woman should
behave – her failure to 'stay in her class', to act her age – has
led (inevitably) to her abandonment and humiliation: 'Where
he left *her*? What he done wid all her money? – Betcha he off
wid some gal so young she ain't even got no hairs' (p. 10).

As Janie (still unnamed) approaches nearer, the community
recognize that her sensual vigour (symbolized by 'the great
rope of black hair swinging to her waist and unraveling in
the wind like a plume'[39]) and personal strength are still in
full evidence, despite her 'faded shirt and muddy overalls'.[40]
These clothes in fact accentuate her sexuality: 'her firm but-
tocks like she had grape fruits in her hip pockets . . . her

pugnacious breasts trying to bore holes in her shirt' (p. 11). This stress on vigour and physical health leads us into Janie's own perspective on her self and her experience – a view from within. And the stress now shifts from castigation ('She's de one been doin' wrong,' p. 12) to celebration. The wearing of the overalls signifies not humiliation but 'liberation'[41] and true self-expression. The overalls are linked to Tea Cake who, in turn, is described as having 'give me every consolation in de world' (p. 18).

Janie's own view of her eighteen months' period as 'delegate to de big 'ssociation of life' is not as a narrative of humiliation and descent. Far from it, she has money in the bank, she has not been ditched by Tea Cake, her tone is self-confident and assured. Both Pheoby and reader find Janie's statement, 'Tea Cake is gone', 'hard to understand'. For we have, as yet, only two contexts for such a statement: the community's assertion that he has abandoned Janie (and Pheoby's reiteration of such a possibility); the earlier less specific reference to 'the sudden dead'. Only later textual segments will provide illumination. Janie's self-presentation, however, expresses womanly strength and self-knowledge. Her narrative will take the form of ascent. This primary effect of presenting us with two Janies – the one subject to the expectations of others; the other self-determined, with emotions and thoughts subject to direct expression – controls our reading of the whole narrative, which is structured on the very swings between these poles. Our reading of Janie and her narrative is strongly conditioned by the tension thus established in the introductory presentation of her.

In my chapter on Cather, I spoke of the way in which we, as readers, continually fill in textual 'gaps' as we read; that all narrative texts are full of holes by their very nature 'because the materials the text provides for the reconstruction of a world (or a story) are insufficient for saturation'. I showed there how the reader goes about filling in, making sense of, such gaps. However, there are occasions when our attempts to fill in such holes founder. Where this happens we get what might be called a jamming of meaning: a text pulling in two directions at once. It is at this point that Iser's model is partially reversed as the reader becomes not just she or he whose construction of meaning is 'pre-structured by the

signs given in the text', but also the one who can point out
the text's reticences, uncertainties and suppressions. It is in
such suppressions that the contradictions masked by the text's
apparent unity emerge. Beneath apparently fixed meanings,
alternative possibilities, ambiguities, incompletenesses, can
always be found.

I have already suggested the presence of one such area
of uncertainty in terms of the presentation of sexual politics
in the novel. Another major gap in *Their Eyes Were Watching
God* exists with regard to the depiction of life in the Florida
Everglades, on the 'muck', as 'utopian fantasy': an 'idyll of
pleasure, work and equality'.[42] For there is a clear problem
in reconciling Tea Cake's statement that the muck is where
'dey raise all dat cane and string-beans and tomatuhs. Folks
don't do nothin' down dere but make money and fun and
foolishness' (p. 192), with the picture of the 'hordes of workers'
who pour in to work (and play) there:

Permanent transients with no attachments and tired looking men with their families and dogs in flivvers. All night,
all day, hurrying in to pick beans. Skillets, beds, patched
up spare inner tubes all hanging and dangling from the
ancient cars on the outside and hopeful humanity, herded
and hovered on the inside, chugging on to the muck. People
ugly from ignorance and broken from being poor.
All night now the jooks clanged and clamored. Pianos
living three lifetimes in one. Blues made and used right
on the spot. Dancing, fighting, singing, crying, laughing,
winning and losing love every hour. Work all day for money, fight all night for love. The rich black earth clinging to
bodies and biting the skin like ants (pp. 196–7).

Working all day for money becomes here part of the 'fun
and foolishness'. A huge textual gap needs filling between
the presentation of pleasure and work as equal aspects of
an 'idyll', and the association of proletarian experience with
ignorance, poverty, ugliness, and defeat. This gap is jumped
in a single bound textually, with the move from 'broken from
being poor' to 'All night now the jooks clanged ...'

What Hurston does here is to marginalize what Houston
Baker calls 'the economic contours'[43] of black experience

as she foregrounds the 'expressive authenticity' of Afro-American culture; the dancing, the tales, the sense of community, the songs. The problem here is that the latter depends on the former – the stories and songs emerge out of the economic conditions of black experience: 'the foundation of the blues is working behind a mule way back in slavery times'.[44] To portray the muck as 'mythic space', Janie's time there as 'arcadian sojourn',[45] is to suppress the importance of that frame which determines the conditions of black life in America. The migrant workers may make 'good money' on the muck, forget the bad times and enjoy the good times as a result, but work for all of them (bar Tea Cake and Janie)[46] is a necessity not a pleasure.

To present the economic constraint of an oppressed racial group as a corollary of 'fun and foolishness' is to radically falsify black experience in America. Hurston's attempt to portray a representational space of free and genuine Afro-American expressiveness clashes with the (almost hidden) economic and political conditions which provide the 'real' (non utopian) frame to black American life. Black forms of self-expression are, in fact, shown to be subject to immediate silencing once the nature of this frame is made explicit. In Palm Beach, both Tea Cake's identity and his legal rights are denied as he is forced, under threat of physical violence, to carry out the orders of his white 'masters'. The very notion of utopian space is shown up as fraud by this narrative sequence; the text works against itself. For white 'masters' similarly frame all functions represented in the novel – it is they who, we can presume, get the profits from the work done on the muck; it is they, too, who presumably employ many (if not all) of the members of the all black community of Eatonville, a community economically and politically dependent on a white superstructure. This is not to deny the validity of Hurston's presentation of black culture, only to point out that the use of the muck as utopian frame raises an important ideological issue. That celebration of black American life and culture within the narration and its glossing over of a 'highly exploitative economic reality'[47] is misleading: black self-expression must fully recognize the (as yet) permanent limitations of this frame.

My final comments in this section relate to the subject of interpretive conventions: the way our framings of a literary text change in response to the changing nature of our political and cultural concerns. When Richard Wright reviewed the novel in 1937, as one whose 'sensory sweep . . . carries no theme, no message, no thought', he was writing from the position of one to whom, in Johnson's terms, 'the black female experience is non-existent'. Johnson goes on to say that 'the full range of questions and experiences of Janie's life are as invisible to a mind steeped in maleness as Ellison's Invisible Man is to minds steeped in whiteness'.[48] The standard histories of American literature have simply ignored Hurston. She has suffered a double exclusion from the critical canon – 'other' in terms both of race and gender – having to wait until Hemenway's 1977 biography for the re(dis)covery of her critical reputation.[49]

We read and make sense of what we read by bringing to the text ways of framing it. The way we look at a text radically affects the way we see it: 'it's interpretation all the way down' (Mailloux, p. 198). Texts lack stability. As metaphorical illustration of how our reading of the text (and the world) can change according to our interpretive position, we can look within the novel itself, where any notion of fixed centre has a way of shifting ground on us. Janie describes herself as 'a real dark little girl' when she sees the photo of herself with the white children; the narrator describes her, through Mrs Turner's focalization, as of 'coffee-and-cream complexion', her looks 'white folkish' in comparison to those 'black niggers' against whom she is measured. Depending on where you stand, depending on your context, so things (even the main protagonist of the novel) look different, so the centre (in this case, the mid-point of the spectrum from black to white) shifts. Thus, from a critical point of view, Noel Schraufnagel defines Tea Cake in terms of his social and economic status, using the criteria of the dominant white culture, in calling him 'a penniless gambler and drifter'.[50] Robert Bone, more aware of Hurston's Afro-American celebration of cultural difference, refers to him as 'an incarnation of the folk culture'.[51]

My own reading of the text is framed by black feminist criticism; one which, in Barbara Smith's words, 'embodies the realization that the politics of sex as well as the politics of race and class are crucially interlocking factors in the works of Black women writers'.[52] This approach, validated

by the reading conventions in contemporary use, leads me
to read the novel in terms both of Janie's negotiation of
the conditions of patriarchal pressure; in terms, too, of
her membership of a black community whose culture is
resistant to the values and modes of expression of the
dominant social group, whose expressive forms constitute a
kind of 'unauthorized center',[53] equally valid, equally vital,
but at one remove from the cultural patternings of the white
majority. Gender role and ethnic identity both overlap and
conflict in the following of such a critical path. Something
of the productive tensions that consequently emerge will be
illustrated in the final section of this chapter.

V

A Barthesian reading

Barthes' model in *S/Z* lies at the far side of reader response
theory. Iser's notion of the reader as responding to 'conditions . . . already . . . structured in the text', the text as stable
entity with its fixed stars between which we make our readerly
moves, is replaced in Barthes by a stress on the instabilities
and pluralities of the text, on the reader as one who 'writes'
the text as s/he reads it, playfully tracing and articulating
meanings released as a result of her or his prior immersion
in other texts, other codes. The reader is thus engaged in an
act of 'collision/collusion' with a text which is not unitary
or stable, rather one which beneath its apparently seamless
surface (the very basis of realism for Barthes) contains in fact
a multiplicity of networks and entrances which the reader
may playfully enter, explore, unravel. As in my chapter
on James and Wharton, my reading, perhaps unavoidably,
strongly connects with my adoption of the conventions of
a particular academic community referred to at the end of
the last section. This reader at least finds it very difficult to
take such play beyond certain limits (perhaps because of my
strong immersion in that cultural code – the book of black
literary theory, of feminist theory). However, it may be that
were I focusing on different, or longer, sections of the text, the

'plurality of other texts' which compose my identity as reader would come more fully into operation. As it is, I feel that the opportunity for the articulation of meaning offered in such a brief section, effectively undermines that part of Iser's theory which stresses the text's structural stability.

In this section, I will therefore take a brief portion of the novel and subject it to Barthesian analysis, cutting the passage chosen into individual segments, discussing these signifying blocks in terms of the overlapping and interweaving of those five codes which Barthes uses as his (arbitrary) organizing base in *S/Z*; adding longer 'divagations' where appropriate. A fuller discussion of the principles of Barthes' approach and a description of his five codes will be found in Chapter Five. As in my previous sections in this chapter, I will be highly selective in my use of material, giving merely a sample of how a Barthesian approach might operate when applied to *Their Eyes Were Watching God*. I wish to discuss the start of Chapter Four of the novel, and in line with Barthes, I will re-cite each unit of text before commenting on it.

(1) *Long before the year was up, Janie noticed that her husband had stopped talking in rhymes to her. Noticed* means *I am going to describe.* The narrowing of the field of observation to a single and partial frame (Janie's focalization as it relates to her marriage). Dissolves of focalization – see the shift to Logan, p. 51, 'There! Janie had put words to his held-in fears . . .' – compose the entire space of the text. * REF. Code of literary art: the (highly artificial) way meaning is produced. ** ACT. 'The disintegration of a marriage': 1: change in mode of communication. *** REF. A version of one of those maxims about love, marriage and romance which make up our 'anonymous Book' of knowledge, part of the handbook of 'traditional human experience'[54] to which the text refers: 'the poetry had gone out of their marriage'. The cultural codes to which this text refers are both Anglo-American and Afro-American. In this case the fixed wisdom is shared, locating the institution of marriage essentially (once the 'poetry' has departed) in relation to the fixity of the social order, the protection of the status quo (security versus romance, property and possessions versus passion, stability versus fluidity). The expression of the traditional wisdom differs, though, according to its specific

cultural context; 'stopped talking in rhymes' being the black vernacular variant of 'the poetry had gone out of . . .'.

DIVAGATION 1. POETRY AND PROSE: METAPHOR AND METONYMY

The prose-poetry antithesis (SYM) is central to the text. Tea Cake and Janie's relationship inhabits the realm of poetry – of romance, wonderment, desire, in terms of the controlling metaphor (poetry and marriage). The prosaic is the everyday, mundane, 'realistic' realm of those determinants (property, propriety, and power) which mark Janie's first two marriages and destroy their 'spirit' (p. 111). Jakobson distinguishes the poetic from the prosaic according to their respective foregroundings of the metaphoric and metonymic modes.[55] With Tea Cake, Janie steps temporarily outside the province of that constraint normally associated with marriage as an institution. The poetry remains foregrounded in a relationship in which the pleasure principle is dominant. She speaks in rhymes of Tea Cake at the very end of the text ('out of each and every chair and thing./Commenced to sing' p. 286). The flood of metaphors with which the narrative closes ('the song of the sigh', 'the sun for a shawl', 'the kiss of his memory', 'love . . . lak de sea') speaks for the retention and celebration of the poetic as the very basis of their marriage to the point of Tea Cake's death and beyond: 'The kiss of his memory made pictures of love and light against the wall'.

The prose/poetry antithesis is, however, unstable from the start. After all, even Logan Killicks, the most prosaic of Janie's husbands (the man who 'look like some ole skullhead in de grave yard', p. 28), speaks in rhymes in the early days of their marriage. And Tea Cake, the bee who fertilizes Janie's symbolic blossom of erotic and romantic desire, cannot exist apart from the world of prosaic reality. His proprietorial attitude to Janie ('you'se mah wife and mah woman', p. 187) speaks for his own conventional base. Their playful relationship is conditioned by Janie's exceptional status as a woman of economic means; is framed by a set of political, legal, and social determinants which may recede temporarily from view, but which cannot be discounted.

Indeed, the instability of this antithesis is suggested by a narrative which bridges the two modes. Janie travels the metonymic roads of Florida, charts her journey in terms of both linear and chronological progression; this journey is, however, capped with metaphoric success. For her talk of reaching the horizon ('Ah done been tuh de horizon') blends metonymic and metaphoric principles, the linear movement from location to location standing alongside the metaphorical signification of fulfilment and completion that the horizon holds throughout the text. Prose and poetry collapse in on each other as Janie's narrative becomes, at its end, a type of prose poem which metaphorically celebrates Janie's love for Tea Cake; and sets against the inevitable end of all human narratives (death) a metaphoric celebration of the power of love, life, memory and imagination.

(2) *He had ceased to wonder at her long black hair and finger it.* * HER. Why does Killicks stop talking in rhymes? Cease wondering at/fingering her long black hair? What will Janie's response be? ** ACT. 'The disintegration of a marriage': 2: loss of the fascination of desire. *** REF. 'The amorous typology of women'.[56] The woman with long black hair is seen (in both male and female eyes) as superior to others. The narrative insists that Janie's valuation is read from a book (of beauty, of desire?) written by men. The part stands for the whole. The Woman, to quote Barthes, 'copies the Book' (p. 33). Janie is 'dismembered' by the male gaze: reduced to her hair, it is this which constitutes her desirability ("Tain't nothin' to her 'ceptin' dat long hair', p. 62).

II. HAM, HAIR AND HEADRAGS

'The code underlying all beauty' Barthes insists, is 'Art' (p. 33). It cannot really be explained, operates in terms of a citation of previous models. Revealed here is an Afro-American dependence on the models of beauty established by a dominant white culture. Janie's difference lies in the fact that she is a mulatta. As mulatta she represents 'white standards of beauty';[57] her 'luxurious hair', her 'Caucasian characteristics', associated with 'divinity' (p. 216) itself by Mrs Turner. This is the source of her attraction to black male eyes, especially to Jody. His imitation of Euro-American models, his possession of a 'sparkly white' house and of power in the community, are well matched by a wife who conforms as far as possible to such standards. Equally, it is the fact that Daisy Blunt's 'negro hair' has 'a kind of white flavor. Like the piece of string out of a ham. It's not ham at all, but it's been around ham and got the flavor' (p. 106) that marks her out as unmarried 'center of the [Eatonville] stage'.

Janie herself makes a move beyond these culturally received patterns. Though she commences the novel using her hair as 'still–bait', aware of what it signified in terms of beauty and desirability, making 'her heavy hair fall down' (p. 47) to catch Joe Starks' initial attention, this hair comes to signify differently for her as the text proceeds. For the hair becomes site of a symbolic battle for authority and power between Joe and her. His ordering her to tie it up in a headrag is a sign of his jealousy and possessiveness which irks her considerably. The hair, then, comes to play a role in the symbolic codes of the text (SYM), the antithesis *under/free from* patriarchal control. She marks Joe's funeral by burning up her headrags, letting her hair swing 'in one thick braid . . . well bellow her waist' (p. 137). From this point on, the swinging and unravelling of her hair are linked to her 'freedom feeling'. Tea Cake fingers her hair as Logan has done, comparing it to 'underneath uh dove's wing next to mah face' (p. 157). He does not, however, make her hide it. Aware of her 'beauty' he is also aware of her need of and right to self-expression. When Janie returns, hair swinging, to Eatonville after his death, it is not beauty which she flaunts, but self-determination, freedom from patriarchal control. Physically, psychologically, economically strong, her hair is like a 'plume', the standard of her autonomous womanhood.

(3) *Six months back he had told her, 'If Ah kin haul de wood heah and chop it fuh yuh, look lak you oughta be able tuh tote it inside. Mah fust wife never bothered me 'bout choppin' no wood nohow. She'd grab dat ax and sling chips lak uh man. You done been spoilt rotten.* * SEM. Aggrieved husband. ** Here lies the partial answer to the enigmas raised in the previous lexia (HER). Killick's change of atttitude to Janie stems from her failure

to fulfil the conditions of the marital contract as he sees it,
(SYM. Male/Female antithesis). His is the purchasing power
('his often-mentioned sixty acres') which enables him to pick
Janie as marital choice. This he envisions as a trade-off; he
buys her youth, vitality and labour, to give her in exchange
status, security, a home, 'uh prop tuh lean on all yo' bawn
days, and big protection, and everybody got tuh tip dey hat
tuh you' (p. 41). Janie refuses this contract. Expecting as
patriarch his demands to be met with little effort on his
part (he won't even wash his feet before coming to bed),
Killick resents Janie's refusal to become a labourer in his
metaphorical employ. He sees the maintenance of traditional
gender roles (men in fields, doing outdoor work, carrying,
lifting) as inappropriate once the marital contract has been
sealed. He hopes his bought labour will work 'lah uh man',
though this certainly is not met by a recognition of any equal
shifting of role on his part. Let alone not chopping wood, Janie
will not even carry the chopped wood inside. Her expectations
of marriage (wanting 'things sweet', wanting love) are quite
out of key with his patriarchal assumptions. *** HER. What
happened to the first wife? Code is formally jammed here:
no solution given. Informally, we might conclude that he
has received full payment on his previous marital contract:
worked the life and energy out of that wife; killed it (Killick),
the black woman who has been 'used for a work-ox' (Nanny's
fears for Janie) until she has dropped in her tracks. **** ACT.
'The disintegration of a marriage': 3: a clash of expectations.
***** REF. Chronology.

(4) *So Janie had told him, 'Ah'm just as stiff as you is stout.* *
REF. Gnomic code. A popular saying drawn from the book
of (Afro–American) common wisdom. ** SYM. Male/Female
antithesis. *** SEM. Stubbornness, strength of will. **** ACT.
'The disintegration of a marriage': 4: the stand-off.

(5) *If you can stand not to chop and tote wood Ah reckon you can
stand not to git no dinner. 'Scuse mah freezolity, Mist' Killicks, but
Ah don't mean to chop de first chip.'* * ACT. 'The disintegration
of a marriage': 5: words of defiance, denial of patriarchal
authority. ** SEM. Determination, self-assertion. *** REF.
Paradigms of Men and Women. Janie's words challenge the

(male) established paradigms which equate femininity with timidity, silence, demureness, etc. So even while Joe later can make 'uh big woman' out of Janie (REF. Genesis. God makes man. Joe, 'I God', makes woman), he still insists on her conforming to the above paradigm: 'mah wife don't know nothin' 'bout no speech-makin' . . .'. Code of Men: the way to a man's heart is through his stomach, here modified to the way to bend a man's will is through his stomach.

III. THE KEYS OF THE KINGDOM

The paradigm of womanly timidity discussed above is countered by an alternative paradigm (REF) drawn from the Afro-American folk heritage, regarding the battle of sexes (SYM. Male/Female antithesis) and weaponry available to women. Mathilda Moseley in *Mules and Men* (1935), Hurston's collection of Afro-American folklore, provides the rare example of a woman 'lyin' (story-telling).[58] 'In de very first days' God made man and woman of equal strength. Man, according to Mathilda's story, finally decides to ask God for more strength than woman 'so Ah kin make her mind'. God awards him this strength thus he is able to coerce her obedience. The devil advises woman to ask God for the bunch of keys hanging from his mantelpiece if she wants to 'come out mo' than conqueror' (p. 35) in this battle. The three keys God gives her are explained by the devil as follows:

See dese three keys? They got mo' power in 'em than all de strength de man kin ever git if you handle 'em right. Now dis first big key is to de do' of de kitchen, and you know a man always favors his stomach. Dis second one is de key to de bedroom and he don't like to be shut out from dat neither and dis last key is de key to de cradle and he don't want to be cut off from his generations at all. So now you take dese keys and go lock up everything and wait till he come to you. Then don't you unlock nothin' until he use his strength for yo' benefit and yo' desires (p. 36).

The man recognizes this source of power and offers a trade-off, half his strength for permission to hold the keys in his hands. The woman refuses, on the devil's advice: 'Tell 'im, naw. Let 'im keep his strength and you keep yo' keys' (p. 37). Man consequently has 'to mortgage his strength to her to live'. Janie uses one of her traditional weapons here. The second key is used, indirectly, with Jody. Her challenge to his masculinity (in response to his ridicule of her own body) leads directly to his departure from the bedroom to sleep in a room downstairs. Humiliated and feeling scorned, he is effectively barred from that space by her words. As to the third key, we are in the presence of a jammed enigma (HER). Is the lock snapped shut? On whom? For how long? A central gap in the text is the lack of any reference to child-bearing. Given the foregrounded reference to fertility in the pear-tree metaphor, and given the fact that Janie has three husbands, this silence may be extremely significant. Does Janie retain her power by keeping the lock firmly turned on this door?

Hurston's knowledge of Afro-American folklore shown here evidences a reliance on cultural models outside what, after Houston Baker, I would call 'the limiting boundaries of traditional American [literary] discourse' (p. 62). The narrative strategy which results from her movement between two traditions is very simply illustrated in the chosen sequence by the shift from the standard American of the narration at the chapter's start, with its normalizing integration of the vernacular phrase 'talking in rhymes', to the use of the black vernacular – which Baker speaks of as 'the privileged domain of Afro-American expression' (p. 213) – within direct speech; the use of words like 'freezolity' which depart considerably from the 'standard' forms.[59] Any notion of antithesis (Black/White?) however, breaks down when we look at such examples. The (apparent) opposition between Euro and Afro-American speech forms cannot be sustained as long as that one term 'American' remains in common. It is, in fact, a false antithesis: 'black' and 'white' rhetorical performance not completely alien to one another (antithesis as, in Barthes' terms, a 'wall without a doorway') but fluid, interconnected, subject to mutual appropriation. A recognition of the fluidity and relativity of socio-linguistic boundaries points forward to my final section.

VI

A Bakhtinian analysis

The world we live in, according to Bakhtin, is 'contradictory and multi-languaged' (p. 275). Language he sees as a site of conflict and contest in which 'historical and social distinctions . . . power relations and hierarchies' are registered. Hurston fits particularly well within such a frame. As black woman writer, her words are in 'antagonistic relation'[60] to those who are seen as oppressors in terms of both sexual and racial politics.

Bakhtin uses the term 'heteroglossia' to describe the flow of separate 'languages' which together compose any national language. The latter he sees as constructed of 'a diversity of social speech types' made up from a 'multiplicity of interacting languages . . . (official, vernacular, technical, literary, the jargons of different age-groups, etc.)'.[61] The heteroglossic nature of Hurston's writing is suggested in a revealing passage from *Mules and Men* where a clear dialogization of different discourses is evident. Collecting 'Negro folk-lore' in Florida, Hurston has returned to the region from 'up North' where her success, according to the standards of the dominant culture (what Bakhtin would call the official American verbal-ideological system) is signified by her possession of 'a diploma and a Chevrolet' (p. 3). Hurston recognizes the awkwardness her presence causes at the pay-night dance held by the workers at the Everglades Cypress Lumber Company. 'They set me aside as different', she says, a difference resulting exactly from her success in this 'official' sphere: 'They were accustomed to strange women dropping into the quarters, but not in shiny gray Chevrolets' (p. 65). These forms of social stratification are then realized in the linguistic interactions which occur as Hurston gradually gains acceptance by the group.

For, though this is non fiction, Hurston presents two languages in a novelistic way: 'the author' in Bakhtin's words 'utilizes now one language, now another, in order to avoid giving himself up wholly to either of them' (p. 314). Hurston gives artistic representation to two forms of speech, and in setting them against each other from a 'third party' position, causes dialogization to occur.[62] Here, the narrator, the 'semifictional' Zora Neale Hurston, is set in linguistic dialogue with the community she enters. She is told a story by a female member of this community, which initially causes shared laughter:

but I knew they were not tickled. But I soon had the answer. A pencil-shaped fellow with a big Adam's apple gave me the key.

'Ma'am, what might be yo' entrimmins?' he asked with what was supposed to be a killing bow.

'My what?'

'Yo' entrimmins? Yo entitlum?'

The 'entitlum' gave me the cue, 'Oh, my name is Zora Hurston. And what may be yours?'

More people came closer quickly.

'Mah name is Pitts and Ah'm sho glad to meet yuh . . . Ah'm makin' mahseff 'quainted.'

'Ah'm glad you did, Mr. Pitts.'

'Sho nuff?' archly.

'Yeah. Ah wouldn't be sayin' it if Ah didn't mean it . . .'

'Miss, you know uh heap uh dese hard heads wants to woof at you but dey skeered.'

'How come, Mr. Pitts? Do I look like a bear or panther?'

'Naw, but dey say you'se rich and dey ain't got de nerve to open dey mouf.'

I mentally cursed the $12.74 dress from Macy's that I had on . . . 'Oh, Ah ain't got doodley squat', I countered (pp. 68–9).

Multiple and conflicting versions of language are apparent here in a passage which moves in two (competing) directions. Hurston's provisional acceptance by this community is marked by her assumption of the vernacular voice which is accompanied by her denial of any official status. For she explains her presence and her car by inventing a tale in which she is 'fugitive from justice, "bootlegging" ', in 'antagonistic relation to the dominant culture'.[63] She switches code from the idiom of the 'high' (standard American English) which both frames in writing the reported speech of this passage ('I mentally cursed . . . '), and which she initially uses ('Oh, my name is Zora Hurston'). This switch entails an assumption of black 'non-standard dialect':[64] 'Ah wouldn't be sayin' it if Ah didn't mean it'.

Bakhtin's notion of language as 'recontextualized, pulled in a slightly different direction, imbued with a different inflection'[65] according to the speaker and his or her ideological position, is illustrated here in the interplay between entrimmins/entitlum/name. For the clash of voices in this passage is not just illustrated in the move between standard American English and black dialect. More than one black voice is heard in this exchange: other conflicts are also evident. Class and/or regional difference is marked by the fact that while Hurston can switch at will between standard English and non-standard dialect,[66] her dialogue with Pitts commences with incomprehension. 'Entrimmins' is only understood by Hurston when he 'translates' it into a form of dialect she understands, 'entitlum'.

Indeed, such a notion of 'translation' raises a key issue here because of its very provisionality. To translate is, in theory, to make language stable, to allow meaning to emerge as what Bakhtin calls in a different context 'a single intentional whole' (p. 297). Dialogization, on the other hand, means that language cannot be made stable, that final 'translation' is not possible in a context where two languages are engaging with one another on intersecting planes. So here, it is exactly the decentering of each form of discourse which is at stake – 'translation' from one idiolect to another is only part of a process which concludes in a thoroughgoing *relativization* of discourse. So Hurston's acceptance into the 'inner circle' of the 'job' relates to her ability to laughingly accept Pitts' 'woofing', to her assumption of the vernacular voice, to her singing of 'John Henry'. All these mark her conscious employment of, and ease in responding to, vernacular forms of Afro-American discourse. At the same time she engages in shifting this discourse into forms of standard American English, the language of the dominant (white) majority. Her phrase 'Ah ain't got doodley squat' is accompanied by a footnote 'translating' black vernacular for such an audience ('Nothing'). These two languages interact constantly in Hurston's prose.

Thus a two-way move occurs, a move paradigmatic of Hurston's prose writing. On the one hand, there is that in the direction of full participation in black community discourse; on the other, towards a separation from such a community in the explaining and framing of this discourse in standard American English. A contest of voices occurs within the prose in which no final 'translation' wins out, only interacting linguistic difference. Dialogization consists precisely in our 'winning out' as readers, able through Hurston's art to understand both languages, and see the contest between them, from a third-person point of view. This, for Bakhtin, is the essence of novelistic prose: its ability to relativize, from a third person authorial position, the 'living mix of varied and opposing voices' (p. 49) which make up any national language.

Thus, here, standard American frames and controls the written text, but foregrounded at the heart and centre of that text (and this goes for *Their Eyes Were Watching God* too), and in contest with the former, Hurston presents the vernacular idiom (as especially represented by the folk tale) in written form. She puts down on paper what Ellison claims to be the 'unwritten dictionary of American Negro usage',[67] an oral culture which, in Gates' terms, stands at the root of the 'signifyin[g] black difference'.[68] In writing the supposedly 'unwritten', Hurston fully recognizes language as a site of conflict, of social and historical change. On the one hand, Hurston's field of production is within a market, and a cultural system, controlled by and serving a dominant white, and middle class, audience. On the other, she writes as a product of the Harlem Renaissance, a 'signal outpouring of black expressive energies', locally rooted in an urban district populated by 175, 000 black men and women, and engaged in a crucial act of Afro-American national self-definition.[69] Out of such a contradiction is Hurston's dialogic prose formed.

Hurston selects her words from a 'tension filled environment'; one, moreover, which extends backwards through the whole history of Afro-American experience and expression in America. Speech difference, for Bakhtin, reflects 'social diversity and the struggle for dominance which is the relation of social classes'.[70] In Hurston's case this conflict operates not just in terms of race, in the dialogic interrelation between standard American and black language throughout her work, but in terms of gender, class and region also. Hurston decentres an official verbal-ideological system by representing in her prose the words which emerge from these marginalized sources (most especially, the first two), words which counter the 'unitary' pretensions of the dominant cultural voice. This representation of both languages in action allows such a decentering to take place.

Thus, in the early stages of *Their Eyes Were Watching God*, a black female ex-slave (Nanny) tells her own story. This story cuts two ways. For while in its historical content it serves to illustrate her own linguistic inadequacy as subjected black woman in an oppressive slave-holding society, in its actual telling it provides a dialogization of exactly that language of racial and sexual domination it initially treats. For, as female slave, Nanny's words never come into dialogic interplay with the authoritative language of an oppressive slave-holding society to which she is subject. Her status as mere instrument of another's will is here reflected in the complete suppression of her voice in the arena of social intercourse. The 'magisterial' authoritative discourse of the Confederate South ruthlessly suppresses any hint of antagonistic verbal exchange. So, when Nanny's mistress speaks, her words represent the 'official-authoritative truth'[71] of Southern culture. The value system inscribed in these words is one which conceives of miscegenation as (officially) taboo activity; of the slave as possession subject to the complete will of his or her owner. Her repeated questioning of Nanny reveals exactly those interrelationships between black slave and white master which might implicitly challenge the governing notion of a hierarchically divided society: she repeats 'maybe twenty-five or thirty times . . . how come mah baby look white'. But such words form mere prologue to her stated intent to obliterate such threat, to re-stabilize the official version of things through fierce and powerful action: asserting that 'as soon as dat brat is a month old Ah'm going to sell it offa dis place' (p. 34).

Nanny is at the mercy of her mistress' authoritative word. As member of an oppressed group she cannot argue with this word, cannot oppose the language of officialdom. In fact, all she can initially do is to echo the discourse of the slave-holding society which would deny her identity, accept the definition of (powerless) self it imposes on her. Her language merely reflects her impotence as she says 'Ah don't know nothin' but what Ah'm told tuh do, 'cause Ah ain't nothin' but uh nigger and

uh slave'. She can put up no linguistic resistance to the power
structure which controls her. She responds to that power and
control of which language is a tool in the only way she sees
open to her, by running away 'to de swamp by de river'; a
strategy simply of evasion and of silence.

Again, it is in Hurston's representation of Nanny's language that dialogization occurs. Her dialect, her narrative,
is here held counter to her mistress' tyrannical voice, in a
way that did not happen in historical fact. In the telling of
her own story Nanny in fact incorporates her white mistress'
words, inflects them with her own accent, strikes back in the
battle for linguistic supremacy which Hurston measures out.
Nanny's telling of her own narrative to Janie registers the
social and historical changes which have occurred since
the Civil War. Her words are now placed 'in quotation
wid' (p. 35) the monoglossic discourse of that earlier time.
Nanny's inflection of 'free' in her phrase 'den we knowed
we was free' recontextualizes it, shifts it from the frame of
Southern Confederate usage. To the latter, freedom – in the
realm of race relations – was accented either in the direction
of radical outside threat (Abolitionism) or, in patriarchal terms,
of earned privilege or gracious gift. Inflections of natural right,
removal of pain and suffering, illuminate Nanny's use of that
word. And so, too, are Janie's words in dialogic interaction
with her grandmother's. The latter's 'text', her 'dreams of
whut a woman oughta be and to do' (p. 31), are not Janie's.
Janie re-accents the latter phrase as a black woman who lives
in changed historical and social circumstances.

Hurston's awareness of the stresses and tensions in the
areas of both race and gender is precisely what animates her
narrative. By placing a black woman's voice at the centre of
her text, she contests any notion of a unitary official language.
For the language of both racial and patriarchal domination
(not, it must be stressed, one and the same) are both subject
to radical critique in this text, dialogized and undermined by
'subordinated languages [trying] to avoid, negotiate or subvert
that control'.[72] It is in representing all these languages to
the reader in their interacting difference that Hurston is so
successful as a novelist.

For the power of the 'official' language, particularly in the
area of race is also recognized. Hurston has figures of white

authority literally invade the text, as if to show how powerful
a white supremacist ideology remained in the American South
in the early 1900s. For the most part, Hurston decentres
such a verbal-ideological system by her concentration on the
representation of a black community, the 'unofficial' voices
as it were of this Southern society. Nonetheless, she gives
sharp reminders of this system's power. Thus Tea Cake, in
the scenes following the flood, is depersonalized by figures
of white authority. Their words, 'Hello, there, Jim . . . We
been lookin' fuh you', if they are – as Bakhtin says all words
are – 'directed towards an answer', are certainly not directed
towards a resisting answer on his part. Tea Cake attempts to
retain autonomy, to negotiate the situation, with his 'Ah'm uh
workin' man wid money in mah pocket'. What his interlocutors
want, though, is but a repetition of Nanny's earlier words, 'Ah
don' know nothin' but what Ah'm told to do . . . '. They meet
Tea Cake's attempt to open dialogue with words of authority,
threat, implied violence, making clear his invisibility in any
but racial terms in their eyes: 'Git on down de road dere,
suh! Don't look out somebody'll be buryin' *you!*' (p. 252).

Both racial and sexual politics come into play in the trial
scene. It is the judge and 'twelve more white men . . . who
didn't know a thing about people like Tea Cake and her'
(p. 274) who try Janie's case. Her words are interpreted
(wrongly)[73] and weighed in a strongly hierarchical context,
and one in which Janie's race and gender are, to the black
male audience at least, voiced as being more important than
the case's rights or wrongs. One such comment, 'she didn't kill
no white man, did she? Well, long as she don't shoot no white
man she kin kill jus' as many niggers as she please' (p. 280), is
repeated almost word for word in Hurston's autobiographical
Dust Tracks on a Road.[74]

The 'official' language of Southern society stifles and
encloses black voices in these scenes. Indeed, the 'anonymous herd' of black people at the back of the court are
officially silenced by the court officers ('Another word out
of *you* . . . and I'll bind you over to the big court', p. 277).
The narrator however suggests the potential power of the
'unofficial' voices of this black community, as well as their
antagonistic relationship to the dominant cultural grouping,
when reporting that 'They were there with their tongues

cocked and loaded, the only real weapon left to weak folks. The only killing tool they are allowed to use in the presence of white folk' (p. 275). For Bakhtin, discourse is 'contested, contestable and contesting' (p. 332). The violence of the metaphor Hurston uses here suggests how central she sees the black voice as being – a 'killing tool', potentially deadly weapon, ranged in conflict against 'the official language of white domination'.[75]

The white power structure, and the language which represents it, can casually destroy accepted definitions of the black self. In the trial scene, for instance, Tea Cake suddenly becomes the alien 'Vergible Woods' (p. 279). The status of the black as 'subjected' race in terms of a hierarchical social structure in the American South is also clear in both burial scene and trial scene. However, the notion of language as a weapon which is used to battle against such forms of social control is vital to Hurston's art. Bakhtin celebrates the novel for its ability to voice all that 'complex choir'[76] of contending languages that are present within any culture. Hurston gives the subordinated language of black America (in antagonistic relation to standard American English – a prestige language, in Allon White's terms, which represents the dominant culture) full hearing in her text. The powerful white voice, with its centripetal tendencies, is not ignored here, as I have shown, but it is the variant voices of the black community that remain Hurston's central concern.

An overturning of the official (what Bakhtin terms 'carnivalization') is represented in Tea Cake's house – the *unauthorized centre* of the "job" ' (my stress, p. 197); in the 'jooks' which clang and clamour all night on the muck. The 'jook', defined by Hurston in *Mules and Men* as 'a fun house. Where they sing, dance, gamble, love, and compose "blues" songs incidentally' (p. 63)[77], is another unauthorized centre where the energies of black cultural life can be freely expressed. A 'culture of laughter' and play is realized on both these sites, strongly opposed to the official culture and the unitary language it would attempt to impose. A 'life-enhancing debunking of the official'[78] occurs. And in *Mules and Men*, Hurston gives examples of the kind of blues lyrics to be heard there, lyrics which irreverently carnivalize the 'high' language of that protestant work ethic which Jody Starks, for example, swallows whole:

'De cap'n say hurry, de boss say run,/I got a damn good notion not to do nary one' (p. 263).

Hurston's novel dialogizes the language of the dominant speech community with another (black) language recognized here as a vitally important part of an American culture. The narrative voice framing Janie's story and speaking to the dominant culture, as well as to a muted black audience, illustrates such dialogization, constantly engaging standard American English with forms of English drawn from a black vernacular context (and alternative 'folk' world view): 'The sun was gone, but he had left his footprints in the sky' (p. 9). Here, Afro-American folk expression is 'translated' into standard written form. Elsewhere, black vernacular ('monstropolous', p. 19) is given direct hearing. Language acts as a weapon in so far as Hurston floods the narrative with direct and indirect speech forms which express the voice and values of black America, voices which compete with the words of white authority (be that in the social or artistic sphere). These black voices are not, of course, coherent or unified. Joe's discourse is saturated with the language of Euro-American success mythology, while Mrs Turner parrots the language of white racial supremacy which would relegate black skin and black cultural forms to the scrap-heap: 'Dey laughs too much and dey laughs too loud. Always singin' ol' nigger songs! . . . De black ones is holdin' us back' (p. 210). But in giving expression to variant forms of black American language in this novel, Hurston counters any notion of American culture as monoglossic. The cocked tongues of her black protagonists represent forms of speech and belief which conflict with the official forms. Language acts as a weapon to counter subjection at both a social and ideological level.

As stressed earlier, however, it is central to note that Hurston dialogizes two forms of dominant languages in *Their Eyes Were Watching God*. Gender, as well as race, is a central issue in the text. And the language of patriarchal power (the revealing transcription of Jody's repeated exclamation as 'I God') is answered by Janie's move from her 'silent rebellions' within her marriage, to the point at which she becomes vocal. Janie's finding of her voice in this context is thus associated with a contestation of patriarchal authority. And her voice has 'killing effect'. She takes 'the middle of the floor to talk right into Jody's face' (p. 122), and – voice now freed – takes the middle of the floor in the novel as a whole, her telling of her story to Pheoby being the structural centre of the entire text. Hurston launches an attack on male discourse from the first, when she writes 'So the beginning of this was a woman'. Janie's grandmother's text speaks of domination and subservience in terms both of race and gender:

> de white man is de ruler of everything as fur as Ah been able tuh find out. Maybe it's some place way off in de ocean where de black man is in power, but we don't know nothin' but what we see. So de white man throw down de load and tell de nigger man tuh pick it up. He pick it up because he have to, but he don't tote it. He hand it to his womenfolks. De nigger woman is de mule uh de world so fur as Ah can see. Ah been prayin' fuh it tuh be different wid you. Lawd, Lawd, Lawd! (p. 29).

The metaphor she uses (black woman as mule of the world) is one of dumbness. Janie, living in different social and historical circumstances from those in which her grandmother was raised, learns to speak openly rather than pray silently. The meanings of the text emerge in the dialogization between her voice, the narrative voice, and those voices, both male and female, black and white, amongst which hers is socially positioned. The voice of the white man as ruler of everything is moreover challenged, at a further level, by the voice of a black woman writer (as well as that of her black woman protagonist) who takes issue with both the racial and the sexual discourses of the period. In Hurston's text a verbal representation of racial, social and gender difference cuts strongly against any notion of cultural centralization, unification. Central issues of literary and social power and access permeate the entire novel.

VII

Conclusion

Henry Louis Gates, Jr., writing of Hurston's *Dust Tracks on a Road*, sums up her achievement as follows:

she employs both the linguistic rituals of the dominant culture and those of the black vernacular tradition. These two speech communities are the source of inspiration for Hurston's novels and autobiography. This double voice unreconciled – a verbal analogue of her double experiences as a woman in a male-dominated world and as a black person in a non-black world – strikes me as her . . . great achievement.[79]

My Bakhtinian frame leads me to pick up that phrase 'double voice unreconciled' in order to say that, of its very nature, language is full of double voices unreconciled, always lacking stability, composed of unreconcilable strata. The 'doodley squat' example at the start of Section Five illustrated how a narrator, using standard English, strategically used black dialect within her prose; but how in the passage as a whole, no clear victory emerged for either linguistic mode. They were placed rather in dialogic (unreconciled) tension, the one with the other. I would see this as the paradigmatic model of Hurston's prose, pointing to Bakhtin's remark that 'it is precisely the diversity of speech, and not the unity of a normative shared language, that is the ground of style' (p. 308). Hurston's great achievement is her ability to constantly dialogize one voice with another, and in doing so, to fundamentally challenge any notion of a unitary American discourse.

Hurston's recognition of different speech communities, different voices, 'double experiences', can lead when raised a level, to a much broader definition of the American literary canon. Paul Lauter analyses the virtual elimination of 'black, white female, and all working class writers'[80] from that canon in the 1920s, a process we are still now engaged in righting. Nina Baym, William Spengemann,[81] Russell Reising, among others, urge the need for such a renegotiation. In concluding with Hurston, I give one of these previously excluded voices its say, and point in the direction of a much more wide-ranging opening out of the canon than I have been able to do in this particular study.

Notes

Introduction

1. Mikhail Bakhtin, *Extracts from notes from the years 1970–71*. Quoted in Tzvetan Todorov, *Mikhail Bakhtin: The Dialogical Principle*, translated by Wlad Godzich (Manchester University Press, 1984) p. xii.

2. Terry Eagleton, *Literary Theory: An Introduction* (Oxford: Basil Blackwell, 1983) pp. 97 and 106.

3. Ibid., p. 103.

4. Shlomith Rimmon-Kenan recognizes the problems that the more rigid aspects of the structuralist approach carry with them in the chapter on 'Story: characters' in her *Narrative Fiction: Contemporary Poetics* (London: Methuen, 1983) pp. 29–42. In Chapter Three, I will modify her model of character construction by my own greater stress on the need to site the subject in the context of socio–historical frames of meaning.

5. Roland Barthes, *S/Z: An Essay*, translated by Richard Miller (New York: Hill and Wang, 1974 [1970]).

6. The phrase is Elaine Millard's. See her 'Feminism II: Reading as a Woman: D. H. Lawrence, *St. Mawr*', in Douglas Tallack (ed.), *Literary Theory at Work: Three Texts* (London: Batsford, 1987) p. 136.

7. David Murray, 'Dialogics: Joseph Conrad, *Heart of Darkness*' in *Literary Theory at Work: Three Texts*, p. 117.

8. Paul Lauter, 'Race and Gender in the Shaping of the American Literary Canon: A Case Study from the Twenties', *Feminist Studies* 9 (Fall 1983), No. 3, p. 435.

9. Sacvan Bercovitch and Myra Jehlen (eds), *Ideology and Classic American Literature* (Cambridge University Press, 1986) p. 1.

10. This is, however, not to suggest that 'new readings' of such authors have not appeared; rather that – in contrast to the recent criticism which has appeared on American Renaissance writers and on particular later authors (James and Faulkner, for example) – such readings are few. Judith Fetterley's *The Resisting Reader: A Feminist Approach to American Fiction* (Bloomington: Indiana University Press, 1978) tackles the masculinist bias of 'classic' American fiction. Nina Baym, in her 'Melodramas of Beset Manhood: How Theories of American Fiction Exclude Women Authors'

(*American Quarterly* 33, 1981, pp. 123–39) extends such arguments to the field of criticism. For those critics who are 're-negotiating' the writings of Fitzgerald, Hemingway, etc., see notes in my chapters on those authors. A more general re-evaluation of the American realist tradition in particular, can be found in Eric Sundquist (ed.), *American Realism: New Essays* (Baltimore and London: The Johns Hopkins University Press, 1982).

11. Russell Reising, *The Unusable Past: Theory and the Study of American Literature* (New York and London: Methuen, 1986) p. 238.

12. See Jonathan Culler's comments on the complexity, subtlety and involution of Proust's *Remembrance of Things Past* and Genette's own approach to it, in Gérard Genette, *Narrative Discourse*, translated by Jane E. Lewin (Oxford: Basil Blackwell, 1986 [1972]) p. 9.

13. Such value is dependent, as Steven Mailloux suggests in *Interpretive Conventions: The Reader in the Study of American Literature* (Ithaca and London: Cornell University Press, 1982), on the nature of that consensus which operates in a particular local, national, and/or international 'literary' community at a particular time.

14. In this view, it is not the work which 'uncovers' meaning, but the reader. Russell Reising seems to me, for the most part, to slide over the issues involved here. He writes of the 'necessary . . . appreciation and understanding of the aesthetic nature of literature' but argues that we must enlarge 'the very idea of the aesthetic' (pp. 222–3). Such a call goes uneasily with his stress on the need to appreciate the heterogeneity of American literature in terms of 'social communities striving to articulate meaning' (p. 235). When he suggests a re-evaluation of the category 'aesthetic/social' in order 'to determine, once the wide range of American writing is accepted for the plurality of voices that it is, where, if anywhere, distinctions between the terms may lie' (p. 229) he does foreground, if briefly, the problems to which I am referring.

15. This appears to be the thrust of Terry Eagleton's final chapter in *Literary Theory: An Introduction*, 'Conclusion: Political Criticism'. See, for example, p. 205.

16. Bercovitch and Jehlen (eds), *Ideology and Classic American Literature*, p. 438.

17. Reising, *The Unusable Past*, pp. 234 and 222.

1. Speech Representation, Focalization and Narration in *The Great Gatsby*

1. Robert Sklar, *F. Scott Fitzgerald: The Last Laocoön* (New York: Oxford University Press, 1967) p. 196.

2. Gérard Genette, *Narrative Discourse*, translated by Jane E. Lewin (Oxford: Basil Blackwell, 1986 [1972]) p. 23. Where appropriate, page references will be given after quotations in the text from henceforth. Where I modify Genette's words on Proust to fit my analysis of Fitzgerald, I make use of square brackets.

3. Terry Eagleton uses this phrase in *Literary Theory: An Introduction*

(Oxford: Basil Blackwell, 1983) p. 92, in describing the intended target of Northrop Frye's critical project.

4. Gerald Prince, *Narratology: The Form and Function of Narrative* (Berlin: Mouton, 1982) p. 163.

5. Ann Jefferson and David Robey (eds), *Modern Literary Theory: A Comparative Introduction* (London: Batsford, 1982) p. 90.

6. Boris Uspensky, *A Poetics of Composition: The Structure of the Artistic Text and Typology of a Compositional Form*, translated by Valentina Zavarin and Susan Wittig (Berkeley: University of California Press, 1983 [1973]) p. 5. Where appropriate, page references will be given after quotations in the text from henceforth.

7. Diana Knight, 'Structuralism I: Narratology: Joseph Conrad, *Heart of Darkness*', in D. Tallack (ed.), *Literary Theory at Work: Three Texts* (London: Batsford, 1987) p. 14.

8. Shlomith Rimmon-Kenan, *Narrative Fiction: Contemporary Poetics*, p. 4.

9. Douglas Tallack, Diana Knight, Bernard McGuirk, Steve Giles, 'New Ways of Reading Old Texts', *English in Education*, Vol. 20 (Summer, 1986), No. 2, p. 15.

10. Eagleton, *Literary Theory: An Introduction*, p. 106.

11. Jonathan Culler, Foreword, in Genette, *Narrative Discourse*, p. 7.

12. Jefferson and Robey (eds), *Modern Literary Theory*, p. 95.

13. Tallack *et al.*, 'New Ways of Reading Old Texts', p. 16.

14. Genette, *Narrative Discourse*, p. 31.

15. Ibid., p. 162.

16. Ibid., p. 167.

17. Rimmon-Kenan, *Narrative Fiction*, p. 107.

18. Seymour Chatman, *Story and Discourse: Narrative Structure in Fiction and Film* (Ithaca and London: Cornell University Press, 1978) p. 147. Telling and showing are terms which develop out of the distinction between *diegesis* and *mimesis* in Plato's *Republic* (see Rimmon-Kenan, *Narrative Fiction*, p. 106; Genette, *Narrative Discourse*, pp. 162–9).

19. Rimmon-Kenan, *Narrative Fiction*, p. 107.

20. Genette, *Narrative Discourse*, p. 167.

21. F. Scott Fitzgerald, *The Great Gatsby* (Harmondsworth, Middlesex: Penguin, 1988 [1926]) pp. 7–9. Where appropriate, page references will be given after quotations in the text from henceforth.

22. Genette, *Narrative Discourse*, p. 171–2.

23. See Chatman, p. 201. All the terms used here are explicated in *Story and Discourse*.

24. Genette, *Narrative Discourse*, p. 171.

25. Ibid., pp. 172 and 185.

26. Ibid., p. 242.

27. William Faulkner, 'Barn Burning', in *Collected Stories of William Faulkner* (New York: Random House, 1950) p. 3.

28. Such a typology can be found in Genette, *Narrative Discourse* and Rimmon-Kenan, *Narrative Fiction*. In accord with the latter's practice, I modify Genette's terminology as I proceed with this chapter where such a modification makes for clarity and consistency. See, for example, Rimmon-Kenan, p. 74, on the use of the term 'narrator–focalizer'.

29. Genette, *Narrative Discourse*, p. 209.

30. Ibid., p. 192.

31. The beginning of Virginia Woolf's *To the Lighthouse* (1927) provides an example of such focalization changes, with its swift initial movement between James, Mr Ramsay and Mrs Ramsay's focalizations.

32. It is Uspensky who develops these different facets most fully; Rimmon-Kenan who, in her chapter 'Text: focalization', adopts his scheme. I follow the latter in attempting to fuse Genette's theory with Uspensky's. I remain aware of the difficulties in so doing, some of which emerge in the section of my chapter on narration.

33. The use of such a perspective (an observer viewing a scene from without) can act as a type of estrangement device (see Uspensky, *A Poetics of Composition*, p. 131). Uspensky is discussing the authorial position here, but his argument can be extended). Something familiar (husband and wife at kitchen table) becomes sinister as a result of its description from outside. See, too, Uspensky's comments on 'The Silent Scene' (p. 65).

34. Uspensky, *A Poetics of Composition*, p. 74.

35. See Rimmon-Kenan, *Narrative Fiction*, p. 79.

36. Ibid., p. 80.

37. Uspensky, *A Poetics of Composition*, p. 88.

38. And it is here that the study of focalization and that of speech representation interestingly overlap.

39. See Uspensky, *A Poetics of Composition*, pp. 25–32.

40. *The Compact Edition of the Oxford English Dictionary* (Oxford University Press, 1971) Vol. 1, p. 315.

41. Richard Godden, '*The Great Gatsby*: Glamor on the Turn', in *Journal of American Studies*, Vol. 16 (Dec. 1982) No. 3, p. 369.

42. John F. Callahan, *The Illusions of a Nation: Myth and History in the Novels of F. Scott Fitzgerald* (Urbana: University of Illinois Press, 1972) p. 45.

43. This definition is one which does not describe the full complexity of the term 'ideological'. Catherine Belsey's 'The subject in ideology' section in *Critical Practice* (London and New York: Methuen, 1980) pp. 56–7, explores the meanings of the word more fully in an accessible manner.

44. Uspensky, *A Poetics of Composition*, p. 15.

45. Quoted in Genette, *Narrative Discourse*, p. 222.

46. See *The Great Gatsby*, pp. 8 and 155.

47. Genette, *Narrative Discourse*, pp. 221–2.

48. Ibid., footnote p. 228. This same footnote acknowledges the difficulties caused by the term 'metadiegesis'.

49. Genette describes the types of relationship which exist between metadiegetic and diegetic events, pp. 232–4.

50. Genette, *Narrative Discourse*, p. 240.

51. See Rimmon-Kenan, *Narrative Fiction*, p. 94, and Genette, *Narrative Discourse*, p. 248.

52. Rimmon-Kenan, *Narrative Fiction*, p. 92. I have modified this quotation to re-introduce Genette's term, metadiegetic. Rimmon-Kenan replaces it

by 'hypodiegetic' to escape the ambiguous connotations of the prefix 'meta'.

53. Genette, *Narrative Discourse*, p. 235.

54. Ibid., p. 195.

55. I am borrowing the term Genette uses to describe 'auctorial' discourse, p. 258.

56. Genette, *Narrative Discourse*, p. 256.

57. Norman Mailer, *The Armies of the Night: History as a Novel, The Novel as History* (London: Weidenfeld and Nicholson, 1968) p. 219.

58. See Uspensky, *A Poetics of Composition*, p. 8.

59. John F. Callahan, *The Illusions of a Nation*, p. 57. This section of my analysis is strongly influenced by my reading of both Callahan and Godden.

60. This quotation is from T. J. Jackson Lears 'From Salvation to Self-Realization: Advertising and the Therapeutic Roots of the Consumer Culture, 1880–1930', in Lears and Richard Wightman Fox (eds), *The Culture of Consumption: Critical Essays in American History, 1880–1980* (New York: Pantheon Books, 1983) p. 8. Lears traces the development of such a sense of self back to the 1890s. Both he and Stuart Ewen, however, apply such a notion to the 1920s too. Ewen quotes, for example, the 'social psychology' of Floyd Henry Allport, who asserted in 1924 that 'our consciousness of ourselves is largely a reflection of the consciousness which others have of us . . . My idea of myself is rather my own idea of my neighbor's view of me'. See Stuart Ewen, *Captains of Consciousness: Advertising and the Social Roots of the Consumer Culture* (New York: McGraw-Hill, 1976) p. 34.

61. Again, see Lears' analysis of the changing meaning of success: *The Culture of Consumption*, p. 8.

62. Ewen, *Captains of Consciousness*, p. 47.

63. A phrase George Harrison Phelps, the car advertiser, used in 1929 as part of what Ewen calls 'an elaborate fantasy of how people around the world would follow and trust the paternalistic suggestions of commercial propaganda'. See Ewen, pp. 74–5. Godden comments (p. 354) that Gatsby 'can look like all the ads – and consequently he invents himself as a shining and empty space'.

64. Godden, '*The Great Gatsby*: Glamor on the Turn', p. 359.

65. See Callahan, *The Illusions of a Nation*, p. 5.

66. Richard Slotkin, 'Myth and the Production of History', in S. Bercovitch and M. Jehlen (eds), *Ideology and Classic American Literature*, p. 70.

67. See Callahan, *The Illusions of a Nation*, p. 48, who rather reads such a narrative in terms of perfection followed by fall.

68. Ibid., p. 13.

69. Slotkin, 'Myth and the Production of History', pp. 74, 83, 86.

70. And the life of his own family. See Godden, '*The Great Gatsby*: Glamor on the Turn', p. 345.

71. The Mid-West, to which Carraway returns, is associated with a type of amnesiac reverie (see Callahan, *The Illusions of a Nation*, p. 40), part of a pre-modern America, a remembered boyhood world of 'street lamps and

sleigh bells in the frosty dark and the shadows of holly wreaths thrown by lighted windows on the snow' (p. 167).

2. Time and Narrative: Faulkner's *The Sound and the Fury*

1. William Faulkner, *The Sound and the Fury* (Harmondsworth, Middlesex: Penguin, 1987 [1929]) pp. 243–4. Page references will be given after quotations in text from henceforth.

2. Paul Ricoeur, *Time and Narrative*, Vol. 2, translated by Kathleen McLaughlin and David Pellaver (Chicago, London: University of Chicago Press, 1985 [1984]) p. 125. Where appropriate, page references will be given after quotations in text from henceforth.

3. Shlomith Rimmon-Kenan, *Narrative Fiction: Contemporary Poetics* (London: Methuen, 1983) p. 44. Page references to follow quotations from henceforth.

4. John T. Irwin examines the repetitions of the novel from a psychoanalytical, formal, and philosophical perspective in *Doubling and Incest/Repetition and Revenge: A Speculative Reading of Faulkner* (Baltimore and London: The Johns Hopkins University Press, 1975).

5. Thomas Docherty, *Reading (Absent) Character: Towards a Theory of Characterization in Fiction* (Oxford: Clarendon Press, 1983) p. 144. Docherty, writing here about Proust, associates such 'cyclical views of time and history' (p. 145) with early modernist writing generally.

6. Jean Verrier, 'Temporal Structuring in the Novel', *Renaissance and Modern Studies*, Vol. 27 (1983) p. 30. Page references to follow quotations from henceforth.

7. See Ricoeur, *Time and Narrative*, p. 83.

8. Rimmon-Kenan, *Narrative Fiction*, p. 45.

9. Christian Metz, *Film Language: A Semiotics of the Cinema*, quoted in Genette, *Narrative Discourse*, p. 33.

10. Eric Sundquist, *Faulkner: The House Divided* (Baltimore and London: The Johns Hopkins University Press, 1983) pp. 14, 9.

11. Frederick L. Gwynn and Joseph L. Blotner (eds), *Faulkner in the University: Class Conferences at the University of Virginia, 1957–1958* (New York: Vintage Books, 1965 [1959]) p. 95.

12. See Genette, *Narrative Discourse*, p. 83.

13. Richard King, *A Southern Renaissance: The Cultural Awakening of the American South, 1930–1955* (New York, Oxford: Oxford University Press, 1980) p. 81.

14. Genette, *Narrative Discourse*, pp. 48–9. 'First narrative' is a term which does cause some difficulty and is best approached pragmatically according to one's immediate critical needs. Rimmon-Kenan uses Genette to give as good a definition as any: 'Both analepsis and prolepsis constitute a temporally second narrative in relation to the narrative onto which they are grafted, and which Genette calls "first narrative". The "first narrative", then, is – somewhat circularly – "the temporal level

of narrative with respect to which an anachrony is defined as such"'
(p. 47).

15. George R. Stewart and Joseph M. Backus, '"Each in Its Ordered
Place": Structure and Narrative in "Benjy's Section" of *The Sound and the
Fury*', *American Literature* 29 (1957–8) pp. 440–56. This dating is not entirely
accurate. Mr Compson's funeral, for example, does not occur on April 26,
1912, as Stewart and Backus claim, p. 453. See *The Sound and the Fury*,
p. 178. Edmond L. Volpe, in *A Reader's Guide to William Faulkner* (New York:
Farrar, Strauss and Giroux, 1964) Appendix pp. 353–77, also matches dates
to events. He, though, wrongly dates Caddy's wedding, April 24, 1910: see
The Sound and the Fury, p. 87.

16. Gwynn and Blotner, *Faulkner in the University*, p. 1.

17. I borrow my terms here from Docherty's comments on George Eliot,
Reading (Absent) Character, p. 195.

18. Edmond L. Volpe, *A Reader's Guide to William Faulkner*, p. 376. From
'They do, when they can get it' to '*did you love them Caddy*', (*The Sound and
the Fury*, pp. 134–5).

19. See Genette, *Narrative Discourse*, p. 48.

20. See Volpe, *A Reader's Guide to William Faulkner*, pp. 373–7.

21. Genette, *Narrative Discourse*, p. 54.

22. Sundquist, *Faulkner: The House Divided*, p. 15. Sundquist extends his
comments to refer to other Faulkner novels, and especially *Light in August*
(1932), *Absalom, Absalom!* (1936), and *Go Down, Moses* (1942).

23. David Minter, *William Faulkner: His Life and Work* (Baltimore and
London: The Johns Hopkins University Press, 1980) p. 96.

24. Faulkner, *The Sound and the Fury*, p. 254.

25. Gwynn and Blotner, *Faulkner in the University*, pp. 262–3.

26. To do so would be to measure it in terms of reading time, which
is, of course, variable. See Genette, *Narrative Discourse*, 'no one can measure
the duration of a narrative' (p. 86).

27. An example of explicit ellipsis (one whose presence is announced in
the text, where the story line elided is indicated) occurs in *The Great Gatsby*,
where Gatsby's story of his 'taking' of Daisy one October night concludes
as follows: 'He felt married to her, that was all. When they met again, two
days later, it was Gatsby . . . ' (p. 142).

28. The details of which are described in the following (analeptic)
sequence, pp. 149–51.

29. Ricoeur uses the phrase 'internal time, pulled back by memory'
(p. 105) in describing Clarissa in Virginia Woolf's *Mrs. Dalloway* (1925).
This description does not quite fit Quentin whose move into 'internal
time' is a product both of memory and of *will*. 'Real time', for Quentin,
exists not in that which is measured objectively by clocks, but in the time
of consciousness. In his father's words, 'clocks slay time . . . only when the
clock stops does time come to life' (p. 81).

30. Genette, *Narrative Discourse*, p. 93.

31. Wallace Martin, *Recent Theories of Narrative* (Ithaca: Cornell University
Press, 1986) p. 124.

32. Henry James, *The Portrait of a Lady* (Harmondsworth, Middlesex:
Penguin, 1976 [1881]) pp. 226–7.

33. Genette, *Narrative Discourse*, p. 109. See, too, his comments on the way in which, in Proust, 'the descriptive piece never evades the temporality of the story' (p. 100).

34. Here, I take issue with Genette, who calls recollection an 'instantaneous flash' (p. 105). For a thought to be processed (come to mind and disappear) some temporal frame is always necessary.

35. Genette, *Narrative Discourse*, p. 97.

36. Myra Jehlen, *Class and Character in Faulkner's South* (Secaucus, NJ: The Citadel Press, 1978 [1976]) p. 43. Jehlen describes this relationship in Bergsonian terms.

37. From 'one minute she was standing' (p. 135) to 'theres a curse on us' (p. 143).

38. Occurring in the late summer of 1909 (see Volpe, *A Reader's Guide to William Faulkner*, p. 365), it lasts – roughly – from supper time to after Benjy's bed-time when it is, however, still dusk. Measurements in terms of textual length and/or chronological duration alone cannot provide a completely accurate reflection of the importance of a particular sequence in a novel which can be seen as a 'vast prose poem' (Sundquist, *Faulkner: The House Divided*, p. 14), and where brief passages of lyrical intensity (see, for example, pp. 77–8: 'Only she was running . . . ') can bear considerable dramatic weight.

39. Volpe, *A Reader's Guide to William Faulkner*, pp. 373–7.

40. Sundquist, *Faulkner: The House Divided*. p. 12.

41. Faulkner, *The Sound and the Fury*, pp. 182–5.

42. Shlomith Rimmon-Kenan, 'The Paradoxical Status of Repetition', *Poetics Today*, Vol. 1 (Summer 1980) No. 4, pp. 152–3.

43. Seymour Chatman, *Story and Discourse: Narrative Structure in Fiction and Film* (Ithaca and London: Cornell University Press, 1978) p. 78.

44. Such effects operate between, as well as within, individual sections; see, for example, Benjy's response to flower(s), pp. 55 and 281.

45. Irwin, *Doubling and Incest/Repetition and Revenge*, p. 37.

46. Shlomith Rimmon-Kenan, 'From Representation to Production: The Status of Narration in Faulkner's *Absalom, Absalom!*', *Degrés*, Vol. 16 (1978) p. 1.

47. Rimmon-Kenan, *Narrative Fiction*, pp. 57–8.

48. Recalls (repeating anachronies), as Genette points out, 'belong to this narrative type' (p. 115).

49. Sundquist, *Faulkner: The House Divided*, p. 11.

50. King, *A Southern Renaissance*, p. 114.

51. Sundquist, *Faulkner: The House Divided*, p. 11

52. See Rimmon-Kenan, *Narrative Fiction*, p. 58. Also, Mark Twain, *The Adventures of Huckleberry Finn* (Harmondsworth, Middlesex: Penguin, 1987 [1885]) pp. 49–50.

53. Ricoeur, *Time and Narrative*, pp. 88–152. Genette, as I have shown, focuses much attention on the two areas of voice and focalization. He does not, however, consider them in his discussion of temporality.

54. See Ricoeur, *Time and Narrative*, p. 86.

55. A full analysis would consist of a comparison of Benjy's voice

and focalization with those others represented in the text and the fictive experiences of time associated with them. Though their approach is not the same as mine, Irwin, King, and Sundquist's examinations of Quentin's voice, and their placings of it within a fuller historical context (by cross reference to *Absalom, Absalom!*) provide an essential complement to my comments on Benjy's section here.

56. Rimmon-Kenan, 'The Paradoxical Status of Repetition', pp. 153–4.

57. Sundquist, *Faulkner: The House Divided*, p. 15.

58. See Rimmon-Kenan, 'The Paradoxical Status of Repetition', p. 155.

59. The argument represented here and the quotations used are extracted from Anika Lemaire, *Jacques Lacan*, translated by David Macey (London: Routledge and Kegan Paul, 1977 [1970]) pp. 51–4, 177, 227.

60. Lacan quoted by Rimmon-Kenan in 'The Paradoxical Status of Repetition', p. 156.

61. Individuality, in Lacan's argument, is marked by language: 'The grammatical category of the 'I' is the index of individuality because it cannot be conceived without the Thou, without the He/it or without the listener to which it is opposed' (Anika Lemaire, *Jacques Lacan*, p. 53).

62. Quentin's interior monologue – the realization of his 'lacerated consciousness' (King, *A Southern Renaissance*, p. 111) – obviously differs considerably from Benjy's. He too however, as John Irwin points out, is condemned to 'an endless repetition of an infantile state' (p. 43) – his desire for incest a desire to shatter the symbolic order of culture itself.

63. See Ricoeur, *Time and Narrative*, p. 148, and Docherty, *Reading (Absent) Character*, pp. 158–9.

64. See Genette, *Narrative Discourse*, pp. 63–7.

65. Docherty, *Reading (Absent) Character*, pp. 140–1. He is quoting Robert Rogers, *Metaphor: A Psychoanalytic View* (Berkeley: University of California Press, 1978), in the initial stages of this statement. The use of the word 'equate' here is perhaps misleading: see my developing argument.

66. Docherty, *Reading (Absent) Character*, p. 159.

67. The phrase is Ricoeur's, *Time and Narrative* p. 107, in referring to Septimus in Virginia Woolf's *Mrs. Dalloway*.

68. Rimmon-Kenan, 'The Paradoxical Status of Repetition', p. 155.

69. Jehlen, *Class and Character in Faulkner's South*, p. 44.

70. King, *A Southern Renaissance*. See especially his analysis of *Go Down Moses*, pp. 130–9.

71. Ricoeur, *Time and Narrative*, pp. 130 and 109.

72. Jehlen, *Class and Character in Faulkner's South*, p. 44.

73. Gwynn and Blotner, *Faulkner in the University*, p. 32.

74. Jehlen, *Class and Character in Faulkner's South*, p. 44.

75. Faulkner, *The Sound and the Fury*, Appendix, p. 285.

76. Sundquist, *Faulkner: The House Divided*, p. 19.

77. This is the phrase Ricoeur uses in his analysis of Proust, p. 139.

78. In *Absalom, Absalom!*. See King, *A Southern Renaissance*, p. 128.

79. Jehlen, *Class and Character in Faulkner's South*, p. 46.

80. This is Docherty's phrase in *Reading (Absent) Character*, p. 135, though he does not apply it to this novel.

3. Slippery Stuff: The Construction of Character in *The Sun Also Rises*

1. Carlos Baker (ed.), *Ernest Hemingway: Selected Letters, 1917–1961* (London: Granada, 1981) p. 249.
2. Ernest Hemingway, *The Sun Also Rises (Fiesta)* (New York: Charles Scribner's Sons, 1970 [1926]) p. 243. Page references to be given after quotations from henceforth.
3. Joel Weinsheimer, 'Theory of Character: Emma', *Poetics Today*, Vol. 1 (1979) Nos. 1–2, p. 190. The full quote runs as follows: 'character, characteristic, and characterization are extraordinarily slippery terms'.
4. Ibid., p. 191.
5. Thomas Docherty, *Reading (Absent) Character: Towards a Theory of Characterization in Fiction* (Oxford: Clarendon Press, 1983) p. xv.
6. Semiology: 'what constitutes signs, what laws govern them'. For a full exploration of this area see Terence Hawkes, *Structuralism and Semiotics* (London: Methuen, 1977). For the above quotation, see p. 123.
7. Wallace Martin, *Recent Theories of Narrative* (Ithaca: Cornell University Press, 1986) p. 116.
8. *The Sun Also Rises* is, as many critics have pointed out, a *roman à clef*, thus Hemingway's comment. See for example Kenneth Lynn, *Hemingway* (New York: Simon and Schuster, 1987) pp. 289–96. To pursue such connections is to make unwarranted moves outside the boundaries of the literary 'system' in terms of strict semiotic analysis.
9. Marvin Mudrick, 'Character and Event in Fiction', *Yale Review*, Vol. 50 (Winter, 1961) pp. 211 and 213.
10. Weinsheimer, 'Theory of Character: Emma', pp. 190 and 195.
11. Roland Barthes, *Image – Music – Text*, translated by Stephen Heath (London: Fontana, 1977) p. 111.
12. Bernard McGuirk, 'Structuralism II: Character Theory: Henry James, *In the Cage*' in Douglas Tallack (ed.), *Literary Theory at Work: Three Texts* (London: Batsford, 1987) p. 33.
13. Martin, *Recent Theories of Narrative*, p. 118–9.
14. Martin Price, quoted by Shlomith Rimmon-Kenan in *Narrative Fiction: Contemporary Poetics* (London: Methuen, 1983) p. 33. Page references from the latter will be given after quotations from henceforth.
15. Roland Barthes, *S/Z: An Essay*, translated by Richard Miller (New York: Hill and Wang, 1974 [1970]) p. 92.
16. James Garvey, 'Characterization in Narrative', *Poetics*, Vol. 7 (1978) p. 76.
17. Seymour Chatman: *Story and Discourse: Narrative Structure in Fiction and Film* (Ithaca and London: Cornell University Press, 1978) p. 138.
18. See Rimmon-Kenan, *Narrative Fiction: Contemporary Poetics* (London:

Methuen, 1983), chapters 3, 'Story: characters', and 5, 'Text: characterization'.

19. Martin Price, *Forms of Life: Character and the Moral Imagination in the Novel* (New Haven and London: Yale University Press, 1983) p. 67.

20. Morris Shapira (ed.), *Henry James, Selected Literary Criticism* (London: Heinemann, 1963) p. 58.

21. For an accessible description of formalism, see Tony Bennett, *Formalism and Marxism* (London: Methuen, 1979).

22. Seymour Chatman, 'On the Formalist–Structuralist Theory of Character', *Journal of Literary Semantics*, Vol. 1 (1972) p. 57.

23. See Vladimir Propp, *Morphology of the Folk Tale*, translated by Lawrence Scott (Austin, London: University of Texas Press, 1968 [1928]) for discussion of role and function.

24. Arnold E. and Cathy N. Davidson explore this area revealingly in 'Decoding the Hemingway Hero in *The Sun Also Rises*'. See Linda Wagner-Martin (ed.), *New Essays on The Sun Also Rises* (Cambridge, New York: Cambridge University Press, 1987) pp. 83–107. So too does Nina Schwartz in 'Lovers' Discourse in *The Sun Also Rises*: A Cock and Bull Story', *Criticism*, Vol. 26 (Winter, 1984) No. 1, pp. 49–69. I acknowledge my indebtedness to these sources.

25. See Rimmon-Kenan, *Narrative Fiction*, chapter 2, 'Story: events', pp. 6–28.

26. This unequal symbolic exchange – something inside the ring for something outside, animal life for human – suggests, in line with the Davidsons' argument, the shortcomings of bullfighting as a metaphor for larger human meanings.

27. A.E. and C.N. Davidson, 'Decoding the Hemingway Hero in *The Sun Also Rises*', p. 97.

28. Chatman, 'On the Formalist–Structuralist Theory of Character', p. 78.

29. See Seymour Chatman, *Story and Discourses*, p. 113. He is referring to Tzvetan Todorov's 'Narrative Men', in *The Poetics of Prose* (Oxford: Blackwell, 1977 [1971]).

30. Roland Barthes, *S/Z: An Essay*, translated by Richard Miller (New York: Hill and Wang, 1974 [1970]) p. 92.

31. Henry James, *Washington Square* (New York: Airmont, 1970 [1880]) p. 8.

32. David Wyatt, *Prodigal Sons: A Study in Authorship and Authority* (Baltimore, London: The Johns Hopkins University Press, 1980) p. 57.

33. See Thomas Docherty, *Reading (Absent) Character*, chapter 3.

34. Ibid., p. 120.

35. Some idea of the context in which such an incident must be seen can be gathered by Hemingway's negotiations with his editor, Maxwell Perkins, over changing the phrase 'bulls have no balls' to 'bulls have no horns', and his refusal to omit the word 'bitch' to describe Brett. Also, in his defence of the book in response to the 'pain and disgust' with which his mother responded. See *Selected Letters*, pp. 211 and 243.

36. Nina Schwartz, 'Lovers' Discourse in *The Sun Also Rises*', p. 52.

37. A.E. and C.N. Davidson, 'Decoding the Hemingway Hero in *The Sun Also Rises*', p. 90.

38. Ibid., pp. 90–1. I am here condensing the Davidsons' more detailed analysis.

39. David Wyatt, *Prodigal Sons*, p. 57. Mark Spilka in 'The Death of Love in *The Sun Also Rises*' points out the resemblance between Jake and Cohn. I am indebted to his seminal essay both here and at other points in this chapter. The essay is reprinted in Carlos Baker (ed.), *Hemingway and His Critics: An International Anthology* (New York: Hill and Wang, 1961), pp. 80–92.

40. Humphrey Carpenter, *Geniuses Together: American Writers in Paris in the 1920s* (London: Unwin Hyman, 1987) p. 15.

41. Walter Benjamin, 'Baudelaire, or the Streets of Paris' in *Reflections: Essays, Aphorisms, Autobiographical Writings*, translated by Edmund Jephcott (New York and London: Harcourt Brace Jovanovich, 1978) p. 156; and 'On Some Motifs in Baudelaire', in *Illuminations*, translated by Harry Zohn (Great Britain: Fontana/Collins, 1977) p. 169.

42. 'On Some Motifs in Baudelaire', p. 177.

43. Ibid., pp. 194 and 196.

44. Linda Wagner-Martin sees the ending in terms of a wry sidestepping by Jake of any further involvement with Brett ('Introduction', *New Essays on The Sun Also Rises*, p. 4). This reading has more justification than one which treats the action entirely outside its 'habitual' context, as does Humphrey Carpenter when he writes of 'Jake and Brett [being] allowed a low-key happy ending . . . enjoying lunch with several bottles of Rioja and cuddling in a taxi'. (*Geniuses Together*, p. 189). It is, though, possible to see the relationship as fundamentally unchanged; Jake's character as static, caught within a *déjà vu* world where habitual action is associated with patterns of repetition carrying no connotations of transcendence (see David Wyatt, *Prodigal Sons*, p. 58). The Davidsons interpret as follows:

> Jake's last words . . . do not simply point to a different future beyond the text. Taken in context, they necessarily return us to the text itself and the possibility of having it all to do all over again. Once more a woman presses against him in the cab. The symbolic policeman is again present, and he isn't smiling this time (p. 103).

45. Wyatt, *Prodigal Sons*, p. 58.

46. Michael S. Reynolds, 'The *Sun* in Its Time: Recovering the Historical Context', *New Essays on The Sun Also Rises*, p. 58.

47. See both A. E. and C. N. Davidson, 'Decoding the Hemingway Hero in *The Sun Also Rises*', and Schwartz, 'Lovers' Discourse in *The Sun Also Rises*', for analysis of how dubious, in fact, is this prop of meaning.

48. Reynolds, 'The *Sun* in Its Time: Recovering the Historical Context', p. 47. See also Malcolm Cowley, *Exiles Return: A Literary Odyssey of the 1920s* (New York: Viking Press, 1971 [1934]).

49. Ernest Hemingway: *Selected Letters, 1917–1961*, pp. 59, 60, 71.

50. Roland Barthes, 'The World as Object', in Susan Sontag (ed.), *Barthes: Selected Writings* (Fontana/Collins, 1983) p. 64.

51. Benjamin, 'Paris, Capital of the Nineteenth Century', *Reflections*, p. 152.

52. Wendy Martin, 'Brett Ashley as New Woman in *The Sun Also Rises*', *New Essays on The Sun Also Rises*, p. 74.

53. This statement might be seen to have particular reference to Jake's position as narrator. Docherty's comment 'the utterance (outer–ing) of characters does not entirely cohere with their interior self', *Reading (Absent) Character*, p. 94, is particularly relevant here.

54. Linda Welshimer Wagner, *Hemingway and Faulkner: Inventors/Masters*, (Metuchen, New Jersey: Scarecrow Press, 1975) p. 48.

55. Docherty, *Reading (Absent) Character*, p. 93.

56. A.E. and C.N. Davidson, 'Decoding the Hemingway Hero in *The Sun Also Rises*', p. 102.

57. Godfrey Kearns of the University of Manchester, to whom I owe much of my enthusiasm for Hemingway and for American literature generally, first pointed out to me the nature and implication of such repetitions. I wish to acknowledge that my critical debt to him extends through much of this chapter.

58. See Wyatt, *Prodigal Sons*, p. 58. Here Wyatt points out that Jake's 'sense of option' is constricted within a 'recurring formula' for movement, 'I walked', 'I passed', 'I read' etc., whose 'unvarying syntax experiences motion as anything but discovery'.

59. 'Words', Frederic Svoboda writes,

are inadequate to the situation, and Brett's rejection of them at once serves to characterize her . . . and to introduce a thematic distrust of verbal communication which is later most clearly shown as the aficionados of the corrida must *touch* Jake before they are willing to believe him as fellow aficionado (*Hemingway and The Sun Also Rises: The Crafting of a Style*, University Press of Kansas, 1983, p. 46).

See, too, David Wyatt on Jake's disbelief in language in *Prodigal Sons*: ' "You'll lose it, if you talk about it". Jake talks about it because he has already lost everything' (p. 60).

60. Susan Gubar, 'Blessings in Disguise: Cross-Dressing as Re-Dressing for Female Modernists', *Massachusetts Review* (Autumn, 1981) p. 483.

61. Sandra M. Gilbert, 'Costumes of the Mind: Transvestism as Metaphor in Modern Literature', *Critical Inquiry*, Vol. 7 (Winter, 1980) No. 2, p. 393. It is this 'connection' which for Gilbert explains the 'intensified clothes consciousness' of female modernist writing.

62. Annette Kuhn, *The Power of the Image: Essays on Representation and Sexuality* (London: Routledge and Kegan Paul, 1985) pp. 66 and 49. See her comments on cross-dressing as 'wilful alienation' from the fixity of gender identity (p. 54).

63. Gilbert, 'Costumes of the Mind', p. 408.

64. Caroll Smith-Rosenberg, *Disorderly Conduct: Visions of Gender in Victorian America* (New York: A. A. Knopf, 1985) p. 289.

65. Ibid., p. 287; Gilbert, 'Costumes of the Mind', p. 398 footnote, quoting Robert Stoller, *Sex and Gender*, 2 Vols. (New York: Aronson, 1975).

66. Gilbert, 'Costumes of the Mind', p. 410.

67. Martin, 'Brett Ashley as New Woman in *The Sun Also Rises*', pp. 66–7.
68. Gilbert, 'Costumes of the Mind', p. 397.
69. For further discussion of Hemingway's use of bullfighting metaphors in the text and the questioning of sexual roles, see Nina Schwartz and Arnold E. and Cathy N. Davidson. Kenneth S. Lynn in his recent biography, *Hemingway*, also considers the novel in terms of 'the sexual turmoil of the twenties, as viewed from Paris' (p. 318). He, however, relates such turmoil to the sexual confusions which he finds in Hemingway's personal life. His reading of the novel in terms of (playful) lesbian parallelism, phallic symbolisms and those particular events which connote sexual unease (p. 323 ff), downplays its constant deep engagement with the subject of gender convention and sexual politics.
70. Kuhn, *The Power of the Image*, pp. 50 and 53.
71. Gubar, 'Blessings in Disguise', p. 479.
72. Martin, 'Brett Ashley as New Woman in *The Sun Also Rises*', pp. 68–72.
73. Gilbert, 'Costumes of the Mind', p. 394.
74. Henry James, *The Portrait of a Lady* (Harmondsworth, Middlesex: Penguin, 1976 [1881]) pp. 201 and 253.
75. Benjamin, 'On Some Motifs in Baudelaire', *Illuminations*, pp. 179–83.
76. Hemingway: *Selected Letters, 1917–1961*, p. 204. To stress war's effects is not to completely downplay Benjamin's focus on metropolitan experience. The two conjoin to deracinate the characters in this text.
77. See Rimmon-Kenan, *Narrative Fiction*, pp. 64–70.
78. And the name Jacob (Jake) does have biblical resonance: 'You've a hell of a biblical name, Jake' (p. 22). Lynn (p. 323) associates the use of this name with the 'lesbian parallelism' in the novel – Jake as one who 'cannot penetrate his loved one's body with his own'. The lesbian Natalie Barney, he points out, lived at 20 rue Jacob; Djuna Barnes at the Hôtel Jacob.
79. Rimmon-Kenan, *Narrative Fiction*, p. 70.
80. Wyatt, *Prodigal Sons*, pp. 58–9.
81. Garvey, 'Characterization in Narrative', p. 76.
82. Chatman, 'On the Formalist-Structuralist Theory of Character', p. 63.
83. Weinsheimer, 'Theory of Character: Emma', pp. 190, 194, 205.
84. Docherty speaks of the 'lack of a single unified intentional centre behind speech-acts' in Beckett and Pinter's drama, *Reading (Absent) Character*, p. 109. Similar effects of 'transindividuality' operate here. Conversational gambits depend on more than one character for full articulation; there seems to be a need 'to help each other out with their lines' (p. 107). Intersubjectivity, not discrete consciousness, predominates.
85. Weinsheimer, 'Theory of Character: Emma', p. 207.
86. Ibid., pp. 206 and 199.
87. Catherine Belsey, *Critical Practice* (London and New York: Methuen, 1980) p. 86.
88. Barthes, *S/Z: An Essay*, translated by Richard Miller (New York: Hill and Wang, 1974 [1970]) p. 92.
89. Rosalind Rosenberg quoted in Daniel Joseph Singal, 'Towards a

Definition of American Modernism', *American Quarterly*, Vol. 39 (Spring 1987) No. 1, p. 10.

90. Belsey, *Critical Practice*, pp. 60–1.
91. Wyatt, *Prodigal Sons*, p. 64.

4. The Dynamics of Reading: *A Lost Lady*

1. Norman N. Holland, quoted in Steven Mailloux, *Interpretive Conventions: The Reader in the Study of American Literature* (Ithaca and London: Cornell University Press, 1982) p. 27. Page references to the latter will be given after quotations in the text from henceforth.

2. Terry Eagleton, *Literary Theory: An Introduction* (Oxford: Basil Blackwell, 1983) p. 74.

3. Wolfgang Iser, *The Act of Reading: A Theory of Aesthetic Response* (London: Routledge and Kegan Paul, 1978 [1976]) p. 220. Page references to be given after quotations in the text from henceforth. References to Iser's other work to be footnoted.

4. Eagleton, *Literary Theory: An Introduction*, pp. 75–6.

5. Elizabeth Freund, *The Return of the Reader: Reader-Response Criticism* (London and New York: Methuen, 1987) p. 5. Page references after quotations in the text from henceforth.

6. Umberto Eco, *The Role of the Reader: Explorations in the Semiotics of Texts* (London: Hutchinson, 1985 [1979]) p. 214. Page references after quotations in the text from henceforth.

7. Stanley Fish, 'Literature in the Reader: Affective Stylistics', in *Is There a Text in This Class? The Authority of Interpretive Communities* (Cambridge, Mass.: Harvard University Press, 1980) p. 44.

8. Wolfgang Iser, *The Implied Reader: Patterns of Communication in Prose Fiction from Bunyan to Beckett* (Baltimore: Johns Hopkins University Press, 1974) p. 284.

9. Ibid., p. xii. I avoid the use of Iser's concept of the 'implied reader' in this chapter. Elizabeth Freund points out the problems associated with the term in *The Return of the Reader*, pp. 143–4.

10. I will continue to make use of the convention which allows me to speak for other readers of Cather's text ('we see', 'the reader is encouraged . . . '). Such practice, though stylistically convenient, is also founded on the notion of shared communal response to texts to be developed later in this chapter.

11. 'The meaning of an utterance . . . is its experience – all of it – and that experience is immediately compromised the moment you say something about it', Fish, 'Literature in the Reader: Affective Stylistics', p. 65.

12. Steven Mailloux, *Interpretive Conventions*, p. 68.

13. Rimmon-Kenan, *Narrative Fiction: Contemporary Poetics* (London: Methuen, 1983) p. 120.

14. Willa Cather, *A Lost Lady* (London: Virago Press, 1985 [1923]) pp. 6–7. Page references will be given after quotations in the text from henceforth.

15. Rimmon-Kenan, *Narrative Fiction*, p. 120.

16. Ellen Moers, *Literary Women* (London: The Women's Press, 1978) p. 238.

17. Fish, 'Literature in the Reader: Affective Stylistics', p. 43.

18. Iser, quoted in Rimmon-Kenan, *Narrative Fiction*, p. 127.

19. Henry James, 'In the Cage', in *Henry James: Selected Tales* (London: Dent, 1982) pp. 125, 119.

20. Iser, *The Act of Reading*, p. 194.

21. See Eco, *The Role of the Reader*, on 'Inferences by Common Frames', pp. 20–1.

22. Ibid., pp. 207 and 32. See also his comments on 'Inferences by Intertextual Frames', pp. 21-2.

23. Moers, *Literary Women*, p. 154.

24. Eco, *The Role of the Reader*, p. 21. By 'overcoded' Eco refers to a narrative situation which has been repeated so many times that the reader knows exactly what she or he can expect to occur.

25. See *A Lost Lady*, pp. 80 and 84.

26. Steven Mailloux, *Interpretive Conventions*, p. 89.

27. Judgements are never, to use Mailloux's term, 'politically innocent'. Because of the focus of Niel's perspective in the text, the reader is tempted to share his judgement of Marian. Such an act squares with his own (or her own – if the female reader has 'assumed the male perspective') position within a patriarchal system. See Mailloux's footnote (p. 89) on his own use of the masculine pronoun with specific reference to Hawthorne's 'Rappaccini's Daughter'.

28. I omit Captain Forrester for reasons of space. His paternalistic values are, moreover, shared by Niel; noticeably the Captain does not follow them as rigidly as he does.

29. Rimmon-Kenan, *Narrative Fiction*, p. 61.

30. Though Indian culture was also threatened by the aggressive expansionism of the railroad companies, for one of which Captain Forrester worked. The opposition between representatives of 'old' and 'new' is not quite as firm as it might at first seem. The pioneer development of 'our great West' (p. 4) depended on a like discounting of native American interests. The Captain's house, after all, replaces 'an Indian encampment' (p. 48).

31. Eco, *The Role of the Reader*, p. 210.

32. Rimmon-Kenan, *Narrative Fiction*, p. 121.

33. This incident is in fact of real significance. For, in mountain climbing, Marian is undertaking direct interaction with the great natural forces of the American continent; behaving, in other words, like a man. The outcome of such 'unnatural' behaviour is that both her legs are broken! Her hubris, in doing what men do, is punished, and she has thereafter to be 'carried' by a massive rock-like man. Marian, like the woodpecker earlier, is associated with the potential inherent in natural beauty and vitality. Both are subject to maiming, one by a male figure (Ivy), the other in the course of an activity which transgresses a 'normal' feminine role (the swimming too?). Marian has 'learnt' to mould her vitality round a male support: this is the lesson which both nature and culture have taught her.

Such an interpretation cuts against the 'gestalt' towards which I have been working as I (re-)read this text. This suggests that texts are, in fact, always to one degree or another unstable, resist totally 'consistent interpretation'. Here the difficulties of transgressing the conditions of a patriarchal culture appear to be enormous; in that its assumptions (the equation of cultural and natural) are seen to be built into basic elements of the novel's contruction.

34. Carolyn G. Heilbrun, 'Bringing the Spirit Back to English Studies', in Elaine Showalter (ed.), *The New Feminist Criticism: Essays on Women, Literature, and Theory* (London: Virago, 1986) p. 26.

35. Annette Kolodny points out in 'Some Notes on Defining A "Feminist Literary Criticism"' the prevalence of images of flight in women's fiction. Cheryl L. Brown and Karen Olson (eds), *Feminist Criticism: Essays on Theory, Poetry and Prose* (Metuchen, NJ.: Scarecrow Press, 1978) p. 38. The possibilities associated with such images are eliminated right at the start of this text.

36. Iser places great emphasis on what he calls 'the structure of theme and horizon' which, for him, is what 'constitutes the vital link between text and reader' (p. 97) in terms of our reaching such a final position. The literary text he sees as marked by 'a shifting constellation of views', in particular, those represented by 'authorial comment, dialogue between characters, developments of plot, and the positions marked out for the reader' (p. 96). The reader, though, cannot take on board all these perspectives at once, 'so the view he is involved with at any one particular moment is what constitutes for him the "theme". This, however, always stands before the "horizon" of the other perspective segments in which he had previously been situated' (p. 97). The horizon 'is made up of all those segments which had supplied the themes of previous phases of reading'. So, to paraphrase Iser's argument and apply it here, if we are at one reading moment concerned with Marian's conduct (theme), our response is 'conditioned by the horizon of past attitudes towards [Marian] from the point ot view of the narrator, the other characters, the plot, the [heroine herself], etc.' (p. 97). These past attitudes have, at an earlier point in the text, themselves constituted the theme. The reader then 'assembles' the text by 'actively synthesizing an assembly of constantly shifting viewpoints' with the 'ultimate meaning of the text . . . transcend[ing] all the determinate elements' (p. 98). As we set one position against another during the time flow of our reading, as theme becomes part of horizon and new theme arises, our attitudes are gradually 'refined and broadened' until we finally end up in a 'transcendental vantage point from which [we] can see through all the positions that have been formulated' (p. 99).

37. Bonnie Zimmerman, 'What Has Never Been: An Overview of Lesbian Feminist Literary Criticism', in Elaine Showalter (ed.), *The New Feminist Criticism*, p. 207. Zimmerman here speaks of Cather's use of the male persona, but her point can, I think, be extended.

38. Charlotte Perkins Gilman, *Women and Economics: A Study of the Economic Relation Between Women and Men as a Factor in Social Evolution* (New York: Harper and Row, 1966 [1898]) p. 5.

39. Heilbrun, 'Bringing the Spirit Back to English Studies', p. 25.

40. Iser, *The Act of Reading*, pp. 48–50, discusses more fully the relationship between overdetermination and indeterminacy. Overdetermination is when a single textual element can signify in several different directions. The term is from Freud, 'to describe the fact that a single element of behaviour can sometimes express a complex motivation' – see Roger Poole, 'Psychoanalytic Theory: D. H. Lawrence, *St. Mawr*', in Douglas Tallack (ed.), *Literary Theory at Work: Three Texts* (London: Batsford, 1987) p. 99.

41. Mailloux, *Interpretive Conventions*, p. 73.

42. Ibid., p. 68.

43. Quoted in Elizabeth Freund, *The Return of the Reader*, p. 142.

44. Eagleton, *Literary Theory: An Introduction*, p. 81.

45. Freund, *The Return of the Reader*, p. 146.

46. Eagleton, *Literary Theory: An Introduction*, p. 134. See, too, Elizabeth Freund, pp. 85–9, and Mailloux on J. Hillis Miller, pp. 140–9. Mailloux here provides a counter-argument to that deconstructionist position which 'purportedly aims at undermining all stable meanings' (p. 147).

47. Iser, *The Implied Reader*, p. 282.

48. Roland Barthes, *S/Z: An Essay*, translated by Richard Miller (New York: Hill and Wang, 1974 [1970]) p. 10.

49. Eagleton, *Literary Theory: An Introduction*, p. 89.

50. David Lodge, *Small World: An Academic Romance* (London: Secker and Warburg, 1984) p. 105.

51. Eco, *The Role of the Reader*, pp. 9-10.

52. The 'informed reader' for Fish is one who does all she or he can to give her or himself literary competence – a full understanding of the way literature works; a knowledge of what to expect when reading a certain type of text; a grasp of the language and cultural signifying systems of the text being read. In his more recent work, Fish has changed his stress from the notion of such an informed reader to focus on the way in which 'communal reading strategies account for similar interpretive responses' (Mailloux, p. 26). This movement is charted, as Mailloux points out, in the introduction and headnotes to the reprinted essays in *Is There a Text in This Class?*

53. Freund, *The Return of the Reader*, p. 107.

54. Edward A. Bloom and Lillian D. Bloom, *Willa Cather's Gift of Sympathy* (Carbondale: Southern Illinois University Press, 1962) pp. 67–8 and 73.

55. Jonathan Culler, 'Reading as a Woman', in *On Deconstruction: Theory and Criticism after Structuralism* (London: Routledge and Kegan Paul, 1983) pp. 43–64.

56. See Nina Baym, 'Melodramas of Beset Manhood: How Theories of American Fiction Exclude Women Authors', *American Quarterly* 33 (1981) p. 134.

57. I paraphrase Mailloux here, p. 191.

58. This is Mailloux's definition of literary 'interpretation', p. 148.

59. Thorstein Veblen, *The Theory of the Leisure Class: An Economic Study of Institutions* (New York: Mentor, 1953 [1899]), 'Introduction' by C. Wright Mills, p. vi. Page references will be given after quotations in the text from henceforth.

60. Jonathan Culler, *The Pursuit of Signs: Semiotics, Literature, Deconstruction* (London: Routledge and Kegan Paul, 1981) p. 51.

5. *The Portrait of a Lady* and *The House of Mirth*: A Barthesian Reading

1. Roland Barthes, 'The Death of the Author', in *Image–Music–Text*, translated by Stephen Heath (London: Fontana, 1984 [1977]) p. 146.

2. Roland Barthes, *S/Z: An Essay*, translated by Richard Miller (New York: Hill and Wang, 1974 [1970]) p. 13. All references to be given after quotations in text from henceforth.

3. Terry Eagleton, *Literary Theory: An Introduction* (Oxford: Basil Blackwell, 1983) p. 136.

4. Henry James, *The Portrait of a Lady* (Harmondsworth, Middlesex: Penguin, 1976 [1881]) p. x. All references to be given after quotations from henceforth.

5. Thomas Pynchon, *The Crying of Lot 49* (Toronto, New York, London: Bantam, 1976 [1966]) p. 137.

6. Richard Cavendish (ed.), *Encyclopedia of the Unexplained: Magic, Occultism and Parapsychology* (London: Routledge and Kegan Paul, 1974) p. 167.

7. Barthes describes in *S/Z* the process by which enigmas in a given 'hermeneutic sentence' are disclosed. The final stage of such a process is:

disclosure, decipherment, which is, in the pure enigma (whose model is always the Sphinx's question to Oedipus), a final nomination, the discovery and uttering of the irreversible word (p. 210).

In Pynchon's text this word is never uttered.

8. Jonathan Culler, *Roland Barthes* (Glasgow: Fontana, 1983) p. 87. Barthes initially distinguishes between the 'readerly' and the 'writerly' in *S/Z*, pp. 3–11. Terence Hawkes explicates in *Structuralism and Semiotics* (London: Methuen, 1977) pp. 113–5.

9. The *Observer*, March 29, 1987, p. 30.

10. Eagleton, *Literary Theory*, pp. 186–7. 'Classic' is synonymous with 'realist' in Barthes.

11. Elaine Millard, 'Feminism II: Reading as a Woman: D. H. Lawrence, *St. Mawr*', in D. Tallack (ed.), *Literary Theory at Work: Three Texts* (London: Batsford, 1987) p. 136.

12. Hawkes, *Structuralism and Semiotics*, p. 114.

13. Steven Mailloux, *Interpretive Conventions: The Reader in the Study of American Literature* (Ithaca and London: Cornell University Press, 1982) p. 125.

14. Millard in 'Feminism II: Reading as a Woman' speaks of the unsympathetic nature of Barthes' critical enterprise from a feminist perspective (p. 137). Her own 'woman-handling' of *St. Mawr* shows how Barthes affirmations of plurality 'allows the opportunism of feminism entry to appropriate the methodology for its own (political) purpose' (p. 139).

15. Ann Jefferson and David Robey (eds), *Modern Literary Theory: A Comparative Introduction* (London: Batsford, 1982) p. 103.

16. Vincent Leitch, *Deconstructive Criticism: An Advanced Introduction* (London: Hutchinson, 1983) p. 200.

17. Culler, *Roland Barthes*, p. 82.

18. Leitch, *Deconstructive Criticism*, p. 200.

19. Millard, 'Feminism II: Reading as a Woman', p. 144.

20. Culler, *Roland Barthes*, p. 84.

21. Rimmon-Kenan, *Narrative Fiction: Contemporary Poetics* (London: Methuen, 1983) pp. 123–5.

22. Hawkes, *Structuralism and Semiotics*, p. 117.

23. Culler, *Roland Barthes*, p. 84.

24. Leitch, *Deconstructive Criticism*, p. 198.

25. Marcus Cunliffe, *The Literature of the United States* (Harmondsworth, Middlesex: Penguin, 1964 [1954]) p. 228.

26. Jay Williams, *The World of Titian* (New York: Time–Life Books, 1968) pp. 70–1.

27. Alfred Habegger, in *Gender, Fantasy and Realism in American Literature* (New York: Columbia University Press, 1982) comments on a later passage, Osmond's view of life as 'a beautiful, late afternoon landscape', as follows:

> the long summer afternoon, as in the book's opening paragraph describing an English tea, stands at the centre of the book in every way, being the best time of the best season, both scene and symbol of an unhurried, contemplative, ceremonial way of life (p. 73).

28. Thorstein Veblen, *The Theory of the Leisure Class: An Economic Study of Institutions* (New York: Mentor, 1953 [1899]) p. 72.

29. Henry James, 'In the Cage', in: *Selected Tales* (London: Dent, 1982) p. 134.

30. Marriage makes Isabel, at least temporarily, 'a motionless feature of the interior of her husband's impressive house' (Habegger, p. 69).

31. Barthes, *S/Z*, p. 20.

32. Habegger, *Gender, Fantasy and Realism in American Literature*, p. 76. Metaphors of fire (white lightning) and water (drowning) lead in the direction of the irreconcilable here. Such metaphoric sundering suggests the (momentary) obliteration of Isabel's psychic stability; cuts against the apparently firm decision making of the text's ending. James's 'frail vessel' (p. xii) is here both scorched and sunk.

33. Habegger calls it 'a deeply anti-masculine book', p. 74.

34. Habegger says of Ralph: 'This passive son of an aggressive Yankee banker has no career; he lovingly cares for his old father . . . he is nurturing and self-sacrificial. In all these ways [he] appropriates an ideal feminine identity . . . like single heroines in nineteenth century novels, [he] is identified by his first name' (p. 75).

35. Mary Suzanne Schriber, in *Gender and the Writer's Imagination: From Cooper to Wharton* (University Press of Kentucky, 1987) writes:

> When a girl is initiated into womanhood in the Victorian novel

and culture, marriage launches the woman and a husband launches a wife. In marrying Osmond, Isabel thinks she creates a reversal of expectations: she will launch her marriage, she thinks, and the wife will launch the husband. Isabel usurps the usual power of the male in choosing Osmond (pp. 126–7).

36. Mrs Mary Wood-Allen, M.D., *What a Young Woman Ought to Know* (Philadelphia: Vir Publishing Co., 1898) p. 224.
37. Schriber, *Gender and the Writer's Imagination*, p. 161.
38. See Judith Fryer, *Felicitous Space: The Imaginative Structures of Edith Wharton and Willa Cather* (Chapel Hill: University of North Carolina Press, 1986) pp. 349.
39. See Cynthia Griffin Wolff, 'Introduction', to Edith Wharton, *The House of Mirth* (New York: Viking Penguin, 1987 [1905]) pp. vii–viii. All references to be given after quotations in text from henceforth.
40. Though see Joan Lidoff's argument for the book to be approached not as social realism but as a 'romance of identity': 'Another Sleeping Beauty: Narcissism in *The House of Mirth*', in Eric J. Sundquist (ed.), *American Realism: New Essays* (Baltimore and London: The Johns Hopkins University Press, 1982) pp. 238–58. Judith Fryer focuses on the way space and imagination interconnect in the works of Wharton and Cather, in her *Felicitous Space*. In Wharton's case, she particularly refers to her 'meticulously conceived interiors, which include all that the eye can encompass' (pp. xiii–xiv).
41. Fryer, *Felicitous Space*, p. 82. In detaching her from such a soil, Wharton 'deprives Lily of a sense of self and makes her like that "water-plant in flux"' (p. 88). My argument is that the reasons for Lily's lack of a sense of self go further than this.
42. Which, however, can be restored if the irony is uncertain.
43. 'The House of Mirth Revisited', in Irving Howe (ed.), *Edith Wharton: A Collection of Critical Essays* (Englewood Cliffs, NJ.: Prentice-Hall, 1962) p. 114.
44. Marshall Berman, *All That Is Solid Melts Into Air: The Experience of Modernity* (London: Verso, 1983) pp. 18-19.
45. Millard, 'Feminism II: Reading as a Woman', p. 144.
46. Elaine Showalter, 'Toward a Feminist Poetics', *The New Feminist Criticism: Essays on Women, Literature, and Theory* (London: Virago, 1986) p. 134.
47. Cynthia Griffin Wolff, *A Feast of Words: The Triumph of Edith Wharton* (New York: Oxford University Press, 1977) pp. 114–5.
48. Judith Fryer, *The Faces of Eve: Women in the Nineteenth Century American Novel* (New York: Oxford University Press, 1976) p. 134.
49. Mary Schriber, *Gender and the Writer's Imagination*, p. 123.
50. Fryer, *The Faces of Eve*, pp. 133–4. She is referring here to Isabel's position prior to the Osmond marriage.
51. And it is the quality of *choice* with which Isabel is identified in the novel: she does have alternatives.
52. Annette Kolodny, 'Some Notes on Defining a "Feminist Literary Criticism"', in Cheryl L. Brown and Karen Olson (eds), *Feminist Criticism: Essays on Theory, Poetry and Prose* (Metuchen, NJ.: Scarecrow Press, 1978) p. 42.

53. Wolff, *A Feast of Words*, p. 109.
54. Wolff points out that to see and to define a woman as 'a beautiful object and nothing more' is 'infantilizing' (p. 110). Part of Lily's 'psychological disfigurement' may be related to her (consequent?) inability to link her beauty to that sexuality which, as Joan Lidoff shows in her analysis of Lily's relationships with Gus Trenor and Rosedale, is 'not an acceptable part of her self-image' ('Another Sleeping Beauty', p. 249). When Lily does express her sexuality, it is in the context of a *tableau-vivant*, and is there contained within the protected frame of artistic representation.
55. Fryer, *Felicitous Space*, p. 92.
56. Cynthia Wolff, *A Feast of Words*, pp. 110–133. See especially Wolff's clear illustration of Selden's 'flawed . . . code'. 'Far from being Wharton's spokesman, Selden is the final object of her sweeping social satire' (p. 132). Page references to follow text where applicable.
57. Henry James, *The American Scene* (London: Chapman and Hall, 1907) pp. 211–12.
58. Wolff, *A Feast of Words*, p. 129.
59. Ibid., p. 127.
60. Toril Moi, *Sexual/Textual Politics: Feminist Literary Theory* (London and New York: Methuen, 1985) p. 130. Moi is here explicating Irigaray.
61. Charlotte Perkins Gilman, *Women and Economics: A Study of the Economic Relation Between Women and Men as a Factor in Social Evolution* (New York: Harper and Row, 1966 [1898]) p. 5.
62. See, too, the excellent discussion of this sequence in Judith Fryer, *Felicitous Space*, pp. 75–82.
63. Lidoff here is referring to the narrator and characters of *The House of Mirth* ('Another Sleeping Beauty', p. 245). Her remark can, though, be extended to James's novel. Ralph's gift of money 'ruins' Isabel. Isabel's 'tenderness' to Osmond relates to her vision of him as 'charitable institution' (p. 427).
64. If both are bourgeois novels in this respect and in their general concern with manners, social ritual, etc., equally the two novels critique bourgeois concepts of reality both in their questioning of the institution of marriage on which such an ideology is based, and in their uncovering of the gaps apparent between the realms of manners and of morals which such an ideology would attempt to conceal.
65. Fredric Jameson, in *The Political Unconscious: Narrative as a Socially Symbolic Act* (London: Methuen, 1981), interprets James' work in the context of a separation occurring between the subject and its 'textual object'. Such a separation results from 'the logic of social development', the process of 'reification', and an attempt on the part of the artist to resist its implications. One of the reasons why Isabel fails to see that Osmond's 'fine gold coin' (p. 228) is counterfeit, is exactly because he represents for her (sited on that symbolic hilltop and associated with 'exquisite taste') the opportunity to keep her subjective 'essence' uncontaminated; the equivalent to that refusal to choose to immerse herself in the world of concrete social reality, that refusal to choose to act, which freedom initially means to her. The knowledge (of her lack of freedom) she gains from the mistake she makes in marrying Osmond, in taking materialistic reality for idealistic

appearance, is, for James, all important. Such knowledge is, though, again finally associated with subjectivism and psychological 'depth'; what Jameson calls a 'desperate myth of the self' which comes into being (I short-circuit Jameson's argument here) as 'a protest and a defence against reification'. See Jameson, pp. 221–2.

66. My reading is an uneasy one here. James does apparently focus throughout on Isabel's gaining of knowledge, understanding, and power to choose. Alfred Habegger argues that 'not what is done to her, but what she herself decides to do forms the novel's proper conclusion' (p. 71). Such self-awareness, however, is questioned in the final pages, where her taking of that 'very straight path' is directly linked to a 'mutilation' of self by metaphorical lightning and drowning – when Goodwood kisses her. The suggestion here is that her subject position is still highly unstable; that her self-understanding must be seen in strongly qualified terms. Such a qualification, though, runs against the current of a novel which appears to chart a process of moral and psychological development on Isabel's part.

67. Schriber, *Gender and the Writer's Imagination*, p. 158.

68. Lidoff, 'Another Sleeping Beauty', p. 242.

69. Wolff, *A Feast of Words*, pp. 110 and 125.

70. Schriber, *Gender and the Writer's Imagination*, p. 158.

71. Fryer, *Felicitous Space*, p. 95.

72. Wolff, *A Feast of Words*, p. 132.

6. The Clash of Language: Bakhtin and *Huckleberry Finn*

1. The term 'posited author' is Bakhtin's. See M. M. Bakhtin, *The Dialogic Imagination: Four Essays*, translated by Caryl Emerson and Michael Holquist (Austin: University of Texas Press, 1981) p. 315. Page references to follow quotations from henceforth. Bakhtin is distinguishing here between the author as represented within the text and he who stands outside it:

he, as its creator, remains outside the world he has represented in his work. If I relate (or write about) an event that has just happened to me, then I as the *teller* (or writer) of this event am already outside the time and space in which the event occurred. It is just as impossible to forge an identity between myself, my own 'I', and that 'I' that is the subject of my stories as it is to lift myself up by my own hair (p. 256).

This statement also has implications for Huck's own position *vis-à-vis* the retelling of his narrative. See Laurence B. Holland, 'A "Raft of Trouble": Word and Deed in *Huckleberry Finn*', in Eric J. Sundquist (ed.), *American Realism: New Essays* (Baltimore and London: The Johns Hopkins University Press, 1982) pp. 73–5.

2. Mark Twain, *The Adventures of Huckleberry Finn* (Harmondsworth, Middlesex: Penguin, 1987 [1884]) p. 48. Page references to follow quotations from henceforth.

3. On the use of surrogate voices in the novel, see Holland, 'A

"Raft of Trouble": Word and Deed in *Huckleberry Finn'*, pp. 76–7.
  4. *The Dialogic Imagination*, p. 23. Bakhtin continues:

> Laughter has the remarkable power of making an object come up close, of
> drawing it into a zone of crude contact where one can finger it familiarly on
> all sides, turn it upside down, inside out . . . break open its external shell,
> look into its centre, doubt it, take it apart, dismember it . . . Laughter
> demolishes fear and piety before an object, before a world . . . is a vital
> factor in laying down that prerequisite for fearlessness without which it
> would be impossible to approach the world realistically . . . In this plane
> (the plane of laughter) one can disrespectfully walk around whole objects;
> therefore, the back and rear portion of an object (and also its innards, not
> normally accessible for viewing) assume a special importance.

This notion can be related to Jim and Huck's inferior status in the
hierarchical world of the novel; to the comic function of their language and point of view. Thus, Jim's 'I knows him by de back'
(p. 134).
  5. Holquist, 'Introduction', *The Dialogic Imagination*, p. xviii.
  6. Terry Eagleton, *Literary Theory: An Introduction* (Oxford: Basil Blackwell,
1983) p. 139.
  7. See the discussion of this issue in the introduction and first chapter
of Tzvetan Todorov, *Mikhail Bakhtin: The Dialogical Principle*, translated by
Wlad Godzich (Manchester University Press, 1984).
  8. Russell Reising, *The Unusable Past: Theory and the Study of American
Literature* (New York and London: Methuen, 1986) p. 234.
  9. Brian McHale, *Postmodernist Fiction* (New York and London: Methuen,
1987) p. 166.
  10. David Murray, 'Dialogics: Joseph Conrad, *Heart of Darkness*', in
D. Tallack (ed.), *Literary Theory at Work: Three Texts* (London: Batsford,
1987) p. 119.
  11. Holquist, *The Dialogic Imagination*, p. xviii.
  12. Allon White, 'Bakhtin, Sociolinguistics and Deconstruction', in
Frank Gloversmith (ed.), *The Theory of Reading* (Brighton: Harvester, 1984)
p. 143.
  13. Mark Twain, *Pudd'nhead Wilson* (Harmondsworth, Middlesex: Penguin,
1981 [1894]) p. 64.
  14. Allan Trachtenberg, *The Incorporation of America: Culture and Society in
the Gilded Age* (New York: Hill and Wang, 1982) chapter six, 'Fictions of the
Real', pp. 182–207.
  15. The phrase is taken from Allon White, 'Bakhtin, Sociolinguistics,
and Deconstruction', p. 136. See also Bakhtin, p. 314: 'The narrator's
story . . . is structured against the background of normal literary language,
the expected literary horizon. Every moment of the story has a conscious
relationship with this normal language and its belief system, is in fact set
against them, and set against them *dialogically* . . . '.
  16. *The Dial*, Vol. 5 (March, 1885) p. 309.
  17. *The Dial*, Vol. 6 (Nov., 1885) p. 185, and Vol. 5 (Dec., 1884) p. 197.
  18. In *My Darling Clementine* (1946), the western by John Ford, the situation

is exactly reversed. Shakespearean prose is there introduced to suggest the insufficiencies of American vernacular discourse and the values associated with it.

19. Mikhail Bakhtin, *Problems of Dostoevsky's Poetics*, translated by Caryl Emerson (Manchester University Press, 1984) p. 122. Unless otherwise noted, all the quotations in the section on carnival which follows are taken from this book, pp. 122–30. It is worth noting that carnival only temporarily overthrows established hierarchies, is made licit by those hierarchies. Bakhtin downplays this point.

20. Though such masqueradings are, as Bakhtin points out (*Problems of Dostoevsky's Poetics*, p. 130), but 'faint reflections' of true carnival with its radical decentering of strict hierarchical orderings, 'carnivalistic shifts of clothing and of positions and destinies in life' (p. 125).

21. He who is apparently graceless and powerless, the lowest of the low, 'a drunk man . . . that sot', is transformed into one with both grace and gaudy authority. Connotations of pleasure and delight are strong in the scene, pp. 211–12.

22. Brook Thomas, 'Languages and Identity in *The Adventures of Huckleberry Finn*', *Mark Twain Journal*, Vol. 21 (Summer, 1982), No. 2, p. 8.

23. Brian McHale, *Postmodernist Fiction*, p. 172. McHale here also associates carnivalized literature with 'the flagrantly "indecorous" '. The 'Royal Nonesuch' incident fits such a category.

24. Katerina Clark and Michael Holquist, *Mikhail Bakhtin* (Cambridge, Mass.: Harvard University Press, 1984) p. 292, and Brian McHale, *Postmodernist Fiction*, p. 166.

25. Holquist, 'Glossary', *The Dialogic Imagination*, p. 427.

26. Harold Beaver, *Huckleberry Finn* (London: Allen and Unwin, 1987) p. 34.

27. See Steven Mailloux, 'Reading *Huckleberry Finn*: The Rhetoric of Performed Ideology' in Louis J. Budd (ed.), *New Essays on Adventures of Huckleberry Finn* (Cambridge University Press, 1985) pp. 113–14.

28. Michael Davitt Bell, 'Mark Twain, "Realism" and *Huckleberry Finn*', in *New Essays on Adventures of Huckleberry Finn*, p. 44.

29. See Tony Bennett, *Formalism and Marxism* (London: Methuen, 1979) pp. 20–5.

30. Beaver, *Huckleberry Finn*, p. 66. Beaver sees Huck's description of the Grangerford's parlour as providing a 'symbolic montage of the South as a gun-happy, fraudulent, sentimental, hypocritical time-warp' (p. 135).

31. The word 'sick' used by itself as an adjective 'connotes a profound psychological shock' in this novel: Beaver, p. 120.

32. Frederick Douglass, *Narrative of the Life of Frederick Douglass, An American Slave* (Harmondsworth, Middlesex: Penguin, 1982 [1845]) p. 124. Page references to follow quotations from henceforth.

33. Henry Louis Gates, *Figures in Black: Words, Signs, and the 'Racial' Self* (New York, Oxford: Oxford University Press, 1987) p. 105.

34. Houston A. Baker, Jr., 'Introduction' to *Narrative of the Life of Frederick Douglass*, p. 13. And see Gates, Jr., *Figures in Black*, p. 117: 'To speak properly was to be proper. But to attempt to employ a

Western language to posit a black self is inherently to use language ironically'.

35. Neil Schmitz, *Of Huck and Alice: Humorous Writing in American Literature* (Minneapolis: University of Minnesota Press, 1983) p. 104. Page references to follow quotations from henceforth.

36. Holquist, 'Glossary', *The Dialogic Imagination*, p. 428.

37. Schmitz, *Of Huck and Alice*, p. 103. In the example which follows Jim thinks he is speaking to himself. However, as Allon White notes, 'Every utterance is for or to someone, even if s/he is not actually present' (p. 128). Jim's speech is thoroughly conditioned by his status in a slave-holding community, even when he is alone. Whether *any* slave would talk in the manner represented here is, of course, a different, and more worrying, question.

38. Bakhtin distinguishes between authoritative discourse and internally persuasive discourse. The discussion on page 342 of the relations, and mergers, between such forms is particularly relevant to Huck's case. See also note, p. 344.

39. White, 'Bakhtin, Sociolinguistics and Deconstruction', p. 125.

40. Ibid., p. 125.

41. Bakhtin, *Problems of Dostoevsky's Poetics*, p. 184.

42. Ibid., p. 252. Bakhtin is referring specifically to Dostoevsky's novels here, but his point can be broadened.

43. Schmitz, *Of Huck and Alice*, p. 96.

44. I here avoid, for reasons of clarity and accessibility, Bakhtin's use of the term *chronotope*. In 'Forms of Time and Chronotope in the Novel' (pp. 84–258), he argues for the concept of the chronotope, the intrinsic connection between time/space relationships in the novel, as a way of approaching the historical development of the novel form. His description of the 'idyllic chronotope' acts as the basis for my argument.

45. Clark and Holquist, *Mikhail Bakhtin*, pp. 310–11.

46. Mailloux, 'Reading *Huckleberry Finn*', p. 114.

47. Joyce A. Rowe, *Equivocal Endings in Classic American Novels* (Cambridge University Press, 1988) pp. 57 and 48.

48. The ways in which Twain's use of the idyllic departs from Bakhtin's description of it (see p. 225 ff) would provide a valuable subject for further discussion. See especially the notion of the family model (pp. 232–3) and Jim's substitution for Pap in the version of it here presented.

49. So, too, with any social grouping. Does Bakhtin's belief in 'the folk' blind him to the fact as he describes the idyllic chronotope?

50. Schmitz, *Of Huck and Alice*, p. 103.

51. Douglass, *Narrative of the Life of Frederick Douglass*, p. 77.

52. Holland, 'A "Raft of Trouble": Word and Deed in *Huckleberry Finn*', p. 70.

53. Richard Godden examines the use of the term 'nigger' in 'Call Me Nigger: Race and Speech in Faulkner's *Light in August*', *Journal of American Studies*, Vol. 14 (August, 1980) No. 2, pp. 235–48. 'Language' as he points out, 'distributes power, even as it pretends to innocent communication' (p. 240).

54. In Schmitz's words (p. 114): 'as Cairo is neared, Jim's voice gets louder and plainer. A word begins to reiterate, ring, in Huck's discourse – *nigger, nigger, nigger* . . . Each time Jim asserts his difference, Huck writes *nigger*'.

55. Holland, 'A "Raft of Trouble": Word and Deed in *Huckleberry Finn*', p. 70.

56. White, 'Bakhtin, Sociolinguistics and Deconstruction', p. 129.

57. Janet Holmgren McKay, ' "An Art so High": Style in *Adventures of Huckleberry Finn*', *New Essays on Adventures of Huckleberry Finn*, p. 78. McKay uses the phrase in a different and earlier context; one which brings out Jim's dependency on Huck's 'friendship' for his continued 'freedom'.

58. Bakhtin, quoted by Tzvetan Todorov, *Mikhail Bakhtin: The Dialogical Principle*, p. 42.

59. Holland, 'A "Raft of Trouble" ', p. 71.

60. Holland, p. 71.

61. Bakhtin, *Problems of Dostoevsky's Poetics*, p. 51.

62. Todorov, *Mikhail Bakhtin: The Dialogical Principle*, p. 104.

63. Joyce Rowe talks of 'Huck's longing for Tom [and his style] as . . . an alternative . . . part of himself'; 'self-division' as 'always the functional principle of Huck's character' (*Equivocal Endings in Classic American Novels*, pp. 65 and 56).

64. His speech, too, is 'infected' by the values of the dominant culture particularly in the way that he *values himself in its terms*: 'I's rich now . . . I owns mysef, en I's wuth eight hund'd dollars' (p. 100).

65. Stephen B. Oates, *Let the Trumpet Sound: The Life of Martin Luther King, Jr.* (New York: Harper and Row, 1982) pp. 259–62.

66. Bakhtin, *Problems of Dostoevsky's Poetics*, p. 6.

67. McHale, *Postmodernist Fiction*, p. 166. I follow McHale in making such a distinction between the heteroglossic and the polyphonic, though this is perhaps to define clear boundaries in Bakhtinian thought which remain somewhat blurred in the original.

68. Murray, 'Dialogics: Joseph Conrad, *Heart of Darkness*', p. 131.

69. M. Pierrette Malcuzynski, 'Mikhail Bakhtin and Contemporary Narrative Theory', *University of Ottowa Quarterly*, Vol. 53, 1983, p. 57.

70. Beaver, *Huckleberry Finn*, pp. 48–9.

71. See Steven Mailloux, 'Reading *Huckleberry Finn*: The Rhetoric of Performed Ideology', p. 108; Louis Budd, 'Introduction' to *New Essays on Huckleberry Finn*, p. 16; Harold Beaver, p. 49.

72. Malcuzynski, 'Mikhail Bakhtin', p. 58.

73. Ibid., p. 52. He is quoting Bakhtin who sees Dostoevsky as 'the creator of genuine polyphony' (*Problems of Dostoevsky's Poetics*, p. 34).

74. Murray, 'Dialogics: Joseph Conrad, *Heart of Darkness*', p. 117.

75. C. Vann Woodward, *The Strange Career of Jim Crow* (Oxford University Press, 1966) p. 6.

76. Steven Mailloux, 'Reading *Huckleberry Finn*', p. 108. Page references to follow quotations from henceforth.

77. Beaver, *Huckleberry Finn*, p. 38. See, too, Chapter Three, 'A Civil War Among Huck's Readers', pp. 37–45.

78. Holland, 'A "Raft of Trouble": Word and Deed in *Huckleberry Finn*', p. 75.

7. A Medley of Voices: Zora Neale Hurston's *Their Eyes Were Watching God*

1. Zora Neale Hurston, *Mules and Men* (Bloomington: Indiana University Press, 1978 [1935]) p. 51. Page references given after quotations where appropriate from henceforth.
2. Paul Ricoeur, *Time and Narrative*, Vol. 2, translated by Kathleen McLaughlin and David Pellaver (Chicago, London: University of Chicago Press, 1985 [1984]) p. 96.
3. Mikhail Bakhtin, *Problems of Dostoevsky's Poetics*, translated by Caryl Emerson (Manchester University Press, 1984) p. 6.
4. Ricoeur, p. 96. I base my argument on what Ricoeur says here, though I modify his analysis to fit my own critical practice.
5. Ricoeur, *Time and Narrative*, p. 99.
6. Nina Baym, 'Melodramas of Beset Manhood: How Theories of American Fiction Exclude Women Authors' (*American Quarterly* 33, 1981) p. 125. See, too, Henry Louis Gates, Jr. (ed.) *Black Literature and Literary Theory* (New York, London: Methuen, 1984) p. 2:

> We overhear the voice of the critic who speaks the word 'canon' to invoke a closed set of texts written mostly by men who are Western and white; a most useful organizing concept for pedagogy becomes another mechanism for political control.

7. Bakhtin, *The Dialogical Imagination: Four Essays* (Austin: University of Texas Press, 1981) p. 411. Bakhtin is speaking here of the novel. His argument, as I suggest, can be extended.
8. Henry Louis Gates, Jr. 'Criticism in the Jungle', in *Black Literature and Literary Theory*, p. 2.
9. Zora Neale Hurston, *Their Eyes Were Watching God* (London: Virago, 1986 [1937]) p. 20. All references will be given after quotations from henceforth.
10. Barbara Johnson, 'Metaphor, Metonymy and Voice in *Their Eyes Were Watching God*', in Henry Louis Gates, Jr., (ed.), *Black Literature and Literary Theory*, p. 218. Though my analysis of Hurston's novel departs considerably from hers, I found Johnson's essay particularly valuable in stimulating my own thinking about Hurston.
11. Virginia Woolf, *To the Lighthouse* (St Alban's: Granada, 1982 [1927]) p. 168.
12. Janie's mother is a week old when Sherman takes Atlanta (1864). She becomes pregnant with Janie when she is seventeen.
13. 'I lived through that terrible five-day hurricane of 1929. It was horrible in its intensity and duration. I saw dead people washing around on the streets when it was over. You could smell the stench from dead

animals as well'. Hurston, *Dust Tracks on a Road: An Autobiography* (London: Virago, 1986 [1942]) p. 195.

14. The terms I use in this chapter are explained in those chapters to which prior reference is being made. Thus, here, see Chapter Two. Consult the index for specific requirements.

15. Houston A. Baker, Jr., *Blues, Ideology and Afro-American Literature: A Vernacular Theory* (University of Chicago Press, 1984) p. 57. This relationship should be seen, too, in terms both of the race-sex-sin spiral which Lillian Smith describes – see Anne Goodwyn Jones, *Tomorrow is Another Day: The Woman Writer in the South, 1859–1936* (Baton-Rouge, Louisiana: Louisiana University Press, 1981) p. 10 – and of Richard King's description of the Southern Family Romance in *A Southern Renaissance: The Cultural Awakening of the American South, 1930–1955* (New York, Oxford: Oxford University Press, 1980) pp. 26–38. From henceforth, references to Houston Baker's book will follow quotations where practicable.

16. See pp. 53, 67. See Barbara Christian, *Black Feminist Criticism: Perspectives on Black Women Writers* (New York: Pergamon, 1985). Christian discusses the stereotype of the tragic mulatta and the move to a more complex view of the black woman in American literature. She notes:

The mulatta usually sits there, regal in her imitation of the white folks' ways, content that she has gotten to the peak of colored society. But Janie cannot stand this isolation (p. 9).

17. Genette, *Narrative Discourse*, translated by Jane E. Lewin (Oxford: Basil Blackwell, 1986 [1972]) p. 93.

18. *Narrative of the Life of Frederick Douglass: An American Slave* (Harmondsworth, Middlesex: Penguin, 1982 [1845]) p. 106. Gates in 'The Blackness of Blackness: A Critique of the Sign and the Signifying Monkey', *Black Literature and Literary Theory*, writes concerning the significance of 'the revision of . . . antecedent texts' in the black literary tradition, with particular reference to this passage (p. 290).

19. Barbara Johnson, in 'Thresholds of Difference: Structures of Address in Zora Neale Hurston', *Critical Inquiry*, Vol. 12 (Autumn, 1985) No. 1, pp. 280–1, examines Hurston's autobiographical writing, where a similar recognition scene occurs.

20. W. E. DuBois, *The Souls of Black Folk*, in *Three Negro Classics* (New York: Avon, 1969) p. 215.

21. Genette, *Narrative Discourse*, p. 97.

22. Robert Stepto, *From Behind the Veil: A Study of Afro–American Narrative* (Urbana, Chicago: University of Illinois Press, 1979). He says that, for Richard Wright for example, 'The North [was both] a destination and a symbolic space' (p. 152).

23. Mary Helen Washington, quoted in Deborah E. McDowell, 'New Directions for Black Feminist Criticism', in Elaine Showalter (ed.) *The New Feminist Criticism: Essays on Women, Literature and Theory* (London: Virago, 1986) p. 215. McDowell calls the black female's journey 'basically personal and psychological', rather than 'political and social'. I would take issue with this in Hurston's case.

24. A repeated rather than a single action, the marriages nonetheless must be classed as 'non-routine' so can, I would suggest, be placed in this category. The way these three marriages change Janie's status and value in her own eyes, and in the eyes of others, is central to the narrative: they constitute significant markers to her self-development as well as providing one of the novel's structural bases.

25. Jones, *Tomorrow is Another Day*, p. 37.

26. Susan Willis, *Specifying: Black Women Writing the American Experience* (Madison, Wisconsin: University of Wisconsin Press, 1987) p. 51. Robert Hemenway, *Zora Neale Hurston: A Literary Biography* (London: Camden Press, 1986 [1977]) p. 233. Willis refers to the scene not in terms of melodrama but as 'a cliché of naturalism', unless a figural reading is taken.

27. Willis, *Specifying*, p. 51. References after quotations from henceforth.

28. Particularly the black female self. As Barbara Johnson says, 'the female voice must be recognized as divided in a multitude of ways'. She suggests some of the divisions of the black female subject in 'Metaphor, Metonymy and Voice in *Their Eyes Were Watching God*', pp. 215–8.

29. Johnson, p. 209. All references are to 'Metaphor, Metonymy and Voice' unless otherwise specified.

30. Mari McCarty, quoted in Elaine Showalter, 'Feminist Criticism in the Wilderness', *The New Feminist Criticism*, p. 263.

31. Barbara Johnson, in her article on Hurston, traces the metonymic/metaphoric relationships between bedroom, parlour, and store, as they relate to Janie and Joe's marriage. I acknowledge my debt to her, though my general argument leads me in a different critical direction.

32. Quoted in Kimberly W. Benston, 'I Yam What I Yam: The Topos of Un(naming) in Afro–American Literature', in Gates, *Black Literature and Literary Theory*, p. 151.

33. Baker, *Blues, Ideology and Afro–American Literature*, p. 59. Baker's 'ideological analysis' of the novel sees Janie's 'striking expressiveness within the confines of Eatonville . . . [as] framed . . . by the bourgeois economics of Anglo–America'. I acknowledge his influence on my reading.

34. Baker, *Blues, Ideology and Afro–American Literature*, p. 59. Baker translates the significance of this to the marginal position of the Afro–American artist in American culture.

35. Steven Mailloux, *Interpretive Conventions: The Reader in the Study of American Literature* (Ithaca and London: Cornell University Press, 1982) p. 68.

36. Further distinctions can be made between the male and female members of the community. Also there is Pheoby, who shares some of the community's beliefs about what has happened to Janie, but who acts as a bridge into Janie's focalization; whose immediate recognition of Janie's well-being ('you sho looks *good*') confirms the authority of Janie's confident voice.

37. Enigmas never fully resolved in the novel.

38. McDowell, 'New Directions for Black Feminist Criticism', p. 194. I use her quotation out of context.

39. See pp. 47, 62, 86–7, 135, 157, etc., in terms of 'reciprocal spotlighting'.

40. The hair is noticed by male eyes; the faded and dirty clothes by female.

41. McDowell, 'New Directions for Black Feminist Criticism', p. 194.

42. Willis, *Specifying*, p. 51, and Johnson, 'Metaphor, Metonymy and Voice in *Their Eyes Were Watching God*', p. 210.

43. Baker, *Blues, Ideology and Afro-American Literature*, p. 59. He uses the phrase in regard to Hurston's position as Afro-American artist. Her 'expressive wholeness', like Janie's in the novel, must be placed, he suggests, within the framework of Anglo–American 'capitalistic economic exchange': artistic expression must be shaped to fit the available market.

44. Bluesman Booker White, quoted in *Blues, Ideology and Afro-American Literature*, p. 8.

45. Willis, *Specifying*, p. 48; Houston Baker, p. 59.

46. Janie works because Tea Cake is lonely without her. They romp and play at work (pp. 198–9). They are, however, in a position to choose to refuse to take work seriously. Nine hundred dollars and a house in Eatonville result from Jody's capitalistic enterprise (in which Janie has shared); give them a secure economic base.

47. Willis, *Specifying*, p. 48.

48. Johnson, 'Metaphor, Metonymy and Voice', p. 215.

49. Robert Bone did write about *Their Eyes Were Watching God* in *The Negro Novel in America* (New York: Yale University Press, 1965) in terms of the opposition between a cramped life and that spiritual fulfilment found through Tea Cake (and the folk culture Bone sees him as representing). Bone's focus on the novel is, though, peculiarly self-contradictory and inconclusive: his critical position uncertain. The quote he introduces as a 'key passage' (p. 131) in the novel is one taken completely out of its original context.

50. Noel Schraufnagel, *From Apology to Protest: The Black American Novel* (Deland, Florida: Everett/Edwards, 1973) p. 17.

51. Bone, *The Negro Novel in America*, p. 130.

52. Barbara Smith, 'Toward a Black Feminist Criticism' in Showalter (ed.), *The New Feminist Criticism*, p. 170.

53. Hurston, *Their Eyes Were Watching God*, p. 197. Showalter's development of Edwin Ardener's description of the relationship of dominant and muted social groups can be usefully applied here: 'Feminist Criticism in the Wilderness', pp. 261–3.

54. Roland Barthes, *S/Z: An Essay*, translated by Richard Miller (New York: Hill and Wang, 1974 [1970]) pp. 205, 18.

55. See Terence Hawkes, *Structuralism and Semiotics* (London: Methuen, 1977) pp. 76–87.

56. Barthes, *S/Z*, p. 35.

57. Barbara Christian, *Black Feminist Criticism*, p. 4.

58. Gates discusses 'signifying' and its particular definition in black discourse in 'The Blackness of Blackness: A Critique of the Sign and the Signifying Monkey', *Black Literature and Literary Theory*, pp. 285–321. 'Lying' also belongs within a specific Afro–American rhetorical tradition: see *Mules and Men*.

59. See Hurston's 'Characteristics of Negro Expression' in Nathan Irvin

Huggins (ed.), *Voices from the Harlem Renaissance* (New York: Oxford University Press, 1976) pp. 222–36. Also Karla F. C. Holloway, *The Character of the Word: The Texts of Zora Neale Hurston* (New York, Westport, Conn., London: Greenwood Press, 1987), especially the chapter entitled 'The Word, Thus Adorned', for Hurston's use of Afro–American rhetorical devices.

60. Allon White, 'Bakhtin, Sociolinguistics and Deconstruction', in Frank Gloversmith (ed.), *The Theory of Reading* (Brighton: Harvester, 1984) p. 125.

61. David Murray, 'Dialogics: Joseph Conrad, *Heart of Darkness*', in D. Tallack (ed.), *Literary Theory at Work: Three Texts* (London: Batsford, 1987) p. 116.

62. Bakhtin sees the distinctiveness of the novel in the fact that it is the site where dialogization occurs (pp. 264, 320). In *Mules and Men*, Hurston uses a non-fictional form as exactly that 'de-normalizing and therefore centrifugal force' with which Bakhtin identifies the novel. The text in fact crosses the boundaries between the non-fictional (anthropology, folklore) and the fictional in its use of 'a semifictional Zora Neale Hurston . . . a curiously retiring figure who is more art than life' (Hemenway, p. 164). The use of such a 'persona' is introduced by a third-party author for precisely the purposes identified by Bakhtin in the given quotation – to present two registers of language in their typicality, thus showing their relativity to one another.

63. White, 'Bakhtin, Sociolinguistics and Deconstruction', p. 125.

64. The terms used here are taken from J. L. Dillard, *Black English: Its History and Usage in the United States* (New York: Random House, 1972) pp. 207, 206. 'Standard' as in 'Standard American English' must be counted a word bearing centripetal implication, suggesting an urge for centralization and linguistic unification which operates to endorse and guarantee the 'official' values of a 'unitary' culture.

65. White, 'Bakhtin, Sociolinguistics and Deconstruction', p. 126.

66. She is not atypical in her ability to code-switch in such a way. See *Black English*, p. 210. Dillard also points out that one of the 'harsher socio-linguistic facts' which must be recognized is that 'the history of the Afro-American languages and dialects correlates with the existence of a caste system' (p. 230).

67. Ralph Ellison, *Shadow and Act* (New York: Vintage Books, 1964) pp. 249–50. Quoted in Gates, 'The Blackness of Blackness: A Critique of the Sign and the Signifying Monkey', p. 293.

68. Gates, 'Criticism in the Jungle', in *Black Literature and Literary Theory*, p. 12.

69. Houston A. Baker, *Modernism and the Harlem Renaissance* (University of Chicago Press, 1987) pp. xiii, 72, 87.

70. Murray, 'Dialogics: Joseph Conrad, *Heart of Darkness*', p. 121.

71. Bakhtin, 'The Dialogical Imagination', p. 344.

72. White, 'Bakhtin, Sociolinguistics and Deconstruction', p. 125.

73. The jury is directed to decide whether Janie is 'a poor broken creature . . . trapped by unfortunate circumstances' or a 'cold-blooded' murderess (p. 279). She fits neither category.

74. Hurston, *Dust Tracks on a Road*, p. 184.

75. Murray, 'Dialogics: Joseph Conrad, *Heart of Darkness*', p. 129.

76. Tzvetan Todorov, *Mikhail Bakhtin: The Dialogical Principle*, translated by Wlad Godzich (Manchester University Press, 1984) p. x.

77. In *Understanding the New Black Poetry: Black Speech and Black Music as Poetic References* (New York: William Morrow, 1973), Stephen Henderson defines 'jook', along with 'roll,' 'jelly', as a 'mascon' word (one containing a '*massive concentration* of black experiential energy'). Such words, he says, 'seem to carry an inordinate charge' in terms of their emotional and psychological weight (p. 44). Hurston discusses the 'jook' in her 'Characteristics of Negro Expression', pp. 232–6.

78. Murray, 'Dialogics: Joseph Conrad, *Heart of Darkness*', p. 116.

79. Henry Louis Gates, Jr., 'A Negro Way of Saying', *New York Times Book Review*, April 21, 1985, p. 43.

80. Paul Lauter, 'Race and Gender in the Shaping of the American Literary Canon: A Case Study from the Twenties', *Feminist Studies* 9 (Fall 1983), No. 3, p. 435.

81. William Spengemann, 'What is American Literature?', *Centennial Review*, Vol. 22 (1978), pp. 119–38.

Index